In the Chamber of
Understanding Risk

Through a new set of detailed case studies, William Leiss shows that while industry and governments have made much progress in responsibly managing risks to health and environment, they remain quite poor at managing their involvements with risk issues, that is, with the often intense controversies about the way in which risks should be managed. This organizational risk, associated with misunderstanding the nature of risk management issues, can have damaging consequences, something that remains poorly appreciated.

The essential problem is the failure to recognize that controversies over risks are "normal events" in modern society and as such will be with us for the foreseeable future. Three key propositions define these events: risk management decisions are inherently disputable; public perceptions of risk are legitimate and should be treated as such; the public needs to be intensively involved in the processes of risk evaluation and management. Leiss and his collaborators chronicle these organizational risks in a set of detailed case studies on genetically modified foods, cellular telephones, the notorious fuel additive MMT, pulp mill effluent, nuclear power, toxic substances legislation, tobacco, and the new type of "moral risks" associated with genetics technologies such as cloning.

WILLIAM LEISS is professor at the School of Policy Studies, Queen's University, and also holds the NSERC/SSHRC Research Chair in Risk Communication and Public Policy in the Faculty of Management, University of Calgary. He is co-author of *Mad Cows and Mother's Milk* and *Risk and Responsibility*.

In the Chamber of Risks

Understanding Risk Controversies

W I L L I A M   L E I S S

McGill-Queen's University Press
Montreal & Kingston · London · Ithaca

© McGill-Queen's University Press 2001
ISBN 0-7735-2238-7 (cloth)
ISBN 0-7735-2246-8 (paper)

Legal deposit third quarter 2001
Bibliothèque nationale du Québec
Printed in Canada on acid-free paper

This book has been published with the help of a grant
from the Humanities and Social Sciences Federation of
Canada, using funds provided by the Social Sciences and
Humanities Research Council of Canada.

McGill-Queen's University Press acknowledges the
financial support of the Government of Canada through
the Book Publishing Industry Development Program
(BPIDP) for its activities. It also acknowledges the
support of the Canada Council
for the Arts for its publishing program.

**National Library of Canada Cataloguing
in Publication Data**

Leiss, William, 1939–
    In the chamber of risks: understanding risk controversies

    Includes bibliographical references and index.
    ISBN 0-7735-2238-7 (bound)
    ISBN 0-7735-2246-8 (pbk.)

    1. Health risk assessment – Canada – Case studies.
    2. Environmental risk assessment – Canada – Case
    studies. 3. Risk management – Canada – Case studies.
    4. Environmental protection – Government policy –
    Canada. I. Title.

    HD30.255.L45 2001   363.17′2′0971   C2001-900478-8

This book was typeset by Dynagram Inc.
in 10/12 Sabon.

For Jeanne

Contents

Figures

Tables

Preface and Acknowledgments

Risk controversies are a maze with an innocent-looking entry and no exit. By now it is well known that intense and protracted public disputes may arise about the decisions made by organizations (largely governments and industry) in managing health and environmental risks. What is less well known is how serious the risks to organizations are in failing to manage competently their involvement in such risk controversies. Failures in what is called here *risk issue management* can not only undo the work of careful risk management, but also have major and sometimes catastrophic consequences for organizations which get caught in the maze when a controversy erupts and they are named as responsible parties.

The main conclusion of the present volume may be stated as follows. There is an underlying common structure to risk controversies and their evolution through distinct stages which has considerable significance for defining competence in risk issue management. At one time or another, intense and persistent risk controversies have affected, or are likely to affect, most major industrial sectors and many different government agencies. The "instinctive" response of managers within those organizations, when a brewing risk controversy first threatens to engulf them, is one of denial: Denial, that the issues as represented by other interested parties are at all significant – and that those parties have any business meddling in such matters anyway; denial, that the management of the risk factors in question is or should be open to dispute by those who are not "experts" in the relevant scientific disciplines; and denial, that "the public" really needs to be involved in the intricacies of evaluating scientific research results and the other messy aspects of doing risk assessments. The case studies of risk controversies to date show, alas, that those instincts are unreliable guides to effective risk issue management. In all cases the opposite propositions are the better guides – namely, that public perceptions of risk are legitimate and must be treated as such, that risk management subsists in an inherently disputable zone, and that the public ought always to be involved (through good risk dialogues) in discussions about the nature of risk evaluation by scientists and risk managers.

The research and initial drafts for seven of the twelve chapters in this volume were done during the period (1994–98) when I held the Eco-Research Chair in Environmental Policy in the School of Policy Studies at Queen's University. For a number of those chapters there were collaborating authors who were attached in some way to the Environmental Policy Unit (hereafter EPU) where the chair program was housed. Thus this volume is a permanent record of the work supported by the chair program, which was sponsored at Queen's University by the federal Tri-Council Secretariat, using funds from Environment Canada, and Imperial Oil Ltd. The single person who is most responsible for whatever success that chair program had is Holly Mitchell, who acted as program administrator for its entire duration and who expertly steered the diverse talents we assembled towards a common set of goals. The originator and champion of the chair program is Keith Banting, Director of the School of Policy Studies, who watched over its activities with a bemused and tolerant mien.

The authorship ascriptions for this book are intended to reflect as fairly as possible the division of responsibilities and deliverables for our shared projects. I designed the research strategy for all but one of the chapters (all except chapter 5) and am responsible for writing three-quarters of the final text, which is why the book appears under my name on the title page. The collaborating authors are listed here in order of priority roughly proportionate to the scope of their contributions:

- *Debora L. VanNijnatten* is the senior author of chapter 6 and the co-author of chapter 9; she was a postdoctoral fellow at EPU and is now assistant professor of political science at Sir Wilfrid Laurier University.
- *Michael D. Mehta* is the author of chapter 5; he was a postdoctoral fellow and senior research associate at EPU and is now associate professor of sociology at the University of Saskatchewan.

- *Stephen Hill,* the senior author of chapter 4, is a doctoral student in the Faculty of Environmental Design at the University of Calgary.
- *Éric Darier,* co-author of chapter 9, was a postdoctoral fellow at EPU and is now a staff member with Greenpeace Canada in Montreal.
- *Greg Paoli,* a contributing author on chapter 3, is the president of Decisionalysis Risk Consultants, Inc. in Ottawa.
- *Peter V. Hodson,* who assisted us on chapter 6, is professor of biology and director of the School of Environmental Studies at Queen's University.

Another who was a valued associate at EPU is Mike Tyshenko, a doctoral candidate in biology at Queen's University and sometime triathlon competitor, who has been working with me on issues in the regulation of genetic engineering under the project title "Winged Pigs: Watching the Gene Jockeys." I am very grateful to Alison Hearn, now at Trent University, who formatted the complete draft book manuscript out of many separate pieces. Christina Chociolko, a doctoral candidate at Simon Fraser University, did a great deal of background research on pulp mill effluent issues (utilized in chapter 6) during the early 1990s in Vancouver, supported by the SSHRC Strategic Grant, "The Flow of Science into Public Policy" (1991–95).

A more recent collaborator at Queen's is David B. Layzell, professor of biology and executive research director of BIOCAP Canada, a research network established to promote a carbon management approach for the terrestrial biosphere as a component in Canada's response to global climate change issues. The then vice-principal (research) at Queen's, Suzanne Fortier, and her associate, Bruce Hutchinson, gave strong support over the years to the Eco-Research Chair program. I am also very grateful for the friendship of Geoff Flynn, professor of biochemistry at Queen's and chair of the Committee on Expert Panels of the Royal Society of Canada, and of my dear colleague John Meisel, professor of political studies emeritus.

For some years now my closest colleagues in the risk management field have been Steve E. Hrudey, professor of environmental health sciences, Department of Public Health Sciences, University of Alberta; Dan Krewski, formerly of Health Canada's Health Protection Branch and now professor in the Departments of Medicine and Epidemiology and Community Medicine, and director of the Institute of Population Health, at the Faculty of Medicine, University of Ottawa; and Len Ritter, professor of biology and executive director of the Canadian Network of Toxicology Centres, University of Guelph. My current collaborators in risk communication projects include Peter Wiedemann, director of the "Human – Environment – Technology Programme" at the Federal Research Center, Jülich, Germany, and Ortwin Renn, Center of Technology Assessment in Baden-Württemberg, Stuttgart; and over the years I have benefited from many exchanges on defining good risk communication practice with Conrad Brunk, professor of philosophy at Conrad Grebel College, University of Waterloo.

The manuscript was completed, including research and writing for the remaining five chapters, during the first two years of operation for my University of Calgary Research Chair in Risk Communication and Public Policy, which was established through the dedication of two individuals: Cooper Langford, professor of chemistry and then vice-president (research) at the University; and Randy Gossen, division vice-president, environment, safety, and social responsibility at Nexen Inc., who agreed to lead the effort to raise industry sponsor funding for the chair. The other industry sponsors of the chair program are Dow Chemical Canada Inc.; PanCanadian Petroleum Ltd.; Enbridge Inc.; the Canadian Chlorine Coordinating Committee; and the Alberta Energy and Utilities Board. Additional funds were provided by the two granting councils, NSERC and SSHRC, which administer jointly the Management of Technological Change (MOTC) program where the chair is located. Three members of the Faculty of Management at the University of Calgary were strong champions in this endeavour: Harrie Vredenburg, distinguished professor of Corporate Environmental Management and director of the Faculty's Institute for Resource Industry and Sustainability Studies; Norma Nielson, chairholder in Insurance and Risk Management; and Jim Chrisman, associate dean – research. I am very grateful to the dean of the faculty, David Saunders, for his strong support since he assumed that post in mid-1999. At Calgary Tim Griffin (environmental design) has been assisting me with original work in website design for innovative risk dialogue projects, and Henry Petersen (Ph.D. candidate, management) is leading new case study projects.

Recently I have had the great pleasure of working at the offices of the Royal Society of Canada/La Société royale du Canada in Ottawa in the company of Jean-Pierre Wallot (president 1997–99), Howard Alper (president of Academy III), and staff members Sandy Jackson, Shawna Lawson, Sophie Buoro, Nancy Lessard, Donna Boag, and Jeanne Salo. The success of the Society's expert panel process owes much to the persons who have served with distinction as chairs of the first five panels appointed under its new procedures: Ken Hare (emeritus, University of Toronto); Conrad Brunk, University of Waterloo (two panels); Dan Krewski, University of Ottawa; Steve Hrudey, University of Alberta; and Brian Ellis, University of British Columbia.

This is my sixth book with Philip Cercone, Joan McGilvray, and the staff of McGill-Queen's University Press, and naturally I find it impossible to believe that any academic author could hope to come upon a better publisher. Judy Williams of Toronto did the copy-editing and Maureen Garvie of Kingston prepared the index.

A number of these chapters, or parts of them, were originally published elsewhere. Some of chapter 2 was published in the autumn 2000 issue of *Isuma: Canadian Journal of Policy Research,* and chapter 3 will appear in the *Journal of Risk Research* vol. 4 (2001). Chapter 7 was published in the collection edited by G. Bruce Doern and Ted Reed, *Risky Business: Canada's Changing Science-Based Policy and Regulatory Regime* (University of Toronto Press, 2000), chapter 3. Some sections of chapter 8 first appeared under the title "Governance and the Environment" in Tom Courchene, ed., *Policy Frameworks for a Knowledge Economy* (John Deutsch Institute, Queen's University, 1996). Chapter 10 combines a text originally prepared for the World Health Organization's *International Consultation on Environmental Tobacco Smoke and Child Health* (January 1999, which appears on the WHO website at: *www.who.int/toh*) with some material from the article entitled "The Censorship of Commercial Speech, with Special Reference to Tobacco Product Advertising," published as chapter 6 in K. Petersen and A.C. Hutchinson, eds., *Interpreting Censorship in Canada* (University of Toronto Press, 1999).

W.L., Ottawa
December 2000

ς

PART ONE

Business in the Labyrinth

1 Risk Issue Management

The chamber of risks is a place of many rooms. The largest and best-appointed of them is the one occupied by professional risk managers, who since the 1970s have refined and codified their approach to health and environmental risks. Their current standards of practice are models of rational decision making, leading the uninitiated in step-wise fashion from the first apprehension of a concern (in technical language, the characterization of a hazard) to its resolution, which itself is usually cast in terms of how much risk is "acceptable" in a particular case.[1] Risk managers are justifiably proud of their powerful instruments, such as toxicology and epidemiology, because risks – the chances that something seriously harmful can happen to us – are notoriously tricky, and individuals often are fooled by them. The best illustration is provided by the delay between cause and effect, known as latency: on average there is a twenty-year delay between taking up regular smoking and the diagnosis of disease, and 30 per cent of long-term users will get a serious lung ailment from smoking. One cannot learn that unpleasant truth just from a casual observation of smoking behaviour; only the analytical tools of risk assessment can sort out what is really happening to our health.

One of the great pioneers of modern epidemiology, Sir Richard Doll, first showed the association between smoking and lung cancer in 1950.[2] Fifty years later the epidemic of tobacco use is still spreading around the world, with tens of millions sentencing themselves to an unnecessary and unpleasant form of early death. What this and much other evidence tells us is that there are other tenants besides professional risk managers in the chamber of risks. In fact risk is multidimensional, and therein lies the basis for the protracted and sometimes bitter fights that erupt regularly among the tenants there.[3]

Many of the other occupants look at risk rather differently from professional risk managers. Many feel much more comfortable with the hazards that are familiar to them, such as car accidents on roads, as opposed to unfamiliar things, such as radiation, and they appear willing to tolerate much higher risks for the former than for the latter. Many do not react in the same way to all consequences, such as fatalities: deaths of children seem particularly troublesome, for example, as do deaths of large numbers of people simultaneously, as in airplane crashes. Not all ways of dying or falling ill are regarded as equal, with cancer or slow neurodegenerative disease being more dreaded than sudden accidental death. Many are offended if, in response to an expression of concern about a particular hazard, such as radiation from nuclear power plants, they are told that, by comparison with many other things that people cheerfully indulge in daily, it is nothing to worry about. And generally many do not understand why, with all the resources of modern science at their disposal, risk managers cannot give clear and unequivocal responses to their concerns, but instead are wont to couch their answers in terms of probabilities, that is, the chances that something bad may or may not happen.

Many simply do not trust the risk managers to tell them the truth. They have seen government and industry spokespersons change their stories on risks, fighting protracted rearguard actions against the revelation of new evidence, and also have seen them add "spin" to data so that it appears less damaging. Europeans heard British politicians loudly proclaim the safety of British beef and denounce those who would close their borders to it in the 1990s, then watched in shock as the evidence of risk slowly trickled out; as of November 2000 the entire sad litany of dissimulation about the human health consequences of "mad cow disease" seemed set to repeat itself on the European continent. The next message the public heard from some of those same government voices was that foods containing genetically modified ingredients are "perfectly safe," and many reacted with contempt. The cellular telephone industry, riding the wave of consumer enthusiasm for their handy devices, insists that "no evidence of harm" is the same thing as "evidence of safety" and keeps quiet about a recommendation in a UK expert panel report in May 2000 that children under age sixteen should use cell phones sparingly.[4]

Professional risk managers are uneasy having to share close quarters with these other tenants. It is hard for them to understand why citizens who evidently cannot grasp the simplest scientific descriptions should want to meddle in such matters at all, rather than leaving them in the hands of capable experts. They are dismayed to hear that they are regarded by many as untrustworthy. It often offends them to be told that their findings and judgments are disputed by those who have no expertise in the relevant technical disciplines. And although these days such professionals are willing to concede that they should make determined efforts to explain to the public how they have arrived at their conclusions, as clearly and honestly as they can, many cannot accept the view that "the public" should have the final say on the acceptability of risks.

Understandable as they are, these reactions by professional risk managers are the initial steps which can, some time later, help to cause the organizations they work for – mostly industry and government departments – to stumble unwittingly into the labyrinth of risk controversy. Then the chamber of risks can turn into a chamber of horrors for business and governments.

Mismanagement of an organization's involvement in risk controversies can be very expensive indeed. An agency of the British government estimated the cost to the national treasury of the fallout from the "mad cow disease" episode, as of fall 1999, at £10 *billion* and still rising. Now this human and animal tragedy is set to repeat itself on the European continent, starting in France and Spain, where governments failed to draw what should have been obvious conclusions from the UK experience, and where the final tally of economic costs will be enormous. The collapse of the East Coast cod fishery in Canada, in which mismanagement of the resource through over-fishing played a significant part, already has a multi-billion-dollar price tag for Canadian taxpayers, in order to maintain those who used to make a living in that sector, a price which will continue to rise as large numbers of people wait for the cod to return, which may or may not ever happen. A global player in the forest industry, Canada's MacMillan Bloedel (now owned by Weyerhaeuser Company), conceded that changing social values about clear-cutting and the logging of old-growth forests had significantly affected its business risk. Silicon breast implant manufacturers in North America have paid out huge sums in compensation to patients for suspected health damage that, if it occurred, almost certainly was not caused by their products. Billions of dollars was lost from Monsanto Corporation's share value on the equity markets in 1998–99, and the long-term prospects of the entire agricultural biotechnology sector were put in jeopardy by the industry's wilful failure to comprehend and accommodate public concerns in Europe.[5] The uproar over genetically modified foods in Europe and the setbacks to that industrial sector occurred over a period of just two years, showing how quickly such controversies can strike and do damage. As corporate concentration proceeds apace with the globalization of industry, the economic stakes in risk controversies are magnified correspondingly, as is the need to discover and nurture a higher level of competence in risk issue management.

Risk is by definition a situation of uncertainty, and as a rule most of us do not handle uncertainties very well. Compounding that difficulty is the fact that the public gets so little help in understanding the basis of risk assessments from those who are keen to persuade them that there is "nothing to worry about." For example, it is very clear that many among the public do not know what genes are. So, when scientists working in the field of molecular genetics manipulate genes in the laboratory, changing the genetic makeup of everyday commodities such as corn and potatoes, and have farmers sow large quantities of the new varieties in the environment, all the while reassuring us that everything will be just fine, many respond: "Not so fast. What's going on here?" Then someone finds a genetically modified corn variety in taco shells that wasn't supposed to be there, and Kraft Foods recalls millions of dollars of products from store shelves in the United States and Canada. Aventis, the corporation which developed the corn variety, following the lead of other large multinationals, decided to get out of the agricultural business entirely after pulling its seed product off the market. At least they did not lose their shirts in the process, which is more than can be said for Monsanto.[6]

GLOBAL CLIMATE CHANGE: A RISK CONTROVERSY IN FORMATION

Consider global climate change as a burgeoning risk issue.[7] At stake is whether there are human-induced effects on climate, caused by the greenhouse gases (GHGs, especially CO_2 and methane) that we emit into the atmosphere, which might have major – perhaps catastrophic – adverse impacts on agriculture, forests, rainfall patterns, violent storms, insect populations, disease vectors, and other domains in our lives. The stakes in *this* game of chance will not long permit us to take refuge in uncertainties as an excuse for either indifference or inaction, for although the relevant uncertainties are indeed huge – including whether the ultimate outcome from "global warming" may be a new Ice Age! – so too are the possible consequences. If the stakes were relatively modest, many of us might opt to wait a while before deciding whether or not to worry. But where the stakes involve some possibility of truly catastrophic dislocations in the course of civilization, are most of us prepared to have our descendants realize that we decided just to wait and see how it all came out? Actually, when the stakes start getting that high, most of us are too risk-averse for the game anyway, and we would (if we could) refuse to play. Alas, we cannot opt out of the climate change game, because GHGs are rising steadily and will continue to do so for the foreseeable future, perhaps even at an escalating pace.

Of course maybe the worst won't come to pass. Certainly we will do more science to get a better idea about what is happening to our climate, as greenhouse gas concentrations in the atmosphere continue to rise, and to be more precise about what types of actions would be required on our part if we wished to stabilize them at some level. Indeed, there is some probability that only good things will happen, because plants love carbon and we could all end up living happily ever after in a botanical paradise. There is also some probability that nothing very bad will happen, as GHG concentrations rise, because offsetting changes in the atmosphere will occur naturally, and everything will stay just about the way it is now. And there are the other, darker possibilities, namely, the advent of catastrophic dislocations in our established ways of life from human-induced climate change. The awkward problem – if we wait, first, for "convincing scientific proof" one way or the other that climate change is or is not significantly related to anthropogenic GHG emissions, and, second, to see whether the net results look all right or alternatively quite bleak to us – is that it may be too late to do anything at all about a bleak prospect. We may not be able to reverse the course of events, despite our technological prowess, should the natural systems thus set in motion turn out to be resistant to further influence from us.

Thus no matter how any of us calculates the risks associated with climate change itself, or the risks associated with our responses to this issue, what none of us can avoid is a confrontation with the unpleasant business of decision-making under uncertainty, where the stakes – including the economic costs and benefits – are enormous. Nations such as Canada have to manage disagreements among their own citizens, over whether to take actions or not (actions that impose real costs to us), and if so, what ones we should take if we wish to be "precautionary" in the face of these risks. Nations will have to participate in international disagreements over who is responsible for what part of this problem, and who should pay to fix it, and whether developing countries should pay anything at all. There will be monumental fights over what actions by various countries will "count" in the way of garnering credits for sequestering carbon: for example, many find rather upsetting Canada's claim that it could be entitled to emissions credits for selling its nuclear power plants abroad, on the grounds that using nuclear power to generate electricity displaces the GHGs otherwise created by using fossil-fuel energy sources. In the meantime everyone is hoping that science will come up with definitive conclusions one way or another, so that all can agree on what we must do, however expensive it proves to be – an expectation that is, unless I miss my guess, certain to be frustrated for a long time to come.

At the time of writing, national governments had left The Hague after the latest (failed) round of negotiations under the Kyoto Protocol, including countries such as Canada, which agreed in 1997 to reduce its GHGs and has watched its emissions rise steadily thereafter, having done almost nothing to honour that commitment. The fossil-fuel industries, including the great multinationals which dominate the petroleum business, are manoeuvring carefully to avoid being tagged with too great a share of responsibility for picking up the slack.[8] But there is trouble brewing in the future for both governments and a variety of industry sectors.

The reason is simple. Most governments in the developed world have told their citizens that they are committed to "taking action" on the climate change issue and that they support the objectives of the Kyoto Protocol, even though few meaningful actions have been taken just yet. But what these governments have failed to tell their citizens is that, *if* present or anticipated future GHG concentrations in the earth's atmosphere are a problem worth worrying about, the Kyoto Protocol will not solve that problem – because the agreed-upon reductions are so trivial. The reductions in GHGs for the developed economies agreed upon at Kyoto (in the range of 5 per cent to 7 per cent below 1990 national emissions levels) would, if fully implemented, just delay the doubling of GHG concentrations in the atmosphere, relative to pre-industrial times, by about one decade.

I suspect that many citizens have been led to believe that implementing the Kyoto Protocol, by stopping further increases in GHG *emissions* in industrialized countries, will therefore "solve the problem" in the sense that global GHG *concentrations* will stop rising, which is most certainly not the case. The reason is straightforward: "Because of the long atmospheric lifetimes of most greenhouse gases, concentrations will continue to rise for a long time even after emissions stabilize or drop."[9] Global CO_2 *emissions* are currently about nine gigatonnes per year (GtC/yr) and in some scenarios will peak at about sixteen GtC/yr around the middle of the twenty-first century before starting a long decline; at that point atmospheric CO_2 *concentrations* are forecast to be above 750ppm, about double the current levels. To achieve an objective such as "stabilizing" global GHG concentrations at some specified level, say 500ppm – which is about 125ppm higher than present levels – would require enormous reductions in current emissions, of the order

Figure 1
Emissions vs. concentration of carbon

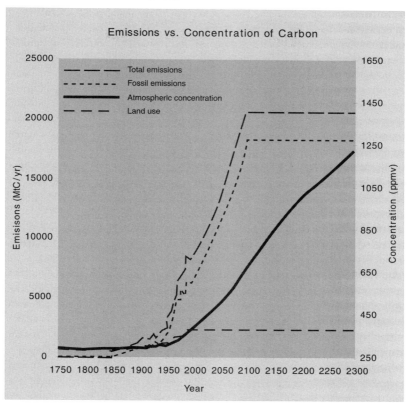

Source: Dr Hadi Dowlatabadi. The carbon emissions and concentration scenarios presented here are based on a simple model developed by Dowlatabadi that uses the neutral biosphere carbon cycle model of Maier-Reimer and Hasselman, together with historic fossil fuel emissions from 1750 to 1997 (Marland, Boden, et al.) and land-use emissions from 1850 to 1990 (Houghton and Hackler). The missing historic emissions and the carbon cycle parameters are calibrated using the Siple ice-core CO_2 record (Neftel, Friedli, et al.).

of *60 per cent* or more below current levels.[10] (See figure 1.) Attempting to meet any such objective would substantially reduce our present standard of living, which is why no politician wants to breathe a word about these scenarios. When the public awakens to these unpleasant truths, the "issue" of global climate change will be considerably hotter than it is now, and there will be much anguished finger-pointing among governments and industry players as blame is assigned for misleading the public.

Whatever the ultimate outcome, the climate change conundrum will demand that all players do much better at risk issue management in the future than they have in the past. And since climate change exhibits in exaggerated form the characteristics of risk issues generally, the baptism of fire we are about to undergo in dealing with it should be beneficial to us in more ways than one.[11]

FROM RISK MANAGEMENT
TO RISK ISSUE MANAGEMENT

There are long-standing deficiencies in the organizational structures and personnel complements among institutions charged with health and environmental risk management. These deficiences stem from a failure to understand the essential difference between *risk management* and *risk issue management*. I will introduce this terminology here and return to it in the concluding chapter.

Risk management for health and environmental risks uses scientific risk assessments to estimate the probable harm to persons and environments resulting from specific types of substances or activities.[12] As such, even when risk managers seek honestly to take into account varying perceptions of the risk in question among different sectors of the public, they are necessarily and properly constrained by the scope and limitations of their scientific assessment in recommending specific courses of action. This is an inescapable part of their duty to protect public health to the best of their ability, taking into account the uncertainties that are always a factor in risk estimates. Mistakes can and will be made in this regard for a whole host of reasons; the public only has a right to expect that the risk management protocols will be sufficiently self-critical and iterative so that serious mistakes are discovered and corrected in the shortest possible time-frame.

Risk issue management is fundamentally different from risk management.[13] The most important difference is that risk issues, as they play out in society at large, are not primarily driven by the state of scientific risk assessments. Rather, such assessments are just one of a series of "contested" domains within the issue. The phrase "risk issue" refers to any of the following types of risk management situations, for example:

- *Stakeholder confrontation*, or the existence of some dispute – about the scope or existence of a risk and how it should be managed – among interested parties, e.g., between environmental non-governmental organizations (ENGOs) and government or industry (such as in the cases of dioxins or genetically modified food crops);

- *Intractable behaviour*, or the persistent inability of professionals to change the public's risk-taking behaviour to some desired degree (cases of drinking/driving by young males or tobacco use);
- *High uncertainty*, or the public expressions of concern over risk factors that are poorly characterized from a scientific standpoint, or where uncertainties in risk assessments are quite large, despite the fact that technologies giving rise to them are already in use or in active development (cases of cellular telephones, cloning, GHG emissions and climate change).

Both public-sector risk management agencies and industries get caught up in such issues daily. Indeed, for professional risk managers this is becoming the stuff of everyday life: a good deal of ongoing scientific review is mixed with some low-level issue management, but the organization never seems to know when or under what circumstances something is going to erupt into a high-profile controversy. This is because it is not aligned or staffed explicitly to deal with risk issue management.

Risk issues are configured by the competing attempts of various stakeholder interests to define or control the course of social action with respect to health and environmental hazards. Issue management refers to the relation between an organization and its larger social "environment," where reigning public policy provides the basic "rules of the game"; and it is inherently governed by *strategic* considerations as developed by an organization or even a loose collection of individuals. (See table 1.) All those who wish to become skilled interveners in risk controversies, such as ENGOs, as well as those who will inevitably be caught up in them, namely industry and governments, become issue managers (by choice or default). To do so entails understanding the internal dynamics of risk controversies and seeking to influence them towards some final resolution; in most cases this will be called the "public interest," although inevitably there will be diverse definitions of what this means in practice. These resolutions may be, for example, introducing a new substance or activity or banning an existing one; changing laws or the regulatory environment; adopting new principles, such as the precautionary approach; introducing changes in business practices; approving a new economic development project or creating wilderness preservation zones; and so forth.

To put the main point a bit differently: Whereas risk management seeks to assess and control a *risk domain*, risk issue management responds to a *risk controversy*. A risk domain is an activity, technology, or environmental hazard that has a unique collection of risk factors associated with it; for example, smoking is a risk factor for cancers of different organs, arteriosclerosis, stroke, emphysema, and many other

Table 1
Contrast between risk management and risk issue management

	Risk Domain	Risk Controversy
Type of responsibility	Risk management	Risk issue management
Type of expertise required	Risk/benefit assessment	Risk communication
Key activities	Hazard characterization Exposure assessment Benefits assessment Uncertainty analysis Options/decision analysis	Science explanations Science/public interface Science/policy interface Explaining uncertainties Stakeholder relations
Orientation of activities	"Substantive"	Strategic
Principal "language"	Technical/probabilistic	Non-technical/graphics

diseases. The risk factors in various risk domains, as assessed or perceived by various parties over time, quantitatively and qualitatively, become the subject of risk management decision making, which may lead to risk reduction strategies or other actions.

A risk controversy, on the other hand, is a risk domain which becomes the subject of a protracted battle among stakeholder interest groups, the outcome of which may or may not be consistent with any set of decision options preferred by the risk managers (in government or industry) who have "official" responsibility for the file in question. The evolution of a risk controversy is determined primarily by the competing strategies of whatever groups or organizations choose to, or are compelled to, enter into it; as mentioned earlier, the objective of these strategies is to steer the outcome of the controversy towards some preferred risk management option.

Since by definition a risk controversy is an area of competing visions about where an optimal resolution lies, competence in risk issue management should not be understood as seeking to "control" the outcome. Rather, it means in general being able to compete successfully with other influential stakeholders within the zone of controversy, in a way that is appropriate to the specific positioning of an organization and its lines of accountability within society as a whole. Industry, ENGOs, and governments all have quite diverse positionings in this regard. Governments' positioning is defined primarily by their role in defining and defending "the public interest" as such – for example, seeking to be as "inclusive" as possible in relation to the spectrum of social interests. Business and industry traditionally are regarded as having the promotion of shareholder interests as their leading, if not sole, aim; however, this view is changing (as is the law of corporate governance), as major corporations wish to acknowledge both environmental and social responsibilities in their areas of operation. Environmental and other non-governmental organizations would appear to be answerable solely to their supporters and funders, although there are efforts under way to hold them accountable for their actions and arguments before some kind of wider public tribunal.

Within the zone of risk controversy, risk assessment and management are strictly subordinate activities, the outcome being determined primarily by which of the participant organizations develop the most successful strategic manoeuvres. Sometimes the scientific assessment is definitive for the issue resolution and sometimes it is not; the outcome is often impossible to predict, and in any case depends primarily on the specific pathway along which the issue evolves. In some notorious cases (such as Alar and apples or saccharin, for example), most observers remain convinced, years or decades after the key events, that from the standpoint of "good science" the wrong resolution occurred. In others, such as BSE and British beef, or health risks associated with radio-frequency fields, the weight of massive and irresolvable uncertainties about the scope of exposure and potential harm hangs like a dark cloud over both the issue and its resolution to date. Even where a broad stakeholder consensus based on scientific evaluation finally emerges, as it has now with a group of chemicals called "persistent organic pollutants," that consensus is the product of a long and tortuous pathway filled with recriminations directed at some parties by others. In all such cases scientific assessment played or plays some role in the issue evolution, but only as one factor among many.

The divide between risk management and risk issue management affects none more seriously than governments. They must do both. Over the past thirty years, coincident with the rise of the modern specialized field of health and environmental risk management, many governments, including Canada's, as well as industry sectors, have developed outstanding expertise in risk assessment and management. But none of them is much good at risk issue management, for a number of reasons, but mainly because they do not accept the legitimacy of risk controversies. I shall return to this theme in the concluding chapter.

Involvement in risk controversies poses distinctive problems and challenges for the organizations which either choose to become engaged with those issues (ENGOs, citizen groups) or are compelled by legal or other mandates to do so (business, governments). On a pragmatic level, the problems include training and supporting competent personnel; allotting adequate resources; understanding the nature of the issues at all organizational levels; maintaining involvement over long periods of time; and relating fairly and effectively to other stakeholders. The challenges are quite severe; they include reacting responsibly to highly emotional situations, handling large uncertainties in decision-making frameworks, and taking into account the often very different values and perspectives that various stakeholders bring to risk issues.

There is very little in the health and environmental risk management literature explicitly dealing with managerial factors as such. A variable called "perceived managerial (in)competence" has been identified, however; it is defined as the "degree to which the public believes that a hazard implies that similar risks are being managed incompetently." The key finding is stated as follows: "Perceptions of managerial incompetence influence the public's response to a hazard to a degree approaching the scale of the event."[14] Here is a finding, derived from the well-known concept of "risk amplification," that is of direct relevance to the mission of risk managers. It means that managers have a lever with which they may be able to influence the outcomes of controversies over risks in society, helping to produce better resolutions to those controversies – so long as they are in a position to operate the lever.

Thus "managerial competence" is a domain where improvement in risk issue management is or ought to be possible, at least in theory. I believe that one primary source of the countervailing perception (to wit, that widespread managerial incompetence prevails) is to be found in a faulty self-assessment and self-representation, by the agencies charged with health and environmental risk management, of their basic mission. To put the point succinctly, they have conceived themselves (over a long period of time) as experts in hazard characterization, and to a lesser extent in risk assessment, whereas what is needed from them above all is expertise in risk issue management. Those agencies naturally also configured their professional staff complement in line with this conception. The commonest example of these faults can be found in the responses of such agencies over the years to public expressions of concern about hazards that fall under their mandates: all too often the representatives of those agencies addressed the hazard characterization (and did so quite fairly, on the whole), but not the concern. What is needed above all is competence in addressing the unity of hazard-plus-concern.

The chapters to follow will illustrate and explain, through case studies and analysis, both the meaning and the importance of the distinction between risk management and risk issue management.[15] In part 1 the studies concentrate on the ways in which industry and business can get trapped in the labyrinth of risk controversy, while part 2 gives a complementary picture where governments are involved. In both sets of cases, however, the other often appears, because governments and business interact so closely in matters of risk management. Indeed because of the close interaction of business and government in today's economy, there are ample opportunities for each to do considerable damage to the other through failures in risk issue management. The chapters to follow illustrate this well. In the cases of genetically modified foods, cell phones, MMT (a manganese-based fuel additive), and nuclear power, serious failings by industry in risk issue management have compromised government's ability to carry out publicly credible risk management. On the other hand, the case studies of pulp mill effluent, toxic chemicals management, tobacco control, and cloning risks show that governments are sometimes paralysed by risk issues and unable to give clear policy direction either to the public or to industry (or in some cases both). Although there is only a brief mention of the issue of global climate change in chapter 1, this risk controversy in formation already shows how some governments are willing to leave industry twisting in the wind, as the controversy mounts, by avoiding their responsibilities to set a clear policy context and to help the public understand the full ramifications of this complex issue.

As well, in many of these cases environmental and citizen groups appear as important players, and their importance is likely to increase in the coming years. The evolution of issues such as genetically modified foods, toxic chemicals management, and climate change have been dictated in part by ENGOs that have shown themselves capable of matching industry's global reach, while in others (such as nuclear power and cell phones) more localized citizen groups have been significant actors in the controversies.

2 Frankenfoods;
or, The Trouble with Science

We think genetically modified material is very good science [but] at the moment, very bad public relations. We've got too many people worried about eating the product and we're in the business of giving our customers what they want, not what we think they should have. (Harrison McCain)

GMOs [genetically modified organisms] are good science, but bad politics. Are GMOs safe, good for the environment, and necessary to support the inevitable growth in the world's population? Yes, but the same arguments can be made for advancing nuclear power. Despite the support of the scientific community, it is unlikely that we will add any new nuclear power plants any time soon. (Deutsche Bank)

The 1-day conference ... was not yet over, and researchers were still heatedly debating whether corn that had been genetically modified to make Bt, a protein toxic to insects, harms monarch butterflies. Yet a [newspaper] headline that day ... seemed to give the meeting's conclusion: "Monarch Butterfly so far not imperilled." ... How could the newspapers have known the upshot of the conference before the researchers themselves did? In fact, they didn't. The stories illustrate how eager interest groups are to spin even preliminary and debated results in the continuing war of words over the risks and benefits of genetically modified crops. (Science)

Those who promote the [GM] foods need to sell their product – to recognize that the opposition comes not from ignorance but from unsatisfied concerns.

Whether the market will hear the message will depend on the commitment, the honesty and, ultimately, the case of the genetic crusaders.

(Editorial, *Globe and Mail*)

By hiding behind the rubric of consumer demand, companies such as McCain's are actually amplifying the social concerns about genetically engineered foods. The successful adoption of any new technology requires a rigorous system to integrate public concerns with scientific knowledge, to maximize the benefits of something like genetic engineering while actively and openly minimizing potential risks.

(Douglas Powell)[1]

MONSANTO'S PATH

In early 1995 Robert Shapiro became the new president and CEO of Monsanto, an old firm best known for its chemicals business, then with a share price of about $10. Shapiro devised a bold course of action which saw Monsanto divest itself of its chemicals business and seek to focus the new corporation on the twin pillars of agricultural and pharmaceutical products, unified under a "life sciences" designation, where new product development was based firmly on applications of biotechnology. With a rising share price and lots of favourable publicity in the business press, Shapiro went on the acquisitions trail in the seed production and distribution sector, spending $6 billion in just three years.[2]

Not everything went smoothly for Monsanto, notably the failed merger attempt with American Home Products in mid-1998, which would have been, if consummated, the sixth largest merger to date in US corporate history. Still, towards the end of 1998 Monsanto's share price had passed the $60 mark. Shapiro also sought to advertise his business strategy widely, saying it exemplified an "environmental sustainability" ethic, with a special focus on meeting the needs of the developing world. This message was articulated in an interview published at the beginning of 1997 in the *Harvard Business Review*: "I offer a prediction: The early twenty-first century is going to see a struggle between information technology and biotechnology on the one hand and environmental degradation on the other." Biotechnology, according to Shapiro, is a sustainable technology because it results in sharp reductions in pesticide use and brings significant increases in crop yields, which reduces demands on land and water resources. Further, Monsanto would "transfer" its knowledge in this area to help the developing world: "The developing economies can grow by brute force, by putting steel in the ground and depleting natural resources and burning a lot of hydrocarbons. But a far better way to go would be for companies like Monsanto to transfer their knowledge and help those countries avoid the mistakes of the past."[3]

North America was the home of the revolution in agricultural production achieved through biotechnology. In the late 1980s the regulatory agencies there had taken the position that foods which contained genetically modified (GM) ingredients should be evaluated according to standard categories of adverse effects, such as whether or not allergic reactions were caused; if no adverse effects were found, the food would be considered "safe." The technology by which these ingredients were created was irrelevant to this evaluation. Therefore, it was unnecessary to require any unique labelling for foods with GM ingredients, and indeed, there was no reason why any special attention should be called to the fact that genetic modification had been used to create the plants and crops which became part of the food supply. With this regulatory clearance Monsanto sought to market its new products aggressively around the world.

The good times were short-lived, for already by early 1997 Monsanto's biotechnology-based corporate strategy started unravelling in Europe. Countries such as Austria, Luxembourg, Italy, and Spain began to ban specific GM crops; then in April the European Commission voted overwhelmingly to prohibit the importation of US corn crops that were genetically modified but were not labelled as such. Greenpeace and other activists launched protest campaigns, including the staging of high-profile events in which test plots of genetically modified crops were invaded and torn up. Greenpeace also played a leading role in June 1999, persuading the prime minister of France, Lionel Jospin, to pressure other European countries to impose a two-year European Union moratorium on new approvals for GM crops, which was indeed done later that year.[4] By mid-1998, opinion polls in the United Kingdom had begun to show overwhelming public support for keeping genetically modified crops segregated from others in the food supply and for explicit labelling of foods and ingredients derived from genetically modified crops.[5] The European Parliament passed a resolution calling for such labelling in early 1999.

Far more damaging, however, and the first clear sign that the pro-biotechnology battle was being lost, were the actions of major food retailers and producers at this time. In March 1999 Sainsbury's and Marks and Spencer in the UK (joined shortly thereafter by Tesco, the largest retailer), together with Carrefour in France and Superquinn in Ireland, said they would stop stocking foods with GM ingredients; in April, Nestlé UK and Unilever UK, the national subsidiaries of the two largest food producers in the world, announced that they would phase out the use of GM ingredients in all their products.[6] Gerber, the world's largest manufacturer of baby foods, followed suit in August of that year. The investment community had been watching these developments and reacted quickly. The research arm of Deutsche Bank issued a report on 21 May 1999 entitled "GMOs Are Dead":

Perhaps we don't yet fully realize it, but genetically modified organisms (GMOs) have just crossed the line. Thirty days ago, the investment community accorded only positive attributes, such as innovation, productivity and progress, to GMO corn and soybeans. The success of GMOs was, to a great degree, the basis for the strong growth rates and the huge public and private market valuations accorded this sector. Today, the term GMO has become a liability. We predict that GMOs, once perceived as the driver of the bull case for this sector, will now be perceived as a pariah. We … would broadly recommend a sale of the seed sector.

The analysts predicted strong growth in the market for non-GMO products.

Monsanto and other companies had fought back vigorously both behind closed doors, in meetings with European regulators, and by massive "public information" campaigns in the media, insisting that it was inappropriate to identify these foods with distinctive labels and rejecting all accusations that there were unacceptable environmental or health risks associated with them. In all this publicity and pressure Monsanto took a leading position precisely because it had made the largest corporate wager on the future of biotechnology. The company apparently was oblivious to the acute sensitivities Europeans had developed to issues of food contamination following the UK scandal about mad cow disease, which had erupted in March 1996, only a short while before the first spreading of news about GM foods. It made no attempt to engage in a reasoned dialogue with the critics of biotechnology (until it was too late to make any difference) and, worse, showed no sympathy whatsoever for those segments of the public which claimed to be worried about the new technology, perhaps because (according to Monsanto) they could not comprehend what it is and how it differs from older technologies. According to Stuart Hart, a US business professor, "the company's inability to listen was pathological."[7] Its basic attitude seemed to be: North American governments have approved these products and we do not need your acquiescence in order to market them.

Gordon Conway, president of the Rockefeller Foundation, tried to warn Monsanto's Board of Governors in June 1999 about the dangers of its confrontational approach to controversy, urging them instead to make a commitment to a very different course of action: "As well as committing to a broad concern for the well-being of the poorest, I think that there are some specific steps that you could take today that would improve acceptance of plant biotechnology in the developing and the industrialized world. These are things that would remove many of the suspicions about abuse of intellectual property to create market domination. They would cost you very little and could allow many poor farmers and others to see your technology as much less of a threat." Ironically, many of those steps could be considered to be fully in accordance with any "environmental sustainability ethic" worthy of its name, so in effect Conway was urging Shapiro just to live up to the vision which he himself had articulated two years previously.[8] Monsanto's board made no public response to this plea. In any case it may have been too late for them to attempt to repair the damage that had been done.[9]

The *Economist* commented at the end of 1999: "A year-and-a-half ago, he [Shapiro] and his firm were flourishing; now both it and his concept of a life-science company – one that applies biotechnology to medicine, food and farming – have been demonised from India to Indiana."[10] Eighteen months from start to finish! Towards the end, too late, Shapiro issued his *mea culpa*: He sent a videotaped address to a Greenpeace conference in London in October 1999, in which he acknowledged that Monsanto had "irritated and antagonized more people than we have persuaded," conceding that he and his company had been guilty of "condescension or indeed arrogance."[11] In December 1999, with its stock price nearly cut in half from its previous high, Monsanto announced a merger with Pharmacia and Upjohn, in which its partner's name would be assumed by the merged entity and where the agroscience business, carrying Monsanto's name, would be spun off and sold. Shapiro was scheduled to leave the new company within a year. During this same period, when the Swiss giant Novartis merged with the UK's AstraZeneca, the new entity also spun off its agrochemicals interests into a new company, Syngenta AG. And Aventis, formed in late 1999 by the merger of Rhone Poulenc and Hoechst, put its subsidiary, Aventis CropScience, up for sale in November of 2000.[12]

Less than three years after the *Harvard Business Review* interview had appeared, both Robert B. Shapiro's bold corporate vision and the corporation itself in which it was to be embodied had been shipwrecked on the shoals of a risk controversy he neither anticipated nor understood.[13]

THE TROUBLE WITH SCIENCE

While the public controversy relating to agricultural biotechnology and genetically modified foods had been gathering steam in Europe and

Japan for some years prior to 1999, it had lain dormant until then across North America. In fall 1999 the campaign against GM foods, led by Greenpeace, moved to Canada.[14] In less than two months the effects had been felt: publicity grew steadily; the Canadian Wheat Board (following similar actions by the US-based Cargill and Archer Daniels Midland) said it would begin thinking about requiring its grain suppliers to segregate conventional from genetically modified crops in the next growing season; and two Canadian firms, McCain's and Seagram's, announced that beginning with the next season's crops they would no longer use genetically modified ingredients (specifically potatoes and corn) in their products. Already beleaguered farmers immediately began feeling the heat from this new threat to their livelihoods, as they faced choices about what types of crops to plant in the coming year amid doubts about whether, if they were to continue to use genetically modified variants, they would be able to sell them at all.[15] And yet, throughout all these events, both the great majority of independent scientists, as well as officials working for government regulatory authorities in all these countries, insisted that the products in question had been rigorously evaluated for risk factors and been found to be "safe."

What these further stages in the controversy over genetically modified foods show is that a failure to engage the public fully and fairly in a dialogue about the science of plant biotechnology and its attendant risks, a failure that can be laid squarely at the doorstep of both industry and governments, can jeopardize the future economic prospects of an industry sector that governments have been very keen to promote. Those responsible for the oversight of this industrial sector – governments and the plant biotechnology industry – have managed the *risks* reasonably well, at least according to the expert scientific consensus (with some dissent), but they have also seriously mismanaged the *risk issues*. In this case in particular, they have failed to appreciate the importance of one key feature of competent risk issue management, namely, the need to establish an appropriate relation between science and the public in risk controversies.

In retrospect it appears that North American risk regulators missed a golden opportunity to "do the right thing" when the need for the regulation of plant biotechnology appeared during the 1980s, namely, to restructure their basic risk management approach so as to overcome the mistakes of previous epochs. When the first versions of modern health and environmental risk management had appeared on the scene, in the 1970s, the new approach had to be applied retrospectively to major industries, such as chemicals and nuclear power, which had grown up and prospered in the absence of society's having proper regulatory structures in place. Much was learned in the battles to impose a new structure on those industries – for example, the differences between "expert" and "public" assessments of risk, and the need to encompass both (the nuclear industry never did learn to appreciate this important point). But, like other nations, Canada failed to seize the opportunity, when the new biotechnology came along, to apply these lessons.

This failing had two aspects, both of which are explored well in two recent doctoral theses done at Canadian universities. Katherine Barrett's work details how governments in North America and some European countries, ever anxious to prove themselves as good economic managers by "picking winners" among new technologies, became obsessed with acting as aggressive promoters of the new biotechnology.[16] Their promotional orientation inevitably dictated the way in which they would approach their responsibilities for assessing and regulating this new industrial sector. Their desire to find an approach which would encourage a fledging sector to develop quickly is illustrated well in the fact that their regulatory rationale, based on the process/product distinction (which is discussed further below), only appeared after the first generation of product development in industrial laboratories was well under way. Elizabeth Moore's thesis has a special focus on the use of "science" as an instrument in regulatory policy formation in the negotiation between industry and government about how to manage the risks associated with plant biotechnology.[17] The discussion to follow shows how this use of science can have unintended impacts on the structure of risk controversy: the subsequent emphasis on science as the *justification* for the chosen regulatory path effectively leaves the public "out of the loop," since most members of the public have no familiarity with what the science of plant genetics is.

Moreover, the chosen regulatory framework was constructed in a secret dialogue between industry and government officials; the public was invited in, and introduced to the subject, only after the fact, after governments were already committed to its basic structure. For example, the first major public consultation exercise on plant biotechnology regulation held by the Canadian federal government took place in 1993, when the federal regulatory framework had already been fully articulated within the bureaucracy. Moreover, the structure of this so-called "consultation" consigned most of the issues of interest to the public to a separate "special session on non-regulatory issues," the very name of which indicated that whatever was discussed there would have no impact on the design of the regulatory system itself.[18] These self-imposed limitations on regulatory responsibility also inhibited Canadian federal departments from freely engaging the public in discussions on a wider range of issues: no communications program from

these departments to date, dealing with products of the new biotechnology, has included a balanced account of risks and benefits, and controversial issues often elicit a response from "official spokespersons"
that is either confrontational or merely inarticulate.[19]

In addition, as Barrett shows, the core concept in that basic structure was founded on an excessively narrow construction of the concept of risk: only risks characterized by the science of plant biology
itself would be admitted into the calculus, and all of them were confined by definition to product-based risks. The structure of regulatory
discourse about the new biotechnology had decided, before the public
was ever invited into the debate, to rule out *a priori* any considerations having to do with the process of using molecular biology to create new organisms. The discussion would be about product safety, and
nothing else. This apparently clever strategy allowed industry to get
its first-generation products into the marketplace with a minimum of
fuss, but it overlooked the fact that, these days, there is no guarantee
that the public will passively accept a "definition of the situation" that
institutions seek to impose arbitrarily on public discourse.

The scientific characterization of hazards is the foundation of modern risk assessment and risk management. However, the epigraphs at
the head of this chapter show the great extent to which science itself –
in this case, the science of plant molecular genetics and its applications
to engineering new traits into food crops – became an explicit theme in
the public risk controversy. This is, in fact, an illustration of one of the
central unifying themes in this book, for questions about the role of
scientific knowledge and expert evaluation can be found at the heart of
all protracted risk controversies. What is especially noteworthy in the
present case is that practising plant scientists themselves decided to
assume a high-profile public role when the controversy about GM foods
finally landed on the North American shores. The record of this involvement is both interesting in itself and significant for the understanding of risk controversies and the tasks of risk issue management.

During fall 1999 three separate attempts were made to persuade
Canadian scientists working in fields related to plant biotechnology to
sign public statements of support for it. One, entitled "Statement by
Scientists in Support of the Responsible Development and Application
of Biotechnology" and dated 1 November 1999, was written by scientists at the University of Guelph and includes the following opening
passages:[20]

As scientists involved with the research and development of biotechnology and
supporters of its use to provide better health and nutrition to people around the
world, we urge Canadians to participate in a dialogue about the technology's

potential. We strongly encourage Canadians to base that dialogue on sound science, on facts and on the results of peer-reviewed research. We hope that Canadians will not be influenced by those who resort to unfounded speculation and discredited science to alarm them ... [W]e expect anyone who chooses to communicate to Canadians about science will do so responsibly using facts and the best available information, rather than unsubstantiated allegations and rhetoric as their platforms.

This statement has certain very serious drawbacks, considered from the standpoint of good risk issue management. First, it is divisive and not "inclusive," for it separates the world into those who have "sound science" (an industry code-word), "facts," and the best interests of the whole world's population on their side, and the others, who are motivated by a wish to alarm the public unnecessarily and who have only "misinformation and fear" on their side. Second, nowhere in the document is any reservation expressed about the whole range of developments in this area to date; thus it fails to concede that there are *any* good reasons for anyone to express any concerns at all. Surely this is going too far. For example, a most reputable source, the Royal Society (London), earlier had included two whole sections in its September 1998 report, "Genetically Modified Plants for Food Use," about areas of concern.[21] Third, it is unwise for anyone to assert that the world of human experience is so simple and transparent such that "facts" lie all on one side of a disputed domain, with nothing but pure "misinformation" on the other.

The second statement was signed by about fifty Canadian plant scientists and sent to federal ministers in late October 1999. It differs from the first in important ways, primarily in implicitly acknowledging the legitimacy of public concerns: "[I]ncreasing concern is being expressed by various groups about the use of genetic engineering for plant improvement, particularly about possible deleterious effects on human health, but also about the concentration of plant variety ownership in the hands of a few multinational companies, and about the impacts of the widespread deployment of genetically modified plants in the environment ... We therefore consider it imperative that the concerns being raised by citizens be openly examined in an appropriate and credible forum."[22] The signatories call for a "national consultative roundtable" in order to air these concerns. This is a much better text than the previous one, because it does not presuppose that the issues to which it calls attention are already settled, or that virtue is the exclusive property of one party in the debate.

The third statement was apparently the product of a well-known international public relations firm; it was drafted in the form of a "Letter to the Editor" of a newspaper and is an unfortunate example of an attempt to manipulate public opinion.[23] The text which the scientists were encouraged to sign and circulate identifies neither its original author nor the individual or organizational client on whose behalf the firm was acting. In asking others to put their names to this statement, its authors (whoever they were) were in effect attempting to enlist Canadian scientists in a double deception. One would have thought that this discredited tactic had gone out of fashion by now. Those who paid for this service may realize too late that they could become their own worst enemies in the court of public opinion. Greenpeace and other opposition groups must have been pleased indeed at having received such help for their cause.

Confusion among plant scientists about how to engage in the public controversy was widespread. For example, in an e-mail message, Professor Peggy Lemaux, of the Department of Plant and Microbial Biology at the University of California, Berkeley, told about having just heard from a graduate student that experimental plants at a university research facility, including some of the student's own research materials, had been destroyed by anti-GM activists calling themselves "decontaminators."[24] This message was widely circulated to plant scientists across North America by the Public Affairs Office of the American Society of Plant Physiologists (ASPP), which appended the following advice to recipients: "ASPP is taking an active role in helping scientists enter the dialogue ... It is best to proceed with letters to the editor, interviews with the media and meetings with editorial boards at which you provide the content of the presentation. You do not need to feel compelled to invite members of the 'opposition,' since this often is more confusing to the audience than it is enlightening." I leave aside any comment on the perhaps unintended irony of the writer, who encouraged others to enter a dialogue where the opposing side had been deliberately excluded. (Seeking closed meetings with the editorial boards of newspapers is a favourite tactic recommended to industry clients by the expensive public-relations "spin doctors" in the United States.)

The anonymous writer of this passage goes on: "The ASPP Public Affairs Office ... can provide background information for use in communicating with the media and the public on plant science issues, such as the relative benefits and risks of plant biotechnology." And yet, on the ASPP website at the time in question, one could find what could only be called an orgy of naked self-congratulation being performed in public by a group of speakers before a Congressional committee, about the miracles being wrought by plant biologists – but precious little about the associated risks.[25]

At the end of 1999, when the first phase of the public battle over GM foods in Europe had ended in victory for the opponents of plant bio-technology, a journalist commented: "And despite the best efforts of the government and the scientific community, the protest has snow-balled." This article also mentioned "that Monsanto revealed last week that GM food has been banned from the cafeteria at its head office in Britain."[26] This stage of the public controversy in Europe had ended, in fact, with the corporate sector, a collection of large multinational com-panies (growing ever larger by mergers in this period), in complete dis-array about the *issue* of genetically modified foods. In mid-2000 the Swiss firm Novartis, one of the world's largest manufacturers of seeds for GM crops, adopted a policy to ban ingredients from these crops from all its own food brands worldwide: "The policy was revealed in a letter the company sent to the Belgian office of Greenpeace in an attempt to get the environmental group to include Novartis in its list of GM-free food producers."[27]

Undoubtedly Greenpeace – arguably, for the time being, the most competent issue managers for risk controversies in the world – made a strategic decision to transplant the campaign against GM foods to Can-ada in the fall of 1999 in order to maintain its global momentum once victory had been achieved, for all practical purposes, in Europe. Among other things this renewed campaign exposed the fragility of public support for agricultural biotechnology in a country where the issue had been dormant. Canada was, after all, the technological home of engineered canola, of one of the leading engineered food crops; and federal government departments which do regular opinion polling had good evidence to show that, down to the early fall of 1999, only one-third of Canadians ever expressed any concerns at all about GM crops and foods. Canadian public opinion reversed itself, however, in a mat-ter of three months once the controversy was brought there. A poll done in December 1999 revealed that almost two-thirds of Canadians opposed having GM foods on store shelves. Some comments by a mem-ber of the polling firm, Pollara, are particularly relevant to the theme which runs through the foregoing paragraphs here: "Mr. Guy, of Pollara, said that the problem is that Canadians simply don't trust the assurances from some scientists that genetically modified foods are safe. 'The big thing among people is, "We don't understand it and we can't control it. So why would we proceed with something like this? If I can't see it and touch it and understand it, then how can I make decisions?"'"[28]

The significance of this perceptive articulation of an underlying pub-lic mood can easily be missed owing to the deceptive simplicity of its form of expression. What it tells us goes to the heart of the relationship between scientists and the public in risk controversies, of the way in which scientists frame their own understanding of their craft, and, as well, of the role of government as an "honest (or not so honest) broker" in the swirling currents where science, technology, industry, and democracy meet. Increasingly, the technologies emerging from the scientist's laboratories which are then commercialized by industry take on more fateful appearances, typified best by genetic manipulation, which undeniably has aspects and prospects that are capable of frightening us. In this context the lack in the public mind of a sufficient understanding about the basic science gives rise to a legitimate set of generalized concerns. But the scientists who leap into the fray, dismissing the activist opponents of their technologies as "mindless Luddites" who "don't have science on their side," are in effect asking the public to take on trust what they say. And trust is one commodity that is in very short supply in contemporary society.[29]

In the end it is the obligation of governments to act as mediators and honest brokers in public controversies. A look at the development of the regulatory framework for plant biotechnology will show that to date in North America they have failed miserably in this role, owing to their decision to act as aggressive promoters of the new technology.

WHY WE NEED A "GENE REGULATOR"

The current regulatory regime for biotechnology products in Canada uses a network of existing legislation and departmental mandates to assess health and environmental risks and to align its evaluation methods with those of its international trading partners. The primary federal departments and agencies involved are Health Canada, Environment Canada, and the Canadian Food Inspection Agency, operating under eight different acts of Parliament. The rationale for this approach is explained as follows: "Biotechnology uses living organisms, or parts of living organisms, to make new products or provide new methods of production. This broad description covers all organisms, their parts and products, whether developed traditionally or through the newer molecular techniques such as genetic engineering ... [D]epartments and agencies now regulating products developed using traditional techniques and processes are responsible for regulating products developed using biotechnology techniques and processes." This approach is also used, entirely or in large part, by many of Canada's trading partners.[30]

The scientific rationale for the approach was enunciated by an expert panel appointed by the US National Academy of Sciences (NAS), in a report published in 1987, and it was reaffirmed by a similar group in 2000.[31] The rationale takes the form of three statements:

1. "There is no evidence that unique hazards exist either in the use of rDNA techniques or in the movement of genes between unrelated organisms."
2. "The risks associated with the introduction of rDNA-engineered organisms are the same in kind as those associated with the introduction of unmodified organisms and organisms modified by other methods."
3. "Assessment of the risks of introducing rDNA-engineered organisms into the environment should be based on the nature of the organism and the environment into which it is introduced, not on the method by which it was produced."

Humans have been doing genetic modification in domesticated plants and animals through selective breeding for millennia; and in this century, before the advent of molecular biology, other modern techniques (such as radiation) have been used as a way of selecting for desired traits. All this may properly be called indirect genetic manipulation, because genetic structures carried within cells could not be accessed as such and the manipulation occurred at the level of the whole plant or animal, in earlier times, or at the cellular level, more recently. On the other hand, genetic manipulation using molecular biology accesses genes directly, which was possible only after the discovery of the structure of DNA; the applications resulting from this new direction are only about twenty years old. I refer to these as the "pre-molecular" and "molecular" phases of plant genetics.[32]

In Canada the lead federal regulators for plant biotechnology applications, first Agriculture and Agri-Food Canada (AAFC) and now the Canadian Food Inspection Agency (CFIA), have argued that there is a strong element of continuity from "traditional practices" (i.e., selective breeding) to the "new biotechnology" (i.e., modern genetic engineering).[33] During hearings on biotechnology regulation held by the House of Commons Standing Committee on Environment and Sustainable Developing in mid-1996, a senior AAFC official provided a general perspective along these lines, where the single phrase "new or traditional biotechnology" was said to cover a process of continuous evolution that has proceeded through four stages: (1) plant cultivation and animal husbandry; (2) selective breeding of plants and animals; (3) gene transfer within the same species; (4) gene transfer among different species.[34]

This perspective reinforces the rationale for the current regulatory approach: "Under the regulatory framework, Agriculture and Agri-Food

Canada assesses the traits of the final products rather than the actual processes of biotechnology, with the belief that genetically engineered organisms are not fundamentally different from traditionally bred organisms."[35] But a slightly different note is struck by the following passage from the same document: "Through new biotechnology techniques, scientists can modify the characteristics of organisms for our benefit in a more controlled way than with traditional practices ... These techniques allow the transfer of genes to be carried out in a very controlled way, so that only one or a few desirable traits are transferred at a time. Furthermore, these technologies can be used to introduce desirable traits from outside the species, something that is not possible with traditional breeding methods."

The first quotation says that "genetically engineered organisms are not fundamentally different from traditionally bred organisms," whereas the second says that the new technology does something "that is not possible with traditional breeding methods." The first statement provides the regulatory rationale for using existing legislation and federal multi-departmental arrangements for the oversight of plant biotechnology applications derived from techniques of modern molecular biology; it is contradicted by the second sentence appearing in the very same publication, and also by the statement by a leading Canadian scientist in the field who heads a firm which actually engineers plants (see note 31). In fact it is a definition masquerading as an argument, or more precisely a contention designed to serve the purposes of bureaucratic convenience.

Another prominent feature of the regulatory stance taken by Canadian federal departments is what may be called a highly restrictive perspective on risk.[36] For the regulators, as expressed in their slogan of "science-based risk assessment," risk is restricted only to those hazards that may be characterized with some precision by scientific practice, such as herbicide tolerance and insect resistance. It is indeed very important for the public to be protected against such risks through the existence of regulatory oversight. However, it has also been known for some time now that among the public, which is not generally expert in the science of molecular biology, or in other sciences, there is a quite different perspective on risk, one that is much broader in scope than that of the regulators and that is permeated by values different from those which govern scientific practice. This differing value structure has been revealed in the series of comprehensive public attitude surveys on biotechnology done in Europe.[37] The main conclusions are: First, perceived usefulness of the biotechnology product is a pre-condition of citizen support. Second, people seem prepared to accept some risk as long as there is a perception of usefulness and no moral or ethical concern. Third, and most important, moral doubts (that is, a sense that something is "wrong") can act as a veto on people's willingness to accept specific biotechnology applications. In other words, the regulator's concept of "safety" (acceptable risk) is not the final or overriding consideration; rather, a looser but also deeply held sense of "right and wrong" is the decisive criterion for public acceptance.

This is where the "process" versus "product" distinction becomes relevant. As we have seen, North American biotechnology regulators maintain that, since there are no unique risks associated with genetic modification, there is no need for a unique form of regulatory oversight for GM applications of any kind. In other words, the regulators say that it would make no sense to regulate the process of biotechnology (that is, directly moving genes themselves among different organisms), as opposed to the various products (for example, herbicide-tolerant canola or insect-resistant corn plants), because the relevant risks are in the end products, not in the process that created them. Moreover, these risks are similar to most of those with which we are already familiar, as a result of conducting regulatory oversight over food products made from "conventional" (non-GM) crops – risk factors such as toxicity (for example, from pesticide residues), bacteria and other pathogens, allergenicity, digestibility, nutritional deficiencies, and so on.[38] Again, this list contains important risks against which the public needs to be protected through competent and diligent regulatory supervision.

But this is not a complete list of risks that are of interest to the public. And the simple fact of the matter is that this regulatory stance has failed to win the confidence of many among the public in Europe and North America.

SCIENCE AS A WEAPON IN PUBLIC POLICY DEBATES

There are many reasons for the policy failure that is occurring before our eyes, including especially some major deficiencies in risk communication.[39] Here I will address only the matters that are relevant to the subject at hand, namely the fault lines in the interface between science and the public. First, there is the cavalier dismissal of deep-rooted, poorly articulated public concerns about GM foods. Second, and more serious, there is the (failed) attempt to use – or misuse – "science" as a weapon or trump card in policy debate, where a declaratory judgment is issued in the following form: Science has spoken and declared these products to be "safe" for human consumption, and therefore there is nothing left to discuss.[40]

The dismissive attitude is nicely epitomized in the following statement by Joyce Groote, president of BIOTECanada, an industry association (the reference is to the labelling of GM foods): "Where in fact they have been demonstrated to be very safe and exactly the same as something that's already been on the market for a very long time, why would we identify that as a different product?"[41] But there are two simple points overlooked here. First, it is simply not true that conventional and genetically modified food products are "exactly the same"; and second, the expression "exactly the same" can have quite different meanings to different people in different contexts. Those who use the phrase "exactly the same" in this context probably have in mind certain unarticulated technical arguments and procedures which underpin the prevailing regulatory structure for the evaluation of food safety. There the phrase "exactly the same" likely means that the molecular composition of the foods, novel trait aside, is indistinguishable. I for one am prepared to accept this as a *plausible* contention, i.e., one that can be robustly defended from the standpoint of scientific evaluation; I am also prepared to believe that it may be vigorously challenged by others who may be able to marshal arguments in their favour that draw as well upon accepted modern scientific principles. However, whatever position one might take on the outcome of such a debate, even in this respect there is a significant failure in terms of public risk dialogue. This is because (so far as I can tell) those who use the "exactly the same" mantra in communicating with the public have not explained clearly what they think it means. Until they find the courage to do so, those persons can expect to encounter some stiff resistance to their messages among their audiences.

It is much the same with the issue of labelling of GM foods itself. Calls for some type of labelling to identify "genetically modified" ingredients have been heard for many years, but on the whole both industry and governments in North America have been adamantly opposed to such labelling, maintaining that information identifying GM ingredients would be "misleading" to consumers.[42] This stance has been maintained stubbornly in the face of steadily increasing levels of consumer demand for labels, as indicated in repeated opinion polling in both Europe and North America. And not just citizens. One could turn to so reasonable and authoritative a source as that of Sir Robert May, when he was chief scientist for the UK government, and find this statement: "We should allow consumers maximum information and choice about what they buy through clear labelling." European governments, joined by others such as Japan and Australia, almost certainly will insist on mandatory labelling, so those still firmly opposed will have to yield at some point, and their resistance – carrying the impression of having "something to hide" – will, I believe, do long-term damage to their own cause.[43]

Now, however, things are changing, and the reason is instructive. The next generation of GM products will have nutritional characteristics that are expected to be attractive to consumers, such as healthier oils and additional vitamins and minerals. Companies will wish to advertise these benefits to consumers, and therefore product labelling will be necessary; all of a sudden, when it is in industry's interest to have such labelling, it appears that it will indeed be possible and feasible to do so.

In a democracy, government is ultimately the guarantor of healthy public debate on issues of policy and values. But governments in Canada and elsewhere have so far failed to discharge this responsibility adequately with respect to agricultural biotechnology and GM foods. This failure shows up in a number of ways. First, there is a notable lack of balance in the presentation of biotechnology on the federal government information sites, where the dominant tone is one of advocacy for the technology. There is much more material on benefits than on risks, by a wide margin; when public concerns are alluded to, usually no clue is offered as to what the nature of the concerns is.[44] Second, the scientific basis of the regulatory oversight of GM products is strongly affirmed, but it is very difficult to find any balanced discussion of the full range of scientific issues, such as (for example) the one offered in the report by the Royal Society referred to earlier.

In this context "science" is used as a weapon against critics rather than as a framework for dialogue. For example, here is the argument against labelling made on an industry pro-biotechnology website: "If biotech products are safe, why are biotechnology companies opposed to labeling them? [Answer:] We are supportive of efforts to ensure that consumers have the information they need to make sound food decisions. The question of consumer product labeling is best addressed by the food industry working in cooperation with regulatory agencies. In the U.S. and Canada, this cooperative effort has resulted in a science-based system that requires labeling if the food differs in safety, composition, or nutritional quality compared to conventional food. No products developed using biotechnology that are currently on the market fall into this category."[45] In other words, government and industry have decided that they are the sole authorities for determining what information consumers need, and that is the end of the matter.

Note especially how the position taken here is justified, namely on the grounds that the food safety regulators use a "science-based system" of evaluation. This carries the implicit contention that anyone who asks for such labelling must be against "science-based" evaluation! Yet surely there are a number of other contexts in which one could reasonably adopt an alternative position – for example, on legal or ethical grounds under a "right to know" or "consumer sovereignty" standpoint. There are two aspects of the Council for Biotechnology Information's statement that are indicative of a deep-rooted inability to understand the rules of fairness in public engagements on risk issues: (1) It does not concede that there is *any* other legitimate way to frame the matter of labelling except the one chosen there. (2) It suggests that referring to something as "science-based" is sufficient justification in itself to clinch an argument.

This mode of presentation inhibits rather than encourages reasoned public dialogue, and as a result both the plant biotechnology industry and the North American governments which have acted as its dedicated publicists have blocked the development of an educated and informed public awareness with regard to these issues. Their approach has played right into the hands of those groups who would like to "own" biotechnology issues for themselves – which they have a perfect right to seek to do in a democracy, of course.[46] From a public policy standpoint, however, it is not an "optimal" outcome when *any* particular stakeholder interest group owns a set of issues. It will take a long time to repair the damage that has already been done in this respect for the issues under discussion here. The responsibility to do so rests squarely in the lap of government. Every delay hereafter in discharging this responsibility will only make the ultimate objective – a reasoned dialogue among a diverse and knowledgeable set of interveners – harder to achieve.

With respect to the risk controversy about plant biotechnology and genetically modified foods, governments should be far more inclusive than they have been so far, with respect to acknowledging the range of public concerns; to facilitating an informed dialogue among stakeholder interests without promoting a preferred decision outcome in advance of meaningful discussion; and to reconsidering the stance that has ruled out even the possibility of the need for a unique, comprehensive, and distinctive legal and regulatory structure for the oversight of all applications of technological processes involving genetic manipulation using modern molecular biology. There has been a significant policy failure here to date, and as always there are "real-world" consequences that flow from such a failure. The most serious is that in persisting along this path governments may have actually undermined the technological and economic prospects of the very industrial sector they have sought to promote so assiduously.

The practices of scientists too have to change, as they take place in the context of public risk controversies, if scientists wish to garner greater respect for their position in these debates. This theme has been nicely articulated by Michael Gibbons, who argues that the traditional relation between science and society is undergoing dramatic change at present. In the traditional relation (over the past few centuries) science worked autonomously and then "spoke" to society, in terms of its dramatic new representation of the nature of the physical world, and it was expected that society would adjust to this new knowledge; but the reverse was not the case. Now science, in its continuing development in laying the basis for new technologies, has brought its discoveries (especially in genetics) right up against the core values on which social institutions and behaviour are based. Gibbons comments: "The old image of science working autonomously will no longer suffice. Rather, a reciprocity is required in which not only does the public understand how science works but, equally, science understands how its publics work."[47] He calls this "science's new social contract with society" and says that it ushers in a new relation between the two, one in which the social legitimacy of science must be continuously re-established rather than being taken for granted. Applying this perspective to the case of the controversy over GM foods, Gibbons urges scientists to recognize that they must take into account the concerns that originate among the public participants in the debate, and not only those that have been defined by the scientific discourse itself.

These observations bring us back full circle to the first two quotations cited in the epigraphs to this chapter, which come from persons in the business sector, who speak of GMOs as "good science" but also as "bad politics" and "very bad public relations." They convey two simple but important messages. First, science itself has been caught up in "contested" social domains; second, there is a radical divide between science and the public (or some part of the public). Within the confines of its laboratories, the scientific community is master of its own domain; once transported into the larger social world, however, its *modus operandi* appears for the most part as an arcane curiosity that violates the precepts of common sense. In that world science has no special standing. Scientists need to learn that their expertise cannot be used as a weapon to dismiss or diminish their opponents; that the phrase "science tells us that this is so" is the beginning of an argument, not its end, and that they cannot unilaterally dictate the terms of debate; and finally that, if their reasoning does not address the specific type of concerns expressed by the public, whether or not the way those concerns are expressed conforms to the conceptual matrix of modern science, their views are unlikely to have an impact on the outcome of the controversy.

TOWARDS BETTER RISK ISSUE MANAGEMENT FOR THE GM FOODS CONTROVERSY

What should be done differently? First, the public risk manager (the federal government) should get out of the biotechnology promotion business *entirely*, in order to rebuild its public credibility as a disinterested risk manager. There are plenty of other bodies which can provide a legitimate advocacy voice for this technology, especially industry associations and those provincial governments that have made this industry a focal point of an economic development strategy. Governments have an important role to play in fostering exchanges of views among the range of interested parties on contentious issues, from the standpoint of a neutral mediator rather than as an advocate. For example, government should invite intensive discussions of the adequacy of its regulatory mechanisms and international trade policy positions, and should provide funding to assist the participation of public-interest groups where necessary.

Second, a massive, long-term risk dialogue program should be launched, especially to enable the public to grasp the principles of the science of plant genetics and to participate in a discussion of its implications. It is imperative that completely independent third parties be commissioned to carry out this task, however, because both industry and governments have shown themselves to be thoroughly incapable of understanding what is meant by a balanced presentation of issues. (I use the term "risk dialogue" project to emphasize the two-way nature of the communications.) Expenditures of something like $500,000 per year (doubled to $1,000,000 in the first year to provide catch-up), and a minimum five-year time horizon, would be entirely appropriate; a substantial part of the cost is the need to prepare high-quality graphics and computer animations for the scientific explanations, since those communicate much better than does text alone. A special emphasis should be laid on clear and thorough explanations of the science of molecular biology, the techniques of gene transfer (including the implications of unintended escape of engineered genes into the environment), and a comparison of molecular biology techniques with others, including mutagenesis and traditional selective breeding.[48]

Third, federal authorities in Canada and the United States should consider following the recommendation made to the British government by the Royal Society (London) in 1998: "[A]n over-arching body or 'super-regulator' should be commissioned by the government to span departmental responsibilities and have an ongoing role to monitor the wider issues associated with the development of GM plants." The purpose of the new agency would be to ensure that more general implications of changing practices in plant biotechnology, which may not be addressed by the specific mandates of existing regulatory bodies, receive careful and ongoing review. For example, the new agency could be charged to "consider the effects of GM crops in comparison with the effects of current agricultural practices in general on ecosystems and the environment as a whole."[49] Australia's Genetic Manipulation Advisory Committee, which has been in existence since 1987, has a number of interesting items in its Terms of Reference ("maintain an overview of the biosafety factors associated with innovative genetic manipulation techniques"; "identify and keep under review classes of work which have undefined risk levels"; and "participate in public discussions about the biosafety of these techniques") that have a similar, overarching thrust.[50]

Fourth, for intense public risk controversies the federal government should always consider referring some current scientific issues to independent expert panels, including those administered under the auspices of national academies. As discussed further in the Appendix to this volume, expert panels can be established with formal procedures which seek to guarantee the objectivity and independence of both the selection of panel members and the production of panel reports. Referring some pertinent, current scientific issues to an independent expert panel – as was done for "the future of food biotechnology" by the government of Canada, commissioning an expert panel report that was delivered in February 2001 – has been demonstrated in a number of cases to be a significant and positive step in achieving broad public credibility.[51]

Clearly organizations caught up in the controversy over GM foods have been shown to need much better capacities for engaging in risk issue management. As used in this phrase, it should be emphasized, the word "management" should not be taken to mean figuring out how to put a clever "spin" on a controversial technology so that one can calm public fears and go about one's business in peace. Rather, it means taking seriously one's responsibilities in the face of public controversy in a risk domain (here, genetically modified foods). In a democratic society, this entails devoting sufficient energy and resources to the needs of an ongoing and fair public dialogue about the nature and implications of that technology. In other words, for an industry or governmental organization to "manage" well in a risk controversy is to do the right thing with respect to what is owed to the public. The concluding chapter in this book gives further guidance along these lines.

All four initiatives presented here are designed to provide better risk issue management for the controversy over GM foods in Canada, particularly for the federal government, and all are oriented around making improvements at the interface of science and the public. First, putting an end to the government's promotional activities on behalf of biotechnology should make it a more credible risk regulator, where citizens are asked to believe that the scientific characterization of the relevant risk factors, and the risk control measures based thereon, is complete, thorough, and responsive to changing information. Second, the arm's-length risk dialogue project has as its primary focus a clear and detailed elaboration of the scientific and technical basis underpinning the genetic modification applications to food crops using molecular biology (including a rigorous self-examination of outstanding issues by a broad range of scientists, in dialogue with members of the public), a comparison with older technologies (summed up as comparative risk/benefit assessment), and reliable and up-to-date information on relevant developments in other countries around the world, with special attention to a continuous re-examination of the adequacy of provisions for keeping health and environmental risks within acceptable limits.

Third, if many governments at least gave serious consideration to implementing the thrust of the recommendation made to the government of the UK by the Royal Society (London), for the creation of a central oversight agency for gene technology, this might give the public greater confidence that the risks were being carefully and thoroughly managed.

The intense and still growing public controversies over biotechnology are a strong indication that many among the public do indeed wish the *process* of so-called "new" biotechnology itself (the engineering of new organisms through molecular biology), and not just the products that happen eventually to appear on grocery store shelves, to be the subject of specific regulatory oversight. This is, I believe, what is implicit in the wide provenance of the now-famous term "Frankenfood" and its cousins (when Japanese scientists first cloned a pig in the summer of 2000, it was immediately baptized "Frankenpig"). The adoption of this terminology reflects the apprehension of a barely articulated set of fears about what may be the ultimate type of creations that emerge from the science of modern molecular biology, and whether or not those creations will be consistent with our moral sense of right and wrong, or instead give rise to a new and troubling dimension of "moral risks."[52] What the public senses, albeit unclearly, to be different about the "new biotechnology" (as opposed to the farmers' conventional and age-old practices of selective breeding) is its inherently unlimited character, the fact that every new stage of understanding leads to an enhanced capacity to manipulate more thoroughly the genomes of all plants and animals, including humans. There are some manipulations imaginable that are so repugnant to our moral sensibility that they must be forbidden. Are we supposed to wait until we are confronted with those actually existing products, along with their makers' assurances that they are "safe," and only then express our repugnance?

On the contrary, what we must have is an anticipatory public oversight that looks broadly at the general features of all the genetic manipulations that are proceeding along the way from laboratory science to new product development, and that applies not only scientific criteria, but also a range of ethical judgments, to those intended manipulations. This requires the creation of a unique, specialized regulatory body at a national level, working in parallel with (but entirely independent of) the existing departmental regulatory agencies that are charged with assuring product safety. Such a proposed agency was described in the 1998 Royal Society statement on genetically modified plants for food use as an "over-arching body" or "super-regulator" that would have responsibility for the "wider issues" surrounding genetic modification.

CONCLUDING REMARKS

Looming in the future are applications of biotechnology far more complex than the ones we have seen so far: genetically engineered food crops involving multiple transgenic insertions, eugenics using genetic screening (modification of inherited human traits), and gene therapy (elimination of undesirable inherited human traits and single-gene diseases). Science will make possible, should we wish to have them, the construction of human-animal chimeras for organ harvesting or of quasi-human living entities. Some of these futuristic biotechnology applications may never come to pass (although it would be unwise to take this for granted), but of some things we can be certain – that scientific research on such things as genetic markers for human disease, aging, and intelligence will continue; that the methods of moving genetic materials between species will be explored and refined; and that the potential commercial applications of any such research that promises attractive medical benefits will be well funded by the biotechnology industry.

There is a certain lack of public confidence in the new biotechnology at present that, in my opinion, will not be easily repaired. A new public institutional structure is required, one which acts truly independently of industrial interests and which is charged with taking the widest possible purview on all the relevant aspects, especially moral and ethical aspects, of the potential social consequences of applications of the new biotechnology.

In the new biotechnology (the "molecular" phase of biotechnology) there is a marked qualitative increase in the human capacity to manipulate genomes of all organisms, plant and animal, including the transfer of genetic material across greatly different species. There is a sufficiently important qualitative difference between these two pre-molecular and molecular phases of genetic manipulation to justify the introduction of a generic oversight mechanism for the latter. In other words, we need a designated "gene regulator" to oversee the processes of molecular biology, with respect to the suitability of specific genetic manipulations intended to be introduced into the environment – that is, an agency which would be a regulatory authority separate from, and superior to, the multi-departmental apparatus for the assessment of product safety previously described.

It is at least possible to see in the present achievements and future promises of molecular biology the prospect of a qualitative change in human technology which also opens up for human societies qualitatively different issues of ethics and sensibility, because there is almost no limit to the genetic manipulations that can take place when science can operate directly on DNA. In this sense the process that is at stake here – namely, the creation of transgenic entities through the direct manipulation of DNA using molecular biology – may be sufficiently unusual, and moreover may have ethical implications for human societies sufficiently profound in nature, that it ought to be the subject of a unique form of oversight.

Finally, whether or not there is any warrant for a new level of oversight based on considerations of health and environmental safety, there is another reason entirely to consider this, namely, as a response to what we earlier referred to as the poorly articulated public concerns about the present and future of genetic manipulation. In other words, given what is thought and imagined about this technology and its ultimate operational capacities, it is advisable to provide another level of regulatory oversight for no other reason than as a means of additional reassurance to the public.[53] This need not be seen as pandering to the lowest common denominator of understanding, or as "giving in" to the current critics of GM technologies, especially those who do not share the basic tenets and values of the modern scientific community, such as the Natural Law Party, which is one of the most active groups in the Internet traffic on GM foods.[54]

It also need not be envisioned as a heavy regulatory burden, duplicating unnecessarily what already exists, but rather – to use the words of the Royal Society report referred to earlier – as a body with "an on-going role to monitor the wider issues associated with the development of GM plants." The purview of such a body should extend to the full range of expected manipulations (plant, animal, human). Obviously, the mandate and operational authority of such a body would require clear description and clear differentiation from the product-based safety reviews which now exist. But in the end, as a practical matter, it may be more efficient to provide this additional layer of public reassurance than to fight an endless rearguard action against the dark shadows conjured up in imagination by fears of what a newly potent science of genetics might bring.

3 Cellular Telephones

WILLIAM LEISS AND GREG PAOLI

"ELECTROSMOG" IN CANADA

Sustained controversy about radio-frequency (RF) fields began in Canada when four networks began to install newer digital personal communications services (PCS) networks, first in the larger urban areas, in 1997. While the older analogue cellular telephones operate at 800–900MHz in the high-frequency band, the PCS systems occupy the ultra-high-frequency band (around 2GHz); this higher frequency allows the latter to operate at very low power. The output power of the base-station antennas is on the order of 100 watts each, and the handsets themselves have a maximum output power of around 1 watt. However, the low-power mode requires a clear line of sight between the antennas in the network, which means that a comparatively large number of antenna installations is necessary (750 antenna sites in Metro Toronto, 500 in Montreal, and 500 in Greater Vancouver).[1] The much larger number of antenna installations, some of which were placed on schools and churches and other locations close to residential neighbourhoods, brought citizens face to face with this technology for the first time, and concerns about health effects were voiced as soon as the installations commenced.

Telecommunications regulation is a federal jurisdiction in Canada, and licences for the transmitter and antenna sites needed for cellular telephony networks are assigned by Industry Canada. Antenna licences for cellular systems are issued in groups of eighty to cover a defined geographical area, but particular sites are not specified. Licensees are required to comply with a set of safety guidelines issued by another federal agency, the Radiation Protection Bureau of Health Canada, and also to undertake consultations with "land-use authorities" (municipalities); obviously, consent of a property owner also must be obtained before an installation can be erected.[2] Except where violation of a valid municipal zoning ordinance (such as height restriction) is at issue, the Industry Canada licence cannot be legally challenged, providing that consent of the property owner has been obtained. Not surprisingly, the perceived lack of community and local government control over such installations, especially in "sensitive" locations (e.g., on schools and churches), is itself a factor in public controversy.

In early June 1997, parents in the Fraserview area of Vancouver learned that Cantel (one of the networks) had made an arrangement to install a PCS antenna on the roof of the local elementary school building. An outcry erupted at a school information meeting and Cantel quickly cancelled the deal; however, as a result of the publicity the community discovered that Microcell (another network) was in the process of installing a 1.2-metre antenna inside the cross atop the Fraserview Assembly Church located across the street from the school building.[3] Microcell refused to cancel this project, and some community members began to mobilize public opinion against it, preparing a news release which was picked up in newspapers and granting TV and radio interviews. Over the next months, protest leaders prepared pamphlets for distribution in the community, wrote letters to papers, held meetings with local government officials, and filed an appeal against the installation with the Vancouver Board of Variance, which deals with zoning matters.

A Health Canada official had been present to discuss health risk concerns at the initial information meeting, but within a week newspapers were citing local school board officials as saying that New Zealand had banned such antennas on school buildings, and the states of Oregon and Washington were considering similar actions. The protest leaders began calling the scientific staff at Health Canada headquarters in Ottawa with requests for more details about the scientific evaluation of risk; a prominent researcher in this field at the University of Washington was also quoted in early media coverage, warning that "there has not been enough research for scientists to know if there are cumulative long-term effects on children from these antennae."[4] As a result of direct contacts with Health Canada staff, university-based researchers, and their first Internet searches, the protest leaders began to inform themselves about the scientific risk assessments for radio-frequency fields.[5]

Within six weeks, the issue was tabled in a formal setting (the Board of Variance meeting) with a structured mode of confrontation. Microcell filed an information package about scientific and regulatory matters with the board in advance, and brought to the board's public meeting not just its own personnel but also a university professor well known in this field, who was acting as a consultant to the company.[6] The Microcell representatives made presentations and were asked questions by the board members. The community protest leaders who had filed the appeal were there too, led by Mr Milt Bowling and Ms Angela Sousi; they had filed a written brief of impressive proportions with the board and made oral presentations, based on documents found through their extensive Internet searches.

The reasons for appeal in the citizens' brief and oral presentations, which had been researched and written within about six weeks, ranged over regulatory and scientific matters and were based on personal discussions with some academic researchers in the field as well as on articles in a leading industry publication, *Microwave News*.[7] Bowling and Sousi opened the "credibility" gap by contrasting what they were being told – about the scientific studies (including animal studies) on which the current risk assessments are based – unanimously by health experts from their own local, provincial, and federal governments, by the company, and by the company's own academic expert, with references to different views apparently held by some Harvard University researchers and by Michael Repacholi, the leader of WHO's EMF risk program. ("EMF" is the abbreviation for "electric and magnetic fields," while "RF" stands for "radio-frequency fields.") Safety Code 6, the federal guideline covering such matters, was said by the citizens to be out of date, being based on the state of research in the 1980s and not having been revised to reflect any of the numerous research results published in the preceding ten years.[8] The Vancouver Board of Variance was in no position to take up matters such as the possibility that recent studies had shown excess lymphomas in laboratory mice exposed to RF fields; in any case, without giving reasons, the board concluded the meeting by revoking the construction permit for the antenna installation in the church.[9]

As mentioned earlier, the federal jurisdiction is paramount in these matters, and Microcell decided not to remove the installation (the church did not require it to do so), which in effect threw the issue back into Industry Canada's lap. For the citizens who had led the fight, the effect of Microcell's perceived intransigence was to prolong the issue, and they responded by redoubling their efforts to prevail. As the issue persisted through the fall of 1997, the role of the WHO program and its director increased in prominence. In October, Angela Sousi remarked on a Vancouver radio program:

[Our] concerns are based on the fact that we feel the scientists in the world can't unanimously agree on the safety of the long term non-thermal bioeffects of non-ionizing radiation and ... when we had a meeting at our school earlier this year, we were told that it was impossible to have non-thermal bioeffects, meaning that if it doesn't heat you, it can't hurt you. There was a study done recently that indicated that is a possibility that we could have non-thermal bio-effects. This was conducted by a doctor, Michael Repacholi, on behalf of Telstra [the Australian national telecommunications company] ... [who] did some experiments with other individuals that suggested that there were some effects. So here we have one group of scientists saying it's possible and another saying it's impossible.[10]

Expert disagreement – and the impacts it can have on the public perception of risk – is not unknown in risk controversies, including all types of EMF risk.[11] The impact it may have under specific circumstances can vary greatly. In this case, it seems to us, the sequence of events and the nature of the actual players made a difference to the outcome.

In the present story, one key event was a press conference in Geneva held on 19 December 1997, at the conclusion of scientific meetings sponsored by WHO and attended by experts from seventeen countries, at which Michael Repacholi called for more research on EMF and RF risks.[12] The lead paragraphs in the wire story ran as follows:

Hoping to sort out "mixed evidence" on the issue, the World Health Organization called Friday for more research into whether mobile phones, power lines and radar might cause diseases that include cancer and Alzheimer's. Dr. Michael Repacholi, manager of WHO's Electromagnetic Fields Project, told a news conference that perceived risks from new technologies have become a serious public health issue. He expressed confidence that existing international standards are adequate for high-level exposure, but said study is needed on the effect of low-level exposure over longer periods.

In the story as a whole there were references to "suggestions," "possible connections," "possible links," and "mixed evidence" between EMF at various frequencies and the following list of diseases: brain cancer, head and neck cancers, childhood leukemia, lymphoma, breast cancer, central nervous system disorders, memory loss, neuro-degenerative diseases, and Alzheimer's. On mobile phones in particular, there was a direct quote from Repacholi: "Mobile phones have only been around for less than 10 years now and the incubation period for cancer is at least 10, maybe 15 years. So we need to set up the studies so that if there is an impact, they [*sic*] can be found in a reasonable time." The public might be excused for thinking upon hearing this that ordinary citizens differed from laboratory rats chiefly in that the latter were used for short-term experiments and the former for the longer-term ones. More to the point, perhaps, citizens in Vancouver might have been excused for thinking that the substantive health-risk basis for their bitter and prolonged fight against PCS antenna siting had been fully validated by an eminently credible international agency.

USE OF THE INTERNET BY CITIZENS AS AN ELEMENT IN RISK CONTROVERSIES

In late April 1998, one of Canada's national newspapers, The *Globe and Mail*, published a front-page story entitled "How the Net Killed the MAI." MAI is the Multilateral Agreement on Investment, a proposed international agreement on investment rules which has been championed by OECD countries for the last few years. A consortium of advocacy groups around the world, opposed to this initiative (partly because it was perceived to be mainly in the interest of multinational corporations), used Internet resources to co-ordinate their campaign, creating attractive websites, maintaining constant communication, and distributing key information instantaneously among their memberships, including leaked official documents. One noteworthy aspect of the campaign is the fact that allies in Third World countries could participate at very low cost. In the context of the announcement that the OECD had suspended its efforts to reach agreement among official government representatives, one diplomat commented: "This is the first successful Internet campaign by non-governmental organizations. It's been very effective." [13] It will not be the last.

One of the major arenas for advocacy-group intervention in global public-policy issues is in the broad area of health and environmental risks, where the "official" players at the table are the same national governments and multinational corporations who were advocating adoption of the MAI. For some time now, organizations such as Greenpeace and the World Wildlife Fund have been active at a global level in "campaigns" about matters such as persistent toxic chemicals, forest management, and wildlife preservation, utilizing competent scientists on their own staffs. Among other things, they have developed interesting Internet websites as a part of their campaigns. One can expect that environmental advocacy groups and others will become increasingly skilled in their use of Internet resources to advance their causes. But as illustrated in our case study here, individual members of the public, who do not necessarily have scientific expertise, but who have concerns about risk issues, also have begun using Internet resources to gather information, establish contact with like-minded people everywhere on the globe, obtain guidance on how to ask questions of experts, and prepare themselves to become skilled interveners in risk controversies. The information-search, documentary retrieval, and networking facilities of the Internet have huge advantages over earlier resources available to the general public (traditional public libraries with books and a few journals), and these advantages will grow steadily in future years. Already all major controversies over risk management decision making are being played out on a public stage with an international cast and audience.

In addition to the aspects already mentioned, such as ease of networking and relatively low cost (including the value of time), the World Wide Web has other important characteristics considered as an information resource. One is the ease with which linkages across related concepts and areas of interest can be tracked, especially types of linkages which very likely would not have occurred spontaneously to individuals or turned up in the cross-indices of the older library card catalogues. Another is ease of access to a wide variety of very different information sources, many of which are interactive – that is, an individual's queries will result in personal responses and offers of further assistance. These and other features can have very important effects on the formation of connections between ideas, on the apparent plausibility of cause-and-effect relations, on the almost imperceptible blending of scientific and anecdotal evidence, and on the basic framing of risk issues. All of these features represent new challenges, discussed later, for those who are responsible for the social management of risk issues. (See figure 2.)

It is very difficult to describe the nature of the information on the World Wide Web in a linear format on paper. Our diagram is an attempt to demonstrate the enormous ability of the Web to capture complex phenomena in ways that normal documents cannot.[14] The diagram is based on an intensive survey of the Web for material on electromagnetic fields, and was carried out in a purely random, experiential mode, by following the links between various sites. The connections indicated by arrows create a map of the thematic linkages which can be "discovered" by anyone who is browsing the Web. This is by no means an exhaustive representation of all of the possible links that may be followed. In other words, ours is only one of many such maps that could be drawn, and the network of connections as a whole is in fact far more complex than this diagram suggests. The figure also reflects the position

Figure 2
Map of thematic linkages on the Web

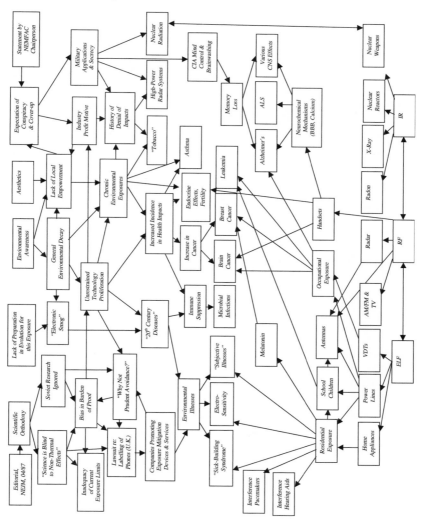

Source: The diagram above (prepared by Greg Paoli) represents one combination of conceptual connections that a citizen might experience in a session of "browsing" the Web for information related to cellular phones and health. The map was generated by noting the principal concepts discussed on Web-pages and then following hyperlinks to subsequent Web-pages. The session spanned approximately twelve hours. A different map would be experienced by another person at another time, though there will be some convergence at key websites. There are alternate methods to capture this type of connectivity. However, this method represents the "conceptual exposure" of a single user.

of health effects within the larger thematic map. Health effects are sand-wiched between technology (at the bottom of the diagram) and the soci-etal variables which drive the public determination of the acceptability of risks and the required interpretation of uncertainty. As an example of the connectivity of issues, the following example describes the path through various concepts that might be followed by browsing the Web.

To take one example of what such a search will encounter, there is one Web page which contains an excerpt from a 1987 editorial in the *New England Journal of Medicine*, suggesting more cautionary ap-proaches to regulatory toxicology;[15] this thought leads to a discussion of the "orthodox" nature of science and the apparent inability or "re-fusal" of the scientific and regulatory communities to accept the possi-bility of adverse health effects beyond those known as thermal effects. This leads to a discussion of the inadequacy of then-current exposure limits and the fact that Soviet researchers had lower limits based on their belief in the possibility of non-thermal effects. Often, commenta-tors will question why the burden of proof is on the government or the public.

Interestingly enough, most sites do not insist with certainty that there are adverse health effects from RF exposure beyond those described as thermal effects. However, there is considerable discussion of "prudent avoidance," which is described as a common-sense precaution in the face of uncertainty. Here it should be noted that the doctrine of pru-dent avoidance is often supported on the websites of companies which provide exposure mitigation devices (such as antenna shields) or con-sultancies in how to measure the home environment for those who are "electrosensitive." Another site featuring prudent avoidance is main-tained by an independent researcher in the UK who has launched a law-suit to require hazard labelling on cell phones; this same researcher offers on the site an elaborate theory that homosexuality, AIDS, and Sudden Infant Death Syndrome (SIDS) are a result of damage to the brain in the area that controls the immune system.

"Electrosensitivity" is a much more mature issue in Europe, and in particular in Sweden, than it has been so far in North America. The "electrosensitive" contributors on the Internet Europe usually refer to "electrosmog" and then make the link to a general concept of pervasive environmental decay resulting from the actions of insufficiently con-trolled industries.[16] The general environmental decay theory is linked to other feared exposures to widely dispersed contaminants and is further linked to any health impact that is, or is perceived to be, increasing in incidence in the population. Correlation between radio-frequency expo-sure and increases in brain cancer, breast cancer, and asthma are fre-quently cited, with the asthma hypothesis supported by some scientific evidence of interference with the activity of antihistamines.

Usually, the discussion returns to what is perceived as denial or cover-up; parallels to the tobacco case are almost always provided, and some sites have exhaustive discussions of allegations about a long history of denial about RF effects – by the US military, for example.[17] This leads in some cases to a discussion of the military/industrial complex and the sheer economic power and momentum of the mobile communications industry. The economic power is in turn seen as explaining how these impacts could be covered up; sometimes the cover-up is linked to the use of RF in brainwashing experiments by the CIA. Finally, RF and power-line (ELF or extremely low frequency fields) issues are closely paralleled on the Web, in particular with regard to the provision of resources (by grassroots activists linking communities with each other) to fight the siting of various types of installations. Any health effect in ELF is a candidate in RF and vice versa; for example, adverse health effects such as Alzheimer's and ALS in the ELF domain are also featured very strongly in the RF domain, and both are linked to findings on memory loss, central nervous system effects, and some so-called "subjective" effects reported by Soviet researchers in past decades.

In early 1998, Microcell "voluntarily" removed its antenna installation from the Fraserview Assembly Church in Vancouver. And in August 1998, the government of Canada asked the Royal Society of Canada to establish an independent expert panel on the health risks associated with radio-frequency fields; the panel issued a public report in May 1999.[18] Within hours of the press release announcing the panel's composition and mandate, the Society began receiving a continuous stream of return messages, including copies of queries sent by Internet activists to a variety of lists asking for an analysis of the panellists, with respect to their "positions" on issues and on sources of their research funding. Two of the panellists immediately were said by the activists to be compromised by close affiliation with the wireless telecommunications or electrical industries.[19]

RISK COMMUNICATION AND
RISK MANAGEMENT ISSUES

There is every reason to think that we are just at the beginning of the period when Internet resources will be used by individuals and groups to enhance their ability to be skilled interveners in social controversies about health and environmental risks. The radio-frequency fields controversy in Canada allows us an opportunity to do an initial assessment of the role of Internet resources in these matters, within the broader context of society's own need for appropriate risk management processes. For it is one thing to observe that Internet-based information resources appear to be vital new aids in the empowerment of citizens, and thus in the functioning of legitimate democratic decision-making processes. But it is equally true that sensible risk management is a complex high-stakes and long-term game in which citizens are obliged to reflect carefully on the assessments and perceptions of risks, as they evolve in protracted risk controversies, and to ask, for example, whether individuals and groups actually are getting the information they need to articulate and assess their concerns. Thus the real heart of the matter is not the uses of Internet resources themselves, but rather the relation between these uses and the ability of individuals to promote their own "best interests" in the positions they take on how our society should manage risks.

The underlying structure of risk controversies is best understood as a state of legitimate and necessary tension between the expert assessment of risk, on the one hand, and the public perception of risk, on the other. Because the gap between the two is an enduring rather than a transitory phenomenon, we require a means of facilitating exchanges between the two domains, and this is in fact the function of good risk communication practices. More often than not, however, we find a systematic failure to employ such practices, leading to the creation of a risk information vacuum which makes sensible and publicly credible risk management decision making virtually impossible to achieve. [20]

The radio-frequency fields controversy in Canada is a perfect case study in the existence of a risk information vacuum and its consequences for risk management. This can be seen clearly once the elements presented earlier are arrayed systematically. In summary, there is clear evidence that governments had authorized private industry (in return for financial considerations) to introduce a new technology across Canada, including numerous installations at sensitive locations within communities, without *first* having in place a clear and credible explanation of the associated risk factors. This is in our opinion undeniably a dereliction of duty for governments, which have the primary responsibility for managing risks. [21] From a practical standpoint it is also asking for trouble. We have organized the issue map into four sectors: risk communication, risk assessment, related "social" issues, and risk management.

1 Risk Communication Issues

Insufficient Explanation of Technical and Engineering Factors

The full electromagnetic spectrum, and its radically different characteristics at various frequencies, are a complicated business. In addition, the trade-off between the frequency and the output power of transmitters (where higher frequencies make it possible to use lower output and thus – arguably – produce a net reduction in total risk, considering multiple risk factors) is directly relevant to perceived risk. Another example: the shape of the beam from a base station antenna has some specific characteristics directly relevant to exposure, and thus to risk;[22] among other things, this is relevant to the application of the "prudent avoidance" maxim (see below). But none of this was explained *in advance* to the public in understandable terms. Once the controversy broke in a specific community in Vancouver, government and industry personnel scrambled to provide some explanations for these and other technical factors; but one cannot hope for much success in persuasive communications under such conditions. (A good time to initiate the dialogue with affected communities would have been when the installation siting was in the planning stage. But this would violate the time-honoured maxim, "Let sleeping dogs lie.")

Explanation of Risk Factors, (a):
Federal Government – Basic Document

Safety Code 6 is an engineering-type document, containing nothing but the barest mention of the health risk factors. Most significantly, the version of the document in existence at the time of the Vancouver controversy did not even name the established risk factor (thermal effect), much less any of the hypothesized, so-called non-thermal effects.[23] Nor did a small Health Canada brochure with the odd title "Safety of Exposure to Radiofrequency Fields: Frequently Asked Questions" mention any specific risk factor. The brochure states: "We hope it provides clear information about a complex and often misunderstood topic." Since the text mentions the possibility of adverse effects, but does not even say what they are, the intended clarity is a vain hope.[24]

Explanation of Risk Factors, (b):
Federal Government – Current Science

Everyone who accesses the Internet on RF issues quickly learns about "non-thermal effects," but (so far as we know) *no document issued by the Canadian government to that time ever used these words*. The published scientific literature includes mention of the following types of such effects (note that any such effect may or may not be substantiated or that, even if it is, an effect is not necessarily an adverse effect in human health terms): brain cancer; other cancers; calcium ion efflux; ocular damage; electrosensitivity; stress; birth defects; headaches; asthma; immunosuppression and immunostimulation; alterations in drug metabolism; memory loss; behavioural changes; learning deficits; Parkinson's disease; Alzheimer's disease; ALS.

The federal government, elected by Canadians, has decided to authorize industry to install technologies in return for handsome payments; information in wide circulation (not all of which is suspect by any means) associates these technologies with certain risk factors. Why is it thought to be appropriate for public authorities in Canada to remain silent on these matters? Canadian citizens could, if sufficiently motivated, turn to the website maintained by the US Federal Communications Commission and at least read a brief discussion on non-thermal effects, and learn that at least two of them (the "calcium efflux" and "microwave hearing" effects) are regarded as well substantiated. They would also find the following general statement: "It is possible that 'non-thermal' mechanisms exist that could cause harmful biological effects in animals and humans exposed to RF radiation. However, whether this is the case remains to be proven."[25] But why should they have to go to a foreign government for such a discussion, however minimal?

Explanation of Risk Factors, (c): Industry

(i) Microcell official quoted in a newspaper: the antenna poses "no risk." (ii) Same official: "There isn't a safety concern." (iii) Cantel official: "There's absolutely no medical or scientific research that indicates any cause for health concerns."[26] The following comments are pertinent: (i) Of course it poses a risk – although the risk may be negligible, vanishingly small, acceptable, or whatever. (ii) Of course there is a safety concern – although that concern could be reduced with more complete or reliable information. (iii) Of course there is such research – although it may not turn out to be substantiated. It is surprising that such officials still do not seem to realize that their statements are both inaccurate and inflammatory.

Timeliness

The lack of advance discussion with respect to the installation of PCS network equipment is a serious risk communication failure, as already indicated. But the next generation of wireless communications technologies is already in the works; are these mistakes likely to be repeated? The terms of reference proposed to the Royal Society of Canada for its review of health risk factors associated with RF fields contain the following statement: "New technologies such as mobile data, wireless local area network (WLAN) in the 5 GHz range, specialized mobile radio (SMR)/enhanced specialized mobile radio (ESMR), wireless local loop and low earth orbit (LEO) mobile satellite service are forthcoming."[27] Indeed, sooner than many may have suspected: "Canada's largest advanced, wireless, broadband telecommunications network will be rolled out in all regions of Canada, beginning in Toronto in the first quarter of 1999 ... [providing] connectivity for data, Internet, voice and video traffic over the air that can be delivered worldwide. The WIC Connexus advanced network represents the genesis of the 28GHz wireless access market."[28] The so-called "local multipoint communications system" (LMCS) wireless networks eventually may put transmitter/receiver equipment in everyone's back yard. This may very well be just fine; but it would be wise to start talking about it with the public without delay.

2 Risk Assessment Issues

Expert Uncertainty and Disagreement
Such matters ought always to be freely disclosed, assessed, and interpreted for the public by the risk managers. There is of course nothing surprising in the back-and-forth among researchers, especially where a relatively new area of research (such as non-thermal effects of RF fields) is concerned. This would be a matter of idle academic curiosity were it not for the fact that governments are collecting monies for allowing others to generate these fields while the research effort proceeds, which gives rise to the corresponding responsibility for *regular* reporting and discussion.

Quality of the Basic Document
Some of the shortcomings of Safety Code 6 as a risk assessment document have been indicated earlier. A revised version was under development for some time and finally appeared in October 1999. But the document format also has many deficiencies, especially in that it treats its subject-matter primarily as a matter of engineering rather than of basic science, and in that it does not explicitly refer to risk assessment methodologies or the incorporation of risk assessment into a "formal" risk management process.

3 "Social" Issues

Equity
This is always fundamental where siting is concerned, and since siting choices are left up to industry, it is industry who should deal with them. Communities are entitled to hear reasons in favour of particular siting choices and an answer to objections to those choices – without having to insist on having them.

Prior Notice

This too should be provided without citizens having to ask for it, but it certainly did not happen with the Fraserview Assembly Church site. Both citizens and municipalities (which are first in line for complaints from their residents) deserve complete disclosure for the entire installation plan in their areas. In November 1997, the municipality of West Vancouver's general services committee approved recommendations for mandatory notification to city council of PCS sites (even when approval is not required), a public notification and information process by companies prior to issuance of permits, and an overall plan for all sites to be requested by a company, so that alternatives could be discussed.[29]

Role of Governments

Both Industry Canada, which has legal authority to approve telecommunications installations by private industry all across Canada, and the various provincial and municipal authorities which are passive partners in these ventures should be far more sensitive than they are now to the potential for community outrage. This is especially so since the actual authorization for licences takes place in Ottawa, far from the localities where the effects will be felt. The advent of the next generations of wireless technologies offers an opportunity for governments and industry to collaborate in designing an enhanced community liaison process.

4 *Risk Management Issues*

Allocating Responsibilities for Enhanced
Risk Communication

Where several agencies of government, in collaboration with industrial sectors made up of many different players, introduce new technologies and new risks, it is unclear who should be assigned responsibility for risk communication. The usual result is that no one picks up the ball. This should be sorted out before the crisis strikes. All these players may be perceived to have some conflict of interest with respect both to the risk assessment and scientific research overview as well as the risk communication activities, but this difficulty can be addressed by using independent third parties for such functions.

Uncertainty

The most problematic aspect of risk management from an ethical and equity standpoint – although it has never been adequately recognized as such – lies in justifying who in society should bear the costs of uncertainties in risk assessments.[30] In the earlier history of innovative risk taking in industrial society, those who could not avoid unequally distributed and often excessive exposures (workers) paid the price for the fact that new technologies were implemented for long periods while massive uncertainties about the associated hazards persisted. Others not so exposed reaped the greatest share of the benefits, but the rising standard of living for everyone also distributed widely a large share of the benefits.

Things have changed considerably on this score. Generally speaking, societal risk management has reduced the excess involuntary risk for sub-populations (e.g., those living in proximity to hazardous waste facilities, RF antennas, or nuclear power stations) to a mere fraction of its former level. Another way of putting this is to say that the benefit-risk ratios in involuntary exposures have widened enormously to the advantage of the former. Those risk levels are not and never can be zero; but they are not necessarily an unreasonable burden on those who now bear them, taking into consideration all of the known risk factors in the lives of people in contemporary society.

But the excess risk (however small) in *every* involuntary exposure it-self, *and* the ever-changing elements of persistent uncertainty in the risk assessments, *and* the rationale for inequitably distributed exposure, *must be* articulated and defended to the citizenry by the risk promoters. (Risk promoters are industries and governments which introduce new technologies.) Such a defence may vary widely in terms of its rationale, but it can be constructed, and, in any democratic society worthy of the name, the risk promoters have the duty to do so.[31] That duty has rarely been discharged at all, much less discharged well, in our own society, and it is past time to change this pattern.

Risk Reduction

In all cases where unequally distributed involuntary exposure is com-bined with a mixture of private benefit and public good, risk reduction to some defensible point (say, "as low as reasonably achievable") is a sound and just risk management option. In EMF and now in RF issues, the phrase "prudent avoidance" has wide currency in this context. It implies that the technology's social benefit is evident and that expo-sures should be minimized so far as especially sensitive populations such as children are concerned. This application of the maxim of pru-dent avoidance was articulated clearly by Milt Bowling: "We want sites located where children aren't going to be exposed for long periods of time every day."[32]

Ironically, the maxim might be applied best by choosing the site which was first the subject of protest, namely, the roof of the local school building. This has to do with the "shape" of the beam in a RF directional antenna (see note 22), which would result in virtually zero exposure in the building itself as well as its surrounding grounds. This point was made by Microcell's expert consultant at the Board of Variance meeting, and also in the circular prepared by the local medical officer of health:

With respect to the particular installation and the specific request to the Board of Variance to institute a moratorium on cell phone antennae sites in the vicinity of schools and day cares, the benefits of a moratorium are at best questionable and at worst non-existent. Given the typical radiation patterns from cellular antennae, there is normally a "radiation shadow" directly beneath the antenna structure with very low levels (well below $1\,\mu w/cm^2$) of radiofrequency radiation. Most of the antenna power is directed outward horizontally (within a $10°$ cone @ 100 ft) usually commencing at a height of several stories above ground level. The practice of "prudent avoidance" in this instance does not result in any increased level of protection as might be the case in requiring buffer zones next to high voltage transmission lines (where both magnetic and electric fields are present as opposed to RF fields).[33]

This is an example of an important point where citizen interveners themselves need to be very clear about their own interests and objectives, first of all, and secondly, about the risk management options that will serve those objectives well. The prudent avoidance maxim itself is not necessarily irrelevant to the RF fields issues; what is at stake here is whether or not it can be applied to achieve some sensible risk reduction objective, and if so, how.

In the end the responsibility to propose such applications – more precisely, to initiate a dialogue with citizens in which the possibility of applying the prudent avoidance maxim sensibly to particular circumstances is raised – does not lie with worried parents, but rather with the risk promoters. In other words, when the industry initiates – as it should – a community dialogue early in its own planning process for new installations, a part of its own contribution to that dialogue is to demonstrate that it has explicitly and seriously reviewed its preferred siting options from the standpoint of the prudent avoidance maxim.

CONCLUSION ON RISK MANAGEMENT: A NOTE ON SWISSRE

One of the most interesting documents yet to appear on RF issues is the booklet "Electrosmog – a Phantom Risk," published in 1996 by Swiss Reinsurance Company (Zurich). The document is also posted on the company's website and thus can be downloaded anywhere, and this is how it was obtained by some of the citizen interveners in Vancouver, who had seen a reference to it in *Microwave News*. It deals in a highly sophisticated way with the business – and specifically the insurance – risk posed by the existence of social controversy over health effects associated with EMF and RF fields, which in SwissRe's view gives rise to

an extremely dangerous risk of change composed of two parts: the classical development risk, that is, the possibility that new research findings will demonstrate electromagnetic fields to be more dangerous than has hitherto been assumed; and the sociopolitical risk of change, in other words, the possibility that changing social values could result in scientific findings being evaluated differently than they have been so far ... We consider the risk of change to be so dangerous because it is evident that a wide range of groups have great political and financial interest in electrosmog being *considered* hazardous by society. If these interest groups prevail, current and future EMF liability suits could be decided in favour of the plaintiffs, thereby confronting the insurance industry with claims on a scale which could threaten its very existence ... In this sense, this publication is a warning.[34]

This warning comes from an industry that is still paying out asbestos-related claims for exposures that occurred up to half a century ago. It carries the implication that liability insurance coverage for the telecommunications industry could be affected by the further development of these issues in "sociopolitical" terms.

Perhaps the most curious aspect related to this publication is that at least some of the citizen interveners in Vancouver who read SwissRe's booklet found succour in it: they thought that it validated their expressions of concern, even though this very carefully written document gives no support to the idea that there are now unacceptable levels of risk associated with RF fields, or that they are likely to be found unacceptable in the future. What can explain this reaction? True, the document has beautiful graphics, including a superb one on the EM spectrum; it has a most intelligent and readable scientific summary of EMF; it takes the matter of persistent uncertainty seriously; it concedes the point that "it is theoretically possible for even the weakest signal to induce biological responses and in this way affect organic processes" (p. 17); it rejects the false comfort of zero risk, stating clearly that "EMF health risks cannot be eliminated entirely ... [but] can at best be reduced, insofar as they are known and measurable" (p. 20); and, above all, it has a sophisticated discussion about the relation between scientific risk assessment and the social evaluation of risk. But none of this explains the reaction of some of the readers in Vancouver. We suspect that their reaction reflects, perhaps subconsciously, a sense of appreciation for the fact that a major industry player had taken the trouble to write about these things at all.

STRENGTHS AND WEAKNESSES OF THE INTERNET AS AN INFORMATION RESOURCE

Earlier we noted that individual members of the public who have concerns about risk issues have begun using Internet resources to gather information, establish contact with like-minded people everywhere on the globe, obtain guidance on how to ask questions of experts, and prepare themselves to become skilled interveners in risk controversies. Those who wish to do so can find on the Web complete copies of many peer-reviewed scientific publications and other documentary material from excellent sources. The advantages of the Internet will grow steadily.

There are some corresponding disadvantages as well. Many sites are maintained by activists who are committed to a particular perspective on issues and who also have (judging by the contents) reasonably good scientific training; individuals visiting these sites who are non-experts in these matters can end up just with a wider array of opinion on what the scientific issues are, without any way of evaluating the relative merits of what they find. Second, much (but by no means all) Internet activism has the tenor of "guerrilla warfare" and conspiracy, a crusade against the large institutional players in government and industry, which influences the presentation of material. Third, straightforward scientific reports are mixed liberally with anecdotal evidence; casual visitors to activists' sites need to exercise some caution in sorting through what they find.[35]

These and other weaknesses are serious matters, but on the whole they do not seem to us to cancel out the offsetting advantages. In any case the Internet as a public information resource is here to stay. Citizens concerned about health and environmental risk issues will derive greater benefit from Internet resources over time as more players set up shop there – including those who have a mission to deliver balanced, disinterested, up-to-date, and credible accounts of long-running risk controversies.

EPILOGUE: THE ONGOING CONTROVERSY

"A Review of the Potential Health Risks of Radiofrequency Fields from Wireless Telecommunications Devices" was commissioned by

Health Canada and carried out by an eight-member independent expert panel appointed by the Royal Society of Canada.[36] The panel reviewed and summarized all of the main lines of scientific investigation relevant to the risks in question, and in general the panel found that the exposure limits in Safety Code 6 provide adequate safeguards for those risks. However, the report (issued in May 1999) went beyond the prevailing rationale for the regulatory framework, breaking new ground in accepting the existence of "non-thermal biological effects":

There is a growing body of scientific evidence which suggestions that exposure to RF fields at intensities far less than levels required to produce measurable heating can cause effects in cells and tissues. Non-thermal effects occur when the intensity of the RF field is sufficiently low that the amount of energy involved would not significantly increase the temperature of a cell, tissue, or an organism, yet some physical or biochemical change is still induced. Whether or not these low-intensity RF mediated biological effects lead to adverse health effects has not been clearly established ... It is possible that users of wireless telecommunications devices, including cell phones, may experience exposures of sufficient intensity to cause biological effects, although these biological effects are not known to be associated with adverse health effects.[37]

And then there is the "spin" that may be put on such a report by interested parties; for example, the Canadian Wireless Telecommunications Association (CWTA), which converted the panel's report to say that it constituted "overwhelming evidence to support the conclusion that exposure will not result in *any* public health risk" (italics added). That is a very strong statement, but it is not what the panel said – namely, that there is no scientifically accepted evidence of a public health risk. The difference between the two (the CWTA's "spin" and the panel's statement) is by no means trivial, and shows just how problematic risk communication can be.

As soon as one says "no scientifically accepted evidence," the fact that one has used the qualifier indicates that there is some evidence. Why would one have to say "scientifically accepted" if there was not *some* evidence – whether it is exactly what one had in mind as scientific or not? Here are some more examples from the CWTA statement: "Findings by the expert panel reaffirm that there is no public health risk." The panel did not say that. "Safety code 6, which provides the guidelines for the installation and the use of wireless technologies, is appropriate." The panel did not say that either.[38]

In fact, the subject of health risks associated with radio-frequency fields is a highly contested domain these days, all over the world, with conflicting interpretations of scientific evidence and allegations of fraud, libel, and various other underhanded dealings.[39] Sensational material involving a dispute between Wireless Technology Research (WTR), an industry-funded group, and researchers Henry Lai and Ross Adey was first reported in the *Sunday Times* (London) in December 1998 and then presented in interviews on a CBC television documentary, "Cone of Silence," in February 1999.[40] In July 1999 WTR released information about expected findings from an epidemiological study of RF exposure and brain tumours, which from the beginning has been a sensitive topic in this domain, eliciting angry rejoinders from the researchers who are actually leading the study. George Carlo, formerly president of WTR, raised the profile of this issue in an open letter addressed to C. Michael Armstrong, chairman and CEO of AT&T, on 7 October 1999:

Today, I sit here extremely frustrated and concerned that appropriate steps have not been taken by the wireless industry to protect consumers during this time of uncertainty about safety ... Alarmingly, indications are that some segments of the industry have ignored the scientific findings suggesting potential health effects, have repeatedly and falsely claimed that wireless phones are safe for all consumers including children, and have created an illusion of responsible follow up by calling for and supporting more research. The most important measures of consumer protection are missing: complete and honest factual information to allow informed judgement by consumers about assumption of risk; the direct tracking and monitoring of what happens to consumers who use wireless phones; and, the monitoring of changes in the technology that could impact health.[41]

A distinguished expert panel in Great Britain, the Independent Expert Group on Mobile Phones (IEGMP), created nothing less than a global news sensation in May 2000 when its report was issued. The "Stewart Report" (named for its chair) is perhaps the most important scientific review document on the subject issued to date, since it not only reviewed the scientific evidence but also gave clear, detailed, and explicit guidance to regulatory authorities based on its expert review.[42] This justifies our quoting extensively from the press release:

The Expert Group has recommended that a precautionary approach to the use of mobile phone technologies be adopted until more detailed and scientifically robust information becomes available ...

The widespread use of mobile phones by children for non-essential calls should be discouraged ...

For exposures from mobile phones a crucial issue is the absorption of energy in the body of the user. This is defined by the specific energy absorption rate

(SAR). The information on SAR from phones should be available to consumers at the point of sale, and on a national web site ...

The Expert Group has heard many concerns about the siting of base stations near schools and residential areas. Although the balance of evidence indicates that there is no general risk to the health of people living near base stations there can be indirect effects on their well-being in some cases. The Expert Group recommends that permitted development rights for all base stations should be revoked and that the siting of all new base stations be subject to the normal planning process ...

A series of measures are proposed which will inform the planning process and provide more information for the general public. These include the provision of information on the siting and specification of new base stations; the establishment of a national database of all base stations which will include details of their emissions; and an independent, ongoing, random audit of emissions from existing base stations. Further, the appointment of an Ombudsman is proposed to provide a focus for decisions on the siting of base stations where agreement cannot be reached locally.

In relation to base stations sited near schools, the Expert Group recommends that the beam of greatest intensity should not fall on any part of the school grounds or buildings without agreement from the school and parents.

The attentive reader will note that these recommendations cover, and at least partially address, many of the concerns expressed by citizens that are recorded above in our Canadian case study. However, it was the single line about restricting cell phone use by children that, not surprisingly, garnered the most attention. The media coverage was so great that Britain's chief medical officer asked the panel for a "clarification" of its report on this point, which was duly issued on 13 June 2000; it reads in part as follows:

"Would the Expert Group be clearer about to what age should children be discouraged from using mobiles for anything other than essential calls?"

As a general rule the Expert Group considers that children less than sixteen years of age should be discouraged from using mobile phones. Children are likely to be more vulnerable to any unrecognised health risks from mobile phone use than are adults. The rationale is as follows. The developing nervous system is likely to be more vulnerable than the mature nervous system to potentially hazardous agents. Because of their smaller heads, thinner skulls and higher tissue conductivity, children may absorb more energy from a given phone than do adults. If there are detrimental health effects caused by mobile phone signals, those using phones for a longer period of their lives will tend to accumulate a greater risk.

The justification for suggesting persons aged less than sixteen years is as follows. Development of the head and nervous system is generally complete by age sixteen years. For example, the density of synapses reaches adult level around puberty and skull thickness and brain size reach adult levels around ages fourteen to fifteen; sixteen is usually recognised as the age at which individuals are sufficiently mature to make informed choices about other "adult" activities.[43]

Canadian authorities, both in industry and government, have failed to react at all to this new and challenging viewpoint, but that failure represents just a continuation of the basic pattern that runs throughout our case study.

As noted, this public controversy in Canada has been going on since mid-1997. Sadly, we must report that a brief new search of information resources undertaken in late 2000 shows that not much has changed with respect to the risk information vacuum. The federal regulator, Health Canada's Radiation Protection Bureau, promised in May 1999 to undertake an "in-depth review" of the Royal Society expert panel's report; as of December 2000 no results were evident on the bureau's website. Moreover, the bureau apparently has no comments to make on the UK expert panel's May 2000 report, despite its dramatic recommendation about children's use of cell phones, nor does it have any guidance in general for the public to assist citizens in interpreting the detailed evaluations of complex scientific evidence undertaken by the two expert panels in Canada and Britain.[44]

The Canadian wireless industry differs little. We have already noted above that it was quick to provide its own "spin" on the Royal Society of Canada's expert panel report. What follows is, so far as we know, the only comment made to date from a Canadian industry source about the issue of children and cell phones raised in the UK expert group report:

Do children using cell phones absorb more radiation than adults? Probably not. Research studies have shown different results, but on balance there does not seem to be significant differences [sic] in EM absorption between children and adults. The Independent Expert Group in the U.K., however, recommended that children be discouraged from using mobile phones for non-essential calls.[45]

These is, again, a bit of "spin" in this retelling, because no further guidance is offered to Canadian consumers about what the UK expert group said, including in its clarification. Saying that children under sixteen years of age should be discouraged from all "non-essential" use of mobile phones is very important, given the usage patterns that are developing among young people for cell phone use in many parts of the world. Equally interesting, the above-quoted statement does not appear on the website of the Canadian industry organization itself (CWTA), but on that of another organization called the Wireless Information Resource Centre (WIRC). This centre lists an address in Ottawa, Ontario, but no other identifying information, except its billing as an "independent non-profit organization that provides up-to-date, impartial and objective information about research on the health effects of wireless technology." In fact, in its present form it was designed, organized, and funded by the CWTA, as can be ascertained by the press release dated May 1999 which can be found on the CWTA website.[46] It is unfortunate that the same information does not appear on the WIRC site, which lists a board of directors but offers no indication about how they were appointed or who pays for the operation.[47]

Perhaps the reason for this excess of caution on the industry's part is that by the end of the year 2000 the issue of cell phones and children's health was very hot indeed and getting more so by the day. On 23 November 2000, ABC Television's "20/20 PrimeTime" program featured interviewees who were critical of the cell phone industry for marketing their products to children when there exists so much uncertainty about the risk factors involved. One of the members of the Stewart Panel, Colin Blakemore, said of the advertising by the industry directed at children: "Personally, I feel that this is irresponsible ... How will you feel in ten years' time if a risk is proven? How would you feel about marketing devices like this, which are so obviously aimed at kids, if in ten years' time we know there is a risk?"[48] In quick response to the ABC story, the Walt Disney Company announced that it would cease licensing its cartoon characters for use in advertising of cell phones. Two days later a new research article appeared in the *Lancet* and itself became the subject of news stories. The article reinforced the view that for these exposures "preadolescent children can be expected to be more vulnerable to any adverse health effects than adults" and complained that "unfortunately some of its [the Stewart report's] greyer areas are now being exploited by the industry to obfuscate the issue."[49] The UK government has accepted the Stewart Report and announced new guidelines that will require cell phones to be accompanied by leaflets containing health warnings (these leaflets will also be sent to all households), including specific advice to parents about discouraging their children from non-essential uses of cellular phones.[50]

In Canada the consumer information resources available from the federal government regulator have been and remain characterized by a serious lack of timely and pertinent responses to new research and the issues being widely discussed in media reports. There is in the communications from the industry what can only be called a lack of full candour about the ongoing health effects controversies. Both types of inadequate responses contribute to the lack of trust in institutions which has been identified repeatedly in the literature as a fundamental theme in risk communication failures. Almost certainly there is trouble ahead on this front.

4 MMT, a Risk Management Masquerade

STEPHEN HILL AND WILLIAM LEISS

The following statement, describing a program aired on "The National Magazine" in late 1998, appeared on the CBC website.

Canada is one of the few countries using a controversial gasoline additive: MMT, a known neurotoxin. MMT has been replacing lead in gasoline since the 1970s in Canada. Canada is one of the few countries using this product. In 1995 the Canadian government proposed banning the trade of MMT to protect health and the environment. However, minister of the environment Sergio Marchi, the MP advocating the ban of MMT, was warned his action would bring him into a NAFTA challenge he would be unlikely to win. The Canadian government eventually withdrew its ban on the import of MMT, and paid Ethyl, the company selling it to Canada, millions of dollars in settlement. Proving the negative effects of manganese [the by-product of the combustion of MMT] on the brain is difficult. However, studies do show that increasing exposure to manganese does result in decreased coordination and memory – symptoms similar to the aging process. Twenty-one different car makers have also lobbied the federal government based on their claims that MMT affects their cars' pollution reduction systems. In the United States, the sale of MMT was banned until 1995, when Ethyl took the government to court. Ethyl won on a technicality. In this case, Canada has fewer rights than the state of California which was able to ban MMT. Ethyl's successful use of the threat of a $250 million suit against the Canadian government illustrates that a foreign corporation had the power to over-rule our own government due to the provisions of the NAFTA trade agreement.[1]

PRELUDE

In April 1991, then Opposition Leader Jean Chrétien penned a series of letters about the dangers of a manganese-based fuel additive to various federal ministers in the Mulroney government. For example, Mr Chrétien wrote to Doug Lewis, the minister of transport: "Two of Canada's top neurotoxic scientists, Dr. John Donaldson and Dr. Frank Labella, have been speaking out on this for several years, and I have letters of warning from the Medical School of Boston University and the University of Pittsburgh, as well as other institutions, warning of the continued use of this insidious toxic heavy metal. I respectfully request that the government ban this substance."[2] Most likely the PM-in-waiting could not have known that he had been given a minor part to play in the staging of a modern Canadian fairy tale, soon to be peopled with an evil agent (an American corporation), noble saviours of the people (Liberal environment ministers), and other ingredients – indeed, all save the most important one, namely a happy ending.

The Opposition leader's letter was constructed so as to give the impression of a consensus among medical science researchers, first, that all uses of manganese should be discontinued, because it is so hazardous that Canadians ought not to be exposed to it at all, and second, that MMT (not identified by name) is the source of unacceptable levels of exposure to that metal. The first such contention, had it been more widely broadcast, would have come as something of a shock to the mining and steel industries in Canada, which for a long time have produced and used rather large quantities of this useful metal. The second is just patently false, based on a series of risk assessments completed by the federal government from the late 1970s onwards. These awkward intrusions of reality never happened, and the tale was allowed to become further embellished, and eventually to be substituted for reality, as is shown in the storyline of the CBC's television program segment, broadcast on "The National Magazine" in late 1998, "Running on MMT."

By the time that program was broadcast, the accumulated confusions were quite extraordinary. The program summary for "Running on MMT," cited at the head of this chapter, after stating that MMT is a "known neurotoxin," goes on to observe: "Proving the negative effects of manganese ... [produced by the combustion of MMT] on the brain is difficult." On the contrary, it is well established that excessive exposure to manganese leads to the neurological disorder called "manganism." The program summary also claims that Ethyl Corporation, the sole manufacturer of MMT, won a 1995 court case against the US government "on a technicality"; we believe that an unbiased reading of the documentary evidence, which is summarized later in our chapter, shows this to be a fanciful construction. Finally, the program reiterates what is now firmly part of Canadian lore, the idea that NAFTA allowed Ethyl unfairly to bully the Canadian government into submission. This carries the astonishing implication that not only did our national government capitulate hurriedly to a rather small US corporation, well before even going to trial, but that Ottawa also lied to the Canadian public about why it agreed to an out-of-court settlement in the statement it issued at the time!

Alas, although the reasons actually given in the government statement do not make as good a tale, they do point towards the truth of the matter (as often happens when a $20 million compensation payment is being made). There is no foreign villain in this story. In our view, the evidence presented below provides sufficient warrant to represent this not as tragedy but as farce, or more accurately as a masquerade: under the disguise of a disingenuous risk management argument, another agenda entirely was played out by the North American automobile manufacturers, an agenda that to this day is not entirely clear in terms of its strategy and objectives. There is bullying in this story indeed, but not by Ethyl; Canada's national government was in fact bullied shamelessly by the auto industry into passing legislation so shoddy and ill considered that only a complete recantation of it settled the matter. What other example is there in living memory of a piece of federal legislation effectively withdrawn in its entirety barely one year after its passage?

The sources of this farce are many, but among them is our inability to put our trust in the process of doing credible health and environmental risk assessments and then having the courage to manage the risks in question in the light of them. The greatest irony in this tale is that a federal department (Health Canada) had done such a competent assessment, in 1994, which was then blithely ignored as the other agenda played itself out. Thus the hapless Canadian taxpayer was twice dunned, once for doing the risk assessment and the second time for ignoring it (when Ethyl had to be compensated). We ought to stop doing this to ourselves.

THE SUBSTANCE IN QUESTION

MMT (methylcyclopentadienyl manganese tricarbonyl) has been used as a fuel additive in unleaded gasoline in Canada since 1976, and the use of MMT increased as lead was phased out as a gasoline additive.[3] Small amounts – in Canada up to 18 milligrams per litre [mg/L] but with an average level around 8 mg/L – are added to unleaded gasoline to raise its octane level between 0.5 and 1.0 units. The sole producer of MMT in North America is Ethyl Corporation at its facilities in Orangeburg, South Carolina; Ethyl imports MMT into Canada, where it is blended at its Corunna, Ontario facility. About forty people are employed at the Canadian plant, and MMT represents approximately 50 per cent of Ethyl Canada's total sales revenue, around $25 million per year. But in the US, MMT could not be used in unleaded gasoline until 1995, when a long battle between Ethyl and the Environmental Protection Agency (EPA) culminated in a series of court rulings won by Ethyl that forced the EPA to permit its use. In the meantime, desired octane requirements in the US have been achieved by refinery technology upgrades, and also by the use of other oxygenated fuels or additives (e.g., MTBE and ethanol).[4] However, MMT is less expensive than the alternatives in raising octane levels in gasoline.

MMT contains the metallic element manganese (Mn), and at sufficiently high levels manganese can cause difficulties with the central nervous system. "Manganism" is the term given to the symptoms displayed by workers and others exposed to excessively high levels of manganese; it is characterized by "various psychiatric and movement disorders, with some general resemblance to Parkinson's disease in terms of difficulties in the fine control of some movements, lack of facial expression, and [other neurological factors]."[5] Although manganese is toxic at high levels, there is still much scientific debate surrounding the health significance of long-term, low-level exposure. Manganese exposure through inhalation is considered more likely to result in toxic concentrations in critical tissues such as the brain than is exposure through ingestion. Because manganese exists naturally in many human foods (manganese is in fact considered an essential trace nutrient required by the body, while, by comparison, lead has no nutritional value), the human body has evolved a very good homeostatic control mechanism that eliminates most of the ingested manganese. Conversely, when fine particles of manganese are inhaled, a very large portion are deposited in the alveoli of the lungs, absorbed into the bloodstream, and made available for deposition to critical target tissues, creating neurotoxic concerns. Manganese does not occur as a free metal, but rather in one of a number of oxidation states; when gasoline with MMT is burned, the main emission products have long been thought to be mostly manganese oxides, but recent studies suggest they are primarily manganese phosphates and sulphates, with only a small amount of manganese oxides.[6]

One of the most important parts of our story, important because of how little was made of it throughout the evolution of the MMT saga, has to do with the range of sources of airborne manganese in the Canadian environment. The principle anthropogenic emissions of manganese to the environment have been from metallurgical processing (47 per cent in 1984) and steel and iron manufacturing (28 per cent in 1984), part of industrial operations located primarily in Ontario and Quebec. Still, the combustion of MMT represented the third largest source on a nationwide basis (17 per cent in 1984), but it is the major source of environmental manganese in all those provinces that do not have industrial sources. In addition, vehicle emissions pose different exposure concerns than do single point-source industrial emissions, owing to their wide spatial distribution and concentration in urban areas.[7] Health Canada estimated in 1994 that use of MMT added 122 tonnes of manganese to the environment in the previous year. Although these numbers are somewhat outdated, as no detailed manganese emissions inventory has been conducted since 1984, a comprehensive 1998 study in Toronto presented some further evidence that sources other than MMT create more serious manganese risks. This study found no correlation between the concentration of MMT in gasoline and personal manganese exposure; the highest concentrations of manganese were found in the subway lines (perhaps from the grinding of the steel rails), where levels were up to 44 times greater than in outdoor areas and in other indoor environments (in the latter case the probable source is resuspended dust).[8]

The main players involved in the MMT debate over the past eight years include Ethyl, the automobile manufacturers, the oil industry, the US and Canadian governments (both federal and provincial), and environmental groups. The substance of the debate had three different themes: (1) the direct effect of MMT on vehicle emissions exhaust, (2) the effect of MMT on emission control systems and the onboard diagnostic systems designed to make sure those systems are working properly, and (3) the effects of manganese from MMT on the environment and human health. Environmentalists, who were mostly concerned that manganese would create health problems similar to those created by lead, sided with the automobile manufacturers in wanting to ban MMT. However, Ethyl, who was conducting its own series of emission and health studies in order to gain an EPA waiver to allow the use of MMT, had been arguing not only that its product was "safe" from the standpoint of human health but that it was also actually good for the environment, because it reduced nitrogen oxide (NO_x) emissions in automobile exhausts. In the meantime, the oil industry remained unconvinced by the car manufacturers' claims about MMT and maintained that it should be kept in gasoline, at least until there was sound evidence that it did cause problems with emission control systems.

Each player had specific interests in the MMT issue. For Ethyl, these were obvious: MMT represented a profitable product line for almost twenty years in Canada that was poised to expand if the US EPA allowed its product to be sold there (it was expected that many other countries would follow the EPA action). Obviously Ethyl's credibility could be expected to be somewhat dubious in the public eye, in that it had been the primary manufacturer of tetraethyl lead for gasoline. The oil industry, on the other hand, was looking for a relatively cheap way of raising octane; if MMT were banned, many older refineries (mostly in eastern Canada) would need to be upgraded or closed and producers would need to switch to other, more expensive, fuel additives such as MTBE or ethanol. The cost to the Canadian oil industry of replacing MMT was estimated by Kilborn Engineering at $115 million for one-time capital upgrades and $69 million annually for increased operating costs.[9, 10]

Whereas it is clear that both Ethyl and the oil industry had something to lose, it appeared that automobile manufacturers did not stand to gain directly from getting rid of MMT. They were seen as an impartial party in this dispute, one whose primary interest was in ensuring that the emission control systems on their vehicles could protect the environment. Because of this perceived lack of bias, their credibility was higher than that of the oil industry, particularly once environmentalists and health advocates took their side (although environmentalists were primarily concerned with the health risks associated with low-level manganese exposure and not with any potential emission control problems). Elizabeth May of the Sierra Club of Canada illustrated these sentiments about the automobile manufacturers at the Senate Hearings on the MMT bill: "The car manufacturers have been adamant that MMT gums up the diagnostic systems of their products ... Ethyl Corp[oration] claims that their product does not have these impacts in their studies. In such a clash of experts and studies, it is useful to ask which party stands to gain or lose in the dispute. Obviously, the automobile manufacturers have no reason to be concerned about MMT unless it does, as they say, compromise the efficacy of the onboard diagnostic systems, including the pollution control devices. On the other hand, Ethyl's interest in promoting contrary studies is obvious."[11] However, as we shall see, the car manufacturers perhaps were not after all the innocent bystanders they were perceived to be.

To recap: The automobile industry claimed that MMT fouled the emission control systems on their vehicles, whereas the oil industry wanted MMT to provide relatively inexpensive increases in octane and to avoid costly refinery upgrades that would otherwise be required. As regulatory requirements for vehicle emissions became more stringent, the battle between the oil industry and the automobile manufacturers intensified. From a public policy standpoint, the goal was cleaner, healthier air from reduced auto exhaust emissions, and there are two technological strategies for achieving this, namely changing the vehicles or changing the fuel. Emissions can be, and primarily have been, reduced through improvements in the catalytic conversion of smog precursors while real-time, onboard monitoring of performance ensures that underperforming catalytic converters can be fixed. On the other hand, fuel composition also has impacts on hydrocarbon, carbon monoxide, nitrogen oxide, and particulate emissions, and reformulated fuel could further reduce them. Over the past few decades, emission reductions have come primarily from improvements in the automobile, and less from changes in fuel composition. Now, the big questions are: What technologies will best achieve the next level of desired emission reductions, and who will be stuck with the tab for them?

The three different issues in the MMT debate overlapped somewhat and the distinctions among them were sometimes blurred. We will repeat the most important differences before taking up the chronological account of events, so that the reader can keep them in mind as the story unfolds. First, there were concerns that exposures to manganese released to the environment upon combustion of MMT might cause neurological and other health impacts. Second, there were persistent allegations that MMT causes problems with emission control systems and a new generation of onboard diagnostic systems (OBD II) that measure the effectiveness of the emission control systems. Finally, there is the impact that MMT in gasoline has on the actual emissions of smog precursors such as hydrocarbons, carbon monoxide, and nitrogen oxides.

Some researchers, environmentalists, and public health advocates worried about MMT's direct impact on human health and the environment. But there was an "official" Canadian government position on the matter, based on a detailed 1994 scientific review by Health Canada, and that position was (and still is) that MMT in gasoline does not pose an unacceptable risk to the health of Canadians.[12] As it usually does with its risk assessments, Health Canada continues to monitor new studies that might cause its officials to reconsider their position.[13] Meanwhile, as we shall see, the US EPA sought to deny Ethyl's 1994 application to permit MMT in fuel because, it was argued, there was a "reasonable basis for concern about the effects on public health that could result if EPA were to approve use of MMT in unleaded gasoline."[14] EPA ultimately failed in this attempt because it tried to use a specific type of administrative action – denial of a waiver under the Clean Air Act based on health concerns – and a US Court of Appeal ruled that this Act did not give EPA the authority to do so, which is the "technicality" referred to earlier in the CBC program summary. (It should be noted that the EPA still has authority under other sections of the Clean Air Act to ban a fuel additive that it believes to be harmful.) Although both government agencies used the same epidemiological studies to arrive at a safe level of manganese in the air and determined functionally equivalent "safe" levels, they used different methods and assumptions to estimate exposure levels. Specifically, ambient monitoring data for respirable manganese were available in Canada for many years during which MMT was in use, whereas future expected levels had to be modelled for the US, since MMT was not being used.

Automobile manufacturers have long claimed that MMT clogged up and fouled emission control systems in vehicles, causing higher emissions of smog-causing hydrocarbons and carbon monoxide (CO). They have contended that manganese oxide deposits accumulate on catalysts and spark plugs, as well as on the oxygen sensors that are used to monitor the effectiveness of the catalyst (the OBD II systems). According to the Canadian government, the basis for its MMT legislation stemmed strictly from concerns about MMT's effect on emission control systems: if MMT indeed kept the emission control systems from working properly, there would be higher emissions of carbon monoxide and hydrocarbons. Ethyl Corporation, through studies it conducted for its EPA waiver applications, claimed that MMT does not affect hydrocarbon and carbon monoxide emissions and actually reduces emissions of nitrogen oxides (NO_x).[15]

The plot thickens when we realize that, *well before Canada's then-minister of the environment, Sheila Copps, brought her draft legislation to Parliament* – the legislation based squarely on the concerns about MMT's effect on emission control systems – EPA had already issued a decision (in November 1993) which contained the results of its own technical assessment on this matter, stating that the "use of HiTEC 3000 [the product name for MMT] at the specified concentration [8.26 mg/L] will not cause or contribute to a failure of any emission control device or system to achieve compliance by the vehicle with the emission standards."[16] On the matter of OBD II systems, the EPA noted that it was "continuing to investigate the question of the potential impact of use of MMT in unleaded gasoline on OBD systems. If after further investigation EPA concludes that the concerns expressed by the vehicle manufacturers are warranted, EPA intends to initiate an appropriate rulemaking under Section 211(c)."[17] In essence, the EPA affirmed that it did not have sufficient evidence to reject the waiver application based on MMT's effect on OBD II systems, while reserving its right to make a different judgment on the matter if new evidence emerged. As of the date of writing, no such judgment has been made.

CHRONOLOGY OF EVENTS: THE AMERICAN CASE

Changes made in the United States during 1977 to the Clean Air Act were the beginning of the battle between Ethyl and the automobile manufacturers over MMT. The EPA acted as a fair, although not always unbiased, referee in this long-running fight. Section 211(f)(1) of the Clean Air Act made it unlawful, effective 15 September 1978, to use additives in unleaded fuel that were not "significantly similar" to those previously certified. Although MMT had been used in leaded fuel, Ethyl was required to apply to the EPA for a waiver under section 211(f)(4) in order to have MMT permitted for use in unleaded fuel. When a waiver application is filed, the EPA has 180 days either to make a decision or to grant a *de facto* waiver. In essence, the onus was on Ethyl to prove to the EPA that MMT did not harm the emission control systems. (See table 2.)

Ethyl applied to the EPA for such waivers for MMT in both March 1978[18] and May 1981.[19] In both cases the applications were denied because of stated concerns that MMT could damage catalytic converters and increase hydrocarbon emissions. In 1988 Ethyl began a new series of discussions with EPA staff to determine a program for developing the necessary data to support a waiver. In May 1990 Ethyl filed its third waiver application, but upon EPA's suggestion Ethyl withdrew this application in November 1990 before the 180-day deadline for a decision had passed. It turns out that the EPA had conducted studies at an Ann Arbor, Michigan test facility that contradicted Ethyl's own data; but it was subsequently demonstrated that EPA had conducted their tests incorrectly and that contaminated fuel had caused erroneous results. As might be expected, this sequence of events did not create feelings of goodwill between EPA and Ethyl. In July 1991 Ethyl resubmitted its waiver, essentially the same application as the one prepared over a year earlier.

EPA denied the resubmitted waiver application on 8 January 1992. Although Ethyl's tests with a statistically relevant sample of 1988 model-year vehicles demonstrated that MMT did not cause increased hydrocarbon emissions, the EPA denied the waiver based on some

Table 2
Chronology of the MMT Case

Date	Actor	Event
Late 1970s	Canada	MMT begins to be used to replace lead as octane enhancer in Canada.
1977	EPA	Clean Air Act prevents the use of MMT in unleaded fuel. Waiver for new additives now required.
1978	Health Canada	Health and Welfare study concludes that there was no evidence at the time to indicate that expected ambient manganese concentrations would constitute a hazard to human health.
March 1978 & May 1981	Ethyl/EPA	EPA rejects Ethyl's waiver application for MMT based on concerns that MMT clogs catalytic converters and increases hydrocarbon emissions.
1986	Royal Commission on Lead	Concludes that MMT is not likely to pose a threat to the environment or human health.
May 1990	Ethyl/EPA	Ethyl submits a third waiver application after two years of testing; this is withdrawn because of EPA tests that show problems with hydrocarbon emissions.
July 1990	EC	Letter from John Buccini to EPA stating that MMT does not cause significant problems with emission control systems in Canada and that manufacturers have failed to submit any data demonstrating problems.
March 1991	NIEHS/EPA	International conference convened to discuss research requirements for assessing possible impacts of MMT on health and the environment.
July 1991	Ethyl/EPA	Ethyl resubmits waiver application after EPA admits that its tests had been conducted incorrectly.
Jan. 1992	EPA/Ethyl	EPA rejects Ethyl's waiver application because of tests done by Ford on 1991 Escorts that showed some problems with hydrocarbon emissions. Ethyl continues to conduct tests.
April 1993	US Courts/EPA	US Court of Appeal orders EPA to re-evaluate the waiver application and take into consideration any new data received since the Jan. 1992 denial. This decision was reached on 30 Nov. 1993.

Table 2
(*Continued*)

Date	Actor	Event
June 93-Sept. 94	Stakeholder meetings in Canada	A series of five meetings on MMT take place between government and industry. These meetings attempt to define the scope of the issues surrounding MMT and to reach agreement on what should be done with respect to MMT in gasoline. By Sept. 1994, failing to reach any agreement, the committee remands the MMT issue to the ministers responsible. The oil industry recommends having an independent panel review the issues – this is rejected by the vehicle manufacturers.
Nov. 1993	EPA/Ethyl	EPA concludes that MMT "would not cause or contribute to a failure of any emission control device or system" but continues to investigate health risks.
July 1994	EPA/Ethyl	EPA denies Ethyl waiver based on unresolved health concerns related to manganese emissions.
Sept. 1994	MVMA/EC	Vehicle manufacturers meet with Environment Minister Sheila Copps and warn of a cost of $3000 per vehicle related to onboard diagnostic equipment if MMT is not removed from gasoline.
Oct. 1994	EC	Minister Copps informs a reporter that unless the oil industry removes MMT voluntarily, she will legislate its removal.
Nov. 1994	Health Canada	Releases health risk assessment that concludes that manganese in the environment does not pose a threat to human health at the concentrations that result from using MMT in gasoline.
April 1995	US Courts/EPA	US Court of Appeal rules that EPA does not have the right to reject a waiver application based on health concerns, although it still has the right to regulate additives under other areas of the Clean Air Act.
May 1995	EC	Bill C-94 (later called C-29), the Manganese-based Fuel Additives Act, is introduced in the House of Commons. The bill bans importation and interprovincial trade of MMT.
Nov. 1995	EPA/Ethyl	EPA is required by Court of Appeals to register MMT as a fuel additive.

Table 2
(*Continued*)

Date	Actor	Event
Feb. 1996	Ministry of Trade	Trade Minister Art Eggleton writes to then environment minister warning of possible trade implications of MMT ban.
April 1997	EC	MMT Bill C-29 becomes law.
June 1998	AIT Panel	Finds that government failed to demonstrate "that there existed a matter of such urgency or a risk so widespread as to warrant such comprehensive restrictions as the *Act* provides on internal trade...The evidence as to the impact of MMT on the environment is, at best, inconclusive."
July 1998	Government of Canada	In response to the AIT panel findings, the federal government announces that the MMT ban will be lifted, they will pay a $13 million (US) settlement to Ethyl, and future investigations into MMT will be reviewed by an independent, third party in consultation with stakeholders and the provinces. If any future action is required, the government will use CEPA.

different testing submitted by the Ford Motor Company. Using a small sample of 1991 Escorts and Explorers under driving cycle conditions different from those carried out in the Ethyl tests (i.e., higher driving speeds), Ford's results showed increased hydrocarbon emissions. The EPA considered the Ford results to be a significant enough data subset to justify denying the application. At the time the EPA also was considering the promulgation of more stringent future emission standards that would take effect for model year 1994 vehicles (around September 1993). In addition the EPA was concerned about the health effects of increased airborne manganese and the lack of knowledge in this area, although this was not the basis for the waiver denial. As a result, the EPA began to study the health issues related to MMT, including jointly sponsoring an international workshop with the National Institute of Environmental Health Sciences in March 1991 to discuss research requirements.

Ethyl filed a petition for review of the waiver denial in the US Court of Appeal for the District of Columbia Circuit and continued to conduct further emissions testing to attempt to resolve the questions surrounding the Ford data. (Why did the Escorts and Explorers show higher emissions? Did the driving cycle have a significant effect on hydrocarbon emissions over the life of the vehicle? What was the effect of the close-coupled catalysts used in the Escorts?) Ethyl conducted further tests with EPA's agreement on six 1991 Escorts and six 1988 Escorts. Based on the data from these tests, the EPA determined that "driving cycle does not contribute significantly to MMT-induced increases in hydrocarbon emissions. However, in addition to addressing the issue of driving cycle, the Ethyl data appeared to confirm the finding by Ford that 1991 Escorts experienced a much higher MMT-induced hydrocarbon increase than that observed in other models tested. The agency was concerned that certain engine and emission control system configurations were more vulnerable to ... emissions increase irrespective of driving cycle."[20]

The EPA required Ethyl to conduct significant further testing surrounding their concerns with the Escorts, which Ethyl did. (Looking forward in time to 8 June 1998, we learn that the EPA reprimanded Ford over emission problems with 1991–95 Escorts, noting that Ford had failed to report changes it made to 1991–95 model year Escorts to improve fuel efficiency. The EPA alleged that Ford used an inappropriately managed fuel-air "enleanment" strategy that caused an increase in smog-producing emissions. Ford was required to purchase and permanently retire 2500 tons of NO_x credits as part of the settlement package making up the consent order.[21, 22] Obviously, knowing that the Ford Escort emission control systems were non-compliant dramatically affects the credibility attached to earlier allegations that MMT was causing emissions problems with those vehicles.) On 6 April 1993 the Court of Appeal ordered the EPA to re-evaluate the waiver application within 180 days and take into consideration any new data received since the 8 January 1992 denial. Based on the new Ethyl data, the EPA changed its opinion and concluded on 30 November 1993 that MMT "would not cause or contribute to a failure of any emission control device or system."[23]

However, the EPA had just established a new Reference Concentration or safe upper limit for manganese in air that Ethyl also disputed. The EPA requested that Ethyl resubmit its application to allow further public consultation on the health effects of MMT. The EPA and Ethyl agreed to extend the 180-day deadline again in order to allow further discussions on the health effects. On 13 July 1994 the EPA, having already ruled that MMT did not cause or contribute to a failure to meet emission standards, denied Ethyl's waiver application based on "unresolved concerns regarding the potential impact of manganese emission resulting from MMT use on public health."[24] The EPA decision also referred to the potential problem MMT might pose for onboard diagnostic systems in 1994 and later model years, but did not actually state that there was sufficient evidence for a decision, reserving judgement on this point. Ethyl promptly filed again with the Court of Appeal, arguing that the EPA did not have the ability under the Clean Air Act, section 211 (f)(4), to deny a waiver based on health concerns.

On 14 April 1995 the court agreed with Ethyl that section 211(f)(4) does not allow the EPA to consider health effects in waiver applications. In waiver applications, the EPA must only consider emission control effects. The court ordered the EPA to "grant Ethyl's request for a waiver," which was finally granted on 11 July 1995. The lawful sale of MMT, however, requires not only an f(4) waiver but *registration* of the additive under section 211(b) of the Clean Air Act. New testing requirements for additive registrations had been adopted on 27 May 1994 and the EPA claimed that Ethyl had not met them. And so the legal battle continued.

In November 1995 Ethyl filed for a second time with the Court of Appeal for the District of Columbia to seek registration for MMT. Ethyl claimed that MMT was already registered with the EPA (because its use in leaded fuel was legal) in 1970. The court ruled that, had the EPA granted the waiver on 30 November 1993 – as it should have, given its own finding that MMT did not cause or contribute to emission control failure – the registration of MMT would have proceeded. (The court had already determined that the EPA had no legal basis to delay the waiver application because of health concerns.) The court ordered the EPA to register MMT for use as an additive in unleaded gasoline.

The EPA issued a press release on 3 July 1996 after an Ethyl advertisement had appeared, touting the benefits of MMT as a fuel additive. The Ethyl ad cites the EPA as conceding that "it has no data showing MMT to be a [health] threat at low levels of exposure." The EPA administrator replied that, "while it is true that EPA does not have data showing MMT to be a threat, the lack of data is exactly the problem. EPA does not have data proving MMT is not a threat ... EPA believes that the American public should not be used as a laboratory to test the safety of MMT. EPA believes more testing should be done before cars across the country begin emitting in the air this additive – which contains the heavy metal manganese."[25]

While the court ruling on section 211(f)(4) prevents the EPA from denying a waiver application based on health concerns, the EPA still has explicit ability to regulate fuel additives based on a different part of the Clean Air Act. Section 211(c) allows EPA to take action to control or prohibit fuel additives that "may reasonably be anticipated to endanger the public health or welfare" (i.e., the health concerns) or that "will impair to a significant degree the performance of any emission control device or system which is in general use, or which the Administrator finds has been developed to a point where in a reasonable time it would be in general use were such regulation to be promulgated" (i.e., the OBD II concerns). Despite this legislative ability, the EPA has taken no action to ban MMT based on concerns that it may interfere with OBD II systems. According to the EPA, the automobile manufacturers have not submitted any further evidence since the 1994 Ford test to back up their claims that MMT prevents the proper functioning of OBD II systems.[26] This, despite the fact that the American Automobile Manufacturers Association (AAMA) is apparently conducting a major study of eighty 1996 and 1997 vehicles to evaluate MMT's effects on OBD II, vehicle emissions, and performance. Meanwhile, as an EPA requirement under section 211(b) of the Clean Air Act, Ethyl is currently sponsoring a series of extensive emission characteristic and health studies to further determine the health and environmental consequences of using MMT in unleaded gasoline.[27] Presumably, the EPA will be in a better position to make a ruling under section 211(c) regarding the health impacts of MMT at the end of this series of studies.

CHRONOLOGY OF EVENTS:
THE CANADIAN CASE

1 Health Aspects of Manganese

The effects of high levels of manganese on the central nervous system have been well documented. While other organs can also be affected, the central nervous system appears to be the most sensitive target, where manganese in excess levels can create symptoms similar to Parkinson's disease. However, research results to date have been insufficient to characterize satisfactorily any potential long-term effects at low levels of exposure.

In 1978 the Canadian federal Department of Health and Welfare published a review of the potential human health impacts from the expected increase of MMT use as lead in gasoline was phased out. The department concluded then that there "was no evidence at present to indicate that expected ambient manganese concentrations would constitute a hazard to human health."[28] The Royal Society of Canada's Commission on Lead in the Environment reached a similar conclusion when it examined manganese and MMT in 1986. The technical study prepared for the commission stated: "The manganese of gasoline origin actually reaching human populations [would] ... be almost exclusively directly inhaled or ingested in incremental quantities, [and would be] insignificant compared with the normal exposure through food and respiration (0.3 µg/day additional intake against an uptake of 120 µg/day without MMT)."[29] In November 1992, Health and Welfare Canada's Health Protection Branch published a three-page document for general circulation, "MMT – Gasoline Additive," in its *Issues* series. It states: "In 1978, Health and Welfare did a thorough study of MMT and concluded that its use in gasoline would not raise airborne manganese levels enough to jeopardize our health. And it hasn't ... Based on current evidence, experts at Health and Welfare are confident that the risk to human health from MMT-derived manganese is extremely small; there is clearly a wide margin of safety between the current intake of manganese from MMT and the lowest concentrations of airborne manganese known to cause any adverse health effects."[30]

Health Canada conducted the most recent and comprehensive federal review of manganese from MMT in 1994, which again concluded that "the combustion products of MMT in gasoline do not represent an added health risk to the Canadian population."[31] The November 1994 Health Canada study was very important from a legal as well as a health policy standpoint, for, as a result of its finding that manganese emissions from MMT did not pose an unacceptable threat to health, the federal government was in effect precluded from taking steps to ban MMT under the "CEPA-toxic" provisions of the Canadian Environmental Protection Act.[32] However, recall that the EPA had denied Ethyl's MMT waiver application in July of 1994 because of unresolved health concerns. What was the basis for the apparent difference in the regulatory risk assessments between the two countries?

In determining the risk of a substance like manganese, two things must be determined: first, a threshold level of safe exposure (often called a health effects assessment), and second, the levels of exposure that people typically experience (often called an exposure assessment). The comparison of these two assessments then determines the risk represented by the compound. In this case, the variance in findings arose from differences in the two exposure assessments. Both the Canadian and US evaluations developed a reference or safe concentration for manganese in air using the same recently published epidemiological study, which had compared 92 Belgian battery plant workers with a control group of 101 workers in a nearby polymer plant.[33] Based on this study's findings, the upper limit for Canada was set at 0.11 µg Mn/m^3, while the US set a similar upper-limit range of 0.09 to 0.2 µg Mn/m^3 (upwardedly revised in 1994 from a previous reference concentration of 0.05 µg Mn/m^3). The EPA gave a "medium confidence" rating to this assessment, since there were unresolved questions about the health effects of manganese on special populations, namely the very young and very old (the workers surveyed in the epidemiological study were predominantly healthy working-age males), although a safety factor was included to account for these uncertainties. In its exposure assessment, Health Canada estimated worst-case personal exposure based on ambient monitoring data from an inner-city, high-traffic location in Montreal, coupled with results from a population-based study of personal exposure to manganese in California. In addition, the report examined small personal exposure studies of office workers, garage mechanics, and taxi drivers in Toronto and Montreal. Although Health Canada conceded that these studies were "not robust in terms of sample size, time frame, or statistical representativeness,"[34] it considered them in its overall risk assessment because the repeated measures of relatively low exposure from the studies gave added significance to the calculations. The most important point was stated clearly: the Health Canada review "indicated that 98 to 99 per cent of the population exposure to manganese (whatever the sources of that manganese) would be below [the] reference value."[35]

The EPA dismissed the Canadian personal exposure studies and instead used a much larger personal exposure study conducted in California to develop its exposure assessment. However, since the use of MMT was restricted to the small amounts of leaded fuel sold in California (as was legal under the Clean Air Act), the EPA had to make a number of assumptions in order to predict the personal exposure to manganese associated with MMT in gasoline. Having done so, it concluded that "the exposure estimates [for a portion of the population] … are in the range of or exceed some candidate Reference Concentration [threshold level] estimates."[36] This left enough uncertainty in the air for EPA to use as a basis for rejecting Ethyl's waiver application.

One of the most interesting findings to emerge from Health Canada's risk assessment was that the locations with concentrations above the reference level were those with large industrial sources of manganese emissions such as steel manufacturing (Hamilton and Sault Ste Marie, for example, have ambient manganese levels much higher than other areas in Canada). In fact, the risk assessment states in its conclusion: "For cities in which there are major manganese-emitting industries (for example steel mills), average respirable manganese exposure of the population is at or above the tolerable level at which it has been calculated that the risk of adverse health effects may begin to increase. This was deemed to be unrelated to the combustion of MMT in gasoline."[37]

Before she made the decision to ban MMT, Environment Minister Copps was aware of this finding, because Environment Canada officials had briefed her about the levels of airborne manganese stemming from steel mills in advance of a meeting with the oil industry.[38] Why did the minister not take action on this threat to the health of some Canadians, which had been established by a thorough scientific review undertaken in another federal department – especially since some of those at elevated risk were very likely to be her own constituents? At least some members of the Senate Standing Committee on the Environment were concerned enough to think action was warranted when they later heard about elevated levels of manganese from industrial steel mills: "Perhaps we should have legislation there instead of here [MMT]," stated Senator Ron Ghitter. And Senator Colin Kenny added: "We could issue a warning today, a news flash."[39] No such "news flash" ever emanated from Ottawa.

The senators had heard extensive testimony at their hearings on the Manganese-Based Fuel Additives Act from Dr Daniel Krewski, then acting director of Health Canada's Bureau of Chemical Hazards and one of the leading risk assessment authorities in the world. We give generous excepts from this testimony, even though it restates the earlier material, because the unsupported claim of adverse health effects goes on and on, down to the present day.[40] This is a great mystery in Canadian public policy: when we have (as we do) world-class scientific expertise, housed in an agency of government charged with protecting the health of Canadians, and when this agency's scientists report consistently *over a period of twenty years* that they have investigated the matter thoroughly, in four separate assessments, and find no basis for concern, why will many of us – including some of our wisest and most experienced politicians – not believe them?[41] Referring to the 1994 risk assessment, Krewski told the committee:

As with most risk assessments, a conservative approach was taken to both the establishment of the toxicological reference level and the exposure assessment. A very conservative reference level of 0.1 micrograms per cubic metre of air was selected … The World Health Organization, in a very recent assessment of the same data, has selected a somewhat higher reference value of 0.15 micrograms per cubic metre as the basis for their air quality guidelines. This gives us increased confidence in the conservative nature of our selected reference criteria …

Much of the opposition to MMT on health grounds is based on the fear that manganese from MMT will prove to be like lead from gasoline in the 1970s and 1980s. However, there are several critical differences between them. Lead is toxic at all concentrations while manganese is an essential element required in small amounts by cells in the body. Lead is toxic by ingestion as well as by inhalation, while manganese is not toxic when ingested even in quite large amounts … In conclusion, the Health Canada assessment, based on a conservative assessment of the scientific data, concludes that the health risks associated with manganese emissions resulting from the use of MMT in Canadian gasoline are negligible.[42]

Throughout the controversy, the concern about manganese's neuro-toxicity always remained in the background, so far as the public was concerned, even though the government finally enacted its legislation on completely different grounds (as discussed in the following section), in part because of the public's familiarity with the story of another gasoline additive, namely lead. What the public did not know was that, when Opposition Leader Chrétien had fired the opening political salvo in this epic struggle in his April 1991 missives, warning Tory federal ministers against allowing the continued use of this "insidious toxic heavy metal," his colleagues had another agenda entirely up their sleeves. One of Chrétien's letters went to the Honourable Don Mazankowski and read in part as follows:

Given the fact that Canadian crude and oil reserves are being rapidly depleted and the government had promised on two occasions ... to bring in Environmentally Friendly ethanol blended fuels since 1984, will you take the necessary action to require that all automotive gasoline based fuels contain 3.2% oxygen content. Such a move would create a market for between 5,000,000 to 8,000,000 bushels of grain, and the by-products can be utilized either as an animal feed or human food that is particularly suited for persons needing a diet of low calories, high fibre and protein ... I respectfully request that you take immediate action on this issue to provide a new market for Canadian Grain Growers, to cut the level of hydro-carbon emissions, and to ban the use of MMT in Canada that will eliminate the use of a substance that threatens the health of millions of Canadians, particularly our children.[43]

One can think of few initiatives in the entirety of Canadian legislative history that could promise to deliver so many valuable benefits at a single stroke of the pen. The minister also was asked to support Bill C-333, a private member's bill put forward by Liberal MP Ralph Ferguson, that would mandate a minimum level of oxygen content in gasoline, thereby encouraging the use of ethanol as an octane enhancer. Three years later, as the Liberal government's legislation banning MMT was being moved relentlessly through the policy process, there was an announcement of a proposed new $170 million corn-to-ethanol plant to be built in Chatham, Ontario (Ferguson's home area) by Commercial Fuels of Brampton.[44]

The campaign for using ethanol as an octane enhancer in gasoline heated up as soon as the Liberals came to power in the spring of 1993. In early May the Liberal party issued a press release, "Liberals

Announce Agriculture Policies," containing a section on ethanol: "For example, if 50 percent of all gasoline sold in Canada contained 10 percent ethanol, its production would require roughly 5 million tonnes of grain per year, which is equivalent to the amount Canada exports annually to our largest export customer ... Liberals are committed to banning the use of MMT in Canadian automotive fuels."[45] One imagines that Canadian prairie farmers, who are of necessity a hard-bitten lot, did not get too starry-eyed over these prospects. But at least the ethanol-in-gasoline theme, which became part of an agricultural policy designed to develop new markets for grain and thus improve the economic lot of farmers, provides a rational – if woefully misguided – basis for the federal Liberal party's campaign against MMT. A close examination of the documentary files, however, reveals that it is much harder to pin down the reasons for the very different, and ultimately politically persuasive, campaign waged by the combined Canadian and United States auto industry against this product.

2 Emission Control System Aspects

In July 1990, John Buccini, then director of the Commercial Chemicals Branch for Environment Canada, wrote a letter to the US EPA responding to EPA's request for a comment on Canada's experience with using MMT, in the context of Ethyl Corporation's waiver application at that time. Among other things Buccini noted the following: "We have had concerns about MMT plugging catalysts. However, while it is certain that some catalysts plug with MMT, we have concluded the number is relatively small. Transport Canada has made repeated requests for data on the incidence of catalyst plugging but no manufacturer has yet submitted any data. Also, examination of the manufacturer's warranty claims did not reveal any abnormal incidence of plugging."[46]

This theme is a consistent thread in the Canadian controversy over MMT use, and its most colourful segment is undoubtedly the astonishing letter written by the president of General Motors Canada, Maureen Kempston Darkes, to the federal minister of the environment, Sheila Copps, on 17 February 1995: "It is with deep regret that I must inform you of the decision we have made to disconnect [emission system] warning lights on our products for the 1996 model year." The reason she gave was that the MMT in gasoline disrupted the normal functioning of that equipment.[47] What could have happened to bring things to such a pass?

The Canadian federal government had set up a collaborative process for making policy decisions about the relative contributions of fuel improvements and emission control technologies to vehicle emissions reductions. Between June 1993 and September 1994 a series of five meetings on MMT took place between government and industry under the auspices of a group called "The Joint Government-Industry Committee on Transportation Fuels and Motor Vehicle Control Technologies," with attendees from various federal departments (Environment Canada, Transport Canada, Health Canada, Natural Resources Canada, Canadian General Standards Board), the Canadian Petroleum Products Institute (CPPI), the Motor Vehicle Manufacturers Association (MVMA), representing domestic automobile manufacturers, and the Association of International Automobile Manufacturers of Canada (AIAMC), representing foreign-based manufacturers. This joint committee, which also had other issues on its plate, was tasked with arriving at a solution to the technical debate surrounding MMT and vehicle emissions.

The first meeting of this government-industry committee took place on 21 June 1993, and the minutes indicate a belief that the fate of MMT in gasoline needed to be resolved by the spring of 1994. The federal government stated for the record that little data existed to substantiate the vehicle manufacturers' claims that MMT might adversely affect the new generation of onboard diagnostic equipment. However, the minutes also note that Ford was conducting new tests on OBD II equipment which would be submitted to the EPA in September 1993 as part of the Ethyl waiver application process. To increase the credibility of these tests, the MVMA agreed to approach Ford about allowing the participation of Canadian government and CPPI observers, but we found no documentation showing any future involvement of the government or the CPPI in Ford's test program. In their attempt to establish a fair and transparent process, federal government participants agreed to develop a paper outlining the technical information that would be required to make a decision on MMT and to "clearly enunciate all the factors that [would] enter into the decision."[48]

In the meantime, the oil and automobile industries wanted to make sure they had their ducks in order for these government meetings. On 30 June 1993, the MVMA and CPPI executives, meeting without government representatives, agreed on the urgency of a decision about MMT, but not on what that decision should be. Since the matter was being presented as a technical disagreement, it was decided that a joint group of CPPI and MVMA technical representatives would be best suited to resolve the issue, although senior executives from Imperial Oil and Ford planned on being there to ensure that strategic business considerations were kept in mind.[49] The MVMA-CPPI technical committee met on 9 August and 1 September 1993 and proceeded to initiate a life-cycle estimate of the environmental impact of banning MMT. This technical committee decided that the CPPI Fuels Group would work with Ford to see what type of practical test program could be carried out to resolve outstanding technical issues, in either Canada or the US, within a one- to two-year time frame. Ford and Imperial Oil were to meet with federal government officials to convey this plan and ask for the extension of the memorandum of understanding between Transport Canada and the vehicle manufacturers, that would be required in order to acquire this test data. The CPPI had stated that if the technical disagreements were resolved in the MVMA's favour, they would remove MMT. Unfortunately, this deal to design a study of MMT's effects fell apart, for when Ford's representative went back to the MVMA board of directors, they rejected it. The CPPI board accepted it.

At the second meeting of the joint committee on 17 August 1993, Transport Canada presented a seven-page federal government paper, "MMT and Motor Vehicle Emissions," that outlined the information that the government felt it needed to make a decision on MMT.[50] Key questions that the government wanted to resolve included why the subset of 1991 Ford Escorts (from the 1992 Ethyl waiver application) were particularly susceptible to emission increases, and what effect MMT might have for onboard diagnostic systems (OBD II). At this government meeting, it was reported that the MVMA-CPPI executive and technical committees were meeting in an attempt to work through their technical differences. The joint technical committee was examining two options for Canada: (1) lowering allowable MMT levels in gasoline from 18 to 8.26 mg/L, and (2) phasing out MMT entirely. (8.26 mg/L was the level specified by Ethyl in seeking a waiver in the US, while 18 mg/L was the level approved for Canadian gasoline, although a CPPI study had shown that actual levels averaged 9 mg/L.) The MVMA and CPPI were not in agreement about the effects of MMT on emission control systems. Everyone agreed, however, that the expected 30 November 1993 EPA decision on the Ethyl waiver application would be a pivotal event. The technical committee was to continue discussion to resolve the issue and provide recommendations at the next meeting, but despite its best efforts, it was stymied by the MVMA board's rejection of its plan.

The minutes of the third meeting of the joint committee (10 December 1993) show that the 30 November 1993 EPA decision – wherein EPA ruled that MMT did not cause or contribute to a failure of existing emission control systems – did not settle anything for the Canadian debate.[51] The vehicle manufacturers continued to press their case against MMT: Toyota made a presentation on how MMT negatively impacted its OBD II system and Ford tabled research that showed a detrimental effect on OBD II. The MVMA stated that despite the recent

EPA ruling, they felt that MMT would be banned in the future because of OBD II problems (recall that the EPA had not made a formal ruling on MMT's effect on OBD II). In the spirit of collaboration, Ethyl and Toyota agreed to get together to discuss the results of their various test programs.

At the fifth meeting on 9 September 1994, Toyota and Ethyl reported that they had met to discuss the differences in their data.[52] The main difference appeared to result from the speed at which the mileage was accumulated in the two programs (i.e., the driving cycle). No consensus was reached as to which was superior, despite the existence of EPA's July ruling that Ethyl's test showed the driving cycle did not affect MMT-induced impacts on hydrocarbon emissions. Environment Canada provided a brief summary of the 13 July 1994 waiver decision by the EPA (denied because of concerns about health effects). Health Canada summarized its most recent risk assessment with the conclusion that MMT did not represent an unacceptable health risk to Canadians. Ethyl presented extensive test data from its own recent research that led to considerable discussion about potential effects of MMT on OBD II systems, whereas GM tabled preliminary findings on the prospect of increased warranty claims that might be caused by MMT use. It was clear that differences of opinion on the status of MMT remained.

The upshot was unusual, to say the least: it was decided that the technical aspects of MMT's impact on emission control systems *could not be resolved*! Although the oil industry wanted a third-party review of the technical debate, the committee remanded the issue to the ministers of environment, transport, natural resources, industry, and health for decision. One might well ask what was preventing resolution of this debate. The series of meetings between the joint industry-government committee, while useful in defining the issues, did not constitute a sound and thorough assessment of the technology, as conducted either by a capable government department or by some independent expert panel. Apart from drafting the seven-page, internal Transport Canada report, "MMT and Motor Vehicle Emissions," the Canadian government conducted no rigorous assessment of the impacts that MMT had on emissions control systems and OBD II. Had it done so, and had it made public any such study, as Health Canada did with its health risk assessment, there would have been a substantive basis to support the government's decision, whatever form it took.[53]

Recognizing this shortcoming, CPPI representatives suggested that an independent, third-party review of the technical data be carried out:

The [CPPI] Task Force has concluded that it cannot reconcile the very strongly held views of the OEMs [original equipment manufacturers] and Ethyl based on the information currently available. While it cannot be argued that the data from either side is inherently wrong, the programs used to develop the data have been designed differently, have been conducted in different ways, under differing conditions and with varying degrees of rigour ... To help resolve the controversy, the Task Force has identified what it believes are key questions that need to be answered. It is proposed that CPPI, the associations representing the OEMs (MVMA and AIAMC), Ethyl, Government and a third party independent technical resource cooperate on a two level program to develop the information needed to reach a sound and proper decision on MMT. The proposed program would combine laboratory work with controlled fleet testing and field warranty monitoring to answer the key questions about potential MMT effects. If initiated promptly, this program could be completed by the end of 1995 at the latest ...[54]

There is a great deal of precedent for using independent expert panels to resolve points of contention in scientific and technological disputes; in the United States, the National Academy of Sciences and affiliated institutions have issued such well-regarded panel reports literally by the dozen for many years now, and a comparable capacity exists under the auspices of the Royal Society of Canada.[55] However, the MVMA replied that such a review would likely not determine anything new and might delay action on MMT.

The CPPI made a series of proposals to the government to provide some resolution of the issue, short of a ban on MMT, as debate around the issue progressed. As noted, it offered to submit all technical matters in dispute to independent panels and committed itself to removing MMT if that was what such panels recommended. In addition, it offered to cut in half the allowable upper limit of MMT in gasoline (average amounts already were at that level, as noted earlier), regardless of the panel outcomes. None of these proposals were accepted. Instead the issue was thrown into the laps of the five federal ministers who had some responsibility for this file (ministers of environment, transport, natural resources, industry, and health), who were obliged finally to "bite the bullet" and take a political decision on the fate of MMT.

At this point any pretence of collaboration broke down, to be replaced by classical political lobbying. The federal ministers truly were caught between a rock and a hard place, for over the next few years they faced one of the worst political nightmares imaginable, a zero-sum game, as platoons of solemn executives and their hired lobbyists, representing two of the most influential industry sectors in the Canadian economy, trooped through their offices with diametrically opposed messages nestled within varied prophecies of doom. From the standpoint of public policy, a good escape mechanism remained even then at hand, although it went unused, the same solution that is now being applied in a different fashion, too late to avoid both the acute political humiliation and the monetary cost of the federal government's subsequent settlement with Ethyl Corporation. That solution was to entrust a thorough re-examination of the two outstanding issues (the performance of auto emissions/OBD II equipment on the one hand, and perhaps the health and environmental risk assessment on the other) to independent expert panels whose reports would be clearly communicated to the public. With such reviews in hand the government might have been able to act responsibly in the matter of MMT, on the basis of credible science and sound risk management principles.

3 A Fully Politicized Process

On 12 September 1994, the vehicle manufacturer executives met with then Environment Minister Sheila Copps, informing the minister that if MMT were still around in August 1995, "they would raise prices by $3000 per vehicle, void parts of their warranties, or close down some Canadian manufacturing units."[56] The bullying had begun. Copps referred to this $3000 figure at different times subsequently (e.g., the press conference for the introduction of Bill C-94), but as might be expected federal officials never were given the slightest hint by the industry as to the basis on which that number had been calculated. In early October the CPPI sent a letter to Minister Copps requesting an urgent meeting with her in the belief that the CPPI deserved the same opportunity as the MVMA had had to present its case. Apparently they were too late. By 12 October 1994, Minister Copps had told a Canadian Press reporter that unless the petroleum industry removed MMT from gasoline, the government would ban it: "I am moving specifically on MMT because we've had complaints from the automotive industry that it could void warranties on Canadian cars," she was quoted as saying.[57]

There is no evidence of how the federal ministers responsible for the MMT file reached this policy decision, but the outcome was clear. Up to this point, the automobile manufacturers and the oil industry had been negotiating on even ground in their technical dispute over MMT and emission control systems. But as soon as Minister Copps let everyone know that MMT was going to be banned if the two industry sectors could not reach a "voluntary agreement" to discontinue its use, the automobile manufacturers had no incentive to continue negotiating with the oil industry. They had won and only had to throw their support behind the government's decision to ban MMT. The CPPI, trying to gain some even footing in the debate, again repeated their suggestion for an independent assessment and review.[58] They offered once more to voluntarily remove MMT from gasoline if an independent review concluded that there were problems with it.

The problem was that the full data set used to substantiate the car manufacturers' claims on emission control impacts had not been made available to the CPPI and certainly not to the public. This was ostensibly necessary to protect commercially confidential information such as warranty comparisons between Canada and the US. Unfortunately, it made the data and research methods impossible for anyone outside of government to review and certainly did not contribute to the transparency of the decision-making process. Further, there were at least some federal officials who had doubts about the quality of the "scientific" evidence being provided to them by the car manufacturers.[59]

A 31 October 1994 CPPI internal memo to its board members reflects some of their frustration with recent developments in the federal process. Regarding the recent meeting between CPPI executives and the minister, the memo contends that Minister Copps informed them "that [the] environmental benefits were not of material consequence in the debate, i.e., the sum game was more or less zero." Further, the federal government made it clear that it would not support the creation of an independent scientific panel.[60] According to the government, any further investigation into the issue would only serve to delay a decision. Moreover, the government apparently still thought that a negotiated settlement around MMT could be reached, for on 18 November 1994 Minister Copps wrote letters to oil and automobile industry executives requesting that the two industries address the issue of *eliminating* MMT in Canadian gasoline and submit a proposed resolution to her by the end of the year.

A month later, CPPI and MVMA executives met to share each other's plans to address the MMT issue. The CPPI again proposed that an independent panel be struck to resolve the scientific debate surrounding MMT and emission control systems.[61] The MVMA presented its latest information about MMT's alleged effects on emission control systems, which had been presented to federal officials the week before. At least some government officials present at this session were not convinced by the MVMA information package. According to an internal government e-mail message circulated shortly thereafter, serious problems were noted with respect to the auto manufacturers' submission:[62] "[The MVMA] presentation, which focussed on the impact of MMT on OBD II effectiveness and vehicle performance, did not make a convincing case. Much of the content was based on confidential warranty repair records and returned components such as catalytic converters and spark plugs ('real world' problems). Not much data was presented. Bar and line charts depicting differences between U.S. and Canadian experiences did not have quantitative scales on the chart axes so the significance of the observations could not be assessed. Experience-based suggestions of cause-effect relationships were not supported by scientific analysis. The weight of the presentation was anecdotal and circumstantial information. If there is 'hard data' beyond the individual cases, it was not being made available." Note that this derisory assessment of the auto manufacturers' own case is made after years of wrangling, and years of their conducting, at least ostensibly, "research" on these problems. Minister Copps extended her deadline for a settlement until 31 January 1995. Although the CPPI continued to push for an independent panel review and in fact approached the Royal Society of Canada about conducting such a review, it became clear that no voluntary settlement would emerge. The vehicle manufacturers dug their heels in deeper: "We didn't see the need for wasting time and money on a problem that was already well-documented," claimed a VP from General Motors.[63]

The documentary files we have examined are littered with complaints from federal officials, members of the Senate who opposed the legislation, the provincial premiers who launched the successful action against the federal government, and representatives of the oil and gas industry, protesting the absence of reliable information to support the auto manufacturers' claims about the effect of MMT on OBD II and emission control systems. As indicated, the absence of reliable evidence is noted as early as 1990, in the letter from Environment Canada's John Buccini to EPA, and it continued down to the point when Bill C-29 (the successor to Bill C-94) became law and even thereafter. The best single overview of this aspect of the MMT controversy is to be found in the Minority Opinion by four senators (Buchanan, Cochrane, Ghitter, and Kinsella) from the Standing Senate Committee on Energy, Environment and Natural Resources, which had conducted hearings on the bill.[64] The Senate Committee had elicited under questioning some of the only evidence on the public record that might explain the real source of the automotive manufacturers' problems with MMT. The testimony is by Mr Doug Bethune, an automotive technology instructor at Nova Scotia Community College:

MR BETHUNE: I work on the front lines and I have seen no devastating effects from MMT residue in catalytic converters, spark plugs or elsewhere ... The question is always whether MMT is really the problem. In 33 years as a technician, I have never seen General Motors be less than very cautious with their science. The manufacturers in general have been very cautious with their science. However, for some strange reason, on every avenue that I pursue to find the science behind these problems with MMT I come to a dead end. As everyone in my area knows, I am a proponent of GM. In my opinion, the MMT

issue was raised when General Motors began putting a base metal in their catalytic converter called cerium, which has the unique property of absorbing
oxygen when it is in plentiful supply and giving up oxygen when it is deficient.
This is when the concern arose for MMT. It is not what MMT has that is the
problem, it is what it does not have [i.e., oxygen] ...

SENATOR KENNY: How do you explain that 21 vehicle manufacturers have
told this Committee that they have a problem with MMT?

MR BETHUNE: As has been mentioned here, there are two giants in this country;
the oil companies and the auto manufacturers. They are at each other on this
MMT issue. These two giants have been pushed to the wall by a greater giant,
and that giant is EPA. The manufacturers are being forced to meet emission
levels ... that are now starting to approach a threshold of unattainable goals. [65]

There are clearly some interesting issues tabled here, ones that would
have benefited from a rigorous and independent examination. Remember that, at the time (early 1995) when the CPPI was pushing the government hard to send the issues to an independent expert panel for
their evaluation, this particular part of the MMT dispute had been simmering for at least five years. Towards the end, as the federal government, pushed harder and harder by the auto industry until its back was
firmly up against the wall, moved on the legislative ban, a number of
provincial governments became active players, because refineries in
their jurisdictions would be forced to make substantial capital investments or even close down.

Perhaps because they were pressured so heavily by a powerful industry sector, the federal politicians never appeared to focus very
much on the provincial complaints, thus setting up a nice irony in the
outcome, because it was the provincial governments' complaints to
the Internal Trade Secretariat that brought the house of cards represented by Bill C-29 tumbling down. Everyone except the auto industry
was looking for an "out," and submission of the technical issues in
dispute to an independent panel appeared to all of them to be the best
avenue towards resolution. As the legislative process dragged on into
early 1997, this option was repeatedly put on the table. For example,
James Ogilvy of Alberta's Ministry of Federal and Intergovernmental
Affairs was asked in the Senate Committee hearings by Senator Kinsella: "Is there an environmental issue here? What is the data? Is there
a health issue? Does MMT gum up the OBD-IIs [sic]? I think that this
committee can answer the first two questions with not much difficulty,
but to answer the third question, where the evidence is so contradictory, I wonder what your government would think, building upon
what your minister has said ... of the idea that, if this committee, in
meeting its requirement from the Senate to produce an interim report

concerning the question of whether or not MMT gums up OBDs, were
to submit the data that we have to a group like the Royal Society of
Canada so that they would become the objective arbiters?" Dr Ogilvy
replied that "the government of Alberta would, in my view, support
that type of process."[66]

The opportunity was never seized, because the federal cabinet had decided to capitulate to the unbearable pressure from the vehicle manufacturers. The 17 February 1995 letter from Maureen Kempston Darkes,
president of General Motors Canada, to Minister Copps, quoted at the
beginning of this section, saying that GM would not honour warranties
for emission control systems in the 1996 model year if the ban on MMT
was not in effect soon, apparently was instrumental in persuading the
rest of the federal cabinet to agree with the ban on MMT, particularly
the minister of natural resources, Anne McLellan, who until then had
been opposing it.

Thus the federal government had no choice but to examine its legislative options for banning MMT. Since Health Canada had stated that
there was no unacceptable health threat from manganese emissions
from MMT, the government could not use the toxic-substance provisions of the Canadian Environmental Protection Act. Further, since direct emissions data showed that MMT did not affect hydrocarbon or
carbon monoxide emissions and actually reduced NO_x emissions, the
government could not act under the Motor Vehicle Safety Act. Finally,
on 19 May 1995, Bill C-94, the Manganese-based Fuel Additives Act,
was introduced in the House of Commons by Minister Copps. The bill
banned importation and interprovincial trade of MMT. This legislation
was functionally similar to the manner in which the Motor Vehicle
Safety Act regulates emissions: no vehicle can be imported into Canada
or across provincial borders for sale without complying with emission
requirements.[67] Although the direct evidence is limited, it appears that
the government felt that using the device of banning not the substance
itself (MMT), but only interprovincial trade in that substance, would
satisfy the NAFTA requirement of treating international firms the same
as Canadian companies.[68]

Of course the price the federal authorities paid for being so apparently clever in their choice of legal authority was to seriously antagonize
many provincial governments, who had been effectively excluded from
the decision-making process and who had in their jurisdictions the oil
refineries producing gasoline, some of which were threatened with
closure by their owners owing to the projected capital costs of equipment changes. Over the next few months, political lobbying became increasingly intense from both industries. And at each legislative stage
(i.e., first reading, second reading, House committee review, third

reading, Senate review), opposition members supported with documents provided by Ethyl and the CPPI challenged the bill. The House Environment Committee, and particularly its chairman, Charles Caccia, resented the way in which Ethyl was challenging the government, referring to the corporation as "bullies in the manner in which they presented themselves and advanced their arguments."[69]

The political battle dragged on until 2 February 1996, when the House of Commons was prorogued. Bill C-94 had not yet passed third reading and so died on the order paper; if the government wanted to ban MMT, it would have to reintroduce the legislation in the next session. During the political battle in Canada, the US Court of Appeal finally ordered the EPA in November 1995 to grant Ethyl a waiver for MMT. The car manufacturers were going to have MMT in the gasoline tanks of their American cars, and the Canadian government's argument that banning MMT worked towards harmonizing US and Canadian fuel standards was greatly weakened. February 1996 also saw a cabinet shuffle, with Sergio Marchi replacing Sheila Copps as minister of the environment.

Early in his tenure Environment Minister Marchi received a letter dated 23 February 1996 from Minister of Trade Arthur Eggleton warning about possible trade implications of a ban on the importation and interprovincial trade of MMT: "Let me stress my department's belief that Bill C-94 should not be reintroduced as it could have many adverse implications for Canadian trade, without compensating benefits."[70] Despite this warning, Minister Marchi reintroduced Bill C-94 as Bill C-29 in the new session of Parliament. Speaking in defence of the bill at third reading in April 1996, Marchi said: "In taking this decision about what has been a controversial, complex issue, I have consulted widely among representatives of auto manufacturers, the petroleum industry, environmental groups, and caucus colleagues. The bottom line for me ... is the potential negative effect on the health of Canadians caused by possible interference of MMT on automobile computer systems which monitor tailpipe emissions."[71] Bill C-29 did not pass third reading before Parliament's summer recess, which gave the government time to pause and reconsider the merits of their plan. On 31 July 1996, Prime Minister Chrétien wrote a letter to the ministers of environment, trade, industry, and natural resources, asking them to review the bill jointly and report back to him in the fall: "This is to advise that, with Bill C-29 not having moved forward before Parliament's recess, it is my view that the issues raised by the Bill should be reviewed in the time available over the summer. I have written to Minister Marchi, asking him to undertake this review ... and to report back to me in the fall."[72] There is no evidence of what was included in this review, or, for that matter, whether it was conducted at all. Bill C-29 was given third reading in the House of Commons on 16 September 1996 and was passed in December.

Bill C-29 became law on 25 April 1997, just two days before Prime Minister Chrétien called a federal election, and was brought into force in June of that year.[73] In April 1997 Ethyl Corporation launched a $250-million NAFTA trade challenge and followed this salvo in June with a lawsuit filed in an Ontario court. Alberta – supported by Quebec, Saskatchewan, and Nova Scotia – launched a challenge under the federal-provincial Agreement on Internal Trade (AIT) in December of 1997. The AIT panel was the first of these bodies to issue a judgment, and in June of 1998 found that the bill represented an internal barrier to trade that failed to demonstrate any legitimate objective recognized by the Agreement. It found that the federal government failed to demonstrate "that there existed a matter of such urgency or a risk so widespread as to warrant such comprehensive restrictions as the *Act* provides on internal trade." It also stated: "It is clear from the submissions that it was the automobile manufacturers who were the driving force behind the elimination of MMT. They claimed that the onboard monitoring equipment in new vehicles would be impaired by the use of MMT-enhanced gasoline. The evidence as to the impact of MMT on the environment is, at best, inconclusive."[74] The report included a dissenting opinion stating that, given the circumstances, the government had acted appropriately.

After the AIT ruling, the government reconsidered its options, and the prime minister asked the deputy prime minister, Herb Gray, to negotiate a settlement between the government and Ethyl.[75] On 20 July 1998, the government announced that it would lift restrictions on interprovincial trade and the importing of MMT. The federal government's press release included the following remarks:

The [AIT] panel noted that the Government's legislation was based on representations by the automobile industry in Canada. The industry maintained that MMT adversely affected automobile onboard diagnostic systems (OBDs). A malfunctioning OBD could fail to detect that a car is emitting higher levels of pollutants into the air. The current scientific information fails to demonstrate that MMT impairs the proper functioning of OBDs. The Government remains committed to protecting the health of Canadians and the environment, and will continue to assess the need for further action as a result of health or environmental concerns. Studies in Canada and the U.S. are proceeding on the impact of MMT and other fuel additives on health and automobile tailpipe emissions. When the results of these studies are made available to the Government of Canada, they will be reviewed by an independent, third party in consultation with stakeholders and provinces. If subsequent federal government action is warranted, it will act, using the Canadian Environmental Protection Act. In light of the Government's response to the panel's recommendation, it has moved to resolve other challenges to the legislation, launched by Ethyl Corporation under the NAFTA and by Ethyl Canada in Ontario Court. The Government has agreed to a payment of $13 million (US) to Ethyl representing its reasonable costs and lost profit in Canada, subject to independent verification. Ethyl will terminate its legal actions. The Government believes this is in the best interests of Canadians because it avoids long, protracted and expensive legal proceedings. [76]

Induced by a powerful Canadian industry sector into embarking on an unwise course of action, unwilling to trust the good scientific work of its own officials in Health Canada on the health risk assessment (always the most critical factor in public concerns about MMT), and having refused (until after its humiliating capitulation) to engage in an eminently sensible process of independent expert review, Canada's federal government had no chips left to play with in the little poker game it had called together – unless we remember the marker left at the table in the form of the compensation payment to Ethyl by the long-suffering Canadian taxpayers.

POST MORTEM

Why was this allowed to happen? The government repeatedly stated that MMT's effect on emission control systems was the basis for its legislation, but there was clear evidence in its possession that the case to back up these claims was at best weak. The final decision to ban MMT was made in the fall of 1994, just after the EPA had denied Ethyl's waiver request on the basis of health concerns. The *Globe and Mail* quotes Minister Copps as saying at the time, "I've seen the evidence," referring to the vehicle manufacturers' claims, to explain her own position. [77] Why did this same technical evidence on OBD II equipment not lead the EPA to deny the waiver, so that it would not have to worry about making any decision at all on the health concerns? On the other hand, if the Canadian government did not accept the EPA ruling, why was the evidence in their possession not published in a publicly available technology assessment, similar to the Health Canada risk assessment?

The allegations about emission control problems became harder and harder to fathom as the industry battle over MMT went on and on. The government thought that it was up against a deadline to ensure that the new OBD II systems worked properly for the model year 1996, and the threats from the car industry to void warranties for new vehicles in Canada were not taken lightly. The North American automobile industry possessed a great deal of inherent credibility on this issue, since it was perceived to be "neutral" by many parties, and it certainly carried a big stick in terms of its privileged place in the Canadian economy. The adding of the magic number $3000 per car to vehicle prices, or alternatively the voiding of all new car warranties, certainly impressed the federal cabinet. The oil industry estimated the cost of replacing MMT at around $5 per year for each vehicle, a mere pittance compared with the alarming number from the auto industry. How could the latter not win out? Finally, these 1994 developments must also be arrayed alongside the Liberal party's long-standing commitment to the banning of MMT, originating in Jean Chrétien's letters supporting a Liberal opposition bill to replace MMT with corn-derived ethanol and continuing with the promise in the 1993 election campaign "Red Book" to carry out this action if the party formed a new government.

Instead of asking the all-or-nothing question of whether MMT should be allowed in gasoline or not, policy makers could have asked how the potentially harmful effects of MMT, such as they are or might be, could be reduced; for example, lowering the allowable concentration of the additive in gasoline, as the oil industry had proposed. At one point in 1993 the CPPI thought that this would be the eventual outcome of the MMT debate and polled its members to see how many would support an upper limit reduction from 18 mg/L to 8.26 mg/L.[78] A second risk-reduction strategy, one with additional environmental benefits, would have been to improve fuel economy standards for vehicles or seek other means to reduce fuel consumption, thereby releasing less manganese, smog-forming, and greenhouse gas emissions into the atmosphere, although this would have been politically difficult. In the meantime, the government could have continued to support research to better understand the environmental and health consequences of manganese. More important, the government could also have addressed the other, higher-risk, anthropogenic sources of manganese, including steel-making and metal-processing operations. In Canada, manganese exposures are routinely above Health Canada's recommended maximum levels in Hamilton and Sault Ste Marie.

From a procedural aspect, the federal government could have ensured that the provinces were satisfied by addressing MMT as part of a more comprehensive solution to vehicle emissions. At the same time that the federal government was planning the ban on MMT, the Canadian Council of Ministers of the Environment had established a Task Force on Cleaner Vehicles and Fuels. Despite the obvious appropriateness of this task force as a means of handling the MMT issue, the group was told to avoid it. In the end, the utterly pointless "politicization" of MMT took time, energy, and attention away from more important tasks – namely, the scientific risk assessment of manganese in the environment (or of other hazards, such as sulphur in gasoline), and the making of informed risk management decisions based thereon, the pursuit of which, for the protection of human health and natural habitats, is the proper business of government.

Even after the government had backed itself into a political corner, had it agreed to undertake some form of independent expert panel review in late 1994 or early 1995, a panel's report might have been able to offer a substantive and broadly acceptable basis for such a decision, whatever it may have been. There is a lesson in all this. If one has been dragged into a contentious and protracted dispute between two other parties (as the federal government was), and one of those parties – in this case, CPPI – offers a way out, promising to abide by the judgment of an independent and credible tribunal, one ought to take up such an offer forthwith. The rejoinder that there was "not enough time left" to pursue that option is absurd, given the size of the stakes: the issue had been "on the table" since the late 1980s, CPPI's formal offer for expert panel adjudication was made in late 1994, and the government's bill did not pass the House until the end of 1996.

The federal government was blindsided by the way in which the MMT case unfolded. It all began with the ethanol caper, and only after that gambit had started to play out, culminating in the Red Book pledge to ban MMT, did an entirely different and unexpected twist emerge, namely the encounter between the auto and oil industries over MMT's alleged effects on equipment. It seems as if the government just could not sort through the many dimensions of this case and focus squarely on what its own responsibilities were. Here is in retrospect how such a focusing might have been done:

1 *Start with the health and environmental risk issues, and get them off the table:*
   • First, deal with the health issue by doing one of two things: Either (a) recognize that the health risk assessment has been done competently by Health Canada, defend that assessment, and state clearly that this is not an issue at this time; or (b), if there were strong reasons to be concerned about the assessment, submit the health issues to an independent expert panel review that includes public consultation and communication, something that was lacking from the 1994 Health Canada assessment.[79]
   • Second, in the absence of any thorough Canadian assessment of MMT's direct impact on hydrocarbon emissions, accept the fact that EPA had passed a competent judgment in this matter (i.e., MMT does not exacerbate this problem), and state clearly that this is not an issue.

- Third, accept the fact that EPA also has credible evidence that the use of MMT yields a benefit for lower NO_x emissions, state this clearly, and present it as an offset to the environmental burden of increased airborne manganese.

2 *Then confront the equipment issue separately:*

- First, in the absence of any thorough Canadian assessment of MMT's impact on emission control systems, accept the fact that the EPA assessment (MMT does not cause or contribute to a failure of any emission control device or system) is thorough and competent. If there had been reason to disagree with the scope and methods in the EPA assessment, then the Canadian government should have conducted its own assessment, or commissioned an expert panel to do so, communicating any results clearly to the public.
- Second, conduct, or commission an independent expert panel to conduct, a thorough assessment of MMT's impact on onboard diagnostic systems (OBD II) and communicate the results clearly to the public. Follow up the assessment by bringing together the two industries and giving direction on how the report's recommendations should be implemented.

3 *Then define how the government will discharge its own responsibilities:*

- First, state that, if there is good evidence of MMT posing an unacceptable risk to the environment, health, or the economy, the government will take action to reduce this risk to acceptable levels. State also that government action will take into account the benefits of using MMT: inexpensive increases in fuel octane, and reduction in NO_x emissions. For instance, if MMT were really causing problems with OBD II systems that led to unacceptable levels of warranty claims for auto manufacturers, state that the government will take steps to ensure at least the availability of MMT-free fuel in Canada.
- Second, state that the government will seek to do this first by negotiation with the gasoline providers, and failing that, by legislative or regulatory fiat.

Only by getting rid of the distraction posed by the unsubstantiated fears of health risk could the government have focused clearly on its main outstanding responsibility, as of 1994, which was to *adjudicate* the dispute between two very important Canadian industry sectors – not, as it did, arbitrarily come down on one side of the dispute. Instead, the risk issues were left to fester in the background, as they had been ever since the then opposition leader wrote his 1991 letters. In essence, the way in which these issues, especially the human health (neurotoxicity) one,

were allowed to function in the MMT case – and still function in the fre-
quent references to MMT now – marks a classic instance of the confusion
between hazard and risk, something which bedevils almost every risk
controversy as well as our legislative instruments (see further chapter 8).
Yes, manganese is "dangerous," i.e., hazardous, if we are exposed to
excessive amounts of it by inhalation, but not at all levels of exposure –
indeed, it is not only beneficial to us (by ingestion) in small doses, but is
an essential nutrient for humans, so that a dietary deficiency of manganese would be deleterious.[80] The Health Canada risk assessments, over a
period of twenty years, stated repeatedly that Canadians are not and
have not been exposed to excessive amounts by inhalation, except perhaps in Hamilton or Sault Ste Marie, where the source of the excessive
exposure is not MMT. But the federal authorities in charge of the MMT
file outside Health Canada never said this, clearly, understandably, and
unequivocally.

Environmental and health public-interest groups supported the ban
on MMT on grounds of unacceptable exposure, but without credibly
countering the Health Canada risk assessment. They also played the
"hazard card" on every occasion, talking about the inherent dangers of
manganese, by which they meant (or should have meant) the dangers
of excessive exposure, if that exposure were found to exist. They never
once mentioned, so far as we know, the existence of other sources of
exposure to airborne manganese in Canada, or the fact that it is an indispensable ingredient in the making of steel. As contributing producers of this charade about hazard and risk they participated without
shame in the scaremongering over health risks, the only upshot of
which is to confuse members of the public about the difference between
what they should worry about, where their health is concerned, and
what they do not need to worry about. This posturing over public
health not only does not serve any useful purpose in the end, but also is
actually detrimental to its ostensible objective, because it does not
allow the public to see clearly the right priorities for risk reduction.

While it is true that a precautionary approach is warranted for many
risk management decisions, particularly those where there are significant scientific uncertainties and potentially irreversible impacts, precaution does not imply ignoring the principles of sound risk management.
Even with respect to the health risks, a precautionary approach would
have been appropriate, had the federal health risk assessment not found
sufficient information upon which to base a decision. This is different
from acknowledging that new information may change the outcome of
a risk assessment, which is always a possibility. Invoking the precautionary principle to dictate the outcome of a technical dispute between
two industries undermines the intention and future application of this
important principle.[81]

If the concern was with something different altogether, say (hypothetically) with the long-term ability of ecosystems to assimilate the anthropogenic sources of manganese, as opposed to the shorter-term human health risks related to inhaling manganese emissions, then the government should have stated clearly that the risks to ecosystems were the issue and should have managed the risk in a comprehensive and responsible manner, rather than by shrouding it in a highly political debate over emission-control technology. (So far as we know, no one ever actually advanced such a concern.) In this case, the government might have sought ways to reduce manganese use in industry that did not seriously diminish the benefits derived from it – in other words, a so-called "win-win" solution. As noted before, these ways might have included improving fuel efficiency in vehicles, thereby reducing not only manganese emissions but those of other substances as well; or seeking ways for the steel- and metal-processing industry to lower their manganese emissions. Finally, the government could continue to collect information needed to inform proper environmental risk management decisions.

The outcome of the government's failure to separate risk issues from the others was the surrender of its strategic advantage in issue management. Instead, as things turned out, the furious lobbying and extended political debate only trapped the government in a zero-sum game without an exit strategy. If by some miracle we Canadians and our governments could learn from the MMT débâcle not to follow such a crooked trail again, but rather to walk the comparatively straight and narrow path of risk management, the $20 million and change we paid out to Ethyl Corporation for the lesson would have been well spent.

5 Regulating Nuclear Power: The Mismanagement of Public Consultation in Canada

MICHAEL D. MEHTA

Nuclear power has been with us for over fifty years. As a relatively mature technology, one would expect it to possess significant social, institutional, environmental, and economic support. However, this is not the case. Nuclear power has generated considerable debate around the world and has strained democratic consultation and decision making to the point of breaking. In Canada a comprehensive debate on the social acceptability of the nuclear option has hidden behind ponderous regulation that systematically excludes the public from meaningful participation. There are several lessons to learn from this failure to practice sound risk issue management. Because newer technologies like biotechnology and developments in future technologies such as nano-technology need to avoid falling into the nuclear trap, much is at stake here. With heightened public awareness of the risks associated with many technological innovations (e.g., genetically engineered foods, wireless communications devices), judging the social acceptability of a technology is eminently a political responsibility. This is especially important, since new and advanced technologies are more complex, have greater levels of scientific uncertainty associated with them, generate impacts over longer time frames, and involve the creation of new risks and benefits. This case study of nuclear power demonstrates how a failure to locate a technology within a broad decision-making process polarizes public opinion and weakens trust.

For years the advantages of living in industrial society appeared to eclipse the dangers created by unsafe industrial practices. This attitude has steadily changed since the early 1970s with the coming of environmentalism. For example, nuclear energy has become both a symbol of industrial progress and energy self-sufficiency and a perceived threat to human health and the ecosystem. The risks associated with nuclear energy have galvanized individuals into two distinct camps: those who support it and those who oppose this energy source and prefer what has been called "sustainable" or "appropriate" technology.[1] In seeking to overcome pervasive risks to human health and environment, democratic societies typically provide citizens the right to comprehend or review and take part in governmental decision making. However, creating mechanisms for the public to assess and debate nuclear energy policy or a nuclear plant licence is difficult when decision making is dominated by technical expertise.[2] Even the language of political debate about nuclear power is highly technical and requires, many argue, specialized knowledge in the assessment and management of its risks. Such specialization raises concern that public decision making will shift from politically responsible authorities to those who best understand the technical issues of a particular hazard.[3] This concern is heightened by our society's tendency to bestow status and legitimacy on those participants in a socio-technological conflict who have scientific credentials.[4]

Such observations suggest that debates about risk are not, in essence, scientific disputes, but rather arenas of social and political conflict, albeit arenas in which the public is kept at arm's length. In Canada most nuclear power plant development and the considerable public debate about its risks have occurred in the province of Ontario. Plough and Krimsky warn "that those who control the discourse on risk, will most likely control the political battles as well."[5] The public policy questions raised by the nuclear energy debate in Ontario are clear: What is the suitable balance between the influence of technical expertise and the influence of citizens in assessing and managing environmental risks? And how much weight should public perceptions of risks have in regulating hazardous technologies like nuclear power?

RISK ASSESSMENT AND PUBLIC PARTICIPATION: A THEORETICAL PUZZLE

Although Krimsky and Plough point out that risk analysis can be traced back to the Babylonians of 3200 BCE,[6] the formal regulation of technological innovations began with the Industrial Revolution. What follows is a skeletal view of how regulation shifted from crude standard setting to dealing with risk. This portrayal is prefaced by my contention that danger exists independently of human activity and innovation, but risk is a social construct designed to help us manage danger.

In the beginning of the industrialized era, satisfactory public protection was assumed to be ensured by the enlightened self-interest of industry.[7] Regulation emerged because of outrage at the insufferable working conditions and loss of life associated with unsafe industrial practices. Standards, the most familiar regulatory tool, were the outcome of a consensus between governments and industry experts. As risks from industrialization became better understood and more dispersed, the movement towards protecting the health and safety of workers in industry shifted to protection of the general population. In both planning and policy, this broader appreciation of risk coincided with scientific research that allowed for the quantification and comparison of specific health and environmental hazards.

One consequence of using science in politics is that complex issues become entangled in a web of epistemological vortices which spin scientific uncertainty into a confusing array of political alignments and incestuous institutional interactions.[8] Politics requires from science its authority – its certainty.[9] Often, debates about risk frame issues to exclude public opposition to hazardous technology by invalidating the public's perception of risk, expunging from their view the influence of the values and visions held by experts and scientists who determine levels of acceptable risk.

It is thus under the veil of modern science that the state acquires legitimacy. Since modern science generates knowledge which is technically exploitable, the nature of real power relations, which cannot be revealed by science, remains not only immune to scientific probing but also hidden from public awareness.

The work of Jürgen Habermas suggests that decision making becomes narrowed because technical issues are excluded from the public domain. Science and no longer religion becomes an "opiate of the masses" by absolving the "public" from the responsibility of making a choice about technologies which in fact are always hazardous and possess uncertain outcomes. Science and morality become indissoluble, wedded in a political arena where cost-benefit calculations and "value-for-life" assessments become the most expedient way to examine both technical and non-technical issues.[10] Presumably, the "free market" and representative government will weed out those technologies and industrial practices that prove unprofitable or unpopular. In fact, profitable – or heavily subsidized – industries that generate risk become exempt from the normal democratic decision-making process and pressures of the free market precisely because of the alienation science engenders in the uninitiated. The use of science in assessing and managing environmental risks has replaced the "will of the people" with the will of industrial élites who exclude and repress the rights of individuals, supposedly for the individuals' own sakes.

German sociologist Niklas Luhmann had the following to say about our trust in science: "Due to the perceived competence and honesty of the entrusted entity, one does not need to bother with assessing the outcomes of actions [policies] and with controlling the decision-making process of that entity."[11] Any critique by public-interest groups about the risks associated with nuclear power becomes futile. Huge disparities in access to resources and less credibility often crush any chance that such groups will win a debate with the nuclear industry on technical grounds alone.

One of the consequences of orchestrating debates about risk using principles of analysis which mirror logico-deductive modes of scientific inquiry is that alternative forms of knowledge carry little or no weight. As such, nuclear risk becomes a tangible product which can be sold, traded, or redefined according to the will of politically active members of society who have access to scientific legitimation. Conceptualizing risk in this manner tends to make risk into an environmental strategy for optimizing current forms of development, not challenging them.[12] Furthermore, environmental policy becomes a risk strategy that serves to minimize the mismatch between economic development and ecological sustainability. Risk becomes merely a minor player in determining how best to ensure profitability and continued growth without creating an obviously dangerous situation that presents a direct threat to human health and environmental quality.

In a depoliticized world, a rationalistic approach to risk would work quite well. Scientific knowledge about hazardous technologies would reduce risk through iteration and trial and error. However, this approach to regulation assumes that science is value-free, that risk is an objective phenomenon that can be systematically controlled and balanced with benefits, that the public has confidence in government, industry, and science, that risk is equitably distributed among those who reap the benefits, and that no collusive relationships exist between industry and regulator.

SOCIAL MOVEMENTS AND PUBLIC PARTICIPATION

Examining the social context of social movements, Joppke[13] finds fault with studies of the interactions between states and social movements, where interaction is depicted as passive sets of opportunity structures that have little influence on mobilizing public concern.

This passive assumption about social movements is unhelpful, and is changing, owing to these groups' controversial interventions about nuclear energy and other hazardous technologies.

Historically, central conflicts within liberal democracies were fought over the implementation of citizenship rights.[14] As Ralf Dahrendorf put it: "The modern social conflict is about attacking inequalities which restrict full civic participation by social, economic or political means, and establishing the entitlements which make up a rich and full status of citizenship."[15] Early citizenship conflicts were founded on political and social inequalities between well-defined groups and classes. Emerging energy and ecological conflicts in the early 1970s, however, created forms of political mobilization that cut across traditional group boundaries.

Transformations in the physical world most likely stimulated a series of changes in the political world of risk processing and environmental regulation. Such changes coincided with a sweeping diagnosis of an emergent risk society as identified by German sociologist Ulrich Beck.[16] Beck believes that we are nearing the end of an era concerned with building an industrial society, and moving into a post-industrial "risk-distributing" society, concerned chiefly with controlling environmental risks created by modern technology.

For Beck, Western society is in a transition period, heading from an earlier towards a second stage of modernity rather than into postmodernity. In such a transition, the logic of industrial production and distribution is becoming increasingly connected to the logic of the "social production of risk." According to Beck, in the first stage of modernity, industrial society was concerned primarily with distributing material wealth. A newly emerging second stage of modernity – called by Beck the "risk society" – is concerned with distributing risk or harm. In essence, this shift represents a redistribution of "desirable items in scarcity" to a distribution of risks that are undesirably abundant. This new modernity involves replacing traditional values of progress and accumulation with an ethic emphasizing risk avoidance, transfer, denial, and reinterpretation.

In this period of acute uncertainty and risk, a reflexive social system (a self-monitoring one) ensures that individuals exposed to particular risks will no longer passively live with them. Beck sums up the process as follows: "In contrast to all earlier epochs (including industrial society), the risk society is characterized essentially by a lack: the impossibility of an external attribution of hazards. In other words, risks depend on decisions; they are industrially produced and in this sense politically reflexive. While all earlier cultures and phases of social development confronted threats in various ways, society is confronted by itself through its dealing with risk."[17] Consequently, a period of transition exists where the distributions of both wealth and risks overlap. Perhaps this exposed surface is where environmental protest groups make their most noticeable dent.

Environmental, anti-nuclear, and peace movements can be viewed as collective risk movements that reject those conventional forms of political decision making which have created ecologically unstable and non-sustainable patterns of consumption. Risk movements are reactions against the encroachments of large-scale technologies on everyday life, as well as other externalities associated with industrial modernization. According to Christian Joppke, citizenship movements are also proactively oriented towards obtaining new resources and expanding civil rights.[18]

For nearly two decades, nuclear power has been embroiled in public controversy.[19] Some reject nuclear power on the basis that it encourages a concentration of political power, social rigidity, and other cultural transformations which they deem undesirable.[20] Defenders of nuclear power are most likely to defend technology in general, as well as economic and industrial growth. Opponents to nuclear power often prefer smaller-scale technologies which are decentralized, environmentally benign, and sustainable, foster more equitable distribution of wealth and political power, and allow citizens to understand and participate in the formulation of social and technological policy. Olsen, Lodwick, and Dunlap would most likely agree that the first set of values matches their definition of an "industrial worldview," whereas, the second cluster of values more accurately belongs to those possessing a "post-industrial worldview."[21]

Differences between proponents and opponents of nuclear power suggest that risk contains elements which activate, or contain ingredients of, sets of values, norms, beliefs, attitudes, and political orientations. If in a democracy consideration of public opinion is a cardinal tenet, then a multiplicity of values should be included in judging risks that affect the health and well-being of many. This way of conceptualizing risk demands that a "democratically open" model of regulation be followed by the Canadian nuclear industry.[22] Such a model permits broad participation in regulation-making, licensing, and compliance proceedings. Public hearings are also part of this model, as are greater opportunities for arbitration and judicial review. Opponents of public participation maintain that it encourages conflict and discord, and that issues are too technical for the public. Douglas Torgerson has written: "In the context of advanced society, there is a distinct and widely noted tendency for public policy analysis to become virtually absorbed in narrow, technical issues. This tendency has been especially noted in the case of efforts to rationalize the operations of the administrative state ... Under sway of positivist logic of inquiry, analysis tends to be guided by an interest in calculating solutions for specific problems – ones which pertain, moreover, to strictly delimited frameworks."[23]

Torgerson goes on to note that "professionalism" may fortify a "technocratic gulf" between expert and citizen, and ally professionals with current administrative institutions. Increasing concern for environmental values has meant the search for political formulations that could broach such a gulf, recognize the limits of science and expertise, and defend a plurality of interests. Ideally, public regulatory agencies should not solely set standards and rules for the environment, but themselves become participants in a trilateral regulatory process, including public interest groups, government, and industry.[24]

It should be no surprise, then, that public distrust of nuclear establishment science and technical expertise has increased as predictions about the reliability and cost-effectiveness of nuclear power plants failed to materialize. The early years of nuclear power were saturated with statements about the certainty of science's ability to solve social problems (e.g., "energy too cheap to meter"), as well as solving technical problems that might ensue following commercialization of nuclear power. Growing evidence of power plant accidents (Three Mile Island, Chernobyl) and waste management problems undermined this credibility, and the growth of activism in the form of anti-nuclear and anti-utility groups is hardly a surprising development.[25]

Paehlke explains that a crisis of legitimation may stem from political movements that insert new values into political life.[26] As people are attracted to new ideals of environmental quality, or a nuclear-free society, this crisis becomes a reaction to the "scientization of politics" – an alienation from politics which has been reduced to arcane technical questions and expert decision making. In this sense, conflict consists of more than competing political interests. It points to the inability of existing institutions to respond and adapt to changes in their environment.[27] Essentially, a crisis of legitimacy occurs when an industry fails to control the environment in which it operates. In the Canadian case, however, the nuclear establishment is doing a reasonably good job of controlling its environment and maintains a fortified position that actively destroys opposition through attrition.

ANTI-NUCLEAR MOVEMENTS AS RISK MOVEMENTS

The literature of social movements is replete with examples of how anti-nuclear groups have mobilized the public and affected government policy.[28] Choice of political action by different anti-nuclear groups is guided by their own distinctive orientations, which include beliefs about nuclear power, social values, and symbols that represent their opposition.[29] Jerome Price suggested that a group's value orientations are intertwined with the motivation of its individual members to act.[30] He adopted a typology developed by Talcott Parsons and Edward Shils to classify social action into four groups that exemplify the most important modes of activity given the existence of specific social values and motives.[31] These are intellectual, expressive, moral, and instrumental types of social action.

Anti-nuclear groups with intellectual patterns of social activism, such as the Union of Concerned Scientists in Cambridge, Massachusetts, critique technical problems associated with nuclear power. This small yet influential type of activist group erodes the public's trust in establishment science by revealing the assumptions used by scientists to support their claims. Expressive activists frequently link anti-nuclear protest to a more general criticism of social and political reality. These groups oppose nuclear power precisely because it is an affront to larger social values they hold. For example, anti-nuclear activists associated with the British Campaign for Nuclear Disarmament were also dissatisfied with the monarchy.[32] Some anti-nuclear groups such as the National Council of Churches react against the moral implications of nuclear technology. For example, they often deal with issues such as the sale of nuclear technology to nations that may use it to develop nuclear weapons. Finally, instrumental activists are interested in changing current political culture through rationally planned mobilization of the public. They have specific goals, such as stimulating changes in environmental policy and provoking improvements in regulatory culture. A variety of examples of anti-nuclear groups conforming to the principles of instrumental activism exist. The Sierra Club values the preservation of the natural environment and therefore attempts to impede future nuclear power plant construction on a national level.

On a larger scale, these protests exemplify a type of diffuse resistance to nuclear technology. For example, Wayne Sugai's case study of ratepayer protest in the state of Washington shows how an anti-nuclear group halted construction of a local nuclear power plant because of concerns about economic viability.[33] A precedent-setting US Supreme Court case between Pacific Gulf and Western (a large US utility company) and the State Energy Resources Conservation League (a coalition of community groups) established that a moratorium on new nuclear plant constructions can be passed by a state, provided that local concern is based on economic reasons alone. Better-known examples, such as the New England Coalition on Nuclear Pollution, Clamshell Alliance of New England, People for Proof, and the Task Force against Nuclear Pollution, illustrate the effectiveness of regional protest.

THE CANADIAN ANTI-NUCLEAR MOVEMENT:
SOME HISTORY

In general, Canadian anti-nuclear activists are not only trying to phase out nuclear energy but are also attempting to change the larger social and political powers behind it. As such, anti-nuclear protest is a product of the emerging "risk society" in that it aspires to replace technocratic power with participatory democracy.

Ronald Babin suggested that two stages characterize the evolution of Canada's anti-nuclear movement.[34] The first stage falls between the early 1970s and the March 1979 accident at Three Mile Island in Harrisburgh, Pennsylvania. This stage is characterized by swift growth and a politicization of the movement. In the second stage, beginning immediately after this accident, the movement becomes more flexible and attempts to forge alliances with other progressive social movements. Babin has suggested that the Canadian anti-nuclear movement first became visible when the implications of nuclear power became evident. However, historical links to earlier alternative lifestyle movements and peace and ecology movements of the 1960s probably laid fertile ground for a host of more focused attacks and protests against identifiable targets like the nuclear industry.

The 1960s heralded the emergence of several alternative lifestyle movements in Canada and elsewhere, although this change in consciousness occurred at a relatively slow pace here.[35] Ripples from ecological battles raging through Europe, Japan, and the United States eventually reached supportive ears in Canada, mostly among the scientific community. In the late 1960s and early 1970s, organized ecology movements began raising public consciousness on a wide variety of issues like air pollution, pesticide and insecticide use, phosphates in detergents, and energy policy. Ecologists became increasingly aware of the interconnectedness of all life, and viewed industrial practices that threatened the harmony and equilibrium of the natural world as a major social problem requiring political action. Adherents of this movement tended to view these problems as emerging from a civilization obsessed with accumulation of wealth and division of labour.

During the 1950s there had been mounting international tension because of the atomic arms race. Scientists helped to found the peace movement when they began communicating their concerns about the risks associated with stockpiling atomic weapons. In the beginning, the "ban-the-bomb" movement was more concerned with raising public consciousness than with mobilizing political protest. In 1959 the Canadian Campaign for Nuclear Disarmament was born in the form of the Canadian Committee for the Control of Radiation Hazards. This organization was concerned with nuclear weapons testing and risks posed by radioactive fallout. A number of other groups also emerged at this time, bringing together people from the scientific, academic, and general communities. The most noteworthy of these Canadian organizations were the Canadian Peace Research Institute, Project Ploughshares, Voice of Women, and the Pugwash Conference. It was not until the early 1970s that these groups and others began criticizing Canada's domestic nuclear power program.

The Canadian peace movement started to rally against the civilian use of nuclear power. In fact, a gradual conversion of the peace movement into an anti-nuclear movement was underway. A paper presented by a Canadian scientist, Fred Knelman, at the 1975 annual Learned Societies Conference stimulated the formation of an anti-nuclear coalition which eventually included a variety of ecology groups and peace groups like Greenpeace and the Voice of Women. This newly constructed Canadian Coalition for Nuclear Responsibility called for a public inquiry into all aspects of nuclear power.

Scientific criticism of civilian nuclear power came mostly from the United States. A host of studies including the Rasmussen Report, studies by the Union of Concerned Scientists and Ford Foundation, and a report by the American Physical Society provided Canadian activists with technical information for lobbying against the Canadian nuclear program. However, much of the criticism of American nuclear technology was quickly dismissed by the Canadian nuclear industry on the grounds that CANDU reactors were substantially different from and also safer than American designs. Access to Canadian content became necessary if the anti-nuclear movement was to succeed in Canada.

The growing number of scientists opposed to nuclear power gave the movement an air of credibility and legitimacy that it had not previously enjoyed. No longer could the movement's adversaries claim that anti-nuclear forces were irrational and ignorant. Dissident scientists began questioning the regulation of Canada's nuclear industry by harshly criticizing the role played by the Atomic Energy Control Board (AECB). Mounting concern about a lack of uniform standards regarding safe levels of exposure to ionizing radiation quickly polarized the scientific community. As well, specific decisions made by the AECB regarding power plant operation came under heavy attack. In 1977 this debate became particularly intense. The four operating generators (there are eight now) at the Pickering Nuclear Generating Station had only one emergency core shut-down system, whereas generators at the Bruce nuclear station have two. These problems and others led to a widespread debate on the safety of Canada's CANDU reactor design.

Concerns about the disposal of a growing stock of nuclear waste resulted in a report by the federal government; the Hare Report,[36] as it was subsequently called, raised considerable debate and criticism from the scientific community, with many opposing the conclusions of the report. This document proposed that medium-level and high-level nuclear waste could be stored in vaults dug into granite formations in the Canadian Shield. The report was criticized on technical grounds regarding the feasibility of deep geological burial of radioactive waste and for its interpretation of the effects of low-level radioactivity on human health and the environment. Some critics also expressed moral indignation about leaving the responsibility to future generations.

Criticisms of the Hare Report in particular, and nuclear industry in general, had an effect on public opinion about the social acceptability of nuclear energy. Opinion polls conducted by the Gallup organization showed a large decrease in public support for continued growth of Canada's nuclear capacity between September 1976 and October 1983. Support dropped from 41 to 23 per cent within this time frame. It was likely that much of this drop in support corresponded with the public's becoming more educated on issues related to nuclear energy. A US study by Olsen et al.[37] on support for nuclear power revealed that 60 per cent of Americans opposed building new nuclear plants, and that 20 per cent wanted existing plants closed down. Concerns about the high cost of producing electricity from nuclear power generation plus the problems of waste disposal accounted in large part for the low support reported. Some have suggested that negative attitudes towards nuclear energy may be due to a failure on the part of the public to understand this complex technology. A national survey by Greer-Wooten and Mitson revealed that 44 per cent of the Canadian population was not even aware that nuclear power was used to generate electricity.[38] Dissident scientific opinion therefore played a significant function in giving the anti-nuclear movement greater momentum. If scientists could shake the public's faith in the infallibility of modern science, then policies that have traditionally relied on technical expertise could be influenced by non-technical considerations too.

Nuclear protest then shifted from large national campaigns to smaller local campaigns. When the Atomic Energy Control Board tried to increase permissible levels of radiation exposure for atomic workers in 1983, several thousand such workers banded together to resist these changes. A variety of unions like the Public Service Alliance, the Canadian Union of Public Employees, and the Nurses' Union forced the AECB to capitulate and withdraw its controversial proposal.

Community protest groups first surfaced in Canada in the early 1970s to resist the location of specific nuclear projects and routing of power corridors on agricultural land. In Ontario the organization CANTDU (obviously a pun on the name of Canada's CANDU reactor) began criticizing the ecological effects of power plants and their associated safety hazards in 1974. Also in that year, twenty activist groups from Nova Scotia, New Brunswick, and Prince Edward Island formed an anti-nuclear coalition named the Maritime Energy Coalition. Their mandate was to oppose construction of nuclear plants in the Maritime provinces and to encourage promotion of sustainable energy and conservation. In 1975 a number of anti-nuclear organizations were formed. These groups were mainly involved in educating the public about nuclear power and mobilizing local populations to resist the construction of proposed nuclear facilities. Ecology groups such as Energy Probe of Toronto and Society to Overcome Pollution (STOP) of Montreal provided educational information to schools, other community groups, and the public in general. Over the next decade, dozens of small anti-nuclear groups would spring up throughout the country. Well-known groups in Canada include Durham Nuclear Awareness (DNA), Canadian Coalition for Nuclear Responsibility, Greenpeace Canada, Ontario Energy and Environment Caucus, and Energy Probe. As well, labour unions have become part of the Canadian nuclear scene, particularly concerning the health and safety of uranium miners. The availability of intervener funding (funds provided by government to groups for fighting proponents of particular projects) made it possible for many such groups to sustain protests within the confines of energy board hearings and Ontario Hydro Demand and Supply Proceedings.

REGULATING THE CANADIAN NUCLEAR INDUSTRY

Nuclear power symbolizes many of the problems of advanced, industrialized societies – namely, rapid technological change, concentration of decision-making power, and incursion of government bureaucracy. The Canadian nuclear industry is even more concentrated, bureaucratic, and inaccessible than most because of its strong public-sector character, protective legislation, and industry-government interlocks. The regulation of nuclear power in Canada closely parallels the corporatist mode of policy making: complex interdependencies between manufacturers, suppliers, and regulators permit nuclear power to be promoted without serious concern for economic, environmental, or safety costs.[39]

In 1946 the Atomic Energy Control Act gave the Atomic Energy Control Board authority to regulate and control atomic energy in Canada. The AECB had broad powers that were exercised through the agency's Atomic Energy Control Regulations. These included the power to license all facilities using radioactive substances, to regulate how such substances are used, stored, transported, and disposed of, to revoke or suspend licences for violations of regulations, to form Crown enterprises, to require that agencies operating under the auspices of the board submit reports and information about their operations, and to give grants for research and development. Canada's participation in the Manhattan Project combined with a security-conscious environment following the Second World War explains the act's proclivity to give the agency a scope and breadth of powers which far exceed those of other federal regulatory agencies. For example, the act does not require public hearings at any stage of its regulatory activities. An independent environmental impact assessment requested by the federal minister of the environment is the sole external mechanism for invoking public review.

In North America, the concept of environmental impact assessment (EIA) was introduced in the United States by the National Environmental Policy Act of 1969. In 1973 the Canadian government adopted a similar approach, the Environmental Assessment and Review Process (EARP), for assessing environmental consequences of construction projects, energy initiatives, and potentially hazardous facilities. During the following decade, several provinces introduced their own environmental assessment processes, and in 1975 Ontario established a comprehensive Environmental Assessment Act. However, since all nuclear power in Canada operates under federal jurisdiction, provincial legislation only applies to non-nuclear projects.

EIA is intended to scrutinize a development scheme while it is still early in the planning stage. Initially the concept of "environment" in EIA referred specifically to the natural world, but was later expanded to include social, cultural, and economic milieu as well.[40] Thus, historically, concern with the social impacts of technology emerged from an analysis of effects on the natural environment. Gordon Beanlands and Peter Duinker have stated: "Environmental impact assessment in Canada, as elsewhere, is a socio-political phenomenon. It is grounded in the perceptions and values of society which find expression at the political level through administrative procedures of government. Science is called upon to explain the relationship between contemplated actions and these environmental perceptions and values."[41]

There are some key differences in environmental assessment between Canada and the United States that can be explained by variations in political culture between the two countries. Barry Sadler wrote: "Compared to the United States, the political culture in Canada is marked by a lesser degree of citizen activism, wide latitude traditionally granted to administrative discretion, and restricted rights to participate in decision making or to challenge the process in court."[42] Essentially, environmental impact assessment in Canada is an administrative rather than a legislative process.[43] Perhaps the Canadian EARP is an instance of what

Seymour Lipset observed, that Canadians are more likely than Americans to rely on the state, and are therefore less inclined to participate as individuals in the environmental policy process.[44]

From its inception the EARP process in Canada was administered by the Federal Environmental Assessment Review Office (FEARO), which reported directly to the federal minister of the environment. Updated in 1977, the process was reinforced in 1984 when the EARP Guidelines Order was issued by an Order in Council. This impact assessment process is primarily a self-assessment process with two phases: an initial assessment phase followed by public review by an independent panel. In the first phase, the government agency responsible for the project – in this case, the regulator (AECB) – reviews a proposal. If the initiating department, agency, or regulator concludes that adverse environmental impacts are unlikely, there is no further review. The second phase of assessment is invoked if, in the regulator's opinion, there is potential for significant environmental problems. In this case, the proposal is automatically referred to the minister of the environment for public review.[45]

In essence, all significant or unacceptable environmental consequences of a specific proposal must be reported to the minister of the environment. This reporting, however, does not mean that a public review will be called. Under section 13 of the Guidelines Order it is up to the regulating agency to determine whether or not public concern is sufficient to recommend to the minister of the environment a public review. Unfortunately, this last requirement is ambiguously worded and may be interpreted differentially by agencies like the AECB. For example, section 13 of the Guidelines Order stated that a proposal for an environmental review could be suggested to the minister of the environment if "public concern about the proposal is such that a public review is desirable." In other words, the AECB must be convinced that public concern is significant enough to warrant recommending a public review. The AECB grants an exemption from public hearings before an environmental assessment review panel if they deem that the environmental impact of the project has not changed significantly from the previous relicensing period, or if expression of public concern about the proposal is not sufficient.

The AECB's interpretation of what constitutes significant public concern, and how levels of concern are linked to the triggering of a public review, is vague. The board has complete authority to decide whether a referral is warranted, and of course the option to decide whether or not the granting of an operating licence, or a renewal, should be a matter of public review.

The case of the 1994 Pickering nuclear generation station relicensing is instructive. Like all nuclear plants in Canada, the Pickering plant is periodically relicensed by the AECB. The local environmental group Durham Nuclear Awareness (DNA) asked for public review and tried to establish under what conditions such a review would be required. What was at issue, in this case, was whether or not this licence was contingent on public review. David Martin, a founding member of DNA, asked AECB staff in a letter of 27 April 1993: "What specific quantitative and qualitative criteria does AECB staff use to judge the type and level of public concern that would make a review desirable or not?" His question raised a variety of unstated issues such as: How many letters must the AECB receive from the public in order to trigger a review? Do all letters carry equal weight, irrespective of the status of writer, gender of writer, region in which the writer resides, pro-nuclear or anti-nuclear sentiments expressed in the text of the letter?

On 7 May 1993, AECB staff member J.G. McManus replied that the AECB "takes into consideration information received from many sources including elected officials at all levels, members of the public, special interest groups, intervenors and license applicants. Of particular interest are representations received from persons living in the vicinity of the facility in question, and anything offering new information." As such, if "sufficient" public concern reaches the ears of the AECB regarding the operating safety of the Pickering plant, then surely a public review should be recommended.

Since the AECB can interpret section 13 of the Guidelines Order according to norms and standards internal to the agency, is it possible that this regulator uses what Bruce Doern referred to as a professionally open model of regulation?[46] Doern described the professionally open model of regulation as being distinguished by a high degree of trust. Its supporters avow that it is internally open, encouraging open criticism and evaluation among professional and technically qualified individuals. Advocates of this model intimate that regulators who use this approach are perceived by regulated industries as professionals trying to achieve collective goals: health and safety, as well as production. As a result, professionals are more prone to divulge to their regulating peers what is working, as well as what is not. This model of regulation is also characterized by minimal reporting requirements and few, if any, public hearings.

In Canada, opportunities for the public to be heard usually come from working on parliamentary committees, royal commissions, and environmental assessment public hearings. Adam Ashford believes that public hearings are "symbolic rituals within the modern state, theatres of power," which legitimate states and allow them to "sit above society as the embodiment of the common good."[47] Brian Wynne[48] views public hearings as rituals that can order and control the public – subverting their goals and values by showing internal contradictions and instability. Wynne believes that the public falls victim to the hearing process technique: "Language, including technical language, can tacitly guide people into seeing the world in certain ways, influencing what is regarded as an accepted value, and what is inevitable, possible, desirable, or at least tolerable."[49] These critiques of hearings give the impression that the public is a passive, unwitting victim of state and corporate manipulation. However, in their study of an environmental hearing, Richardson, Sherman, and Gismondi show that the public can challenge expert knowledge and stop development projects, although, as they indicate, the Alberta government and industry quickly reasserted a technological solution and used another "expert review" to overturn the original decision which favoured the public.[50]

TWO RISK PARADIGMS: THE TECHNICAL AND THE SOCIALLY CONSTRUCTED

The polarized nature of debate about the social acceptability of nuclear power in Canada may be characterized as a competition between two risk paradigms: a technically inclined, positivist-oriented concept of risk and a socially constructed, culturally embedded concept of risk. Awareness of the differing impact of each competing risk paradigm for protection of health and environment allows us to reframe how risk is subject to social, economic, and political processing, and provide another understanding of modern social movements where risk is central to political conflict.

The technically oriented way of conceptualizing risk demands that decision makers, and members of the public, trust scientific authority and expertise. Furthermore, there must be a willingness to limit boundaries of analysis so that risks can be compared quantitatively to one another in a rational and depersonalized manner. That is, risks from hazardous technologies like nuclear power stations can be understood in terms of statistical probabilities which are based on engineered doses and cost-benefit calculations for large populations but not for individuals. In this sense, risk is the relation between decision and damage where scientific knowledge-claims are true to the extent that they adequately reflect reality.

Government agencies and regulators such as the Atomic Energy Control Board attempt to assess and manage risks from our modern world by "objectively" analysing the physical world through an iterative process of approximation. However, the social and political ramifications of their decisions ensure that safety guidelines or regulations for protecting human health and environment are the inevitable consequence of technocratic decision making. A reliance on expertise and a belief that "objectivity" and "neutrality" are possible only through the scientific method ensure that this remains so.

The assumption is that risk, treated as an objective phenomenon, can be assessed using scientific techniques that reveal its deepest, most complex secrets to the best scientific minds. Empirical testing, peer review, and internal standards should consistently yield the best possible risk estimates. Managing hazards with access to such knowledge should also be a fairly straightforward process. In this case, public input and debate would not add anything valuable to these assessments: interference from the "ignorant" masses would only waste time and money, according to this way of thinking.

The AECB's interpretation of the EARP Guidelines Order, its dealings with anti-nuclear protest groups, and its technically oriented approach to assessing and managing risks clearly generate a democracy-technocracy quandary. Although not directly linked to the erosion of democracy in post-industrial societies, a reliance on technically oriented approaches to risk assumes that liberal individualistically oriented policy making cannot deal with modern, communal risks. Furthermore, such an approach also assumes that production and distribution of risks are independent from economic and political forces whose actors may prefer to avoid input from the public in the form of consultation. This is where technocratic decision making shines brightest. If public participation distracts regulators from making the "right" choices using tools of science and scientific modes of thinking, then too much public participation will paralyse the state and public policy process.

The concept of a "public" out there somewhere waiting to be heard from implies that those who actually make decisions do so without wide-scale support, and that such decisions are in the interest of an elite keen on maintaining control over ever-scarcer resources. In a democracy, public opinion needs to be considered as a reflection of the "will of the people."[51] Unfortunately, the role of public opinion in shaping environmental policy is often peripheral in technical debates that tend to accord greater weight to "expert" scientific opinion.

The rise of environmentalism, the growing number of arguments for appropriate, manageable technologies, and increasing antipathy towards social institutions are, in part, by-products of this struggle between competing risk paradigms and their respective supporters. In a sense, two opposing camps have evolved, one supporting and promoting large technologies and further economic growth, and another opposing large-scale technologies, supporting conservation efforts, and favouring a zero- or low-growth economy. Generally speaking, the former can be represented by the AECB and Canadian nuclear industry and the latter by anti-nuclear groups. In addition, the nuclear constituency relies on a technically oriented concept of risk while anti-nuclear groups more closely follow an approach consistent with a socially constructed concept. Opponents of nuclear energy are challenging the assumption that nuclear technology is in the best interest of the whole of society. Furthermore, those who oppose nuclear power do so not just because they view it as unsafe, unnecessary, and uneconomical, but because they see it as producing a range of undesirable social consequences. The failure of science to handle ever more menacing risks of modern industrial life is accelerating an erosion of trust in science and authority. As it becomes more apparent that management of risks is increasingly reliant on political decisions, new forms of public participation will be demanded. Technocratic decision making cultures are no longer able to ignore the will of the public when benefits of industrialization pose socially unprocessed risks.

The developing literature on risk poorly addresses organizational behaviour, political processes, and social movements. This is probably due to a tendency to view risk assessment and management as tasks that require logical and rational decision making rather than as forums for addressing issues of public acceptability and participation. However, the presence of modern risks heightens the necessity of rights-based democracy, and requires a renewed commitment to equal rights in public dialogue and enhanced citizenship rights within a participatory, communal, and co-operative decision-making environment.[52] Such an environment would evaluate risk in terms of its political and social consequences, such as possible disruptions in the social fabric or a loss of communality, rather than exclusively considering a hazard's possible effects on human health and environment.[53]

This alternative form of decision making is aptly illustrated by a concept of risk that is sensitive to social constructions of reality and an understanding of risk through scientific knowledge. Like all social reality, risks are socially constructed to a certain degree. This is the classic insight of the sociology of science and more recently the direction in which research on risk and social movements is headed. In other words, all reality, ideas, and meanings including ideologies are socially constructed. A cultural perspective on risk sensitive to these social constructions can address larger social issues that its technically oriented counterpart must ignore. Moreover, this approach to risk requires widespread trust in the democratic process, since there exists an important difference between public acceptance and public participation. Expanded citizenship rights need to keep pace with change if risk is to be de-scientized, and consequently withdrawn from technocratic decision-making environments, where an appeal to expertise is of little help, since experts disagree on many scientific questions, let alone social ones.

Habermas uncovered a set of political problems which demonstrated how the public interest has been absorbed and subverted by an expansion of subsystems of purposive-rational action, where objective exigencies of technological progress become key problems for democratically controlling technology. Communication between politician, expert, and "lay" public is, for Habermas, a critically interacting set of relations between expert and politician which are necessarily dependent on "mediation by the public as a political institution."[54] Since social conflicts involve the presence of differing values, visions, beliefs, and political orientations, Habermas suggested that communication between competing agents should be "based on a historically determined preunderstanding, governed by social norms, of what is practically necessary in a concrete situation."[55] This "preunderstanding" is a type of social consciousness shared by all members of a community. Consequently, public opinion can be considered as a "discourse of citizens in a community" where "removing restrictions on communication" encourages "communicative action" which is "governed by binding consensual norms, which define reciprocal expectations about behaviour and which must be understood and recognized by at least two acting subjects."[56]

Social movements like the anti-nuclear movement in Canada attempt to inject new values (such as environmental sustainability) into the political sphere by questioning and criticizing the trajectory of contemporary society and its reliance on purposive-instrumental rationality. Furthermore, such social movements question our decision makers' tendency to privilege science and expertise in an uncritical fashion while simultaneously excluding the public from the political process.

For individuals in such social movements, believing in the power of "tribes of experts"[57] leads to an inevitable erosion of democracy by according privileged status and enhanced legitimacy to participants with scientific credentials in socio-technological controversies. As well, a romantic view of the scientist as a modern magician or miracle worker is often paralleled by the negative image of "Dr. Faustus, Dr. Frankenstein, Dr. Jekyll ... a fear that our scientists will go on being titans who create monsters."[58] For anti-nuclear protest groups like DNA, nuclear reactors represent the ultimate "monster" which has been unleashed on an unwary and trusting public. To make matters worse, this "monster" has been repackaged ideologically as a gift from nature and science to humanity giving us the potential for unlimited economic growth with minimal environmental and health impacts. Halfmann and Japp say that social movements emerge as a defence against threats to "life-chances" generated by risky technologies like nuclear power.[59] More-over, risks allow social movements to develop protest communication strategies that ensure internal solidarity and provide social movements with targets for collective action.

For the anti-nuclear movement, the nature of nuclear risks over the past twenty-five to thirty years has led to a shift in emphasis from a "ban-the-bomb" movement to an anti-reactor movement and now to-wards a soft energy path, pro-conservation movement which empha-sizes regional energy self-sufficiency, solar power, and technologies like solar and co-generation. As risks from nuclear technology became more local and immediate in their consequences, citizen protests against nuclear reactors, waste disposal sites, and research laboratories replaced a more diffuse concern about global thermonuclear warfare. In a sense the moribund state of the Canadian nuclear industry and the reduced need for active opposition have led to a decline in the number and strength of opposition movements. This is why the anti-nuclear movement can be seen as a "mature" social movement where "middle-class politics" is used to transform what are perceived to be the defi-ciencies of what Beck has called the "risk society."

The opposition of anti-nuclear groups like DNA to the Canadian nu-clear industry and the AECB is not just a resistance to nuclear technol-ogy. Rather, it is more fundamentally emblematic of a larger social undercurrent composed of a wide range of individuals frustrated with a democratic system clogged by technocratic procedure.

BRINGING THE PUBLIC BACK

The regulation of nuclear power in Canada, and subsequent exclusion of the public through mechanisms which confound the intent of section 13 of the Environmental Assessment and Review Process Guidelines Order, do not have to produce such a gloomy picture. In democratic nations throughout the world, bringing the public into the arena where debates on the social acceptability of technology unfold has varying de-grees of success. The technocratic decision-making culture of regulators like Canada's AECB is an extreme example.

In the United States nuclear power has been heavily criticized for sev-eral decades by citizen activist groups who use political lobbying and court challenges to ensure that they have a voice. The litigious culture in the United States combined with a strong history of resisting central-ized authority resulted in successes for anti-nuclear groups that are un-paralleled in Canada. In the United States an amendment to the Atomic Energy Act (1954) included a provision for ensuring that the public has a right to be heard in all nuclear licensing decisions. This amendment – known as the Government in the Sunshine Act – requires that all federal regulatory bodies act as though they were living in "glass houses." In Canada no such condition for facilitating either public observation or scrutiny of regulators exists: regulation of nuclear power in Canada involves primarily the establishment of parliamentary or legislative committees, Royal Commissions, and environmental assessment reviews that typically include only "token" citizen participants.

In parts of Europe such as France, Germany, Switzerland, and Finland, the role of the public in debates on nuclear safety is somewhat different from both Canada and United States. For example, in France – one of the most heavily nuclearized countries in the world with approximately 80 per cent of electricity production coming from nuclear reactors – a public inquiry must be held by the national government before any nuclear facility can be built. The French use a concept known as *la concertation*, roughly translated as developing a common understanding as a basis for future projects, to ensure that civil liberties and constitutional rights for a majority of French citizens affected by a particular project are not violated. In Germany, citizens participate in public hearings primarily as a "third party" in a "multi-party" legal system that includes the licensing authority, applicant (also known as proponent), and members of the public. In Germany the legal system protects the rights of interveners to participate without any fear of civil litigation. "Altruistic" objections in the interest of nature or creation can be raised in such hearings.

In Switzerland, federalism and direct democracy make it impossible to impose a decision on a determined minority. Using cantonal referendums, the Swiss ensure that approaches for defining and solving risk problems are more democratic than technocratic. As a final example, Finland's Nuclear Energy Act requires that a first step in licensing any new nuclear facility involves obtaining a "decision in principle" to proceed with a project. As in Sweden, consultative referendums are used to ensure that the majority support, in principle, a planned facility. As well, municipal councils can veto the siting of such industrial facilities within their communities if they are perceived to have negative or dangerous impacts.

These examples of how the public can be brought into the decision-making process demonstrate how public participation varies with different approaches to public consultation. The Canadian nuclear industry and its regulator the Atomic Energy Control Board are not doomed to a life of technocratic decision-making. As a technologically advanced nation with an excellent communications infrastructure, Canada has the potential to change the character of its public policy process. Perhaps an increased penetration of computer networks such as the Internet will allow Canadians to exercise their democratic rights more directly through computer-mediated channels so that implementation and cost of regular referenda and plebiscites become more viable. Technological innovations do not necessarily have to lead to decision making that is technocratic, elitist, and closed. Regulation of the Canadian nuclear industry can only become more open and thus more accurately reflect the will of the people. Thus decisions on risky technologies can be seen as a two-way street where citizens are not expected to make choices based on technological criteria, but where regulators are expected to make socially "correct" decisions.

Future research in this area of inquiry can proceed in many possible directions. At a theoretical level, research on how modern society is moving towards being a "risk society" should be given more attention by social scientists. In the same vein, the relation between production of industrial risks by capitalist societies and the necessary synthesis of competing participatory and expert-based risk paradigms should also be examined. On a more applied level, questions about public participation and mechanisms for including the public in techno-social debates should also be examined. Some of the topics that need addressing are summarized by the following questions: Who is the public and how should they be recruited for participation? At what stage should this public begin participating in the consultation process, and when should such participation end? How much weight should public perceptions of risk have, relative to the opinions of scientists and experts? What types of evidence and arguments are considered permissible and valid in these public forums? Should public funds be used to support groups in the form of intervener funding? Research dealing with these questions may also consider some specific questions on social movements. For example, do modern risk conflicts lead to competition between different social movements such as the anti-nuclear movement and a fast-growing "anti-environmentalist" movement? Will such competition lead to a "backlash" from governments, regulators, labour, and industries, resulting in greater environmental and health risks? These questions suggest that modern social conflicts that involve risk are really debates about the future form of society and the role of citizens in shaping this future.

NUCLEAR POWER TODAY

At present the Canadian nuclear industry is in a state of crisis. There is a moratorium on new plant construction in Ontario and Quebec and weak sales of CANDU reactors abroad. As well, escalating costs associated with maintaining and repairing existing power plants, a huge debt at Ontario Hydro (estimated to be $38 billion), concern about the disposal of an ever-increasing stockpile of radioactive waste, anxiety about who will be financially responsible for decommissioning costs incurred when closing power plants, and declining demand for electricity all conspire to make nuclear power less attractive.

In August of 1997 Ontario Hydro was forced to shut down seven of its nineteen reactors in the province. An independent consulting team brought in from the United States by Ontario Hydro's president Allan Kupcis determined that safety was being compromised at many plants, including the Pickering plant, by a rash of accidents and related safety problems. It is estimated that the costs associated with bringing these plants back on line could exceed $8 billion. In the province of Ontario, reliance on nuclear power as a source of electricity has been steadily decreasing. From an environmental perspective, this shift in the overall energy mix has implications for acid rain formation, particulate matter emissions, and greenhouse gas production. From a social perspective, reduced trust in those who support and regulate nuclear power corresponds with reduced social acceptability, and no amount of "spin-doctoring" and risk communicating appears to be able to help. In a sense, the failure of governments to explain technically complex nuclear science with due regard to uncertainty propels risk issues forward into a vacuum where public opinion is strongly polarized. This case study demonstrates how a failure to include the public in debates on the environmental impacts of the Pickering nuclear power plant led to internal tensions at Ontario Hydro which ultimately threaten the future of this energy source, a form of institutional suicide.

Thus nuclear power in Canada has finally begun a downward spiral from which it is unlikely to recover. Ironically, the anti-nuclear activists, including members of DNA, were not the ones responsible for the decisive step in this shift in attitude. A group of nuclear "experts" decided on their own that many of Ontario's nuclear facilities were unsafe and uneconomical.

6 Environment's X-File: Pulp Mill Effluent Regulation in Canada

DEBORA VAN NIJNATTEN
AND WILLIAM LEISS,
WITH THE ASSISTANCE OF
PETER HODSON

This chapter reviews the decade-long discussions about the regulation of pulp mill effluent in Canada from a specific perspective, namely, the interplay of scientific research and policy choices.[1] Those discussions began with the discovery of worrisome organochlorine compounds in the effluent – namely dioxins and furans – and towards the end of the 1980s had shifted to the so-called "AOX parameter," used as a regulatory instrument to measure the entire class of organochlorines.[2] As early as 1990 serious questions were being raised about the appropriateness of AOX as an indicator of effluent toxicity; along the way, however, it was realized that pulp mill effluent can still be toxic to aquatic life at zero AOX.[3] For most of the 1990s, a vigorous debate ensued among stakeholder interests and federal and provincial governments, whereby the issue of pulp mill effluent toxicity got caught up in the larger battles over chlorine chemistry generally. Meanwhile, some scientists were conducting what has been called "the search for Compound X," that is, the one or more compounds that might be the source of the residual effluent toxicity.[4]

In late 1991 Environment Canada published its view that the AOX parameter should not be used as a regulatory standard. Instead, the department placed severe restrictions on levels of dioxins and furans in the effluent – having the effect of lowering total organochlorine loadings appreciably – and introduced further measures to reduce acute toxicity through the installation of secondary treatment in all mills. In addition, the department undertook major research and began Environmental Effects Monitoring (EEM) programs aimed at more adequately characterizing the residual toxicity of the effluent and the adequacy of new regulations. At about the same time, the British Columbia government moved in exactly the opposite direction and directed that effluent in the province be at zero AOX by 2002. Ontario followed suit in using the AOX parameter, although it did not mandate a zero level.

However, Environment Canada, which rejected the AOX parameter, has yet to devise an alternative policy framework to deal with the residual (non-organochlorine) toxicity of pulp mill effluent. To be sure, its regulations controlling acute effluent toxicity have delivered considerable environmental benefits; and it might be argued that the EEM program provides a *de facto* ultimate objective – namely, discharges that have no discernible impacts on fish, fish habitat, and the use of fishery products. The program is intended to test whether the present regulations governing pulp mill effluent are adequate and, as such, may provide impetus for regulatory reform. EEM does not, however, define a set of policy objectives. On the other hand, given the reality of non-organochlorine toxicity, is there any justification for other jurisdictions in Canada to continue using the AOX parameter as their primary regulatory standard?

Currently, a consensus seems to be emerging that designing and adopting "systems closure" or "minimal impact" technologies, which would reduce or even eliminate effluents, is preferable to continued regulation based on identifying and controlling particular substances in the effluent's constituents. There does not exist conclusive information, however, concerning the achievability and affordability of systems closure technology. More important, there exists little consensus within the policy community as to whether a "zero effluent," or the alternative "minimal impact," result should be the goal and how quickly the chosen goal should be pursued.

The end result is that we do not have in the public domain a clear policy vision guiding the future direction – including the research and development, capital investments, and environmental priorities – of a major industry whose operations continue to have a significant impact on the receiving environment and on Canada's economy. Nor do we have a concerted attempt to construct such a policy vision. Instead, we are fighting various battles – dioxin, organochlorines, "Compound x" – which have been inspired by scientific studies embodying varying degrees of certainty and which are not necessarily geared towards preventing pollution in the first place.

The following discussion of federal and provincial strategies is organized chronologically and is divided into three time periods: the rise of scientific and public concern over dioxin contamination in North

America during the 1980s; the shift in Canada to a broader focus on organochlorine compounds in the receiving environment in the late 1980s and on AOX as a parameter to regulate these; and, beginning in the early 1990s, a growing consensus that AOX is an unsuitable regulatory parameter and, as a consequence, the search for a non-chlorinated "Compound X" in effluent linked to environmental effects. Each stage begins with scientific research which propelled the policy debate concerning pulp and paper mill effluent and environmental protection in a new direction.[5] The chronology which follows describes in detail these specific scientific developments which set each stage apart from the next. Developments in the political sphere are then delineated for each scientific period. The final section reflects on the interplay between scientific research and policy choices.

PRELUDE TO THE PULP AND PAPER MILL EFFLUENT STORY: THE DIOXIN ISSUE

Dioxins had become a public issue during the 1970s and early 1980s as a result of extensive media coverage of a number of high-profile events: the claims of health damages by Vietnam veterans who had handled the herbicide "Agent Orange"; the evacuation of the entire community of Times Beach, Missouri; the explosion of a chemical factory in Seveso, Italy; and the discovery of the buried chemical wastes at Love Canal and Hyde Park, New York.[6] By the mid-1980s scientists had honed their ability to measure dioxins down to parts per trillion, and an extensive scientific knowledge base had begun to accumulate, with widely publicized accounts especially of the acute lethality and carcinogenicity of 2,3,7,8-TCDD as demonstrated in laboratory tests on a number of animal species.[7] (See table 3.)

On 20 August 1987, Greenpeace released its report "No Margin of Safety," which contained evidence from US Environmental Protection Agency (EPA) documents leaked to the organization, as well as documents obtained by Greenpeace activists under a Freedom of Information Act lawsuit, that pulp mills were discharging dioxins into the air and water.[8] The report began by outlining the current science on the effects of dioxins on human health and the environment: "The release of even minute amounts of dioxin into the environment may therefore have severe repercussions, not only because such low levels may profoundly affect generations of human and animal health, but also because dioxins simply may not go away. Minute amounts released over time will accumulate and move in both predictable and unpredictable ways through the environment and food web."[9]

Table 3
Chronology of key events in the pulp mill effluent case

Date	Scientific Developments	Policy Developments
PHASE 1		
1970s, early 1980s	Scientific knowledge base (acute lethality, carcinogenity) for dioxin grows.	With Love Canal, Seveso, Italy, and Times Beach, Missouri, dioxin becomes public issue.
August 1987	Greenpeace releases "No Margin of Safety" report alleging pulp mills are releasing dioxins into water, US EPA and industry trying to keep this from the public. Greenpeace Canada takes sediment samples from Harmac, BC mill, lab results show high levels of dioxin, and press release is issued.	
January 1988		Environment Canada announces a pulp mill monitoring program, which results in fisheries closing on BC coast.
Late 1988	PAPRICAN researchers discover that formation of dioxin in bleaching process can be prevented by substituting ClO_2 for molecular chlorine, which sparks widespread industry substitution.	
PHASE 2		
Late 1980s	Research Council of Swedish National Environmental Protection Board releases initial results of its "Project Environment/Cellulose I." Researchers find effects on fish downstream of bleached kraft mills and attribute these to chlorinated compounds. Specific compounds are not identified. Findings are questioned in North America, as standardized toxicity tests on secondary-treated bleached effluent show no detrimental effects. Scientific panel concludes that Swedish findings can not be extrapolated to US mills.	In 1987, Swedish government regulates all chlorinated compounds using the "AOX" parameter, with plans for reaching zero AOX by 2000.

Table 3
(*Continued*)

Date	Scientific Developments	Policy Developments
1987-89	Environment Canada's NWRI launches major research program to analyse effects of bleached kraft mill effluent. Initial results analogous to those in Sweden, but effects also observed near mills discharging low AOX.	
1989-90	Follow-up studies for "Environment/Celluose II" show reduced effects with reduced AOX but effects also observed near unbleached mills. Correlation between effects and AOX in doubt. Studies in NA confirm lack of correlation.	In 1989, BC announces limit on organochlorine discharges of 2.5 kg AOX/tonne by 1993. A new environment minister unilaterally declares lower limit of 1.5 kg, but premier vetoes this.
Fall 1991	PAPRICAN researchers show that ClO_2 substitution has reduced dioxins and AOX in effluent by 90% and 50% respectively.	Canadian Pulp and Paper Association announces plan to "virtually eliminate" persistent, bioaccumulative compounds in effluent.
November 1991	Environment Canada releases CEPA Assessment of "Effluents from Pulp Mills Using Bleaching" and concludes that, even when dioxins are removed, effluent is toxic. States there is no scientific basis for setting federal AOX standard.	CEPA Assessment findings accepted by ministers of health and environment.
December 1991		Federal government announces regulations requiring elimination of dioxin, not AOX, from effluent by July, 1992. Industry required to carry out an Environmental Effects Monitoring (EEM) study on each mill every 3 years, with first due in 1996. Environment Ministry holds workshop for ENGOs to explain regulations, their scientific basis. Federal officials reject call from ENGOs to endorse AOX parameter on basis of precautionary principle.

Table 3
(*Continued*)

Date	Scientific Developments	Policy Developments
January 1992		New NDP government in BC releases regulations limiting AOX discharges – with target of zero AOX by 2002. Industry responds that science and current technology can support only 2.5 kg limit. BC government attempts to begin stakeholder consultation on new regulations, but fails. Swedish government announces it will adopt a low-chlorine focus but abandon zero AOX target.
June 1992	BC Council of Forest Industries (COFI) releases report finding that AOX is poor parameter for measuring environmental impact.	Industry-commissioned report shows that market demand for chlorine-free pulp is flat. No other country has mandated zero AOX target.
September 1992	Conference Board of Canada releases review of literature noting scientific consensus that AOX is not good indicator of environmental damage. BC Ministry of Environment releases report "AOX as a Regulatory Parameter," which concludes that AOX is a poor indicator of persistent, bioaccumulative, toxic organochlorines, but there is no alternative.	
October 1992	PAPRICAN releases results of minnow study showing that effluents have little impact. Greenpeace criticizes study on grounds that it does not address long-term effects. PAPRICAN research evaluating the feasibility of bleaching without chlorine compounds is ongoing. An H.A. Simons study indicates that a total chlorine ban would increase cost per tonne of pulp by 18–29%.	Speculation grows in Ontario that the NDP government may model its effluent regulations on those in BC. A coalition of Northern Ontario majors, pulp industries and unions – the Alliance for Responsible AOX Regulations – forms to oppose the adoption of such an approach.

Table 3
(*Continued*)

Date	Scientific Developments	Policy Developments
PHASE 3		
January 1993	NWRI releases final results of its effluent research program, which indicates effects on fish unrelated to the presence or absence of bleaching or levels of AOX discharge. Studies indicate that natural components of wood, "Compound x," are at least partly responsible for effects. Greenpeace releases report by a British biologist, who criticizes NWRI's methodology but agrees that effluent, chlorinated or not, has effects.	Federal officials note, in response to NWRI findings: "this is a strong scientific argument on why not to use AOX to regulate." Greenpeace argues that the federal regulations only reflect a concern for industry, not the environment. Industry supports the federal research findings. BC's environment minister notes that other effects may be linked to the AOX family of compounds.
February 1993		Ontario's environment minister presents a Draft Effluent Limits Regulation setting an AOX limit of 0.8 kg/tonne by 1999, with a nonbinding goal of zero AOX by 2002. Federal officials argue that these are "politically expedient" but not based on science.
March 1993	University of Toronto's Pulp and Paper Centre releases report criticizing Ontario's regulations, as scientific research has not established a relationship between effects and AOX, and there is no evidence that AOX is persistent or toxic.	
July 1993		The Alliance for Responsible AOX Regulations demands to see the science on which the new Ontario regulations are based. Ontario officials respond that certain organochlorines have been found to be toxic and the regulations support the IJC's call for a phase-out of chlorine in the Great Lakes region.

Table 3
(*Continued*)

Date	Scientific Developments	Policy Developments
October 1993	Scientific review panel brought together by the Alliance for Environmental Technology finds that AOX should not be equated with persistent, toxic chemicals, it is misleading to combine all organochlorines in one class, and sufficient evidence exists to suggest that non-chlorinated compounds are responsible for some effects.	
November 1993	*Pulp and Paper Canada* suggests it is time for the closed cycle mill. PAPRICAN, Ingersoll-Rand, and Air Products Canada announce a pilot experiment with ozone bleaching.	The final version of the Ontario regulations are released and contain the nonbinding zero AOX target.
April 1994	D.W. Schindler, Killam Professor of Ecology at University of Alberta, argues that despite its non-specificity, AOX is a useful regulatory tool resulting in pulp mill emission reductions.	
July 1994	The Society for Environmental Toxicology and Chemistry (SETAC) holds a scientific workshop on chlorine-containing chemicals and releases a press statement asserting that organochlorines should not be treated as a single class and that steps taken to manage such chemicals are adequate.	
November 1994	During the Second International Environmental Fate and Effects of Bleached Pulp Mill Effluents conference in BC, scientists note that effluent from unbleached pulp mills is still causing effects in fish.	BC's environment minister, in response to reports at the conference, notes that if the science crystallizes "one is never adverse to reconsideration." However, at present, he prefers to "err on the side of caution."

Table 3
(*Continued*)

Date	Scientific Developments	Policy Developments
April 1995	The consensus of 500 scientists/ experts at a conference in the US is that elementally chlorine-free (rather than totally chlorine-free) pulp is better as it uses less wood while addressing dioxin problems adequately.	
1996	An H.A. Simons report reviews developments in closed-cycle technology and notes that, despite some progress, significant obstacles to total closure remain. The first EEM cycle is completed, cycle 2 begins.	The Progressive Conservatives take over the reins of government in Ontario and decline to enforce the province's AOX regulations. The zero AOX goal is officially abandoned.
1997	COFI sponsors a government-industry-ENGO workshop on "science and AOX," at which it is acknowledged that a non-chlorinated substance, Compound X, is still causing effects.	
1998	Interim results from EEM cycle 2 suggest considerable improvement in effluents.	
1999	COFI commissions report into the utility of the AOX discharge limits. The authors encourage a revisitation of the AOX question, since a relation between AOX and toxic effects is inproven at these levels; also, the toxicity of non-chlorinated compounds is a matter of concern Industry reaches AOX average of 0.5 kg/tonne.	
2000		BC's NDP government, at a historic low in terms of public support, faces an uphill electoral battle against the Liberals, known opponents of zero AOX.

Documents cited in the "No Margin of Safety" report indicated that EPA officials had known by 1980 that pulp mills were potentially major emitters of dioxin pollution and that this suspicion was confirmed in 1983 when fish collected downstream from several mills by agency officials showed heavy contamination. Then, in 1986, samples from sites slated for "control" sampling by the agency and predicted to have only "background" dioxin levels consistently revealed high levels of dioxin contamination downstream from or near pulp mills. Greenpeace charged that senior EPA officials and the pulp and paper industry were working together to limit public knowledge about the presence of dioxin in pulp and paper mill effluent, and that industry was lobbying the EPA behind the scenes to delay regulatory action. Following the release of Greenpeace's report, EPA officials acknowledged the seriousness of the findings and announced that the agency would conduct further study of the effects of mills using chlorine bleaching. The EPA also released the results of the long overdue "National Dioxin Study," documenting dioxin emissions at more than a hundred chemical industry plants, in fish populations at over a hundred different sites, and from municipal incinerators.

In Canada, the British Columbia Council of Forest Industries (COFI) arranged for Greenpeace Vancouver to meet with pulp mill managers in August so that the findings of the "No Margin of Safety" report could be presented to them before its release. The report, which had focused on American sources of dioxin, appeared more significant in the Canadian context in mid-September when West Coast Canadian newspapers were flooded with reports that high levels of dioxin had been discovered in the eggs of a Great Blue Heron colony near a pulp mill in Crofton, BC. The sampling had been deemed necessary when all of the colony's two hundred eggs failed to hatch that spring. Shortly thereafter, Greenpeace took sediment samples from an area near MacMillan Bloedel's Harmac pulp mill in Nanaimo, BC and sent them to Sweden to be analysed. The laboratory results indicated high levels of dioxin in the sediment samples. Greenpeace informed Environment Canada officials of their findings and then issued a press release in January of 1988 revealing that dioxins had been found at the mill.

On 25 January 1988 the federal minister of fisheries and oceans confirmed Greenpeace's results and announced that a national study was to be conducted. Federal officials then began the regular monitoring of mills in British Columbia. Initial data documented elevated levels of dioxin and furans in edible fish and shellfish tissues near nine coastal mills. The federal government responded in 1989 by issuing restrictions on various crab, clam, prawn, shrimp, and oyster fisheries. Further sampling was carried out at other mills and more areas were closed for fishing. Sampling and subsequent closures continued over the next year, accompanied by extensive media attention.[10] Very quickly, a province-wide coalition of fifty-four trade unions, environmental groups, Native peoples, and consumer groups established a well-organized and very vocal Pulp Pollution Campaign. The West Coast Environmental Law Association (WCELA), on behalf of the campaign, began pressing federal and provincial governments to adopt regulations or permit standards to completely eliminate the discharge of persistent, toxic chemicals from pulp mill effluent.

By the end of 1988, researchers at the Pulp and Paper Research Institute of Canada (PAPRICAN), the research arm of the industry funded by both industry and the federal government, had determined that dioxins and furans were formed when certain precursors were introduced into the pulping and bleaching processes as chemicals used in the process or present in the wood or water used by mills.[11] These researchers also found that this process could be prevented by substituting chlorine dioxide for molecular chlorine in the bleaching process, which sparked a widespread movement towards chlorine dioxide substitution in the pulp and paper industry.

THE SHIFT TO ORGANOCHLORINES AND AOX AS A REGULATORY PARAMETER

In the late 1980s, research carried out in Sweden attributed observed effects on fish downstream of pulp mills to organochlorines formed in the pulp-bleaching process generally, rather than merely dioxins. These widely published findings spurred an international focus on the entire class of organochlorines – of which dioxins are only one example. A substantial Canadian research effort into the effects of organochlorines in the receiving environment yielded contradictory results, however. The effects observed in Sweden were present in Canada, although effects were also seen in the area of mills discharging low levels of organochlorines. In the absence of scientific certainty concerning organochlorine effects on aquatic life, various jurisdictions in Canada chose different regulatory approaches.

SCIENTIFIC DEVELOPMENTS

In the mid-1980s, the Research Council of the Swedish National Environmental Protection Board initiated its "Project Environment/Cellulose 1" to study the physiological, pathological, and ecological impacts of primary-treated effluent from bleached kraft mills on fish communities in the Gulf of Bothnia.[12] Prior to this, there had been little published information on the sublethal effects of pulp mill effluents on wild fish populations.[13] Instead, most work assessing the impacts on fish and fish populations had measured acute lethality. The "Environment/Cellulose" researchers found chemical contamination, increased activity of mixed function oxygenase enzymes (MFO induction),[14] pathology, altered responses to stress, changes in energy use and storage, and impaired reproduction in fish populations sampled in 1984–85.[15] Moreover, the sampling had been carried out along a dilution gradient and many of the physiological changes followed an exposure-response relationship, with responses most pronounced at two sites nearest the discharge and some responses as far away as ten kilometres. Significantly, these effects were not observed in fish in the area of an unbleached kraft mill. Researchers attributed the observed effects to organochlorine emissions from the bleaching process, although this linkage was not conclusively demonstrated.[16]

It is notable that the Swedish scientific findings suggested only that the effects were caused by chlorinated compounds; the findings did not show which compound(s) was or were causing the effects. Despite the lack of conclusive cause-and-effect evidence, and rather than trying to identify all of the toxic compounds in effluent as well as estimate individual interactions and effects, the Swedish Environmental Protection Board regulated all chlorinated compounds using the AOX parameter beginning in 1987. The Swedish regulations limited AOX discharges to 1–2 kg AOX/air dried metric tonne (ADT) of pulp by 1993, with plans for reaching zero AOX by 2000.[17] Achieving the zero AOX goal would require a discontinuation of the use of chlorine in the pulping and bleaching processes. It should be noted here that most Swedish pulp and paper mills did not even employ secondary treatment of effluent at that time.

The applicability of the Swedish findings to the North American context was immediately questioned by government officials and industry, as North American research on pulp mill effluent prior to 1988 had not yielded similar findings. For example, a series of standardized toxicity tests conducted in the mid-1980s by the National Council of the Paper Industry for Air and Stream Improvement (NCASI) in the US had concluded that secondary-treated bleached kraft mill effluent had little or no detrimental effect on receiving water environments.[18] A "Scientific Panel on Pulping Effluents in the Aquatic Environment," convened by Procter and Gamble Cellulose Company in the US to address discrepancies between the Swedish and available North American studies of effluent impacts, concluded that the Swedish studies could not be extrapolated directly to American mills because of physical, chemical, and biological differences in situations, and the fact that secondary

treatment at many North American mills effectively reduced or eliminated sublethal effects in the receiving environment.[19] In addition, the
panel cautioned against inferring cause-effect relationships about chlorinated organic compounds from the two cases used by the Swedish
researchers, as the unbleached mill had operated under different
conditions from the bleached kraft mill.[20] However, it was also true
that the type of study conducted by the Swedes had not been done in
the United States or Canada. In fact, the Swedish studies represented a
paradigm shift in the way testing was carried out; rather than relying
on standardized effluent toxicity tests in artificial environments using
small population sizes, as NCASI had done, the Swedish research represented an attempt to measure actual ecosystem effects.

In response to the Swedish findings, Environment Canada's National
Water Research Institute (NWRI) in Burlington, Ontario launched a
major research program to analyse the effects of bleached kraft mill
effluents on the receiving environment. The "Environmental Impacts of
Bleached Kraft Mill Effluents Study," headed by Dr John Carey, was to
determine the following: (1) whether the same type of effects the
Swedes reported were occurring in Canada; (2) whether these effects
were indeed associated with chlorine bleaching; (3) whether these effects were typical of mills with secondary treatment or only of older
mills; and, consequently, (4) whether changes in process and effluent
treatment in more modern Canadian mills could effectively eliminate
these effects. The study would thus investigate whether a cause and
effect relationship existed between organochlorines and any observed
effects and aid decision makers in choosing the most appropriate regulatory approach.

In 1988–89, NWRI, in co-operation with the Department of Fisheries
and Oceans, and to a lesser extent the Ontario Ministry of the Environment, studied the effects of effluent from mills using primary treatment
in Lake Superior and in the St Maurice River in Quebec. The results
were analogous to those observed in Sweden. However, studies tracking the effects of a mill near Espanola, Ontario utilizing oxygen deligni-
fication, chlorine dioxide substitution, and secondary treatment – and
thus discharging low amounts of AOX into the river – still showed
effects, though it was noted that the low dilution factor in the river
might account for these results. Further studies at different sites in Ontario in 1990–91 also found effects analogous to those observed by the
Swedish researchers.

In 1989–90, follow-up studies for "Environment/Cellulose II" in
Sweden showed reduced levels of effects following improvements to
effluent treatment, ClO_2 substitution, and reduced AOX discharges;
however, MFO induction in fish was still evident and more widespread

than previously believed.[21] The Swedes also found that similar effects were caused by unbleached kraft pulp mills using no chlorine. This placed the correlation between the observed effects and organochlorines as measured by AOX in doubt. One of the project leaders, Karl-Johan Lehtinen, later claimed that whole mill effluents give no evidence that chlorinated substances are any more hazardous than non-chlorinated ones: "In some instances the effect of effluents from unbleached production are the same as or greater than those from bleached production."[22]

In late 1990 researchers at Beak Engineering in Brampton, Ontario presented a paper at the Pacific Paper Expo which cast doubt on the role of adsorbable organic halogens as meaningful parameters for measuring the toxicity of pulp mill effluent. The paper noted that AOX was a much less sensitive and specific measure of the potential for biological impacts than a toxic equivalence measure based on "recognized toxicological endpoints."[23] In a later paper which reviewed various external treatments for removing AOX, the researchers argued that "the discrepancy between removal of the bulk organochlorine feature, AOX, and the removal of more toxic, lower MW [molecular weight], chlorinated phenols observed across a wide range of treatment systems brings into question the value of a nonspecific measure such as AOX as a regulatory parameter … The variable concentration of individual chlorinated organics within the AOX group and, in particular, the highly toxic chlorinated phenolics, implies that AOX, in itself, is not a dependable indicator of effluent toxicity."[24]

The authors also referred to several other studies which noted the difficulties of using AOX as a regulatory tool,[25] as well as those citing a poor correlation between acute or chronic toxicity and AOX.[26] However, a study examining levels of chlorinated organic compounds in wastewaters from bleached kraft mills in Ontario found that AOX as a surrogate parameter represented well the specific halogenated organic compounds surveyed for the study.[27] The authors of the study concluded that "for this reason the use of AOX as an indicator for the presence of halogenated priority pollutants is recommended." In 1991, a comprehensive review of research on the effects of pulp mill effluents in the aquatic environment was published.[28] The review concluded that "no complete mechanistic link had been demonstrated that relates exposure to contaminants in pulp mill effluents to 'within organism' responses, 'whole organism' effects, and effects at the population and community level."[29] The author called for a multi-disciplinary effort to combine chemical, toxicological, and biological studies of adverse effects and to identify the responsible chemicals.

The federal government also released its assessment under the Canadian Environmental Protection Act (CEPA) of "Effluents from Pulp Mills Using Bleaching" in November of 1991. The assessment concluded that the effluent was toxic, even when dioxins were removed, and that it was entering the environment in a quantity or concentration having immediate and long-term harmful effects on the environment.[30] The background report and discussion papers written by Environment Canada scientists were reviewed by industry, environmental organizations, Fisheries and Oceans Canada, Health and Welfare Canada, Environment Canada, and several university researchers. The ministers of health and welfare and the environment accepted the assessment, and bleached pulp mill effluent was considered "toxic" under paragraph 11(a) of CEPA. The report recommended controls on organochlorines, but no standards were suggested. Significantly, the report stated that, although the effluent was toxic, a scientific basis for setting a federal AOX standard could not be established, since AOX as a measurement did not provide estimates of the potential toxicity, persistence, or bioaccumulation of the effluent in the aquatic environment. Further, several information gaps were identified about exactly which compounds in AOX were creating the biological effects and what control measures were needed. The backgrounder accompanying the assessment noted that, when research currently underway by federal scientists, the provinces, universities, and industry was completed within the next two years, the federal government would be in a position to determine whether it should regulate AOX levels.

In September of 1992, a report prepared for the Industrial Waste and Hazardous Contaminants Branch, Environmental Protection Division, British Columbia Ministry of Environment, Lands and Parks was released. "AOX as a Regulatory Parameter: A Scientific Review of AOX Toxicity and Environmental Fate" concluded that AOX was a poor indicator for the presence of persistent, bioaccumulative or toxic organochlorines and thus limited in its use for regulating the discharge of toxic chlorinated organic compounds from bleached kraft mills. It was noted that AOX as a bulk parameter did not allow for the distinction or quantification of individual organochlorine compounds. Thus, more research was needed to assess the toxicity of chlorinated and non-chlorinated compounds, both alone and in combination, as "some specific chlorinated organic substances included in the AOX measurement may need to be regulated to control potentially harmful impacts on the environment and human health."[31] Yet the report concluded that no other better parameter was available to regulators and that organochlorines did need to be regulated because of the suspected harmful effects of some constituent compounds. The best solution, according to the report's author, would be to eliminate organochlorines altogether through a closed loop process.

Moreover, a study on the life cycles of minnows living in various concentrations of treated effluent from mills using chlorine, conducted by PAPRICAN, showed that the treated effluent posed no problems for fish at concentrations typical of receiving environments. The institute did find, however, that minnows in high concentrations of the effluent had difficulties producing eggs and showed a trend to gender imbalance. The institute's president said that research would now focus on identifying the responsible components in the effluents, as the study indicated that fish abnormalities could not be linked to the bleaching process. Significantly, the tests conducted by PAPRICAN researchers on a variety of bleached and unbleached kraft mill effluents[32] showed that there was no correlation between AOX release and effluent toxicity to minnows for mills releasing more than 2.5 kg AOX/ADT of pulp.[33]

POLICY DEVELOPMENTS

Thus, the ongoing research could not conclusively link effects observed in the aquatic environment to organochlorines. In fact, some studies suggested that organochlorines might not be responsible for the effects observed. However, in the face of intense pressure from environmental groups and daily media coverage, governments in Canada set about formulating regulations to control the release of hazardous substances in pulp mill effluent. Successive federal environment ministers had promised that a pollution law restricting the release of chlorinated organics, not just dioxins and furans, would be instituted. Provincial premiers and ministers of the environment also began indicating that they would regulate in this area.

Industry was monitoring regulatory developments closely. The president and CEO of Fletcher Challenge Canada Limited, Ian Donald, noted in an address to the Canadian Pulp and Paper Association (CPPA) that it was important for the national industry trade associations to get together to develop common environmental protection standards based on "good science" for the regulation of the global industry.[34] Failure to do so, he warned, would lead to "some arbitrarily imposed standards and huge capital investments – for only modest environmental improvement – a result inconsistent with the concept of sustainable development and with the survival of large parts of this industry."

As early as 1989, British Columbia Environment Minister Bruce Strachan had announced the province's intention to limit pulp mill organochlorine discharges to 2.5 kg AOX/tonne of pulp. A cabinet shuffle in 1990 brought John Reynolds to the environment portfolio and he expressed his support for the government's commitment to the 2.5 kg limit. However, a few months later, Reynolds unilaterally announced that the limit would be lowered to 1.5 kg AOX. Industry was surprised by the new target. Fletcher Challenge's president said: "Research suggests that the benefit to the environment [of further reducing AOX] will be minimal" and he thus questioned the wisdom "of spending an additional $500 million [to reach the 1.5 kg limit] to clean up chlorinated organics."[35] In December 1990, Reynolds resigned when Premier Bill Vanderzalm, under pressure from the CEOs of BC's major forest companies, refused to endorse the new, tougher targets.[36] The premier then appointed backbencher Cliff Serwa to the environment portfolio and a bill was enacted that set an AOX discharge limit of 2.5 kg/tonne pulp to be met by 1993, while also requiring that all mills install secondary treatment equipment.

The BC cabinet also announced that it would consider toughening the provincial pulp mill pollution standards when research on organochlorines being conducted at BC's three universities was completed.[37] This was deemed a "political footdragging move" by Greenpeace's toxic chemicals campaigner.[38] However, the province's political landscape changed dramatically just months later with the installation of the New Democrats in the seat of government and the appointment of John Cashore to the environment portfolio. Cashore was well known for advocating the total elimination of organochlorines from pulp mill effluent while in opposition and during the election campaign.

By the fall of 1991 the CPPA had launched a plan to "virtually eliminate" the amount of persistent, bioaccumulative compounds released into the environment by its mills, although implementation was to be tempered by its economic impact on the industry.[39] The CPPA's president noted that "the major expenditures required to pursue virtual elimination must be shown to have a clear environmental benefit." The association also cited recent environmental successes achieved without regulation. The results of a comparative analysis by three PAPRICAN scientists between 1988 and 1991 showed that dioxin control measures, i.e., the substitution of chlorine dioxide for molecular chlorine, had been "very effective" at reducing both dioxins and the formation of organochlorines (the AOX component) more generally. In fact, average national dioxin and AOX effluent emissions into the receiving environment had decreased by over 95 per cent and 50 per cent, respectively. Further, the authors predicted that these values would increase to over 99 per cent and 70 per cent, respectively, after the technology to meet the proposed CEPA regulations was fully implemented.[40]

On 14 December 1991, the new package of federal regulations was announced. There were three regulations in the package which became law on 20 May 1992: The Pulp and Paper Mill Effluent Chlorinated Dioxins and Furans Regulations, promulgated under CEPA; the Pulp and Paper Mill Defoamer and Woodchip Regulations, also promulgated under CEPA; and the Pulp and Paper Effluent Regulations, promulgated under the Fisheries Act. The first-mentioned of these required that pulp and paper mills using chlorine bleaching implement process changes to prevent the formation of dioxins and furans. These regulations were to come into effect on 1 July 1992, but allowed for transitional extensions for mills built before 1971 of up to a year and a half. In actuality, the regulations largely reflected the changes already taking place in the industry, as noted in the preceding paragraph. The Pulp and Paper Effluent Regulations (PPER), developed with the aid of industry, environmental organizations, labour groups, and the provinces, required that all mills have an effluent that was not acutely toxic and mandated the implementation of secondary treatment at all mills.

Significantly, the federal regulations did not include a regulation to specifically control organochlorines using the AOX parameter. However, secondary treatment of effluent as mandated by the PPER would eliminate many of the AOX compounds, particularly the lower molecular weight chlorinated compounds, to yield a non-acutely lethal effluent. This regulation would work in concert with the Chlorinated Dioxins and Furans Regulations to eliminate those specific compounds known to be dangerous. As noted by both federal officials and industry, reducing dioxin levels by means of chlorine dioxide substitution would also reduce AOX discharge levels to below 2.5 kg/tonne AOX, a level believed to have minimal environmental impact. Moreover, as continuing NWRI research indicated that effluent was still having effects even at low organochlorine levels, further reductions in AOX were unlikely to solve the problem.

The PPER also required that all mills conduct an Environmental Effects Monitoring (EEM) study every three years to measure the impact of effluent on fish and fish habitat. Each mill was expected to gather information on a wide range of substances and characteristics of receiving water quality set out in the requirements. For mills beginning operations before 1 January 1993, the first EEM had to be presented to the federal environment minister by 1 April 1996, whereas for later mills the first study had to be available within three years of start-up. The average cost of gathering the information for each mill's EEM study has been approximately $85,000. Since these costs are conducted over a three-year study cycle, the average cost is approximately $28,000 per study per year.[41] The first three years (cycle 1) were deemed preliminary, primarily to identify baseline conditions and problems and set the stage for future cycles. No conclusions regarding cause and effect were to be drawn.

At the time of the release of the new federal regulations, the federal environment minister, Jean Charest, had spoken with several key non-governmental organization representatives and committed the ministry to holding a technical workshop to present NGOs with the research on which the regulatory package was based. The workshop was organized by NWRI and led by Dr John Carey of NWRI with participation from other DOE and DFO officials, as well as university scientists. It was co-chaired by a representative of the West Coast Environmental Law Association (WCELA) and NWRI's executive director. Twenty people were invited to attend on behalf of numerous interests, including environmental, labour, and aboriginal peoples' organizations. The workshop began with a presentation on recent federal research into the effects of pulp mill effluents and its implications for effluent regulations. In the afternoon, NGO representatives were invited to meet privately to discuss the findings and provide comments on the program.

Immediately after the workshop, a WCELA representative wrote to Environment Minister Charest to inform him that the meeting had been "very productive" and that NGOs "strongly support federal research in this area and we encourage you to continue your search for the cause of the reproductive and enzyme problems in organisms exposed to pulp mill effluent." The letter encouraged federal officials to stress in their statements to the public that "the main result of the studies is that pulp mill effluent is affecting fish and that the precise cause is not yet known; the reduction in organochlorines ... will have a positive environmental effect; and this research has not proven that organochlorines are harmless."[42] As the NGOs were attempting to point out, while it was evident that organochlorines were not essential for effects (i.e., non-chlorinated compounds could cause effects), the toxicology of the organochlorines was still not well understood. The letter closed with the notion that the precautionary basis for eliminating organochlorines was the most appropriate course of action. John Carey replied to this letter as follows:

The precautionary approach may have some validity when we have no observable effects and want to be careful, but in this case, we have observable effects that will not be eliminated by the proposed reductions. Whether they will be eliminated by eliminating organochlorines depends completely on the means by which we eliminate the organochlorines. It can just as easily be imagined that the elimination of organochlorines will increase the effects, if they originate in a part of the process that is unconnected with the bleaching process, or if the compounds causing the effects are partially decomposed during bleaching. The precautionary basis for eliminating organochlorines is based on inappropriate models of organochlorines (such as PCBs and DDT) that do not compare chemically to the vast majority of the organically bound chlorine present in effluents.[43]

As if to underscore this point, the Swedish government announced soon after the workshop that it would adopt a low-organochlorine focus in its new legislation directed at pulp mill effluent, rather than a zero discharge policy for chlorine. The legislation also shifted its focus to specific compounds in pulp mill effluent regulation and away from the more generic AOX parameter.[44]

In January of 1992, just one month after the federal regulations were announced, BC's Pulp and Paper Mill Liquid Effluent Control Regulations were released by the province's newly installed New Democratic government, and, unlike the federal regulations, the province set strict limits on the discharge of AOX. The new regulations required that BC's pulp and paper mills completely eliminate chlorinated organic compounds in mill effluent within ten years. The new regulations were to be implemented in two stages: the first, effective 17 January 1992, required that pulp mills using chlorine to bleach pulp submit to the ministry, by 30 June 1995, a time schedule to ensure that the AOX produced in the bleaching process and discharged into the environment was eliminated. The second stage, which was to come into effect as of 1 July 1992, required that pulp mills reduce their actual AOX discharge limit from 2.5 kg per air dried tonne (kg/ADT) to 1.5 kg/ADT of pulp produced by 31 December 1995. All mills were required to eliminate AOX by 31 December 2002. Thus, industry in the province would have to discontinue using chlorine and chlorine dioxide bleaching processes. Mills that proposed an alternative plan to eliminate AOX produced in the bleaching process by 31 December 2000, two years ahead of schedule, would be exempt from the 1995 deadline. At the same time, the province released its second Pulp Mill Effluent Status Report covering the period from 1 April 1991 to 31 August 1991 and outlining the industry's progress in complying with a schedule of upgrading under the existing Effluent Control Regulations. The report noted that eleven mills had complied, ten had "somewhat complied," and two mills were not in compliance.[45]

The new regulations were touted as "another signal that the New Democratic Party is prepared to be tougher on industry than the former Social Credit regime, which had bowed to pressure against a similar standard proposed more than a year ago." Industry immediately announced, however, that it would not be able to comply with the new regulations. A MacMillan Bloedel representative stated: "There's no technology right now in the marketplace to meet the zero discharge." He also noted that "current data indicate that we will be able to meet the 1.5 kg limit, but lower, I don't know. It's going to be a challenge, and nobody knows what it's going to cost." According to a representative of the BC Council of Forest Industries, "complying with the zero-discharge target could force major technological and process changes in bleach plants," which would add to the $1 billion already invested in equipment changes to bring the province's twenty-three mills to the 2.5 kg limit prescribed for 1993 as well as to install secondary equipment. Moreover, the representative stated: "We question the need to go beyond the 2.5 mark ... Science is not telling us that there is any reason to go beyond this level. AOX is not a very good parameter for measuring environmental impact."[46]

In response, the industrial waste branch of BC's Ministry of Environment, Lands and Parks denied that it acted without due cause and explained that the new regulation represented a "precautionary" approach to the pulp mill effluent problem: "Pulp mill effluents contain about 30,000 different chemical compounds, of which only 10% have been identified. Environmental regulations can't wait for unequivocal data, particularly when it's been demonstrated that effluent poses a hazard to sea life."[47] Proponents of regulating on the basis of the AOX parameter argued that the regulation would force a rethinking of pulping and bleaching processes and lead to the development of more environmentally friendly technology.

The BC minister of environment, lands and parks had also committed the agency to holding consultations during the months following the amendments. Dr Gerald Cormick, an American mediation and negotiation expert, was brought in to assist the ministry with consensus building. At the end of February 1992, Cormick circulated a "Proposed Consensus Process: AOX Regulations," which outlined suggested procedures for the establishment and functioning of a task force.[48] Matters for discussion included the level of AOX in pulp mill effluent and dates for reaching prescribed levels (although "It is recognized that the Minister of the Environment has announced proposed standards and dates"), and the assessment of current and review of emerging and prospective scientific evidence and technologies and their relationship to the regulation, present and future. The task force was to be composed of "caucuses" of industry, environmental, commercial fishery, First Nations, labour, federal, and provincial representatives. Each caucus of stakeholders would be expected to represent its constituents and to ensure their support. Consensus was defined as "the substantive agreement of the caucuses represented on the Task force, such that all can support the recommended regulations." Task force meetings were to be closed to all except caucus members.

Cormick began by meeting one-on-one with individual interests to canvass support for the task force and encountered divergent views on what the goals of the process should be. Environmental representatives were satisfied with the new AOX regulations and were loath to commit themselves to a process which might result in any changes to these regulations, while industry was reluctant to take part unless changes to the regulations were a possible outcome. After a few unsuccessful and poorly attended meetings with some of the stakeholders, Cormick informed the ministry that the "necessary preconditions to a successful consensus-building process are not met" and recommended that attempts to establish such a process be discontinued.[49]

In fact, a Multi-Stakeholder Working Group on Research Needs for Pulp Mill Effluent Regulation in BC (hereafter MSWG) had already been convened almost a year earlier by Simon Fraser University's Centre for Policy Research on Science and Technology.[50] Its purpose was to compile information about pulp mill effluent research then underway, identify issues that the government should look at when making regulatory choices in this area, and highlight areas that needed further research. The MSWG contained representation from those interests that would have participated in the BC Ministry of the Environment's Advisory Group and the MSWG process was thus given support from the ministry. The MSWG's consensus recommendations, submitted to the ministry, identified areas for further research and increased monitoring by governments, and suggested ways of increasing public participation as well as continuing multi-stakeholder input into the regulation of pulp mill effluent.[51]

These activities were interpreted by a *Globe and Mail* journalist as proof that the BC ministry "is keeping open the option of relaxing the chlorine ban"[52] and that "some of BC Environment Minister John Cashore's senior staff accept the latest [scientific] findings."[53] To each of these pronouncements, however, the minister reiterated his commitment to zero AOX on the basis of the precautionary principle.

A great deal of study was conducted on this policy issue throughout 1992. In June, an industry-commissioned report entitled "Market and Economic Research on Current and Future Demands: AOX Free and Low AOX Kraft Pulp" concluded that demand for "Totally Chlorine-Free" (TCF) pulp was primarily limited to the German market and that even German paper producers were "strongly resisting" TCF price premiums unless they were sure these could be passed onto consumers.[54] Markets were better for "Elemental Chlorine-Free" (ECF) pulps producing a very low amount of AOX content (0.3 kg AOX/ADT) during manufacturing. Also in June, the BC Council of Forest Industries (COFI) released a paper entitled "Position on Zero AOX." The paper stated that "AOX is a poor parameter for measuring environmental impact" and cited various PAPRICAN and international studies as supporting documentation.[55]

In addition the paper noted that, although a number of countries including Finland, Sweden, and some European Community member countries had adopted AOX regulations, none was presently mandating the total elimination of chlorinated organics. As a result of the capital expenditures for the pollution equipment required to meet the zero AOX target, the paper added, BC mills would be producing pulp at a significant cost disadvantage relative to other pulp-producing nations. Then in September 1992 the Conference Board of Canada released "The Case of Effluents from Pulp Mills Using Chlorine." This report reviewed the scientific literature and went on to state: "In terms of environmental decision-making, some of it is being done on public pressure more than scientific evidence," since "the jury is out on whether further reduction of chlorine compounds from pulp-mill discharges will benefit the environment." It noted: "So far, the scientific consensus is that AOX is not a good indicator of prospective environmental damage." The report quoted extensively from studies conducted by the pulp and paper industry and, specifically, Procter and Gamble. In response, Greenpeace stated that the Conference Board could not have done a thorough review of the literature "or else they would know there are stacks and stacks of scientific papers showing organochlorines cause harm to waterways."[56]

Two weeks later, PAPRICAN released the minnow study which had found no difference between the development of minnows hatched from eggs and reared in clean aquaria and those which spent their entire life in the aquaria containing effluents. Industry cited these results as supporting their claim that the new BC regulations were not justified by science. Greenpeace criticized the study on the grounds that it did not deal with long-term effects: "Most of the science on organochlorines shows us that the reason they are of concern is that they build up and move through the foodchains and have an impact on the progeny and on predator species," a representative of the organization said.

In October 1992, an H.A. Simons study, commissioned by the BC government and based on four hypothetical mills considered representative of the BC industry, concluded that a total chlorine ban would increase the cost per tonne of pulp by between 18.4 and 29.4 per cent. The study supported COFI's view that this would adversely affect the competitive position of the BC industry, as no other jurisdiction in the world had imposed a chlorine ban. Even Sweden had backed away from its intended ban and had instead settled on an AOX level of 0.5 kg by 2000, a target achievable with chlorine dioxide substitution.[57] Simons estimated that applying this same standard to the BC industry would mean production cost increases of between 5.5 and 21.8 per cent per tonne, lower than would be the case with a total chlorine ban.

The BC Ministry of Environment released its report "AOX as a Regulatory Parameter: A Scientific Review of AOX Toxicity and Environmental Fate" in September of 1992. The report concluded by noting that "A review of the scientific adequacy of pulp mill effluent regulations is required and has been initiated by the BC Ministry of Environment, Lands and Parks."[58] In a letter which accompanied dissemination of the H.A. Simons and ministry reports, an environment ministry assistant deputy minister noted: "There are remaining uncertainties regarding the achievement of the longer term goal of AOX elimination in the bleaching process. The uncertainties relate mainly to technology to achieve totally chlorine-free bleached pulp and the scientific knowledge regarding the environmental effects of low concentrations of AOX in the environment."[59] He continued: "However, the government remains committed to the goal of eliminating AOX compounds produced in the bleaching process by the year 2002. The Ministry believes, based on the current state of knowledge on the environmental impacts of pulp mill effluents, this precautionary approach is the correct one. We also recognize there is a strong divergence of opinion on this matter and that it is imperative for us to continue our search for knowledge of both the environmental effects and new technology."

The BC environment minister invited comment on the reports disseminated and noted that he remained "committed to a multi-stakeholder consultative process to facilitate better communication among various stakeholders." He also indicated that a Pulp Mill Advisory Group might be established to achieve this. In a further communication to interested parties, the ADM, environmental management, invited nominations to a steering committee of five to six stakeholders, which would finalize the terms of reference of the group. In the draft terms of reference accompanying the communication, it was emphasized that "scientific knowledge and technologies which reduce AOX are advancing rapidly" and that "we expect scientific research to provide us with the additional insights into the interrelation and accumulation of chemical compounds with the environment and improved means of monitoring those impacts." The advisory group was to monitor the evolving nature of knowledge "in order to ensure the effective application of the AOX regulation." Particular attention was to be paid to scientific advances, technological advances in achieving AOX elimination, and experience in applying the new regulations.[60]

Meanwhile, in Ontario speculation was growing that the province's NDP government was modelling its new pulp and paper effluent regulations on the BC legislation. The regulations had been under development since 1988 under the province's Municipal-Industrial Strategy for Abatement (MISA). Industry officials were mounting an intense campaign in the province against regulations which followed BC's lead on AOX, as it was estimated that installing another bleaching system to eliminate all AOX discharges could cost up to $100 million. In fact, a coalition of Northern Ontario mayors, unions, and pulp and paper companies, calling themselves the Alliance for Responsible AOX Regulations, had formed in June 1992 to oppose new pulp and paper regulations mandating a zero AOX goal. Environmentalists, however, were lobbying equally hard to back up the BC government's position. Ontario announced its own version of AOX-based regulations in the spring of 1993.[61]

In the midst of these debates during the fall of 1992, the first full-scale ozone kraft bleaching plant in the world, which also utilized chlorine dioxide bleaching, came on line in the US The plant was based on fifteen years of company research, cost $113 million US, and was designed to greatly reduce the effluent flow from the mill, which was situated on a small river.[62] In Canada, research at PAPRICAN to evaluate the feasibility of bleaching hardwood and softwood kraft and sulphite pulps without chlorine compounds was continuing.[63] In its "Alternative Bleaching Technology and the Environment: A Summary of Research and Development at PAPRICAN," the institute pointed out that 15.3 per cent of its research effort was being directed towards "new chemical pulp bleaching systems," with 7.3 per cent aimed at technology to achieve "effluent systems closure." However, the report also noted: "The majority of markets continue to require fully bleached pulps which meet stringent standards of strength, cleanliness and uniformity. At present, this combination of properties cannot be commercially met without using at least one chlorine compound – chlorine dioxide."[64] The report explained that reductions in chlorine use and advances in the engineering sciences had renewed interest in effluent systems closure, but that the total elimination of organochlorine discharges would involve "a considerable risk to the overall investment."

With the release of further research results from the ongoing federal "Environmental Effects of Bleached Kraft Mill Effluent" study, doubt about the need to regulate the whole class of organochlorines using the AOX parameter reached a new high. In fact, both Canadian and international research linked sublethal effects in fish to the presence of a non-chlorinated substance or substances in pulp mill effluent.

Moreover, a scientific consensus that reductions in AOX levels below 1.5 kg were unlikely to provide greater environmental benefits gradually solidified. In this context, the Ontario government introduced regulations mandating a reduction in AOX levels, though it did not actually require that industry achieve a zero target.

SUBSEQUENT SCIENTIFIC DEVELOPMENTS

In January 1993, Environment Canada's NWRI released a major report entitled "Recent Canadian Studies on the Physiological Effects of Pulp Mill Effluent on Fish," which summarized the results of the $2.3 million research project into the environmental effects of pulp mill effluent originally begun in 1988. The research, conducted independently of industry, had been financed by the federal Departments of Environment, Fisheries and Oceans, and Industry, Science and Technology, and carried out with the help of researchers at the universities of Guelph, Waterloo and Laval. Samples of effluent and fish had been collected at twelve sites in Ontario in the summer of 1991 to assess receiving water quality and the responses of fish to pulp mill effluent. The study considered effluents from bleached kraft mills both with and without secondary treatment as well as effluent from three sulphite mills. It found effects on native fish that were unrelated to the presence or absence of bleaching and unrelated to the levels of AOX in water and of chlorinated dioxins and furans in fish. It thus concluded that chlorinated compounds were not solely responsible for effects and that more study was needed to discover what unchlorinated substance was causing effects. Follow-up studies in Canada, as well as some in Sweden, had shown that effects were caused by black liquors created in the pulping process, indicating that natural components of wood might be at least partly responsible for the effects.

In October 1993, a scientific review panel brought together by the Alliance for Environmental Technology (AET), a coalition of chemical producers and forest products companies, released "A Review and Assessment of the Ecological Risks Associated with the Use of Chlorine Dioxide for the Bleaching of Pulp." The panel had been asked to prepare an expert opinion on the chemistry and potential biological impacts of bleaching effluents produced from pulp and paper mills using substantial quantities of chlorine dioxide in the first stage of bleaching. It was also asked to examine the likely results of increasing this proportion. The panel found that substituting chlorine dioxide for elemental chlorine resulted in a five- to ten-fold reduction in organochlorine discharges and a decrease in the degree of chlorine substitution, which in turn reduced the persistence and toxicity of the effluent, the potential for bioaccumulation, and overall adverse effects. For the most part, the compounds that make up AOX were considered to be water soluble, non-hydrophobic, and non-bioaccumulative.

Thus, the panel believed that AOX should not be equated with hydrophobic and persistent chemicals and that it was misleading to combine all organochlorine chemicals in one class. Furthermore, the panel was of the opinion that sufficient evidence existed from responses observed at non-bleached mills to suggest that non-chlorinated compounds were being released or formed during the production of pulp and were responsible for adverse effects. The identification of these compounds and the elucidation of their mechanisms of action should thus be a priority. Indeed, the panel identified a number of scientific uncertainties regarding the actual levels of chlorinated compounds in effluents and their variability under normal operating conditions, as well as the toxicity of some of the compounds identified in these effluents.[65]

In July 1994, the Society for Environmental Toxicology and Chemistry (SETAC) held a scientific workshop on the "Environmental Risks of Chlorine-Containing Chemicals" in Alliston, Ontario. The workshop was attended by more than fifty scientists from nine countries. Based on a critical review of the scientific evidence, the SETAC workshop released a press statement asserting that chlorine-containing chemicals should not be treated as a single class of chemicals; that current approaches used to estimate the environmental risks of most chlorine-containing chemicals were adequate; and that steps taken to manage the risks of chlorine-containing chemicals had already improved environmental quality in some regions. It was noted that additional controls on highly toxic, persistent, and bioaccumulative chemicals were needed to eliminate their release. However, the workshop agreed that calls by environmentalists for a total ban on chlorine use to protect the environment were not supported by the available scientific evidence.

The SETAC workshop was followed by the Second International Environmental Fate and Effects of Bleached Pulp Mill Effluents conference in Vancouver, BC in November. The conference was organized by Environment Canada and Fisheries and Oceans, and partly sponsored by BC's environment ministry as well as by two sodium chlorate producers, Canadian Occidental Petroleum Ltd. and Sterling Pulp Chemicals Limited. Papers presented by Swedish and Finnish researchers supported the Canadian findings that untreated effluent from chlorine-free mills was still toxic to fish. Dr Carey of NWRI noted: "The studies haven't shown a major difference between ECF and TCF pulping processes with respect to their environmental impacts." Dr Keith Solomon of the University of Guelph cautioned: "With chlorine dioxide, we've peeled back the onion's layer we call dioxin, revealing effects that may be caused by natural compounds in mill wastewater." And as Peter Hodson (then a fish toxicologist with NWRI) said: "The basic message is good news; that is, it's not chlorine. The bad news is, it's the wood."[66]

SUBSEQUENT POLICY DEVELOPMENTS

Provincial and federal officials, industry, and environmental groups had been aware of NWRI's findings in the "Recent Canadian Studies" report for some months prior to its public release. The research was not formally presented to the public earlier, since some of the work was still under peer review. After its release, one of the authors of the report, Dr John Carey, stated: "This is a strong scientific argument on why not to use AOX to regulate for a given set of effects ... [and] there is extensive evidence supporting the belief that chlorine is not the culprit and that it could be some other unknown agent."[67] However, a Greenpeace Canada representative charged that the government's claims had less to do with science and more to do with the policy that Canada was trying to promote – to protect the pulp and paper industry – a charge vigorously denied by Environment Minister Charest.[68]

While acknowledging that other dangerous compounds could be contributing to the problem, the Greenpeace representative argued that chlorine was still hazardous and that the "Recent Canadian Studies" report had not provided evidence to the contrary. Instead, according to Greenpeace, the report had been produced to justify the course of action chosen by the government. In response, a federal source explained that the report was based on years of research and that preliminary findings from the research had formed the basis for Environment Canada's decision to ban the release of only chlorinated dioxins and furans, rather than the whole class of organochlorines. In addition, Greenpeace believed the report to be replete with unpublished studies or reports that had not yet been peer-reviewed and, in January, Greenpeace released a critique of NWRI's research methodology by a British biologist. The scientist raised technical questions about the laboratory analysis and took issue with the fact that the findings of the NWRI report had been discussed in the media before the formal peer review had been completed.[69] The biologist also noted, however, that pulp mill effluent, whether chlorinated or not, had a dramatic impact on the environment.

The federal findings were welcomed warmly by industry. A representative of E.B. Eddy Forest Products Limited mill at Espanola, Ontario, one of the ten mills producing bleached and unbleached pulp that were studied by NWRI, said: "We have to have answers. We have to be guided by science. There's only so much money, so we have to do it right the first time." BC's pulp producers responded to the research: "It's time to bring science into the debate ... When we do find the problem, there won't be any money available to fix it."[70] BC Environment Minister Cashore said that he would be monitoring the emerging science: "If we were to come up with a measure that's better than AOX, I would be the first to celebrate that." But he added that other effects might be linked to the AOX family of compounds and that industry had plenty of time to develop alternatives to chlorine use before it came up against the 2002 deadline.

In the midst of public furor over NWRI's findings, Ontario Environment Minister Ruth Grier presented a "Draft Effluent Limits Regulation for the Pulp and Paper Sector" on 2 February 1993. The draft proposed that by the end of 1995 the limit should be 1.5 kg AOX per tonne of pulp, and by the end of 1999 the limit be 0.8 kg per tonne. Further, mills would be required to prepare an AOX elimination plan specifying a schedule for decreasing AOX discharge to zero by 2002, although it was not mandatory that these plans be fulfilled. According to Environment Minister Grier, the government would be "flexible" if companies could not meet that deadline. The justification for the AOX regulations was set out in a document accompanying release of the draft: "Organochlorines are a large family of chlorine-based compounds which are generally toxic and include mutation and cancer-causing agents ... Organochlorines (AOX) ... are a parameter of special concern due to their toxicity and possible persistence. These stable chemicals can build up in the tissues of plants and animals with chronic and irreversible effects."[71] The minister also told reporters when presenting the new regulations that "human health is at risk" because of pulp mill discharges and that industry had been using the Great Lakes, the source of drinking water for six million Ontarians, "as a dumping ground ... They can no longer sustain this kind of toxic overload."

An Ontario official interviewed concerning the proposed regulations said that the government wanted "to get rid of chlorine" but stopped short of a ban because "we're conscious of the problems with the recession" in the forest industry. A federal source argued that Ontario's decision to pursue the elimination of AOX was not based on establishing a scientific link between organochlorine discharges and effects on fish. Instead, phasing out AOX had been "politically expedient." In response, an Ontario government source argued that NWRI's research was problematic, as it reversed the findings in the earlier CEPA assessment of pulp and paper mill effluent that organochlorines posed a danger to fish.[72]

On 25 March 1993 a report was released from the Pulp and Paper Centre at the University of Toronto which set out reasons why "banning AOX" was not an appropriate regulatory response on the part of the Ontario government. The report began by arguing that, "while the chemistry of AOX is complex and not yet fully described, most, if not all AOX, is not toxic, not persistent and not bioaccumulating. There is no justification for the elimination of substances which are not toxic, not persistent and not bioaccumulating." The report cited studies which had shown harmful effects caused by pulp mill effluent, yet had not found a relationship between these effects and AOX. Thus, the proposed regulations were "not justified by presently available scientific evidence and would be prohibitively expensive using presently available technology." Moreover, the report argued that "no evidence is presented [in the government's documentation] that AOX is a persistent, toxic substance." It went on: "The science of the environmental fate and effects of chemicals is highly complex, involving a vast array of variables. As a result, there is often confusion and conflict in the data. However, there is clear guidance concerning AOX and environmental effects, toxicity, persistence and bioaccumulation."[73]

In July of 1993, the Alliance for Responsible AOX Regulations demanded to see the scientific information on which Ontario's new regulations were based. Requests were made under the Freedom of Information and Protection of Privacy Acts and preparations were made to force the Ontario government, through the courts, to subject its AOX regulations to the Environmental Assessment Act. The alliance, which had argued for an AOX limit of no lower than 1.5 kg per tonne of pulp produced, said that scientific information did not warrant the elimination of chlorine use in its plants. Ontario officials said the province's draft regulations were based on evidence that some organochlorines had been found to be persistent toxic compounds and that the regulations were in accordance with the Canada-US International Joint Commission's (IJC) 1992 call for the phase-out of chlorine and chlorinated compounds in the Great Lakes region. An official in Ontario's Ministry of the Environment stated that the ministry's position was "really one of acting in a precautionary manner." Ministry officials also noted that there was still much research needed to understand the cumulative effect of organochlorines found in pulp mill effluent. In response to the requests of both environmentalists and industry that the Ontario government clarify whether it intended to force mills to eliminate organochlorine emissions, ministry officials reiterated that the ministry was "highly desirous" of mills meeting plans to phase out the use of chlorine, but that "the actual legal requirement was not there."[74]

Indeed, the final draft of Ontario's new pulp and paper regulations, released in late November, did not force the province's mills to eliminate all chlorinated compounds from their discharges, although the goal of elimination by 2002 was still contained in the legislation.

Neither would industry officials have to sign a commitment to try to meet the government's zero discharge goal, a provision included in the initial draft. Instead of plans, Ontario mills would file reports allowing them to include evidence of the pros and cons of the province's goal, rather than just how they would achieve it. A government source noted that "a final decision will be made in 1999 when the matter has been studied further."[75]

At approximately this time, it was suggested to the editors of *Pulp and Paper Canada*, an industry periodical, that the idea of the closed-cycle mill and the complete elimination of effluent deserved serious debate in the Canadian industry: "It may be a good way to avoid bans on AOX, and could mean the continued use of ClO_2 in a way that is safe for the environment." In fact, research into totally chlorine free (TCF) bleaching methods was continuing in pace with the campaign against chlorine and as government AOX deadlines drew nearer. PAPRICAN, Ingersoll-Rand Canada, and Air Products Canada announced a pilot-scale experiment with totally chlorine free bleaching of pulps using ozone.[76] The primary objectives of the project were to optimize the oxygen-, ozone-, and hydrogen peroxide-based bleaching sequences, thereby enabling pulp manufacturers to meet government requirements for chlorinated compounds.

Back in British Columbia, the *Vancouver Sun* reported a source in the Council of Forest Industries as saying that the forest industry was not worried about BC's AOX zero discharge by 2002 regulation, as "there are a bunch of elections between now and then." Environment Minister Moe Shihota responded in kind: "I'm appalled that, rather than work to clean up the environment, the industry would rather wait for a government that will let it off the hook." Industry argued that the province did not have the scientific evidence to prove that zero discharge was truly needed. The minister claimed, however, that "our government's regulations for chlorine discharges have been based on the best available scientific knowledge, on present and anticipated market demand, on a precautionary approach to environmental and health risks, and on strong concerns expressed by British Columbians."[77]

In April of 1994, D.W. Schindler, Killam Professor of Ecology at the University of Alberta, sent a letter to MP Clifford Lincoln outlining his opinions on AOX and chlorinated compounds. He began as follows: "Despite its non-specificity, I believe that AOX has been a rather useful regulatory tool for halogenated compounds. It is simple and relatively inexpensive to perform on a routine basis. Regulation of AOX has allowed us to greatly reduce the content of dioxins, furans and other toxic chlorinated compounds in pulp mill effluents ... by regulating AOX, we have caused pulp mills to control their emissions of both man-made halogenated compounds and superconcentrated ones."[78] Schindler also noted that "the implications of [Dr John] Carey's work [at NWRI] for AOX and other measures to regulate chlorine have been misinterpreted," for although "industry has quoted Carey's studies as showing that chlorinated effluents were not toxic, examination of his work shows another story." He went on: "The battery of indicators used in fish should be regarded as early warning signals, even though they cannot presently be linked directly with adverse effects." Moreover, Schindler noted that "the concept of taking preventative health measures is now thoroughly incorporated in human health ... I do not see why we are reluctant to apply such precautionary measures to address ecosystems." He concluded: "industry should be given incentives to explore effluent-free technology more diligently. At the present rate, I believe that we will continue to find problems with effluents for many years to come, while paying a very expensive price for the science to conduct such examinations."

In responding to this letter, Dr Carey noted that Schindler "arrives at the same conclusion we have that effluent-free processes are the best bet."[79] He added: "He is correct concerning the recent improvements [in pulp mill effluent] but incorrect when he atttributed these results to AOX regulation. In fact, the driving force for the improved performance of pulp mills was dioxin and furan control ... When we chose dioxin and furan regulations, we were well aware of the relationship between AOX production and production of harmful chlorinated substances in pulp mill bleaching and we fully expected substantial reductions in all chlorinated substances to result from our regulation." The last sentence is the key to the regulatory strategy championed by Carey and adopted by Environment Canada some years earlier. Carey also noted that industry had "publicly stated that they will act to eliminate the effects when we have identified the most appropriate way for them to do it" and that the federal government and industry were discussing incentive programs to explore effluent-free technology. In fact, a memorandum of understanding had been signed by the government of Canada and the Pulp and Paper Research Institute that future research efforts would be directed towards developing technologies for closed-loop circuits. Then, in November 1994, DFO finalized criteria for the reopening of contaminated fisheries in BC And, in February 1995, some areas closed to fishing owing to dioxin/furan contamination were reopened. Several more coastal and river fisheries were reopened or upgraded in the following months and BC's Ministry of Environment, Lands and Parks reported that the pulp and paper industry was a year ahead of schedule in eliminating the whole class of organochlorines by 2002.[80] On the other side of the border, it was reported that the EPA had removed dioxin advisories on fifteen water bodies since 1991.

That same month, at the Environmental Fate and Effects of Bleached Pulp Mill Effluents conference in Vancouver, a scientific consensus emerged that organochlorine was not the sole, or even the main, cause of effects in fish.[81] In response to the conference discussions, BC Environment Minister Moe Sihota said: "If the science on this issue crystallizes, one is never averse to reconsideration." However, he also noted that until all the evidence was in, he preferred to err on the side of caution rather than rewrite the province's pulp and paper regulations in the face of developing science. In addition, environmentalists pointed to the scientific uncertainties highlighted at the conference, including the non-chlorinated compound believed to be causing effects in fish. Pulp industry executives attending the conference indicated that the latest findings "add urgency to the work of developing effluent-free mills."[82]

A January 1995 "w5" show entitled "Science vs. Politics" opened with the following characterization of the AOX/chlorine debate by commentator Eric Malling: "Hang science, the politics, it seems, just ploughs ahead. This reprise takes place in BC, but across the country we're spending billions on environmental faith and dogma with little regard for effectiveness."[83] In response to criticism of the BC government's stance on AOX from fellow interviewee Dr Keith Solomon, the province's (then) environment minister, Moe Sihota, also a guest on the program, claimed: "The overwhelming preponderance of science is saying that the direction the government is moving in is correct. I should have brought every study that is on my side of this thing, versus the side that you will now advocate, and then stacked them on the table, which I did a couple of months ago for industry. And I had about four feet on this side and they had about four inches."[84] For his part, Dr Solomon noted: "there are a number of interest groups out there that have agendas and beliefs that they take to the public, and the public likes them because they're often simplistic and easy, but this becomes faith, it becomes religion, it becomes perception, but most of the time it's not science."

On 13–15 March 1995, the American Forest and Paper Association's annual Paper Week Conference took place, reiterating the benefits of Elemental Chlorine-Free (ECF) bleaching based on chlorine dioxide technology for the environment. Market figures showed that demand for Totally Chlorine-Free Pulp (TCF) had not taken off as some had expected. The Alliance for Environmental Technology (AET), in a news release of 11 April 1995, claimed that whereas ECF pulp had captured 40 per cent of the world pulp market, TCF market share remained negligible, at less than 7 per cent.[85] Moreover, research into TCF bleaching was showing that the TCF process would increase wood consumption by 9 to 11 per cent because of lower pulp yields.[86]

Also in April, about five hundred scientists and technical experts debated the merits of TCF vs. ECF pulping processes at the pulp and paper industry's International Non-Chlorine Bleaching Conference in Amelia Island. Many agreed that the future was dim for TCF pulp, as TCF bleaching appeared to offer no water quality improvements over the ECF method. Instead, the use of substitution of chlorine dioxide in the paper-making process appeared to address dioxin problems sufficiently. A spokesperson from the American Forest and Paper Association noted: "Ninety percent of our mills are now at non-detect levels of dioxin." The executive director of AET claimed that "ECF is the answer to the riddle of dioxin" and said further, "ECF bleaching has a number of advantages ... It makes strong pulp, which enables the material to be recycled more often. It is more economical to manufacture, and it preserves forest wood resources because not as much wood is needed to make the same amount of paper ... If all of North America's bleached pulp mills were TCF, an additional 100 million mature trees would be required for today's pulp and paper market."[87]

CONCLUDING OBSERVATIONS: TOWARDS THE MINIMUM IMPACT MILL

The AOX case is marked by many of the usual features of environmental policy controversies: first, sharply polarized stakeholder viewpoints; second, some significant uncertainties in the cause-effect relationships for environmental impacts; and third, massive investments in both basic research and environmental monitoring which often do not seem clearly directed towards broadly acceptable policy solutions. The unique feature in the case of pulp mill effluent, which compounds the general difficulties just mentioned, is the extraordinary complexity of the chemical composition of this effluent.

Indeed, the degree of scientific understanding concerning the environmental impact of the effluent constituents considered in the preceding chronology has differed considerably, as has the policy response of different levels of government in Canada. In the first stage, a scientific consensus concerning the acute toxicity of dioxins formed quickly and the political response in different jurisdictions was similar, if somewhat delayed. In the second, however, contradictory results from different studies attempting to determine the link between organochlorines and toxic effects resulted in some scientific uncertainty and, in this context, governments in Canada chose different approaches to the regulation of pulp mill effluent. Whereas the BC and Ontario governments chose to regulate on the basis of the AOX parameter, the federal government chose to focus on reducing acute toxicity through the regulation of specific endpoints and secondary treatment, while continuing its research and gathering of data. In the third stage, a scientific consensus developed that a non-chlorinated substance, Compound x, was still causing effects in fish even when chlorinated substances were greatly reduced in effluent. This consensus appears to have solidified at a 1997 Science and AOX workshop sponsored by COFI and attended by environmental representatives, the major pulp unions, and provincial environmental officials.

This scientific consensus did not result, however, in any overt change in government policies. The federal government continues its research and monitoring efforts, but British Columbia's zero AOX regulation has become "an untouchable political symbol," at least for the government now in power.[88] Ironically, the industry's efforts to decrease the AOX content per tonne of pulp have already resulted in an industry average of 0.5 kg/ADT, which is lower than the limit recently imposed by the US Environmental Protection Agency in their pulp mill effluent regulations.[89] Finally, there simply does not exist suitable market interest in TCF pulp. Thus, the BC government – if it upheld the zero AOX goal – would be forcing the province's pulp industry to produce a product (TCF pulp) for which there are no buyers. In Ontario, the Conservative Harris government has declined to enforce the AOX regulations inherited from the New Democrats and has officially abandoned the zero AOX goal.[90] However, the existing requirement of 0.8 kg/ADT remains in place, and there are indications that the Ontario industry is already in compliance.

The BC Council of Forest Industries commissioned another AOX report in August 1999, which concluded: "It is important, however, to re-visit the use of AOX beyond the year 2000, now that dioxins and furans have been eliminated as contaminants of concern." Other highlights of the report are:

- The great majority of mills in BC have less than 0.5 kg AOX/ADT in their final effluent.
- While there was an earlier correlation between the reduction in dioxins and furans or higher chlorinated phenolics and a decrease in AOX, a continued relationship is not expected between AOX in general and the toxicants of concern for ecosystem function and for higher, keystone predators.
- The focus of studies on pulp mill effluent effects has shifted away from chlorinated compounds to primarily non-chlorinated plant extractives and their transformation by-products, which are not included in the measurement of AOX. These other non-chlorinated compounds are of greater scientific concern.
- There is a misconception about the potential for biomagnification of all organochlorines, which appears to be the driver behind BC's zero AOX target.

- There is no way to define a single toxicological threshold for such a complex mix of potentially toxic and virtually non-toxic compounds, especially where the mix is likely to be different for each mill.

For nations (such as Canada) having a large pulp and paper sector, pulp mill effluent represents a significant regulatory challenge in the domain of industrial emissions. All the more problematic, therefore, is the fact that Canada is employing various regulatory strategies which do not appear to constitute a cohesive policy vision guiding the future activities – including the research and development, capital investments, and environmental priorities – of this industry sector. Different policy routes have been followed and argued over, but neither the strategies employed by the federal government nor those of provincial governments deal with the specific nature of the effluent problem as it was known as of 1992. Nor do these various strategies in combination provide a policy framework for the industry now.

The federal government, having opted for the route of controlling acute effluent toxicity through the Pulp and Paper Effluent Regulations (PPER) requirement that secondary treatment be implemented in mills as well as through the dioxins and furans regulation, has achieved the environmental benefits it sought through this regulatory approach. Almost all effluents are non-acutely lethal to fish on a regular basis, and discharges of chlorinated dioxins and furans have been sharply reduced; as a result, closed fisheries have been reopened. However, Environment Canada has known for more than five years that there is residual toxicity when dioxins and furans are at non-detectable levels and it is not clear what policy framework is in place to respond to that knowledge. Certainly, PPER and the dioxin/furan regulations were not designed to eliminate all of the chronic, sublethal effects caused by pulp mill effluents.

The EEM program and continuing research at NWRI are geared towards evaluating current regulations and providing direction for future regulation of specific endpoints, if any.[91] Interim Cycle 2 EEM results for Ontario mills suggest substantial improvement in effluent quality, although different types of secondary treatment processes appear to be linked to different levels of sublethal effects. The EEM results appear to be providing some very important information about the relationship between individual facilities and their receiving environment. It would also appear, as with ARET (see chapter 9), that some are now advocating the adoption of an "environmental management systems" approach, to further reduce outstanding impacts and tie environmental improvement specifically to mill processes. The focus appears to be shifting to a more holistic approach to environmental management by individual mills (taking into account the impacts on all environmental media).

Yet, some policy discussion concerning future directions for the industry is required; the "more research is needed" mantra is not itself a policy choice. Certainly the policy options in environmental regulation must be informed by pertinent scientific findings, but this does not mean that all policy discussion must be on hold indefinitely (science is endless, of course). At the same time, however, those who have remained committed to regulating via the AOX parameter have not addressed the pointed scientific critiques, by NWRI's John Carey and others, directed at the AOX-based approach. These critiques have shown that *all* of the environmental benefits contemplated in the AOX-based approach are already achieved in the dioxins and furans regulation. The consensus of scientists is that, below the levels of AOX already achieved a number of years ago, there is no incremental environmental benefit gained from further AOX reductions. Judging from what is on the public record, nothing is being done to formulate the policy choices that can deal with the residual toxicity in pulp mill effluent.

The inescapable fact is that there is an unknown compound or combination of compounds in pulp mill effluent which continues to affect aquatic life. Moreover, toxicity *per se* is only one of the problems; other effects also may be of importance. More generally, and more fundamentally, the currently dominant approach of searching for the particular compound or compounds having an impact on the ecosystem represents an end-of-pipe mentality rather than a pollution prevention approach. Even the AOX regulation represents the mind-set that, if the right compound can be discovered, monitored, and treated, the problem will be solved. What is needed, however, is a broader, longer-term, preventative approach.

The chronology presented above indicates that the emphasis on scientific research increasingly has been accompanied by a search for achieving a technological solution through closed-loop systems. A March 1996 paper from H.A. Simons, "Mill Applications of Closed-Cycle Technology," reviewed developments in closed-loop technology to date. The paper provided details of mill applications of closed-cycle technology, by organization and mill, in the US, Sweden, and Finland, and pointed out that there were a number of bleached kraft mills currently pursuing closed-cycle operation, including some with and some without ClO_2, and with and without ozone as bleaching agents. Tentative plans for increasing bleach plant closure were being conducted for many mills to identify options and develop strategies on a mill-specific basis, though these studies were generally confidential. The authors noted, however, that a number of technical challenges to total closure remained, specifically in the areas of reducing water use to enable collection and treatment, and dealing with the corrosive effects of recycling chemicals, referred to as "cationic trash," on mill equipment. Moreover, recent research being carried out at Queen's University on the recycling of wastewater through mill equipment indicates that there may be some problems in this area as well.[92]

In current discussions of systems closure, the term "zero discharge" often comes to the fore. This concept is problematic, however. Zero may seem an attractive policy choice for many people because of its simplicity and popularity with the public. As a regulatory goal, however, "zero" is very difficult to work with and raises unrealistic expectations on the part of politicians, citizens, and interest groups. What technology would one base a zero discharge requirement on, as technology is constantly changing? In addition, has it been determined from an overall perspective that zero discharge is desirable in terms of energy utilization and other impacts? Moreover, will a movement to zero discharge make some of the investments in pollution control equipment already made by industry potentially redundant? These questions remain unanswered.

Some have embraced the concept of "minimum impact manufacturing." The "minimum impact mill" has been defined as one which:

- maximizes pulp yield and produces high-quality products that are easily recyclable, and/or safely combustible;
- maximizes the energy potential of the biomass;
- minimizes water consumption;
- minimizes wastes – gaseous, liquid, and solid – and disposes of them optimally;
- optimizes capital investment; and
- creates sustainable value to shareholders, customers, and employees, and to local, regional, and national communities.[93]

The minimum impact mill is not one which strives to achieve zero discharge; in fact, it does not confine itself to dealing with effluent. Instead, it is one which minimizes all releases from the pulping and recovery processes.

The minimum impact approach, if it is indeed the appropriate strategy to achieve our environmental protection goals (which remains to be seen), would require that both short- and longer-term goals are set for the industry; in other words, that a policy vision is formulated for the pulp and paper industry in Canada. Precisely this is lacking. Neither the federal nor the provincial governments have constructed such a policy vision. Some federal funds have been devoted to systems closure technology, but it is unclear to what extent and at what speed the federal government desires that industry move in this direction. Proponents of regulating on the basis of the AOX parameter argue that freeing pulping systems from a reliance on chlorine will also remove one of the major barriers to systems closure. Proponents of the minimum impact approach argue that the elimination of chlorine compounds from processes is "not necessary for environmental protection, nor is it necessarily the place to start" as "both ECF and TCF based bleaching strategies are compatible with a high degree of system closure."[94] Still others point to investments already made and currently being made by industry to comply with existing regulations at the federal and provincial levels and ask if they will be wasted.

What we have at present is a collection of regulations placing restrictions on different endpoints. And not only do we not know where we are going, but we do not know how to get there. We do not have in place some type of stakeholder consensus-building process which might address these outstanding issues and questions and aid governments in defining a policy direction for the coming years. Pulp mill effluent regulation in Canada is another example of wandering in the policy wilderness.

PART TWO

Governments in the Labyrinth

7 Between Expertise and Bureaucracy: Trapped at the Interface of Science and Policy

INTRODUCTION

Environmental policy and its stepchild, environmental risk management, wander the political landscape in permanent disarray, hounded by coteries of special interests awaiting the next swing of the public mood in their favour. There are two very different reasons for the disarray. One has to do with the irreducible uncertainties in environmental risk assessments, which for the most part forestall clear attributions of blame for harm done and, often, even a clear sense of just how serious the hazard itself might be. (Was it seals or birds which ripped out the stomachs of the Atlantic cod strewn on the ocean floor that were pictured in a notorious videotape shown by Newfoundland's minister of environment?) The other is simply a reflection of the public's deep and abiding ambivalence about the need for environmental protection measures at all, when economic advantage beckons or remediation cost looms: Let's just get the gold out of the mine near Yellowknife, and worry later, if at all, about how to deal with the huge repository of arsenic waste left behind when it closes or who should pay to clean it up.[1] Moreover, do grizzlies and cougars really need that much territory to call their own, if the land in question happens to include the site of the proposed Cheviot Mine in Alberta?

For whereas the public is well aware these days that adequate health protection is expensive, the environment traditionally has been perceived as a "free good," there for the taking, which needs little regard from us and will always adjust somehow to the demands we place on its resources. Nature is nice to have, but we really don't see why we should have to pay to use it.

Judged by the way we ordinarily behave in such matters, it appears that to many of us the need for assiduous environmental management is rather dubious, and the reasons why we should care all that much about human impacts on nature not very clear or compelling at all. Then why was the renewal of what is actually a rather inconsequential piece of federal legislation, the Canadian Environmental Protection Act (CEPA), so bitterly contested for so long during the 1990s, among the phalanx of federal departments; in the social arena, particularly between environmental groups and industry; and, rarest of sights, even publicly among politicians within the governing party? Since so little turns on the outcome – a reflection of the minor role in environmental management assigned to the federal power by the Canadian constitution – what explains the passion? And was it really a passion play at all, or rather just a political soap opera, since the roles of the actors seemed so conventionally scripted and the story-line took so painfully long to unfold?[2]

The answer is that what we observed in the battle over CEPA was a symbolic contest, and this is the type of contest about which an essentially peaceful people, such as Canadians are, can get very excited. (Other examples that spring to mind are the protection of Canadian culture and the definition of an authentic Quebecker.) The essence of symbolic contests is the disparity between the scale of portentous rhetoric and the lack of any perceptible changes in the prevailing state of affairs after each episode is finished. After six years of agony the new CEPA turned out to be pretty much like the old CEPA with a few new bells and whistles added.

In everyday life, Canadians appear to be highly ambivalent about environmental issues. On the one hand, in recent times these issues dropped far down the citizens' list of political and social priorities for action by governments, seemingly overwhelmed by concerns over employment security, health care, balanced budgets, and national unity.[3] Yet the public polling experts who track the shifting sentiments of our citizens insist that those same issues remain "top of mind," matters of deep and abiding concern, ready to be transformed at any time into broadly based demands for resolute actions to "clean up" the environment. The president of the polling firm Environics told a meeting of the National Round Table on Environment and the Economy in spring 1998 that 73 per cent of those surveyed said they would choose environmental protection over economic growth, if the two conflicted, and he predicted that the next "great green wave" would hit the political system early in the new century.[4] We shall see.

Looked at from the standpoint of national politics and the federal policy-making capacity, the public management of environmental issues goes beyond mere ambivalence and approaches a state of acute schizophrenic disorder. As noted in the 1999 *Report* to the House of Commons by Canada's commissioner of environment and sustainable development, "federal departments are deeply divided on many key issues. They do not share a common vision of how toxic substances should be managed. They disagree strongly on such issues as the degree of risk posed by some industrial chemicals, the interpretation of federal policy and the need to take action on it, the relative merits of voluntary and regulatory controls, and their own respective roles and accountabilities."[5]

Although surely we cannot be unaware of how prominent environmental issues are or can become in these times, in Canada we appear to wander into their orbit half-consciously, as if sleepwalking. Think of the implausible federal-provincial "agreement" on climate change thrown together just before Canada sent its negotiators off to Kyoto in 1997, which had begun to unravel before their flight landed; or the half-hearted regulatory oversight of Ontario Hydro's nuclear plants; or the regrettable decision to exempt the sale of CANDU reactors to China from an appropriate risk assessment; or just nonsensical little things, such as the abortive attempts to ban the export of PCB wastes or the import of the gasoline additive MMT. Not entirely surprisingly, these episodes in the decade just ended turn out to be symptomatic of more general underlying weaknesses in our policy-making competence in environmental matters, weaknesses that have plagued us for many years. Some of them are listed in the following paragraphs.[6]

POLITICALLY INDUCED ORGANIZATIONAL
CHAOS AT ENVIRONMENT CANADA

This department, already among the smallest in the federal system, suffered severe personnel and budgetary reductions under "program review" during the first Liberal mandate in the 1990s. These cuts exacerbated the long-standing structural woes of Environment Canada as a department – the adding and subtracting of bits and pieces from other departments, the revolving door of ministers, and, above all, the endless turf battles with other departments.[7] These bureaucratic troubles began with the creation of the department in 1971 and have persisted down to the present; they are politically induced in the sense that the core leadership of various prime ministers and their most powerful ministers, in both governing parties, never bestowed full legitimacy on the department's mandate, never gave it clear originating legislative authority, and never put it on a firm organizational footing.

During the 1990s, the seemingly endless review of the Canadian Environmental Protection Act was marked by some furious backstage bureaucratic manoeuvring between Environment Canada and the "resource management" departments (Natural Resources, Industry, and Agriculture), in particular over authority for the regulation of biotechnology products.[8] And although from an issue management standpoint Environment Canada should be the authoritative lead agency for global climate change policy, so far it has been forced to share this mandate awkwardly with Natural Resources Canada, which has quite different interests in this matter, producing at one point in time the embarrassing spectacle of then-Environment Minister Christine Stewart literally sitting speechless during Question Period in Parliament as this policy was being debated. Finally, Environment Canada "carried the can" on behalf of the entire federal system for one of the most humiliating political losses in recent memory, the withdrawal of the legislation banning MMT. The fragmentation of authority reaches into the departmental organization itself, where protracted turf warfare over the internal ownership of issues (such as pulp mill effluent) among Environment Canada headquarters and regional units is not uncommon.[9]

FEDERAL-PROVINCIAL JURISDICTIONAL SQUABBLES

The historical record in this matter is interesting, especially against the backdrop of the attempt to "harmonize" federal and provincial initiatives on environmental matters during the last few years. There is some reason to think that, if the so-called "harmonization initiative" succeeds, it would effect a restoration of the *status quo ante* in federal-provincial interjurisdictional relations in this domain. Before the period of endemic conflict between the two, the start of which, in the latter half of the 1980s, was marked by an assertion of a larger federal presence, the provinces had the leadership role in environmental regulation, with the federal government playing a "backup" role, especially in providing scientific research capabilities.[10] If we should witness such a restoration, it may not bode well for Environment Canada's situation in the context of the "program review" cuts carried out after 1993. Doern and Conway have described in detail how the department tried to wrap itself in the mantle of science before 1985, and how this strategy continually fell victim to the budget cutters.[11]

ENVIRONMENTAL ASSESSMENT GAMES

The long-overdue Canadian Environmental Assessment Act (CEAA) was finally proclaimed after many delays at the beginning of 1995 – yet it arrived, after a truly agonizing birth, over the strong objections of all provinces and the open defiance of Quebec in particular! Can we ever hope to get anything right in this area?[12]

The question is necessary because, simply stated, Canada has an embarrassing and consistent record of failures in credible environmental assessment for high-profile, large development projects, which include, in just the past few years alone, the "Windy Craggy" site and Alcan's "Kemano Completion Project," both in British Columbia, both of which have cost that province considerable sums in the way of monetary settlements and political capital. And there is the long-running Cheviot Mine saga in Alberta, where in a recent episode a federal court agreed with the claim by the Sierra Club of Canada, to the effect that a combined federal/provincial assessment panel did not carry out the act's requirements for a cumulative impact assessment.[13] Passage of the CEAA followed the farcical episodes in the 1980s involving the Rafferty-Alameda Dam in Saskatchewan and the Oldman River Dam in Alberta, where courts ordered environmental assessments to be done on major projects already under way, thus discrediting the assessment process itself, and where, in the first-mentioned case, "Canadians witnessed the spectacle of federal and provincial ministers challenging each other's version of a backroom deal in Court."[14] Since the act has not been fully tested yet, it is too early to tell whether we can hope ever to get anything right in this area. But the determined opposition of the provinces does not augur well for success.[15]

THE MYSTERIOUS FATE OF ECONOMIC INSTRUMENTS

Despite a steady stream of reports and studies, with overwhelmingly positive findings suggesting clear benefits from implementing this approach, Canada seems unable to take even the most tentative steps in the direction of using market-based instruments for environmental regulation (e.g., tax regimes, emissions trading). Why not?

The concepts on which such instruments are based have been around for at least twenty-five years.[16] In 1992 Environment Canada issued a comprehensive discussion paper, entitled "Economic Instruments for Environmental Protection." In November 1994 the Department of Finance and Environment Canada issued "Economic Instruments and

Disincentives to Sound Environmental Practices," the output of a multisectoral task force. In all of these sources can be found strong reasons for utilizing market-based instruments. In June 1995 the House of Commons Standing Committee on Environment and Sustainable Development said, "the Committee strongly urges the federal government to continue the important work begun by the Task Force to ensure that barriers are eliminated and appropriate economic instruments are implemented."[17]

Despite all this, for all practical purposes, *nothing has been done.* How many more reports will be commissioned, laboured over, submitted, and praised, only to be shelved by policy makers?[18] Canada's ill-prepared state in this respect is now much more serious than in the past, since emissions trading regimes will be a crucial part of global action on reductions in greenhouse gas emissions. The promise to utilize economic instruments has been reiterated once again in the brand-new Canadian Environmental Protection Act; does this mean that we shall actually see some of them in operation before, say, the onset of the fourth millennium?

THE TENSION BETWEEN SCIENCE AND POLICY

Is it reasonable to think that environmental policy should be "science-driven," in the sense that "good policies" ought to be rooted in "good science"? Or, in other words, that "ecosystem management" – which means regulating human impacts on the biosphere in such a way as to assure a sustained basis for the satisfaction of human needs – should be based on ecosystem science, that is, a detailed understanding of how ecosystem interactions among species and their habitats actually happen?

It is certainly true in general that, if we wish to do intelligent ecosystem management, we must have a continuous growth in our scientific understanding of ecosystem dynamics. But this is not the same thing as saying that ecosystem science can or ought to be the *primary "driver"* of – as opposed to being a *primary component of* – environmental policy making. The reasons are fairly straightforward, and among them are the following. First, policy requires "yes/no" decisions, whereas science often is continually evolving from one level of uncertainty to another (in many cases, the more we learn, the more questions we have). Second, and even more important, environmental policy making is often driven in a political context by just those issues for which we have at that time the most imperfect scientific understanding. (The anthropogenic contribution to global climate change and the possible health effects of radio-frequency fields are two current cases in point.) As a general rule, the cause-and-effect pathways in broad ecosystem impacts are difficult enough to isolate scientifically, whereupon there is added the further requirements of a level of "proof" that will satisfy evidentiary standards for legal and regulatory purposes that have been adapted from quite different realms.

Third, environmental issues usually lack "immediacy" in that they are based on long-term trends, whereas, in the total context of government policy making, economic, jurisdictional, political, legal, and other factors have a stark immediacy that simply cannot be overlooked by politicians. In this context, policies driven primarily by long-term ecosystem trends framed within inevitable scientific uncertainties are doomed to disappointment or crippling compromise. None of this means that science is irrelevant to the environmental policy-making process, however. But these factors do point to the tendency for science to become entangled within the nets of institutional inertia and interest-group conflict. These nets become "policy traps" which can lead to protracted policy warfare; a prime example is toxic substances policy, which is discussed at length in the following chapter.

This entanglement in policy traps has had and continues to have a telling impact on the organizational structure of government departments of the environment everywhere, but perhaps on none more than Environment Canada. As Doern and Conway have shown, "the DOE from the outset ... saw its scientific and technical capacity as a central pillar of its hoped-for influence."[19] DOE (Environment Canada) filled its professional staff slots with scientists, sought to align many of its program delivery functions in terms of the scientific description of reality, and sent forth these highly trained legions into policy battles – but it was unable to "translate" scientific competence into policy competence, as perceived by many others within the federal bureaucracy: "[To] the rest of the Ottawa system, the [DOE policy] ideas seemed too quixotic and intermittent, too frequently unrelated to economic realities, and too uninformed by a coherent view of where the DOE ought to be going."[20]

To the extent to which the scientific personnel drop their primary focus on actually doing scientific research, and get drawn into protracted policy warfare, they are asked to perform functions for which they have had no decent training or experiential background whatsoever, becoming easy prey for the professional policy specialists in the system, especially those who haunt the central agencies of government. And to the extent that they retain a primary focus on remaining practitioners of ongoing scientific practice, they are often ill equipped to negotiate safely the quicksands of policy development.[21] The lesson for

Environment Canada is that scientific competence alone is not a sufficient basis for policy influence. Indeed, policy competence, which means being able to find ways to defeat institutional barriers to needed changes in our ways of doing business, is probably independent of scientific competence, even in environmental management.[22]

We find a clue to the supposition that something important is going on here in the low credibility that governments today generally have in the eyes of citizens. Governments (and those working for them, including scientists) are not perceived to be "neutral" in matters such as environmental management, or to be positioned "above the fray" in relation to conflicts among interest groups in society. Instead, government scientists share a relatively low credibility ranking with their compatriots in industry, while environmental groups occupy with academics the upper end of the spectrum, apparently because both are perceived to be "disinterested" parties. The relative standings are shown in results from surveys.[23] (See figure 3.)

Of all the actors portrayed here, only governments have seen their standing change materially over the last two decades, dropping from the top to the bottom half of the perceived credibility spectrum, where they now appear to be stuck. This credibility problem limits the room governments have to manoeuvre through difficult policy issues, especially those at the interface of science and policy.

The discussion to follow contends that, as recent experience in Canada shows, there is some serious misalignment in the interplay between science and public policy within government. Indeed, one might conclude that the two appear to be fundamentally incompatible with each other, so much so that their respective outcomes could be expected to dovetail only by pure chance. This experience is useful, for it tells us that an old pattern – where government departments do scientific work directly which is then applied to policy choices – is obsolete. The case for a new paradigm is argued here, one where governments manage health and environmental risks, and draw upon independent scientific bodies for the risk assessment expertise they need in order to carry out their risk management mandate effectively. The strict institutional separation of science and policy is good for both of them. Science is only useful to policy when it is completely true to itself, which requires autonomy in the setting of research questions and an unconstrained peer-review and publications process, with its often brutal questioning of methods, experimental procedures, and findings. On the other hand, even in the area of health and environmental risk management, where scientific research is indispensable to sensible decision making, good policy does not and cannot flow automatically from science itself.

Figure 3
Credibility of scientists by affiliation

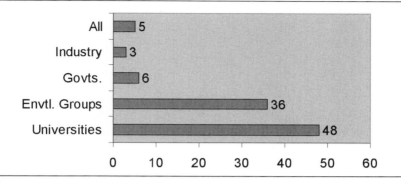

Source: Environics Environmental Monitor Survey, December 1993.

In what I call the older model, governments thought it wise to provide for in-house science expertise so as to translate risk assessments into policy choices for everything from food safety to wildlife conservation. Like everything else in the civil service bureaucracy, the scientific advice was given in secret and was thus unchallengeable by the public, a fact which was especially useful for covering up the existence of huge uncertainties and the lack of essential data to support a preferred policy choice. Although the risk management decisions emanating from this model had some successes as well as spectacular failures, other changes in society now have rendered it obsolete.

The newer and still-emerging model requires that governments should concentrate on being accountable for managing risks, especially where the risk factors are publicly controversial – a duty that is generally discharged poorly these days – and leave the provisioning of science relevant to those risk factors to independent institutions. In fact until the realization dawns about where the real duty of governments lies in the area of health and environmental risk management, we will continue to waste scarce resources on sub-optimal risk reduction ventures. Until governments are able to focus their attention on their inescapable duty to carry out credible risk management, and to staff their professional ranks with the requisite skills for this purpose (which a training in the sciences alone cannot provide), they will not have resolved the real nature of the dilemmas that exist for them at this zone of the science/policy interface.

These issues are attracting a good deal of attention within government these days. In 1999 the government of Canada's Council of Science and Technology Advisors (CSTA) issued a report entitled "Science Advice for Government Effectiveness."[24] The governments of the UK and New Zealand also have sponsored some important new work in this same area, and the US National Academy of Sciences regularly issues relevant reports as well.[25] Clearly this subject is recognized widely among Western governments as one of current and pressing importance. The CSTA report, for example, provides clear guidance with respect to some of the most important principles and best practices relating to the procurement of expert advice by governments. However, it is also painfully obvious in this report that Canadian governments are still very far from knowing confidently how to apply these principles under "real-world" circumstances in actual cases.[26] And there is an abundant supply of both recent and current cases, concentrated in the domain of risk management broadly defined, which, I suggest, is just the domain where problems in the science/policy interface have the most onerous and expensive consequences for governments. One important reason for this is that risk management is decision making under uncertainty; the relevant uncertainties are often quite large, which is a problem for citizens because risks cause people to worry. "Good policy" should seek to fill the blanks represented by those uncertainties, by managing well the *issues* that arise while scientists work to reduce the scope of the uncertainties. Alas, this simply doesn't happen. In the following pages I suggest how serious this shortcoming is, by way of urging that further work be done on closing the gap between theory and practice in this area.

SCIENCE VS. POLICY

Three fisheries scientists created a stir some time ago when they published a journal article entitled "Is Scientific Inquiry Incompatible with Government Information Control?"[27] What was perhaps most surprising about the ensuing contretemps was that anyone thought that the question itself was scandalous – or that the answer to it was less than obvious. The answer to the question they posed is "Yes": Of course scientific inquiry is incompatible with the management of information within government bureaucracies. The fact that the question even had to be posed provides the backdrop for this chapter.

Perhaps the source of misunderstanding lies not in some uncertainty about the nature of scientific inquiry, but rather in an unfamiliarity with the needs of governments as they pertain to the use of information (including scientific research findings) in public policy formation. In this latter domain there is no question whatsoever that good government practice requires that the bureaucracies which serve ministers manage the flow of policy-relevant information.[28] A look at any major policy issue in the broad area of health and environmental risk management will confirm the truth of this contention.[29] If we consider for the moment only the aspect of uncertainty in risk analysis, and ignore all other dimensions of risk management, we can see why the policy development process must include information management.

In most cases where public concern about risk factors leads to demands for government action, there are insufficiently definitive results in the risk analysis to justify a single path of risk control at any particular time. (This uncertainty can persist for decades, even where expensive, large-scale research programs are under way; some illustrations are given later.) In other words, reasonable persons legitimately can and will disagree on the type of policies and control measures (including none at all) that are called for, on the basis of the "facts" or the evidence at hand, to protect human health and the environment.[30] To make intelligent policy choices under such circumstances, ministers and their senior advisors should hear vigorous arguments in favour of various interpretations of both the scientific data and the risk assessment assumptions, as well as the full range of risk control options and their likely impacts – economic, social, political, and institutional. Many risk issue domains are extremely contentious, where interested parties of all kinds have strongly opposed viewpoints and "solutions" which they are desirous of impressing upon governments. A sane policy development process must to some extent insulate itself from the rough play of social interests. To this end the policy-relevant information flow must be managed, by which I mean that confidentiality is needed during the policy deliberation period.[31]

That said, should these same policy advisors be running down the hallway to the offices of the government's own staff, in order to get a quick-and-dirty version of what the state of science is? No: at least, not any more. For it is naïve in the extreme to think that the institutional system of official bureaucracy, which has over the centuries raised the craft of information control to the level of high art, would shrink from doing everything in its power to shape and channel what it hears from its servants, whether they be scientists or janitorial staff.[32] Neither governments nor anyone else can do health and environmental risk management without the aid of science. However, in all risk management domains it is clearly in the interest of governments today, as well as of scientists, for that assistance to be provided in every instance at arm's length (and governments these days need scientists primarily for risk management). Science can serve policy best – indeed, can only serve it at all – in our era by coming to policy with expert advice from an independent standpoint.[33]

This was not necessarily always the case, for things have changed over the last thirty years or so, and there is a specific explanation as to why in our own era, and hereafter, only independent science can serve the needs of policy in risk management. There are two different reasons for this transition. One has to do with the different type of risk management challenges we face, and the other with the changing role of the public and interest groups, including their access to expertise in risk matters.[34]

THE OLDER MODEL: SCIENCE IN THE (SECRET) SERVICE OF POLICY

In the older model, beginning in the early twentieth century and continuing through the 1980s, government-employed scientists in both regulatory and non-regulatory matters produced confidential risk assessments that became the basis of policy choices.[35] In the cases of ministries responsible for natural resources, such as agriculture, forestry, fisheries, mining, and wildlife, the government-owned scientific research establishments could be (and sometimes still are) substantial indeed. These establishments generally worked in applied science areas, ultimately in the service of economic development; their specific tasks covered such areas as occupational health and safety, control of environmental factors (e.g., insect pests), and yield management.

The public health services were perhaps the only science-based government units that did not have primarily an economic development function under the older model. But there as elsewhere the refrain was and is the same, when public queries are raised: "Trust us, we (as scientists) have the necessary expertise and we also (as civil servants) have your best interests at heart. It is unnecessary for you to trouble yourselves about the messy details of scientific investigation or risk assessment – besides, you would be utterly unable to understand all this even if we tried to explain it. We can assure you that you are 'perfectly safe' [to use the line about British beef fed to politicians by their advisors during the BSE crisis]."

The only other institution which had complementary resources invested in applied science, as well as some basic science, was private industry. Thus in practice both the risk assessments and the risk control strategies – in the many cases where industry and government interests overlapped – were negotiated behind closed doors between these two parties. The innate secrecy of government bureaucracies was reinforced by industry's insistence that commercial confidentiality also was at stake in many cases. With respect to all health and environmental risk factors related to economic activity, which covers a huge range of such factors, there was and is a direct relationship between choices among risk control options, which for human health are primarily a matter of controlling exposures, and "the bottom line" for industry: generally speaking, the more stringent the risk control, the higher the monetary cost.

This direct relationship between risk and economic interest had a number of consequences. First, there was a strong urge not to know if unacceptable occupational or other risks were present. This urge was satisfied first by simple denial that evidence of harm existed; second, by demands for proof of cause-and-effect relations (and a legal standard of proof at that), where any sort of proof was difficult or impossible to obtain; or third, by blaming the victim (for carelessness at work or immoral behaviour at leisure). So the scope of the damage only emerged after the fact, when the body count could be tracked in epidemiological data. Typical of this pattern was the finding of a significant correlation between vinyl chloride and liver cancer in rubber-plant workers; after the studies were done, the exposure limits were lowered. Most of the effective standards for occupational exposure to both natural and industrially created hazards that we have today came about in this way.[36]

The older model remains strong. Within the past decade there is no better example than the mismanagement of the risk of "mad cow disease" (bovine spongiform encephalopathy, BSE) by the UK Ministry of Agriculture, Fisheries, and Food. The new type of pathogen that is implicated in this disease remains a great challenge for scientific research itself. But the public risk management of the disease was fatally compromised by other agents entirely, namely, the pathological secretiveness of the British bureaucracy, aided and abetted by the farm lobby, which feared for its livelihood and conspired to bring down ruin upon itself.[37] Every stage of the work of British government scientists over the decade 1986–96 was tainted by the overriding "policy" need for information control, accompanied by completely ineffective animal disease control measures, blockage of access to information for external researchers, misuse of uncertainties, and, above all, provisioning of false reassurances of "safety" to the public.

It is perhaps too easy to list the high-profile events of a similar nature in Canada during the preceding two decades: the catastrophic contamination of the blood supply from the viruses that cause AIDS and hepatitis C; the vanishing of the North Atlantic cod, originally a natural resource of prodigious abundance; the imperilled state of the equally prodigious Pacific salmon fishery; and the fact that the safety and performance status of Ontario Hydro's nuclear power system appears to have been a mystery to the engineers who ran it.[38] In all of these cases, government-controlled science had some role to play, if not as the author of the tragedy, then at least in failing to prevent it. In some of these cases a noisy cabal made up of provincial governments, industry, and labour also sought to ensure that no one looked too closely at the uncertainties in the risk assessments.

A bitter controversy surrounds the case of the Atlantic fishery, but in my opinion a strong and plausible case has been made for the view that Canadian fisheries science was abused over a long period of time as a result of short-sighted economic and political considerations.[39] In the case of the Atlantic cod fishery the indictment is a severe one: "Nonscientific influences on fisheries research incompatible with normal scientific inquiry included: (i) government denunciation of independent work, (ii) misrepresentation of alternative hypotheses, (iii) interference in scientific conclusions, (iv) disciplining of scientists who communicated publicly the results of peer-reviewed research, and (v) misrepresentation of the scientific basis of public reports and government statements."[40] None of the replies published to date seriously challenge the evidentiary basis of this indictment, and those taking the contrary position are content to make light of the complainants' alleged belief in a right to do "pure science" while being supported from the public purse.[41]

And whereas the Atlantic cod fishery débâcle has garnered most of the attention to date, many are perhaps unaware that Hutchings et al. examine another case in their article, namely, the fate of fisheries science over a period of more than a decade during Alcan's ill-fated "Kemano Completion Project" in British Columbia. Here the evidence of bureaucratic interference with scientific evaluation is, if anything, even stronger than in the case of the Atlantic cod fishery – indeed, the political pressures on government fisheries scientists in this case displayed unrelenting contempt for the work of science.[42]

The most significant failure of the older model, however, was in the domain of occupational health and safety, and no case illustrates this better than asbestos risk. As it developed under the older model, asbestos was an appalling story of deceit and cover-up for a lethal occupational risk, as awful diseases took their toll on thousands of workers and their families. When the full history of this tragedy finally emerged into the light of day, largely as a result of class-action litigation in the United States, we understood how industry science had concealed what it knew and feared, and how governments committed to economic and technological benefits had turned a blind eye to the human health costs.[43] In the area of environmental risks, pesticide regulation provides the best example: until the early 1980s decisions emerged from a secretive and cozy relationship between industry and government scientists, and those who dared to dissent, such as Rachel Carson in *Silent Spring*, were subjected to frenetic attack. And of course the Long March of tobacco industry prevarication, helped along by legions of politicians, shows best the uses to which a science crafted in secrecy can be put.[44]

Sometimes the failings under the older model take a tragicomic form, although the show still can be expensive for the public to watch, as the notorious case of MMT (chapter 4) demonstrates well. All in all, this was a very ugly business. What if the government had chosen from the beginning to play out the confrontation between science and policy in full public view, rather than behind closed doors? What if the government simply had asked two different and equally independent scientific panels – one on health and environmental risk issues, the other on risk to the emissions systems – to review the scientific basis of the various positions? And if it had done so sometime before making up its mind to pass legislation in this area?[45]

It would be churlish not to concede that the older model was – and is – capable of achieving outstanding results and of serving the public interest. An excellent example of this in recent times is the work of Environment Canada scientists on environmental impacts of pulp mill effluent, as we saw in chapter 6. Strong initiatives by that department beginning in the late 1980s had been concentrated on ensuring sharp reductions in dioxin and furan residues in the effluent, and the departmental scientists came to the conclusion that their approach in this matter provided a wide range of environmental benefits, especially in controlling the production and release of chlorinated organic compounds generally. By the early 1990s they had decided that further attention to chlorinated organics derived from industrial sources alone – the so-called "AOX parameter" – was unwise, and they turned their attention to other substances (including natural sources) in the effluent which were still giving rise to unacceptable levels of adverse impacts on aquatic organisms. This stance proved unpopular with those who believe that industrial chemicals alone are the root of all evils, and some nasty confrontations ensued, during which the integrity of the government scientists was unfairly called into question. These scientists stood their ground, however, and in subsequent years the consensus of expert opinion supported their position.

So there were notable successes as well as failures in the older model, bringing gradual and important improvements in managing risks. There were many dedicated scientists and regulators in both government and industry who waged campaigns for more enlightened practices out of public view. Especially notable have been the conservation biologists in fish and game departments, who often were leaders in the fight for protection of wildlife and its habitat. The fact that this older model is obsolete is not the result of its high-profile failures, all of which simply illustrate its inadequacies without proving its inherent unworkability. The need for a new model is grounded elsewhere: in the changing capabilities of the public and public-interest groups with respect to expertise; in the nature of the specific risk management challenges that we face now and will face even more in the future; in the merging of disparate risk issue domains into a unified sequence of both opportunities and resource constraints for optimal risk reduction programs; and finally, in our relation to the environment and its resources itself. In every one of these four dimensions, in the zone where science and policy meet, an independent science is more useful and indeed necessary than is a government-employed science.

We face utterly different risk management challenges now as compared to the past. This changes the roles of both science and government, and the relationship between them, at the science/policy interface. I shall explain this change with reference to the four dimensions listed above.

TRANSITION TO THE NEW MODEL

1 The Public and Interest Groups

With few exceptions (notably in the public health area), neither individual members of the general public nor public-interest advocacy groups can or did interfere with the secret service of science to policy under the older model. This began to change in the late 1970s, beginning in the United States, although it will be some time yet before that change is complete. One of the notable steps, for example, was the victory in 1984 by the US Natural Resources Defense Council, when it persuaded the federal courts to crack open the long-standing, secretive process of pesticide registration.[46] Now in the United States major advocacy groups regularly take on both industry and governments over health and environmental risk management, and (as we saw in chapter 2) some like Greenpeace operate on a global scale.

The effective newer players have the resources to bring their own staff scientists to the table and to confront the original participants on equal terms. Industry has adapted to the new rules, but, by and large, governments have not, for they are caught between their original mandate and their new one. In the former (which has evaporated), governments were the sole players with scientific competence representing the public interest; in the new one governments must act as brokers in risk controversies (including brokering the different representations of science offered by other players), a role that requires a completely different set of professional skills. These skills are not now widely available in the ranks of civil servants, alas.

Over the past few decades, university-based scientists have taken on intervener roles in risk controversies, both as members of independent expert panels and also as individuals with strong views on appropriate risk management. New journal publications also try to bring science to a broader public. But as well, and increasingly, individual members of the public who do not necessarily have scientific expertise, but who have concerns about risk issues, use Internet resources to gather information, establish contact with like-minded people everywhere on the globe, ask questions of experts, and prepare themselves to become skilled interveners in risk controversies, as in the case of the radio-frequency fields issues reviewed in chapter 3. The information-search, documentary retrieval, and networking facilities of the Internet have huge advantages over earlier resources available to the general public, and these advantages will grow steadily in future years. From now on, all controversies over risk management decision making will be played out on a public stage with an international cast and audience.

The game is up for the older model. Today the only response that makes sense to the public's demands for a full accounting of the risk management decision making is to put all the science and the risk assessments "on the table."[47] As a practical matter, in all countries except the United States, government is the only party which can be accountable to the public for risk management decisions in the final analysis (because only in the US is it feasible for private groups to take on industry in the courts). But then governments cannot "do" the science itself, because today they will be perceived – and rightly so, in my opinion – to be an interested party in that regard.[48] And, because they are still staffed to carry out the older mandate rather than the newer one, they have not been able to deliver – in many high-profile cases – credible risk management decisions to the public.

2 *The Changing Nature of Risk Management Challenges*

In Western industrial societies, with respect to the intrinsic difficulties of carrying out credible risk management decision making itself, all of the low-hanging fruit has been picked, so to speak: the easier victories have been won and the harder ones remain. These easier victories amounted to drawing firm conclusions from toxicology and epidemiology that unacceptable levels of risk exist, that exposures should be reduced, and that either governments or industry should pay the costs for risk reduction without further ado. Again, occupational risks provide the best illustration: for workplace accidents and for exposures to metals, hydrocarbons, minerals, heat, particulates, gases, and industrial chemicals of all kinds, unsafe conditions tolerated earlier by workers (primarily because they had no choice but to do so) and social institutions are no longer acceptable. Exposure to most of these same substances and new ones as well still occurs in industrial plants, but at levels many, many times lower than in the past.

These were relatively easy victories for risk management, but not in terms of the institutional battles that had to be waged to secure them. The direct relation between risk reduction and incremental cost was apparent to every industrial corporation. In the worst cases, such as the dye industry earlier and asbestos later on, every conceivable obstacle to risk reduction measures – advocated by labour unions and independent medical scientists – that could be devised by the industry's own scientists and lawyers was employed.[49] But the struggle was actually about the balance of power in society, not about competing risk assessment methodologies (although the latter could become implicated indirectly in it). The same was true in the case of public health: huge risk reductions and increments in human welfare were achieved at relatively low cost in the battle against infectious diseases.

Now our risk management battles are almost entirely different, sometimes because the risk reduction gains are purchased at much higher prices, but even more importantly because the reasons for carrying on the battles themselves are so much murkier.[50] This is a complex and contentious matter, so two examples must suffice.

The first is asbestos. Although the earlier occupational risk battles have been won, in the sense that industrial exposures in Western countries are now at levels considered to be appropriate, there remains much controversy over the risks to the general public posed by the continued marketing of asbestos products (which have many highly desirable and useful properties) and by the fact that the nearly indestructible asbestos fibres are found everywhere in our environment from past uses. It is not at all clear that anyone should worry about this level of risk, or that measures such as the removal of intact asbestos insulation from buildings are warranted, but the expert disagreement can be furious on these and other points.[51] It is also most unclear whether there are substitutes for asbestos that present lower levels of risk. Canadian governments have a high stake in these disputes, since Canada is one of the two largest exporters of asbestos in the world, and some countries have instituted total bans on the importation of asbestos products. But one lesson is already very clear: governments should stay out of direct involvement in the scientific research on asbestos hazards and allow the further studies by independent scientists to take their own course, wherever they may lead. Governments should confine their involvement to the risk management of asbestos, which takes the balance of expert opinion on acceptable risk into account, and factors in economics, relative risk, evaluation of substitutes, and so forth. In other words, they are accountable for deciding whether further risk reduction measures for asbestos are or are not warranted, and they can safely leave the ongoing scientific investigation of the health risk factors themselves to university-based experts.

Then there is the case of dioxin.[52] Publicly labelled "by far the most toxic compound known to mankind" by a US EPA scientist in 1974, dioxin (the shorthand name for several families of organochlorine compounds) became thereafter an emblem for the concerns about risks associated with industrially produced chemicals felt by many people, and especially about potential adverse health effects from toxins at extremely low doses. As is often the case, industry first learned about dioxin as a result of relatively high occupational exposures in chemical plants, often as a result of accidents; later there were other terrible accidents affecting the public, notably two in Asia involving contaminated rice oil, where thousands became ill. After a decade of new research in the 1970s, industry and governments began to act relatively quickly (compared with similar episodes in the past) to lower dioxin emissions from industrial facilities. For example, dioxin in pulp mill effluent became a public issue in 1987, and by 1995 Canadian mills in British Columbia had lowered such emissions by about 95 per cent. The North American chemical industry has taken similar steps. Scientific research has demonstrated that the total environmental burden of dioxin-like compounds, which had risen steadily around the world during most of the twentieth century, had begun a slow but uninterrupted decline around 1980.

But no one cheered, and the reason for this tells us a great deal about the systematic failure of governments to develop publicly credible risk management frameworks.[53] The absence of cheering can be explained thus: For something that is "by far the most toxic compound known to mankind," 95 per cent emissions reductions arguably are not good enough, and only 100 per cent will do; on this reasoning if entire industries (pulp mills or PVC plastic, say) must be shut down, no matter how many useful products they market, so be it. Yet there is no credible evidence at hand to suggest that either worker or public exposures to dioxin after 1980 represent an unacceptable level of risk. So why does the dioxin issue still have such a high profile on the public's risk agenda? The answer is that the scientific characterization of dioxin-like compounds (which by now must fill whole libraries) is exceedingly complex. Beginning around 1970, governments allocated substantial budgets to this scientific area, including their own expert staff resources. On the other hand, they allocated no resources whatsoever to an attempt to explain dioxin science and risk assessment credibly to the public, or to engage the public in a dialogue about dioxin risk.

And so the controversy goes on, apparently indefinitely, now accompanied by a related one, involving what are called "endocrine modulating substances," where there are also widespread fears of serious adverse health effects that may result from exposures to these substances at extremely low doses.[54] These can be expensive as well as frustrating episodes, because the costs for risk reduction rise exponentially as environmental concentrations of the targeted substances fall.[55] But we are condemned to go on along this path unless and until governments recognize that their real duty in this regard is to facilitate the public dialogue on risk rather than to help in doing the science.

3   The "Synthetic" Nature of Risk Management Today

Traditionally, government departments have been watertight compartments where ministers vigorously defend their allotted turf. Responsibility for risk management has been no exception to this rule.[56] This allocation of discrete mandates under the older model worked equally well for both the political order and the public interest, in so far as there were (as indicated earlier) notable successes in risk management. But whereas it still may provide comfort to civil servants and their political masters, it no longer serves the public interest at all, for reasons advanced in the preceding section: the nature of the most important risk management challenges facing governments has changed dramatically and permanently in the meantime.

During the first half of the twentieth century, the great victories that were won for risk reduction – in occupational health and safety, public health, air pollution, even environmental risks – , were achieved initially by dealing with each of them separately.[57] There are many reasons for this – for example, the fact that in each case the skills for characterizing very diverse types of hazards and for identifying sometimes convoluted routes of exposure (i.e., the toxicology and epidemiology) were still in their infancy. In addition, although governments had accepted responsibility for some types of hazards early on, such as infectious disease and threats to food safety, other mandates – especially for environmental risks – were added much later, layer by layer, down to the present. Now there is no significant risk factor in the lives of the population for which government cannot be expected to be called upon for a policy response.

The shift in the pattern of dominant risk factors themselves, as noted earlier, comes into play here. Now with far broader sets of responsibilities for risk management, with ever-increasing public expectations for risk control, and faced with the iron law of exponentially mounting costs for incremental risk reduction, in principle governments should look at risk factors synthetically, i.e., from the standpoint of comparative efficiencies in resource allocations for risk reduction opportunities. But by and large they are paralysed, prevented from doing so both by the legacy of bureaucratic turf allotments and by their unwillingness to confront an apparently resistant public – who, to be fair, have not yet been introduced to the idea by their governments.[58]

The costs for reducing risks vary by many orders of magnitude. It is not uncommon for policy choices requiring risk reduction actions to be made, in one area of government responsibility, while other areas under the jurisdiction of the same government are relatively neglected. The important costs are in lost opportunities for enhanced health benefits.[59] With every advance our society makes in collective risk reduction, there are distinctive benefits to be reaped, both in terms of enhanced quality of life and longevity. But in most cases the marginal costs for risk reduction inexorably keep rising, so that with each passing day it becomes increasingly more important to allocate risk reduction resources wisely. This must mean, quite simply, that some public alarms would be addressed with dollars, while other concerns, however loudly expressed, would be answered only with explanations as to why the expenditures would not be made. Addressing this awkward state of affairs is such an enormous challenge for the government policy domain that it is perhaps unsurprising no one wants to be first in line to do so. Sooner or later, however, it must and will be done.

4 Society's Relation to the Natural Environment and Its Resources

Earlier I referred to the mismatch of science and policy in the older model: science usually couches its answers to cause-and-effect questions in "maybe" (probability) terms, whereas policy demands a "yes" or a "no." Over time the dilemma posed by this mismatch becomes increasingly onerous. This is because, with relentless population growth and resource-intensive lifestyles, we inevitably erode the margins of safety between our demands on natural resources and the recuperative powers (sustainable carrying capacity) of natural ecosystems. The disaster in the East Coast fishery is the most dramatic illustration, but quite apart from its singular meaning, it is also a metaphor for the more general category. A risk management approach informed by modern applied sciences is, in the case of (once) renewable resources such as fish or forests, designed to maximize long-term sustained resource yield indefinitely, but it can only do so by giving estimates, ranges, or scenarios with various probabilities attached to them.

At the same time, in a country such as Canada, where the state has a huge and continuing role in natural resource policy, pressure builds at various times to maximize short-term yield, which exploits the inevitable element of uncertainty in the probabilistic scenarios. In the West Coast forests (and now soon perhaps in its salmon fishery), as in the East Coast fishery, the modern science of yield management has been crushed at least in part by policies of over-cutting and over-fishing, as the necessarily cautious voices of at least some resource managers were drowned out by the loud cheers of all interest groups – politicians, business, and labour.

It is now generally recognized that the relentless growth of human populations and their economic systems challenges the sustainability of natural ecosystems – in so far as the capacity of those ecosystems to serve human interests is concerned.[60] Another way of phrasing this point is to say that humanity has eroded the once-substantial margin of error it had, vis-à-vis the natural environment, with respect to the extractive technologies it employs in the service of its needs. For example, the long-term fluctuations in the populations of North Atlantic cod and Pacific salmon species certainly respond to purely natural forces, such as food supply and ocean temperature;[61] however, almost certainly the technological power of the modern commercial fisheries also had a major part to play in their recent collapse. The margin of error in agriculture has to do with how much fertile land we can afford to convert to other uses, and also allow to erode and deteriorate, before the food supply is imperilled – no matter what manipulations of industrial technology or genetic engineering we can deploy. The global climate change debate is based on the presumption that, in highly complex natural phenomena such as global weather patterns, a relatively small incremental impact from anthropogenic greenhouse gas emissions might be sufficient to trigger alterations in those patterns that otherwise might not have occurred (at least within the same time-frame), alterations which can have adverse consequences of enormous scope for human societies.

Modern scientific risk management is based on the idea that we can derive significant new human benefits by becoming increasingly cunning in shaving the margin of error in our manipulations of nature. Chemotherapy regimes, for example, depend on fine-tuning the medicinal dose so that aggressive cancers can be destroyed without an unacceptable level of risk of collateral damage (killing the patient). In general, since everything we encounter in nature is toxic at some dose, but so many of those same things are also extremely useful to us, we try to find the dose at which some limited exposure is "safe" while we use them.[62] But we will not tolerate now the level of human costs for our technological manipulations that obtained in the past when, as mentioned earlier, we did the body counts retrospectively and adjusted the exposure limits after the data was in. At least, not on the same scale.

So with decreasing margins of error the risk management exercises – the inescapable responsibility of governments – demand much more exacting attention than was bestowed on them earlier. In part just because the assumptions, data quality, risk control options, and evaluative judgments brought to bear in risk management decision making are more complex and nuanced than they used to be, and become progressively more so with each passing year, they all must also be presented and defended to the citizenry, in a never-ending public dialogue. A truly daunting task, to be sure, but an equally inescapable duty – as yet unacknowledged.

THE NEW MODEL: SCIENCE, GOVERNMENT, AND THE PUBLIC DIALOGUE ON RISK MANAGEMENT

In the absence of this ongoing public risk dialogue, we face obstacles to sensible risk management that simply cannot be overcome. One is what I call the "tyranny of small and unfamiliar risks." One of the surest findings in the risk perception research is that we underestimate the probability and consequences of familiar risks and overestimate those same dimensions for unfamiliar ones. The thought that minuscule doses of obscure chemicals called "endocrine modulators" (EM) may be having devastating effects on reproductive and immune systems of both humans and wildlife is very worrying to many people now. There is a huge, worldwide research program under way to test the relevant hypotheses; in the meantime, while we are awaiting the results, the most responsible provisional conclusion might be that EM risk factors are unlikely to turn out to be as significant for us as are many others with which we are quite familiar.[63] But if, for the sake of argument, that is indeed the appropriate message from a risk manager, it cannot be just tossed off in a press release.

To be credible, such a message must be accompanied by an elaborate "translation" of the current state of good science into publicly understandable terms; also by a framework that relates possible outcomes from the scientific research programs to a set of feasible risk control options; also by a decision matrix in which various probabilities of adverse health effects are arrayed against achievable risk reduction scenarios and their costs. These are some of the nuts-and-bolts components in the foundations of sensible policy choices in risk management domains. And all of this must be done over and over again, because it is also unlikely that we will be in a position to make definitive judgments about EM risk management strategies for another ten, twenty, or more years.

To be sure, the most secure part of those foundations is the painstaking assembly of scientific research findings through which the nature of the hazards in question is characterized with precision. But for every risk domain that is now or may become controversial, the scientific research enterprise itself is clouded in suspicion – simply because basic and applied scientific research is the source of that technological innovation, past, present, and future, that engenders many risk factors. The rising level of public awareness of and participation in risk controversies means that there is simply no reasonable expectation that governments which are directly involved in doing or even promoting that research in terms of its economic development potential can be regarded as credible sources of information about it.[64]

Another obstacle is what I call "premature policy closure," and there is no better illustration of this one than the conduct to date of the public conversation on global climate change issues. Long before the public was afforded the opportunity to grasp the nature of the exceedingly complex risk factors at stake here, or the implications for their future lifestyles of the kind of greenhouse gas emissions reductions agreed to at Kyoto, they have been asked just to believe that the government which negotiated at Kyoto on their behalf knew what it was doing.[65] Public opinion polls show that two-thirds of Canadians apparently are convinced that Canada should have insisted on even further reductions for ourselves and other nations. Perhaps so, although it would have been nice if the pollsters had gone on to inquire what these same citizen respondents thought this would mean for their expected lifestyles.

Since we are unable as yet even to assign any reliable probability numbers to the potential adverse effects implicit in global climate change scenarios, would it not be kinder to the public for the government to engage citizens first in a comprehensive dialogue about the relevant risk factors, risk control options, and risk reduction scenarios? The Kyoto conference had been scheduled years in advance. Why did the impenetrable policy fog lift only briefly at the penultimate moment, when the hapless citizenry learned that we had to "beat the Americans"?

Clearly we have a long way to go. But at least – so I have argued – we have the right map in hand which indicates the path we need to follow. If we do so we will forget about doing science in the public sector and concentrate instead on taking the steps that will enable governments to deliver credible risk management decisions to a public who will eventually be grateful for the gift.

A recent internal review of these matters within the federal government considered whether the science capacity now resident in government departments should be transferred to independent organizations, and answered in the negative, on the grounds that, if it were, research would become irrelevant to the policy process.[66] That incorrect answer is based on an elementary mistake in the analysis. The relevance of scientific research to the policy process in risk management is in no respect whatsoever a function of its organizational proximity. Rather, science's continuing policy relevance and indeed its indispensability are grounded simply in the fact that governments must manage risks and that health and environmental risk management cannot be done without it. Period.

In the reference to "independent organizations" we should have in mind primarily universities or other entities that draw upon the independent expertise resident in universities.[67] One well-established way of organizing this expertise for risk-related issues is the convening of expert panels; this is done in many parts of the world but nowhere more systematically than in the United States, under procedures administered by the National Academy of Sciences and its related institutions.[68] The Royal Society of Canada set up comparable procedures in 1995 and has carried out expert panel reviews in the areas of asbestos; the future of the primate colony at Health Canada; and health risks associated with radio-frequency fields.[69] Two further studies, one dealing with setting environmental standards for particulate matter and ground-level ozone, the other on the future of food biotechnology, are under way at the time of writing.

Another outstanding recent example is the 1998 Report of the Federal Environmental Assessment Panel on the Nuclear Fuel Waste Management and Disposal Concept released by the Canadian Environmental Assessment Agency. This panel first generated a thorough and credible technical review using independent scientific experts, but it also argued that the waste management framework must meet "social" as well as "technical" criteria, and it explicitly included ethical and equity dimensions in the former. Its conclusions are: "From a technical perspective, safety of the AECL concept has been on balance adequately demonstrated for a conceptual stage of development, but from a social perspective, it has not. As it stands, the AECL concept for deep geological disposal has not been demonstrated to have broad public support. The concept in its current form does not have the required level of acceptability to be adopted as Canada's approach for managing nuclear fuel wastes." These conclusions are supported in the report by careful and sophisticated reasoning, making this arguably the most balanced environmental assessment document produced in Canada since the famous 1977 Royal Commission report by Thomas Berger on northern pipeline development. Its main recommendations have been accepted.[70]

To return to the main theme: governments could still insist on cloaking in unnecessary secrecy the applied scientific studies they might purchase as contract research from universities under the new model. But they would run a number of risks in doing so. First, the most senior researchers, who have the best access to unrestricted grant monies, would have nothing to do with them. Second, it would defeat the basic purpose, because it would not be responding to the changed nature of the challenges in risk management decision making, as outlined above. Under today's conditions the science itself should be thrown on the table for everyone to see as soon as it comes out of the peer review process, every time, without exception. Even when a particular study result is subsequently found wanting and is superseded or withdrawn, the credibility of the entire scientific enterprise is enhanced. This credibility will also be transferred to the risk management process within which such science is utilized – if only the civil service and its political masters can be persuaded that the obsessive secretiveness which, they believe, serves them well does not do so here.

8 The CEPA Soap Opera

PRELUDE: WHAT'S TOXIC?

The province of British Columbia's Waste Management Act includes Regulation 300/90, the Antisapstain Chemical Waste Control Regulation, which is intended to prevent harm to aquatic organisms from stormwater run-off discharges to receiving waters originating at sawmill sites. The regulation, promulgated in 1990, sets numerical limits for stormwater concentrations of the specific chemicals (fungicides) used at those sites to prevent softwood lumber from succumbing to "sapstain," a discolouration of wood produced by the activity of micro-organisms that reduces its marketability.[1] The regulation also has an overriding provision to the effect that effluents from sawmill sites "shall not be toxic," as measured at the point of discharge (end-of-pipe) at the site; compliance with this criterion is monitored using a rainbow trout bioassay.

Some years later, the British Columbia Ministry of Environment, Lands and Parks initiated discussions on proposals to lower drastically the allowable concentration limits for some of the antisapstain chemical fungicides used at sawmills. In this context a report on compliance with the regulation was made to the BC Stakeholder Forum on Sapstain Control, a multi-stakeholder group, as follows: "Stormwater effluents from lumber mills [in 1995] had a high frequency of acute toxicity (assessed by the standard 96-hr LC_{50} rainbow trout bioassay) despite evidence of good antisapstain control. For example, 65% of a stormwater data set with 676 samples, did not pass the 96-hr LC_{50} bioassay, while only 9% of the samples contained antisapstain chemicals in excess of their reported 96-hr LC_{50} concentrations."[2]

Although the situation appears to be complicated, it really is not. What the statement above means is that the chemicals are not the cause of the toxicity, and that, despite having designed the regulation and put it into place five years earlier, the ministry did not even *imagine the possibility* that there could be other causes, since no other potential agent is mentioned or controlled in the regulation! Further investigation was initiated, and there gradually emerged solid evidence for alternative causes, namely leaching of zinc due to the pH value of rainwater (low hardness) from roofs at the sawmill sites and, at some sites where timber has been stored for long periods in water before being milled, leaching of naturally occurring resins and phenols from the wood itself.[3] The irony with respect to the first (zinc) is that extensive roofing at sawmill sites was mandated earlier as an environmental protection measure, since it was thought that this could inhibit the process whereby rainfall would otherwise wash newly applied antisapstain chemicals off unprotected wood and into receiving waters. An even more delightful irony emerged when it was found in an informal test that "pure" BC rainwater did not pass the 96-hr LC_{50} rainbow trout bioassay on account of its pH value! The province and the softwood lumber industry are now collaborating on an appropriate research program, including the investigation of remedial technologies.

Is there a moral in this story? One sincerely hopes so, because not only has there been inadequate environmental protection in the province for ten years and counting, as a result of this little oversight, but also the mistake was only discovered by accident, and one cannot tell how many more similar cases there might be. To draw the lesson we have to know first why it happened, and to find this out we have to ask: How could a regulator seek to prevent harm to aquatic life and imagine this could be done absent any examination whatsoever of the possible causes of that harm? There may be multiple reasons for this lapse, but almost certainly one of them has to do with a persistent and unfortunate propensity in some quarters to assume that *all* the most serious cases of environmental damage originate with industrial chemicals, otherwise known as "toxic substances."

The moral in this story is as follows. What is shown by the review of toxic substances policy undertaken in this chapter is that governments get cornered by risk issues in a number of specific ways. First, inadequate constitutional authority: In Canada the federal authority is severely constrained in terms of a broad environmental management mandate and therefore is preoccupied by default with its power to ban (or "virtually eliminate") particular substances, in itself an enormously cumbersome process; the result is that the federal government remains a minor player in environmental management generally. Second, both this chapter and the next show how federal authorities in Canada have tied themselves in knots by stubbornly refusing to employ a variety of governance mechanisms to encourage industry to achieve the highest possible level of environmental responsibility. Unlike the first, this is a self-imposed constraint. It results from adopting an empty rhetorical stance of "command – control – punish" more appropriate to ENGO strategies than to government itself, which makes for entertaining ministerial speeches but little else in the way of concrete accomplishments.

TOXIC SUBSTANCES

Government departments with a general mandate for environmental protection date from the early 1970s. Since a number of related but more limited mandates had existed for some time in a bureaucratic form (in matters such as air and water quality, wildlife protection, etc.), these units typically were rolled into the new departments. In terms of distinctively new legislative and regulatory mandates, it is arguably the case that "toxic substances management" is primarily what is new and different about the mandates of environment departments themselves in the ensuing quarter-century. (Environmental impact assessment mandates are also relatively new, but where they are in place, they tend to be lodged in separate structures.) Both Canada and the United States passed legislation along these lines in the mid-1970s, and Canada renewed this thrust with both the first CEPA in 1988 and the second one in 1999.

The fact that toxic substances management was front and centre is not particularly surprising, given the origins of modern environmentalist protest in the 1960s, which had focused on the dispersion of industrial chemical pollutants in air, water, and soil. Industrial development to that time (in both market-oriented and "socialist" variants) treated the environment by and large as a limitless receptacle for the hazardous by-products of goods production and use. Moreover, the receptacle was freely available for this purpose, and polluters did not have to worry about internalizing the costs that otherwise would have been incurred if preserving environmental quality had been an obligation of producers. Since the cause-and-effect chains in environmental degradation can be long and convoluted, when they can be established at all, both in general and for specific polluting sources, denial of culpability was always the easy rejoinder to allegations of harm.

The structure of all legislative frameworks to date for toxic sub-stances management (TSM) requires the regulator – that is, governments – to take the following steps:[4]

- First, to discover some harm in the environment that may be imputed to a polluting substance.
- Second, to confirm the cause-and-effect link between the harm and the substance, using scientific methods and risk assessment protocols.
- Third, to devise control measures for the substance that will confine the harm to acceptable levels.
- Fourth, to detect violations of these controls and punish the offend-ers – using an onerous standard of proof, since these are not civil but rather criminal code matters.

Each one of these steps is fraught with immense difficulty. Each one may be hotly contested between the regulator and the regulated. The history of toxic substances management in North America is littered with titanic and expensive battles of this sort.

In a legal and administrative sense this way of proceeding – what I shall call the "old paradigm" – all has to do with burden of proof. But at a deeper level the old paradigm incorporates by default a managerial ethic according to which protecting the environment is, simply speak-ing, not the responsibility of a polluting industry. Rather, environmen-tal protection is the business of the public at large, and of governments. The structure of the relationship among social interests that is implied by this ethic may be summarized as follows:

1 The polluter has no responsibility to know what harm is being caused.
2 Governments and private citizens are responsible for detecting the existence of environmental harm and its causes.
3 The existence and causes of such harm must be proved "beyond a reasonable doubt" before remedies may be demanded.
4 The threat of punishment for causing harm after it has actually occurred is the best way of assuring that harm will be averted.

In fact practices in Canada and elsewhere have been moving away from the old paradigm for some time now. Yet the basic legal and adminis-trative framework for achieving environmental protection has changed little in that time.

The old paradigm may be labelled "discover (if you can) and pun-ish." In its very structure it inevitably polarizes stakeholder interests where protecting the environment is at issue. Industry is positioned to deny harm, remain ignorant if it can, conceal whatever it can, and throw up roadblocks to controls on its activities at every turn. The public – represented by private citizens and environmental organizations – is positioned to ferret out hard evidence of malfeasance and to demand severe punishment for the same under the powers of the law. Governments, sitting squarely in the middle, devise administratively complex regulatory regimes, conduct endless consultative exercises with stakeholder groups whose outcomes are known perfectly in advance, and throughout it all try to find some way of avoiding being too badly wounded by the crossfire between the other parties.[5]

The old paradigm has long been known by the phrase "command and control," but this is a misnomer. Considering the number and chemical complexity of the (ever-changing) set of industrially generated toxic substances, governments have never had – *and never will have* – the resources which would be required to "command" the field of environmental protection as such. The well-known proportion between the number of substances in commercial use, on the one hand, and the number of those assessed and controlled by formal regulatory processes, on the other, is a standing and definitive rebuke to the toxic substances management approach under the old paradigm.

THE FEDERAL POWER

Toxic substances management is the cornerstone of CEPA, the Canadian Environmental Protection Act, in both its first (1988) and second (1999) incarnations.[6] It is also the reason why this "flagship" legislative authority for Environment Canada is such a cumbersome and ultimately ineffective instrument to serve the cause of environmental protection. Moreover, since that ineffectiveness is attributable squarely to the limitations of federal power in environmental matters imposed by the Canadian Constitution, it cannot be repaired, but only bypassed. How to do so is suggested in the concluding chapter in this volume, in the concluding section of this chapter, and in the "Addendum" that will be found at the end of chapter 9. I begin with a brief look at the constitutional framework.

In *Canada v. Hydro-Québec* (1997) the Supreme Court gave a clear statement on the federal power and its limitations in environmental management, in the context of a challenge to the constitutionality of CEPA's toxic substances provisions. Although the court was badly split (5–4) on the particular question before them in this case, both the majority and the minority agreed on their interpretation of the underlying constitutional framework relevant to it.[7] Writing for the majority, Justice La Forest said:

Part II of the Canadian Environmental Protection Act [1988] does not deal with the protection of the environment generally, but simply with the control of toxic substances that may be released into the environment under certain restricted circumstances, through a series of prohibitions to which penal sanctions are attached. There was no intention that the Act should bar the use, importation or manufacture of all chemical products, but rather that it should affect only those substances that are dangerous to the environment, and then only if they are not otherwise regulated by law ... This is a limited prohibition applicable to a restricted number of substances. The prohibition is enforced by a penal sanction and is undergirded by a valid criminal objective, and so is valid criminal legislation. Specific targeting of toxic substances based on individual assessment avoids resort to unnecessarily broad prohibitions and their impact on the exercise of provincial powers.

The sobering statement that CEPA "does not deal with protection of the environment generally" is reinforced in the dissenting minority opinion by Chief Justice Lamer:

... [P]rotection of the environment is also a valid purpose of the criminal law. While the impugned provisions [sections 34–5 of 1988 CEPA] have a legitimate criminal purpose, they fail to meet the other half of the test. They are not intended to prohibit environmental pollution, but simply to regulate it, and so do not qualify as criminal law under s. 91(27) ... The prohibitions in s. 113, such as they are, are ancillary to the regulatory scheme, not the other way around. This strongly suggests that the focus of the legislation is regulation rather than prohibition ... Finally, granting Parliament the authority to regulate so completely the release of substances into the environment by determining whether or not they are "toxic" would inescapably preclude the possibility of shared environmental jurisdiction and would infringe severely on other heads of power assigned to the provinces.

All nine justices agreed in effect that Parliament can only prohibit, not regulate.[8] In essence, therefore, the justices believe that the federal power can deal with hazards, but not with risks. And this means in turn that the scope of the federal power in environmental management is pretty much useless.[9]

What I mean is this. A hazard is "in principle" a threat to health or the environment, in the sense that under certain conditions it can cause adverse effects which we wish to avoid. Those conditions are represented by two things: first, what is known as the "dose," that is, variations in the *amount* or type of contact with the hazard required in order to induce the harm, and second, the type of exposure to that dose. When we know the hazard characteristics (i.e., what kinds of harm something can do), the dose, and the exposure of specific populations or processes, we can estimate the probability that particular types and intensities of adverse effects may occur to certain humans, wildlife, or biophysical processes in the environment. What is necessarily implied here is that there is almost always some uncertainty in the outcome, for various reasons, especially our inability to pinpoint what exposures have occurred or what level of toxic insult was actually present, as well as the variations within populations that produce varying responses to the same level of insult.

"The dose makes the poison," in the famous phrase from toxicology; indeed, there is reason to believe that, at least in many cases, some exposure at low levels to substances that at higher doses are lethal to us may be good for us, in that our immune system is stimulated and develops protective mechanisms. In addition, there is the awkward fact that so many hazardous things which are undeniably harmful to us at certain doses also have enormously useful properties; such things include almost all chemicals, radiation, minerals, metals, and gases. Indeed, everything is hazardous to us at some dose, including the essentials of life such as water and oxygen. The bottom line for all this is an excruciatingly simple proposition: As a general rule, for our own good we must regulate toxic substances, not prohibit them.[10] Another way of putting this point is to say that "prohibition" is almost certainly the least applicable instrument in our arsenal of responses to health and environmental risks of all sorts.

"Regulation" means identifying the particular conditions under which exposures to hazardous substances are or are not allowable. This exercise in discrimination serves – when we get it right, which we often do not, or at least not in time to forestall tragic consequences – to enhance our well-being immeasurably. The benefits cannot be realized, obviously, if we prohibit any use of them at all, but can be if we regulate those uses wisely. To be sure, there may always be some unavoidable "downside," represented by randomly occurring adversities to small numbers of people or wildlife, even when all "reasonable" precautions have been mandated, that occur when society permits the use of hazardous things – whether they be automobiles, radiation, asbestos, or chlorine, or any of tens of thousands of others – in an effort to derive benefits from them. If we are sufficiently knowledgeable and compassionate about these unavoidable circumstances, we compensate the unfortunate victims. This is what we generally mean by "acceptable risk," a concept not allowed to be mentioned in polite company, but one which governs the everyday behaviour of every one of us, whether we care to admit it to ourselves or not.

Our need to operate on the basis of risks, not hazards, means that the federal power derived from the Canadian Constitution is largely irrelevant in environmental management. This irrelevance, rarely if ever recognized explicitly over the course of the lengthy CEPA review process, cast a dark shadow over the entire proceedings. Only the constitutional lawyers among us could have clarified all this, but they were largely silent on the matter.

CEPA REVIEW

During the tortuous CEPA review process, begun in 1993 and finally concluded on a bizarre note in late 1999, the contending interests fought each other to a standstill, and as a result the new CEPA is pretty much like the old one. In the period that will run from the new CEPA to the next CEPA we should all try a little harder to find a way to agree on fundamental changes in orientation that might enhance the federal role in environmental management.[11]

In this spirit it would be instructive to try to estimate the value of the investment in personnel time and ancillary expenses made by all stakeholders in the review process. First, the preparation of submissions – including internal consultations among federal government departments, and ENGO and industry association caucuses – for delivery to the initial hearings before the House of Commons Standing Committee on Environment and Sustainable Development, held in 1994; second, the committee's own labours in producing *It's about Our Health!* in 1995; third, the long-running dogfights (largely held out of the public view) among numerous federal departments, up to and beyond the formulation of the *Government Response* in December 1995; fourth, stakeholder commentaries on the *Response*; fifth, manoeuvring during spring 1997 before the election was called and the session prorogued; sixth, more committee hearings and a bitter struggle between the committee and the government during 1998 and early 1999, culminating in the defection of the committee chair and three supporters when the legislation came to a final vote. Finally, throughout all this, the intensive lobbying of officials in a number of different departments.

The monetary costs of this exercise are easily in the millions of dollars, and perhaps in the tens of millions. It would be nice to say that the result had repaid the costs, but it would be difficult to make such a case. Indeed, the greatest difference between the new CEPA and the old one is a purely rhetorical: most of the potentially innovative concepts are stuffed into the "Preamble" to the new act, where they stand ready to be trotted out as grand phrases on ceremonial occasions, without the risk of having them actually change the ways in which the business of environmental regulation is carried on.

This was undoubtedly a great disappointment, especially to those who saw *It's about Our Health!* the 1995 "Report of the Standing Committee on Environment and Sustainable Development," as promising a breath of fresh air in an otherwise stale debate. And yet they were bound to be disappointed in any case, if they thought that it was possible (using this report) to drive a powerful "pro-environmentalist" wedge through the jaded federal department bureaucracy. For the Standing Committee's report accepted the underlying logic of CEPA itself (old as well as new), namely, that the words "CEPA-toxic" arm us with a potent administrative weapon for ensuring adequate environmental protection. Alas, this is, as the Bible says, "a snare and a delusion" which produces with much sweat little more than an elaborate confirmation of what everyone else already knows. If we cannot take the trouble to ask why this is so, and to do things better next time, then the lead-up to the next CEPA, in five years or so, inevitably will be an exercise in utter futility similar to what we have seen in the immediately preceding period.

That the word "futility" is an apt descriptor for the 1994–99 CEPA review process is best revealed by the reactions of key stakeholders in Ottawa to the bill's first tabling in the House on 10 December 1996. At a news conference on that day, an ENGO spokesperson remarked that, if the bill (in that version) were thought of as a nicely wrapped Christmas gift, then it could be said that "industry" got the present while "environmentalists" got the wrapping. Meanwhile, in the very same city, some of the key industry association analysts were already preparing for their colleagues a strong critique of what were in their eyes the serious deficiencies in that same bill, from a business standpoint, and a recommendation to press for the inclusion of many changes during the final committee hearings process.[12] If anyone (apart from the civil servants who had the assignment) was actually happy with the monumental 228-page text tabled that day, we never heard from them.

As the Canadian polity slipped into disarray over the Quebec secession issue during the summer of 1995, in the nasty backstage skirmish being waged over the CEPA review a large bone of contention was the set of recommendations contained in the 357-page "Report of the House of Commons Standing Committee on Environment and Sustainable Development," issued in June 1995 and entitled *It's about Our Health! Towards Pollution Prevention*.[13] Even its title could be considered to be a deliberate provocation, for it carries the suggestion that environmental pollution is directly implicated in threats to human health. But as a general statement this is not true, at least not for Canada (environmental pollution is not among the most significant risk factors in the health of Canadians as a general rule) and, in any case, the report itself provides no evidence to substantiate this implied threat.

The Standing Committee Report proposed to "strengthen" CEPA by retaining its core structure – especially part II of the act, entitled "Toxic Substances" – and by adding a great number of new, general principles and specific operational mandates to that original structure.[14] But the core section of the original act itself (and its operational component, the "Priority Substances List") is fundamentally flawed, as the Standing Committee Report itself acknowledged in passing, and the changes recommended probably would have made it worse, not better. The original CEPA has done almost nothing to achieve better environmental protection in Canada, and a CEPA revised along the lines suggested by the Standing Committee Report conceivably might do even less. All of these problems are rooted in the fact that CEPA simply repackaged the basic thrust of its predecessor legislation without changing it, despite the fact that its predecessor was widely acknowledged to be unworkable, even by officials at Environment Canada.[15]

The predecessor legislation was the Environmental Contaminants Act (ECA), proclaimed in 1975; its core element was the "screening" of "toxic" chemical compounds for adverse health and environmental effects. It reflected the same regulatory approach as the US Toxic Substances Control Act (TSCA), passed in 1976. In this type of legislation, "toxics" are a subset of the whole range of physical, chemical, and biological agents – naturally occurring or industrially created – which we encounter and which are thought to be, in common-sense terms, intrinsically and especially harmful to human health or the environment. Obviously the idea of screening toxic substances implies a process of perhaps quickly canvassing the scientific databases to identify at least the worst cases among all those that might fall into this category and then, of course, promptly doing something useful with this information.

Such screening may sound easier than it is, at least when, in principle, *all* chemical compounds currently in use are candidates for this process, since such compounds number in the tens of thousands, and the scientific knowledge base on them is sometimes vast and complex, making the screening effort time-consuming and sometimes minimal or non-existent and making the screening practically impossible to carry out. Although the screening exercise is only meaningful as a prelude to regulatory action, this prelude appears to overwhelm the rest, which somehow never gets done. The experience in the United States provides the most telling evidence on this point: applying to this toxics screening task its considerable scientific resources and funding, which far exceed those of any other nation, the US Environmental Protection Agency, in the eight years between 1976 and 1984, placed regulatory controls on exactly four chemicals.[16] Under similar provisions for the separate legislation for pesticides in the United States, "only six of some six hundred active ingredients mandated for reregistration under the 1972 amendments had been fully tested" by 1985.[17] Doern and Conway quote a comment made by two knowledgeable Canadian authorities in 1979 on the comparable situation here: "The Environmental Protection Service [of Environment Canada] lacks the resources to be able to administer the *Environmental Contaminants Act* effectively."[18] Operating under the ECA, in a period of ten years Environment Canada managed to assess just five chemicals.[19]

By the time the policy consultation process on CEPA began in the mid-1980s, the inherent difficulty in the "toxic substances" approach to the regulation of environmental pollutants ought to have been readily apparent. Ross Hall, a biologist who worked closely with Environment Canada for many years, argued this position strenuously throughout the 1980s, at the time when CEPA was first going through the drafting and hearings process, to no avail. He offered the following whimsical analysis:

The single-chemical approach breaks down under the sheer weight of the 60,000 existing industrial chemicals. To illustrate the absurdity of trying to regulate industrial chemicals in this manner, let's do a simple calculation. The 19-member bureaucrat team of the Contaminants Control Branch took 10 years to assess five chemicals. That is, it took 19 x 10 = 190 bureaucrat years to write five regulations – 38 bureaucrat years per chemical. Imagine that Environment Canada puts *all* its 10,000 employees – from janitor to deputy minister – to work writing regulations. At that rate, the department would write 260 a year. The department wouldn't keep up with the 1,000 new chemicals that enter commerce every year.[20]

Nevertheless the policy process steamed ahead, making the identification of toxic substances the core part of CEPA, which was proclaimed in 1988; the shorthand expression for substances which fit its criteria is "CEPA-toxic." By that time regulators elsewhere had been busy making up lists of chemicals ranked in some order of priority, using various criteria; so, following suit, CEPA incorporated the concept of a "Priority Substances List" (PSL). "CEPA-toxic" is flawed for two reasons: first and foremost, because it reaffirms the toxic-substances approach itself, which already had been shown to be fruitless by the time the act was drafted; and second, because it confuses the concepts of hazard and risk. I will deal with these points in reverse order.

" CEPA-TOXIC "

Part II of the original CEPA defined "toxic" as follows (1988 CEPA, section 11, "Interpretation"):[21]

11. For the purposes of this Part, a substance is toxic if it is entering or may enter the environment in a quantity or concentration or under conditions
(a) having or that may have an immediate or long-term harmful effect on the environment;
(b) constituting or that may constitute a danger to the environment on which human life depends; or
(c) constituting or that may constitute a danger in Canada to human life or health.

"Harm" and "danger" (as well as "hazard") are synonyms for the ordinary dictionary meaning of "toxic." Indeed, what can only be called the perverse affinity of the act's drafters for the vagueness of everyday usage is the prime reason for its incoherent and unworkable character. In phrasing this complaint one could not do better than the Standing Committee Report itself: "The use of the word toxic in CEPA has given rise to a significant amount of confusion, and no small amount of consternation, in both the scientific and lay communities."[22]

What is the source of the confusion? The explanation may appear to be terminological hairsplitting, but I hope to show that using the correct terminology is indispensable for effective environmental management. The *Government Response* says: "The Government of Canada is committed to a risk-based approach to decision-making."[23] Then why is it afraid to use terminology that is commonly accepted around the world? Risk is a product of "hazard" (the intrinsic properties of a substance or event that can cause harm) and "exposure," the extent to which individuals or groups are likely to encounter that hazard and thus be harmed. The term "toxic" is misused in CEPA because it incorporates the possible encounter with a substance (exposure) instead of referring only to the properties of that substance. A brief from Health Canada made this point to the Standing Committee: "In scientific parlance, toxicity is the inherent capability of a substance to cause harm, which does not take into account exposure."[24] There is a marvellous irony in this brief, since ministerial responsibility for CEPA is shared by the minister of environment with the minister of health; a perhaps uncharitable interpretation of the above-quoted sentence is that one federal department is telling another that the latter doesn't quite know what it is doing.

Is this terminological confusion important? Yes, it is. As a practical matter, we should not care if something is toxic or not, so long as no one (human or non-human) is exposed to it in sufficient quantities to do harm. In other words, to take action to regulate a substance, we want to know not that it is a *hazard* – because just about everything is hazardous under some conditions – but whether it is a *risk*, or more precisely, an unacceptable risk. Virtually everything used in industrial settings is hazardous, that is, can cause harm under some conditions. But exactly the same stricture applies to virtually everything that we use or encounter in everyday life – cars, gasoline, electricity, stoves, stepladders, tools, toys, prescription and non-prescription drugs, foods (bacteria and moulds), and razors. The list is literally endless. We try to take steps, through good product design, hazard information, consumer education, and so on, in order not to eliminate the risks, which is impossible, but to contain them within broadly acceptable bounds, as defined ultimately by community standards. In short, everything is hazardous, but not everything is unacceptably risky.

The Standing Committee Report, having acknowledged (i) that the original formulation of section 11 amounts to a risk-assessment approach, although it is not called such, and (ii) that the use of the word "toxic" in section 11 is confusing (because that usage is inconsistent with a risk-assessment approach), then proceeds to compound that confusion by introducing the notion of "inherent toxicity." The report had just quoted Health Canada to the effect that "toxicity is the inherent capability of a substance to cause harm," which makes the phrase "inherent toxicity" inherently redundant. "Toxic" *means* "inherently harmful": why replace a confusing term ("toxic" in section 11) with a new, equally confusing phrase ("inherently toxic")? Well, there is a method in this madness, as we shall see.

When regulating for health and environmental safety, we cannot confuse hazards and risks – which is exactly what "CEPA-toxic" does. So, in rewriting CEPA, why not just "simply replace the word toxic because of the confusion its use has engendered," as the Standing Committee Report puts it? This option was rejected, because the Standing Committee was not overly troubled with the "confusion and consternation" created by "CEPA-toxic." What it *was* troubled about was the failure of the risk assessment approach to catch enough substances in its net: "We are concerned that some potentially dangerous substances are not being adequately addressed by the current risk assessment-based PSL system ... First, extensive amounts of data are required to conduct a full risk assessment. For some substances, these extensive data requirements may be extremely difficult to satisfy with the result that the PSL process may be fatally compromised. For 13 substances on the first PSL, the assessment process, unfortunately, could not be completed for this reason. Second, the Committee believes that, in some cases, such exhaustive information is not required in order to justify their regulation."[25]

Now we are at the heart of the matter! The "agenda" here is self-evident, and so are its inadequacies. What does it mean to say that "some potentially dangerous substances" are not being adequately addressed by CEPA's risk assessment approach? Does it mean that Canadians are being exposed to unacceptable threats of harm from "some" *unspecified* dangerous substances? Which ones? And if so, how would we know this to be true, unless we had reliable results from a scientific risk assessment? For it is irresponsible to suggest that "some potentially dangerous substances are not being adequately addressed" at present without giving *any* examples of such alleged threats. If there were a real basis for perceived harm, CEPA had provided an adequate response capability under section 35; as stated there, "if the Ministers believe that immediate action is required to deal with a significant danger to the environment or to human life or health," an interim order providing for regulatory action may be made at once, and that order may remain in force for as long as two years.

The PSL 1 list required risk assessments to be done on 44 substances; this mandate was carried out, jointly by Environment Canada and Health Canada, and 25 were found to be "CEPA-toxic."[26] Fine. Since the mandate was carried out, what is the problem? What is the basis for the allegation, quoted above, that "the PSL process may be fatally compromised"? No basis is stated. Why then add the assessment of "inherent toxicity" to the CEPA mandate? The report answers as follows: "Removing the exposure criterion from section 11 and using 'inherent toxicity' as the criterion for a new schedule of toxic substances under CEPA could mean that as many as several hundred to a thousand or more, of approximately 28,000 substances now on the Domestic Substances List (DSL), may be classed as toxic." So, without any idea whether or not we are confronting unacceptable risks for this huge list of additional substances, we should, in effect, create a major makework project for the bureaucracy, all in the name of "protecting the environment." The report is explicit on the "bottom line" for the changes that it advocates: "Our overriding wish, however, is that a larger number of substances of concern should become subject to the regulatory process under CEPA."[27]

After twenty-five years of accumulated futility, it is past time to admit that the toxic-substances approach is a massively inefficient path towards good environmental management. The original form of part II of CEPA was bad enough; the Standing Committee Report's approach would have compounded its existing defects.

Referring to the established toxic substances approach, the *Government Response* acknowledged the "complaints that the current system is slow, inefficient and prone to delays." At the same time, the government announces its agreement with the thrust of the Standing Committee Report and accepts the need to "identify, screen, assess and control larger numbers of substances." How are we to reconcile these two sentiments? The government appears to believe that it can process more substances more quickly by greater efficiency in its screening operations. It starts with a priority on those that are shown to be persistent, bioaccumulative, and toxic, but then immediately adds "other criteria." This is what was proposed:

(i) substances currently on the Domestic Substances List, estimated at 23,000 substances, would be categorized with respect to persistence or bioaccumulation and inherent toxicity in environmental organisms ...

(ii) substances on the Domestic Substances List with the greatest potential for exposure to Canadians would be categorized.

(iii) substances categorized as indicated above would be candidates for screening level risk assessments based on science ...

The document further promises that "the criteria for persistence and bioaccumulation ... would be prescribed in regulations."[28] So we will have to wait and see whether such criteria allow for an "efficient" search through the 23,000. In addition, (i) and (ii) are completely different types of criteria; it is not at all clear what kind of data would be used to assess exposure. Since there exists only a meagre approximation of adequate data for such an exercise, at least it should be conceded that rough estimates will be used. Nevertheless, what is proposed is to run through the list of 23,000 not once but twice – and then to do something called "screening level risk assessments." What is a "screening assessment" anyway, which reappears undefined in section 74 of the 1999 CEPA?

Based on the history of the toxic substances approach to date, this is not a plausible scenario. Based on this history, it is incumbent upon the authors of this scenario to persuade us that something meaningful will result from it. Until they do, no one should wait around for anything to happen.[29]

Note the use of the phrase "inherent toxicity" above, which the authors of the *Government Response* adopt cheerfully from the Standing Committee Report, and which is defined in the *Response* as "the intrinsic ability of a substance to cause harm."[30] Perhaps the authors of that definition did not read the Health Canada brief, which is quoted in the report, and which gives the equivalent of the quoted phrase as the accepted definition of *toxicity*? They go on: inherent toxicity is "most often determined from the results of laboratory studies and accordingly, a substance can be considered inherently toxic regardless of whether there is any actual exposure." A little later on, we encounter the words "inherent toxicity (i.e., laboratory studies)," which makes it appear as if those two phrases are equivalent.[31]

This little game finishes in the new CEPA, section 77(3)(a), where it resurfaces as one of the three criteria that will entitle something to a place on schedule 1, the List of Toxic Substances (i.e., certified as "CEPA-toxic"); to qualify, a substance must be "persistent," "bioaccumulative," and "inherently toxic to human beings or non-human organisms, as determined by laboratory or other studies." Since almost all risk assessments are based in large part on laboratory studies, as everyone knows, the mention of such studies in this context is a bit puzzling. Much worse, however, is the circularity of the definition: something is deemed to be toxic (section 64) if it has been found to be inherently toxic (section 77). As already mentioned, the government proposes to define in regulations the meaning of both persistence and bioaccumulation, but it apparently will not do so in the case of "inherent toxicity," and the term is nowhere defined in Bill C-32. Which is, all in all, based on what has been said above, probably a good thing.

Perhaps this elaborate dance around the concept of toxicity in the original version of "CEPA-toxic" was based on the mistaken presumption that one cannot estimate the exposure of organisms in the environment to toxic agents. If so, this is a high price to pay for the confusion that was engendered thereby. Of course we can do environmental exposure estimates: they are not easy to do, and in many cases they must be done by sheer educated guesswork, but in fact estimating exposures even in human health risks is often done under many of the same limitations, which results in harsh criticism for many epidemiological studies. Despite this criticism, when the toxicity profile justifies concern, the acknowledged limitation of the exposure estimates does not prevent risk managers from taking action based on the best available evidence and suppositions at their disposal.

Looked at from another angle, the now officially blessed notion of inherent toxicity, as it appears in the *Government Response*, may have been designed as a solution to the conceptual problems inherent in the original version, although if so it is not successful. In the passage quoted above from page 69 of the *Response*, the three criteria of persistence, bioaccumulation, and "inherent" toxicity in item (i) amount to what should be referred to as the hazard identification phase of a risk assessment process; item (ii) breaks out exposure separately, as is conventionally done in proper risk assessment procedures (but which section 11 of the old CEPA pointedly failed to do, becoming the source of that confusion and consternation referred to in the Standing Committee Report, and which goes unrepaired in section 64 of the new CEPA). In other words, if we really wanted to base environmental management on a risk assessment approach, as we pretend, we should just forget about "toxicity" altogether, and use the terms "hazard" and "exposure" as the basic building-blocks for a risk management scheme.[32] But that is too much to ask, evidently.

On the other hand, the idea of doing "screening assessments" by sifting twice through a list of 23,000 substances before any action towards risk reduction becomes feasible means that the CEPA forces will still be spending most of their time listing and assessing, rather than getting on with the job of overseeing actual reductions in environmental risks.

THE BILL OF LISTS

Events since 1988 fully justify the charge that CEPA demonstrates once again the futility of the toxic-substances approach. CEPA operationalizes this approach in three steps: one, the compilation of a "priority substances list" of candidate substances; two, the scheduling of substances as "CEPA-toxic" following a completed scientific risk assessment; and three, taking regulatory action once a substance has been scheduled.[33] So, you might well ask, what has happened on this front in the eleven years since CEPA was first proclaimed?

The first round of step 1 resulted in what is known as "PSL 1," the first Priority Substances List. Forty-four substances (which can include "families" or groups of chemicals) found their way onto this list, in ways which I do not have time to detail here.[34] In effect these 44 were a subset of the approximately 28,000 substances appearing on the so-called "Domestic Substances List," which is a compilation of substances known to have been manufactured in or imported into Canada in commercial quantities as of about ten years ago. Step 2, the risk assessments on the 44, was completed by 1994, and 25 on the original list (currently 45 in all) have been certified as "CEPA-toxic."[35]

What kinds of substances were initially declared "CEPA-toxic"? Of the original 25 in total, many could almost have been regarded as household names, by which I mean that their "problematic" nature had been widely reported in the media, in some cases for many years: PCBs and PBBs; dioxins and furans; the ozone-depleting family of chemicals (chlorofluorocarbons, bromofluorocarbons, carbon tetrachloride, methyl chloroform, others); and quite familiar ones – asbestos, lead, mercury, vinyl chloride. PCBs, dioxins, and the ozone-depleting chemicals had been the subject of especially intense media reporting at different times. The well-known ones in the list above compose at least 20 of the 25 PSL 1 substances. The ozone-depleters alone make up about half of the total PSL 1 list, as finished in 1994, but the "Montreal Protocol on Substances That Deplete the Ozone Layer" predates CEPA, having been signed with great fanfare as long ago as mid-September of 1987. Most of the others listed (PCBs, asbestos, lead, mercury, and vinyl chloride) had been regulated, at least in certain settings, under earlier legislation, prior to CEPA. The question is: What specific, incremental environmental benefit was gained by reprocessing a list of quite familiar "bad" chemicals through the CEPA-toxic classification mill? The answer is not at all clear. Certainly this bureaucratic labour could not be justified on the basis of the amount of *new* regulatory action taken in the period since the first CEPA came into effect.

Regulatory action is step 3 in the CEPA process. What has been carried through to step 3? As of early 1995, exactly four PSL 1 substances had been newly regulated: "Regulations for four of the toxic substances – polychlorinated dibenzo-dioxins, polychlorinated dibenzofurans, effluents from pulp mills using bleaching, and 1,1,1-trichloroethane – have already been implemented ... Of the remaining 21 substances, two ... were proposed for regulation, while the other 19 substances are subject to a Strategic Options Process that will determine measures needed to reduce exposure to them."[36] This statement can be misleading: pulp mill effluent, containing (literally) tens of thousands of different chemical compounds, is regulated under CEPA *only* in so far as its dioxin and furan components are concerned;[37] and, conversely, dioxins and furans are regulated *only* in so far as they are components of pulp mill effluents – the many other anthropogenic sources of these compounds are not regulated.[38] With these clarifications in place, the CEPA-driven regulatory structure for environmental protection is even thinner than it appears at first glance.

Nevertheless the CEPA battalions soldier on. The PSL 2 process is well under way, and Environment Canada announced courageously some time ago that the "Government plans to finish assessing 100 substances by the year 2000" (that target was not met).[39] If the authors of this promise expected it to be greeted by thunderous applause from the citizenry, they may have been disappointed. Those citizens certainly will be disappointed, if one of the many recommendations in the Standing Committee Report were to be adopted, the one which, by changing the definition of "toxic," "could mean that as many as several hundred to a thousand or more of approximately 28,000 substances now on the

Domestic Substances List may be classed as toxic."[40] For the only substantive result of such a move would be to widen enormously the gulf between the list-making exercise on the one hand and any actual steps implemented to achieve better environmental protection in Canada on the other.

The main problem we face is this: the "operational" mandate for Environment Canada under CEPA is grounded in the making of "priority lists," but *this is not a priority-setting process with respect to actually achieving for Canada the highest possible level of environmental protection*, taking into account available resources at a given time.[41] What I mean is this: the protracted process of listing, assessing, and (possibly) regulating substances or sets of substances goes on entirely in the absence of any calculus of where the best trade-offs may be found. There are at least two types of relevant trade-offs: (i) cost-effectiveness in one domain of risk reduction versus others; (ii) the relative "efficiency" of reaching agreement and securing quick co-operation, among interested parties, on risk reduction opportunities. I shall comment briefly on each.

Like other toxic-substances approaches, CEPA provides no *legislative* basis for deciding how to assign priorities for action within the group of things assessed as excessively hazardous or risky. And because there is no public defence or scrutiny of relative priorities among the listed substances, we have no idea whether or not it makes sense for the bureaucracy to be dealing with them in the order which they happen to choose: like its predecessor, the group assigned to develop the PSL 2 list worked behind closed doors. Moreover, the criteria for screening candidates for the PSL 2 list are based on risk alone; yet we know that the costs of achieving comparable amounts of risk reduction across the whole range of applicable health and environmental risks vary enormously.[42] Applying comparative cost-effectiveness tests (i.e., balancing of costs and benefits) to the results of a robust, publicly defended priority-setting scheme would at least enable us to debate openly the merits of different ways of allocating risk reduction budgets. To date no government in Canada has been willing to trust its citizens sufficiently to engage with them in this necessary debate. So our environmental protection budgets in the public sphere, never robust at the best of times, continue to be applied with apparent randomness.[43]

My second point has to do with the relative "efficiency" of reaching agreement and securing quick co-operation among interested parties on risk reduction opportunities. In other words, some environmental protection battles required protracted warfare, others do not; a sensible rule is to fight where some clear and compelling reason demands taking a stand. Where less combative methods will do, ensure that they receive the utmost encouragement. A case in point is a process in Canada known as "ARET" (Accelerated Reduction/Elimination of Toxics), launched in late 1991.[44] Based on a negotiated and co-operative approach, the stakeholder group identified its own priority list of substances and, more to the point, has sought commitments for reduction targets from emitters of those substances. ARET sought the virtual elimination of emissions of 14 persistent, bioaccumulative, and toxic substances and substance groups over the long term, with a 90 per cent reduction [from pre-1990 levels] by the year 2000. For 87 less hazardous substances, it sought emission reductions to levels that are insufficient to cause harm, with a short-term reduction of 50 per cent by the year 2000.[45] It is arguably the case that this single exercise has achieved a greater amount of actual environmental and health benefit than all of the activities under CEPA during the same period.[46] But if one had thought that, in the ten years that have elapsed since 1991, we would have seen many more such initiatives as ARET, with clear encouragement from the federal and other governments, one would be wrong. To date it has been neither repeated nor much encouraged.

In summary, the original CEPA lacks utterly the two elements that might provide some assurance that we were getting maximum impact for our environmental protection efforts: a way of evaluating and demonstrating the relative cost-effectiveness of different risk reduction scenarios, and a way of stimulating and indeed "prodding" industry to devote the largest possible amount of its own resources to reducing environmental pollutants.[47] And very little in the CEPA review process encourages us to think that we will get either of them anytime soon.

WHAT SHOULD BE DONE ABOUT SOMETHING THAT IS "CEPA-TOXIC"?

The answer is, to use a phrase now found in the policy literature on toxic substances: We should "virtually eliminate" it. This is a curious phrase with a checquered history of development, but one which does seem appropriate to an age of virtual reality. Virtual elimination (VE) is now for the first time anywhere in the world enshrined in legislation, namely in section 65 of the new CEPA: "[V]irtual elimination means, in respect of a toxic substance released into the environment as a result of human activity, the ultimate reduction of the quantity or concentration of the substance in the release below the level of quantification specified ... which means ... the lowest concentration that can be accurately measured using sensitive but routine sampling and analytical methods."[48] Below the level at which we can "accurately measure" something, we have no idea whether or not it is present in the environment, except if it shows up again with the deployment of newer instrumentation: once we could measure at the level of parts per million, then billion and trillion and quadrillion and so on down the microscopic scale eventually to the molecular level. But for all practical purposes, if we could once pinpoint something but now can no longer do so, we do not know if any of it remains or not, so we cannot chase it any more. In other words, in effect it shows up on our current detection equipment as "zero concentration"; another way of expressing this is to say that the substance is now at a "non-detectable level." On the other hand, if it reappears again under the scrutiny of more powerful equipment we could, if we wished, take steps designed to push the concentrations down again to a newer non-detectable level.

In the late 1980s this occurred when dioxins showed up in cardboard milk containers because brand-new laboratory equipment for the first time broke through the testing threshold of parts per quadrillion; process changes were implemented in the pulp and paper industry that resulted in dioxins' disappearing again from the test results. But it is a virtual certainty that dioxins are still present in those containers, as well as in everything else we use, since dioxins from various sources (industrial and natural) are ubiquitous in the global environment at very low levels. Should we care? The only way to answer that question is to do a risk assessment, starting with the latest hazard characterization for dioxins, the detectable levels in the environment, a dose-response model, and exposure data, and coming up with an estimate of the probability of harm. But the nice thing about VE is that it saves us all the bother of having to redo the risk assessment, which is a rather complicated business: if it's on the list to be virtually eliminated, and we detect it, we can then initiate a process to drive it away again.

The list in question is schedule 1 of CEPA, which is made up of substances that have been declared "CEPA-toxic"; some dioxin compounds are on the list, along with (as of now) forty-four other compounds or groups of compounds, including the ozone-depleting substances and some familiar ones, namely, asbestos, lead, and mercury. It is especially interesting to find asbestos on this list, since Canada remains the second-largest producer of one form of asbestos in the world (all of it mined in the province of Quebec). Our country has vigorously defended the continued use of this toxic substance in industrial applications – subject to appropriate controls on human exposure as determined by a risk assessment – against recent bans and proposed bans by European countries such as France and Britain. Asbestos is a virtually indestructible mineral fibre that, like dioxin, can be detected everywhere in our environment as a result of past commercial uses, but our risk assessment tells us that, on the basis of current understanding, we do not have to take any further actions to reduce asbestos concentrations in ambient air. No call has been heard in Canada, so far as I know, to "virtually eliminate" asbestos.[49]

VE was championed most strongly in the reports and publications after 1985 sponsored by the International Joint Commission (IJC), the binational body that oversees boundary waters along the entire Canada-US divide; later it was adopted in the federal government's "Toxic Substances Management Plan" and the US EPA's "Virtual Elimination Pilot Project." The odd thing about all the references to this concept is how infrequently it has been defined. One of the few places one can find a reasonably clear account of it is in a 1994 Canada-Ontario agreement: "The ultimate goal of Canada and Ontario is to achieve the virtual elimination of persistent, bioaccumulative and toxic substances from the Great Lakes Basin Ecosystem by encouraging and implementing strategies consistent with the philosophy of zero discharge ... Continued application of the zero discharge philosophy, both in the Great Lakes Basin and outside the basin, will be necessary to eventually achieve the long-term goal of virtual elimination."[50] It is instructive to find this approach described as a "philosophy," rather than a risk management strategy. The unwitting candour here at least helps us to figure out what is going on. For the "philosophy of zero discharge" is in fact inconsistent with the risk assessment approach, which is based on a dose-response concept of harm, an approach which the Canadian government is ostensibly committed to for fulfilling its responsibilities for health and environmental protection.

It is in any case not a very comprehensive philosophy, at least not when it appears in its legislative incarnation in CEPA. The following exchange took place with an Environment Canada official during the Senate hearings on Bill C-32, the final version of the new CEPA:

SENATOR SPIVAK: Am I correct that this ["virtual elimination of releases"] deals with the 12 most persistent [toxic] chemicals, and does not refer to the 23,000 which currently exist [in commercial use]? ...
MR LERER: That is correct. There are now 12 on the list, nine of which have been banned in Canada. They are not used domestically. The environment is still exposed to some of them because of global wind currents ... Nine of the twelve have already been banned. Our best scientific guesstimate is that, over the next five to ten years, we may see another dozen of these among the 23,000 that the bill commands us to categorize and assess.[51]

It is indeed refreshing to hear the witness using the word "ban" to describe the objective of virtual elimination. And indeed appropriate, for it brings us back to where we started in this discussion, to the federal power – as elucidated by the Supreme court – as it pertains to environmental management. As noted earlier, the court has stated clearly that this power is limited to acts of "prohibition," and thus VE, if it is subjected to and survives any legal challenge, will do so as the functional implementation of the authority to prohibit.

Alas, as thus circumscribed, virtual elimination will never be applied to more than the tiniest fraction of the substances introduced into the environment by human activity which require some kind of management strategy. As the culmination of a toxic substances management strategy, therefore, VE is and will remain functionally impotent. The price that is paid in constitutional terms for the court-sanctioned authority to ban toxic substances is a very heavy one: namely, a restriction of its practical applicability to a small subclass of potentially harmful agents, a subclass on which there is already near-universal agreement about the wisdom of discontinuing use. We need a somewhat wider purview for environmental management than this.[52]

In the end it all goes back to the constitutional basis of the federal power. The cumbersome nature of the toxic-substances authority is rooted in the power to prohibit, as affirmed by the Supreme Court; the very quality that makes it constitutionally valid also dooms it to ineffectiveness and irrelevance for risk-based decision making. No one who is in the federal policy system and who also wishes to be regarded as sane would, these days, advocate a redistribution of constitutional authority for the environment between the federal and provincial governments, but, alas, that is what is needed. But what about striking a "win-win" deal? The federal power could receive paramountcy and full regulatory authority in environmental matters in return for ceding complete control over health care to the provinces. Thus two endemic sources of fruitless irritation and squabbling could be eliminated at a single stroke. There is even some logic in the idea, in that environmental protection needs increasingly cross regional, transboundary, and international regimes, so that vesting the authority to address them squarely in the federal power makes sense. Realistically, however, this scheme has low probability of success, perhaps because the continuation of intergovernmental squabbling is a highly prized endeavour in its own right.

TWO VIABLE STEPS

Sometimes it seems that departments of government responsible for "the environment" take too literally the meaning of environment as "everything," especially if they have enshrined that meaning in their legislative instruments.[53] Responsible in principle for everything, they appear to have difficulty in deciding just what they can and should do about anything in particular. A solution for the problems diagnosed above lies precisely in picking – even arbitrarily – out of that universal mandate a very limited set of things that can be done, comfortably and consistently, with whatever resources are available. I have in mind just two such things; if they were to be done well, very few would mind that some other things must wait. The two are: (i) orienting *all* programs around a single focal point, defined by pollution prevention and an appropriate precautionary principle; (ii) delivering these programs largely through co-operative and negotiated arrangements and, to the greatest extent possible, market-based instruments.[54]

In spring 1995, Environment Canada released a consultation document entitled "Pollution Prevention: Towards a Federal Strategy for Action."[55] It defined pollution prevention as follows: "The use of processes, practices, materials, products or energy that avoid or minimize the creation of pollutants and waste, without shifting or creating new risks to human health or the environment." Ontario's Ministry of Environment has led the way in Canada in seeking to win acceptance for this approach, and the US Environmental Protection Agency has championed it for some years now.[56] When a definition reappeared in Bill C-32 (section 3), the word "substances" was added to the first part, and the last part (after "pollution and waste") was dropped and replaced with the words "and reduce the overall risk to the environment and human health."

The rewording in Bill C-32 is a vast improvement over the earlier formulation. Using a risk management approach, we should always be on the lookout for good (cost-effective) bargains in risk reduction. On the other hand, we also need to be on the lookout for apparent solutions that merely shift the *same* (or greater) burden of risk from one medium, area, or population group to another. (For example, eliminating effluents to water by transferring them to the air.) However, provided there is no surreptitious or otherwise unacceptable risk transfer, a prohibition on the creation of *any* "new" risks unnecessarily reduces the potential benefits from pollution prevention, because almost always, by definition, new technologies create new risks.[57] The only relevant questions are: Has a risk been shifted unacceptably? Is there a demonstrable net risk reduction? And are the new risks acceptable according to prevailing community standards?[58] If the first answer is "no," and the next two "yes," there is no reason not to proceed.

A NOTE ON THE DESIRABILITY OF CREATING NEW RISKS

As a practical matter, since by and large technologies advance incrementally, we witness gradual improvements in our ability to produce useful things, using hazardous materials, with progressively lower environmental and health risks. Since all of our technological manipulations induce risks, the creation of new (lesser) risks is generally a salutory process, in that they are intended to replace older and greater risks – and, since there is no such thing as a risk-free technology, the creation of such new risks is a necessary aspect of progress in environmental protection. Thus, contrary to the view that pollution prevention ought to outlaw new risks, the contention here is that the creation of new risks of lesser magnitude ought to be not just tolerated, but rather positively encouraged. Since this is a potentially controversial standpoint, I want to provide some additional support for this notion here.

We can start with the common assumption that existing technologies entail specific types of risks, which become more or less adequately recognized and quantified and which also generate specific types of benefits. Over time the types of general benefits we seek (such as comfort, adequate nutrition and shelter, good health, and personal mobility) tend not to disappear, but rather to be amplified in scope and elaborated in detail, requiring newer technologies to provision them. At the same time, reflecting our greater awareness of risk factors themselves, as well as the urge to protect our attained state of well-being from unacceptable levels of risk, we require those newer technologies to produce greater benefits with lesser risks, which is generally possible with more sophisticated technologies. An example is a medical technology that can target tumour tissue directly as opposed to flooding the entire body with toxic therapeutic chemicals; another is a pesticide which, when broadcast into the environment, can attack target organisms while minimizing or eliminating impacts on non-target ones.

Such sophisticated technologies achieve their results through innovative mechanisms of physical, chemical, and biological action. For example, the group of chemicals known as "statins" can reduce blood cholesterol levels by suppressing the liver functions by which the body produces cholesterol, which was not possible before these chemicals were devised. *But this is virtually the same thing as saying that they create new types of risks.* Generally speaking, in incrementally advancing technologies the sum total of potential adverse effects on health and environment will be progressively smaller than it was previously, except where qualitatively new types of benefits are involved. Some of the risks associated with newer technologies will be less damaging versions of earlier ones, and some will be completely new, the result of those innovative mechanisms of action referred to above; however, the risks will never be zero. Because new technologies are by definition new types of actions, and by definition new types of actions are virtually certain to have unintended adverse effects as well as the sought-for beneficial ones, new types of risks will be created in the pursuit of a generally lower overall risk profile for available technologies as a whole. Q.E.D.

"CREATION" VS. "RELEASE"

Another issue sometimes raised is the difference between "creation" and "release" of (potential) pollutants. Both the Standing Committee Report and the federal consultation document opted for "creation," but without giving an adequate picture of what is at stake in choosing one or the other of these two terms. If it is understood literally, the "creation" of pollutants applies to any substance that is formed in an industrial process, *whether or not it is released to the environment*. For example, if a new substance – say, in a pulp mill process – were created as a direct result of introducing a fully closed-loop (zero discharge) system, even though that substance would not escape into the environment, presumably this would violate the preferred formulation of the pollution prevention principle. But surely this is nonsensical and self-defeating. What should we care if some new hazardous substance is created, so long as it is not released (i.e., there is no exposure to it)?[59]

Let us be clear on this point. Most of the hazardous substances that are industrially created exist because they are useful in themselves or because they are feedstocks for other useful things; a good example of the latter is phosgene, which is extremely hazardous, and which is also a feedstock chemical for a huge number of ultimately useful things. Obviously we must carefully manage the exposures of humans and other entities to these dangerous things. On the other hand, materials that are *only* "pollutants" are not created deliberately, but arise as accidental and (at a particular time) possibly unavoidable by-products of other processes. It is not only common-sensical but also cost-effective to seek to avoid the creation of pollutants, which, unless they can be discharged without hindrance into the environment (a course of action that is progressively more tightly circumscribed), give rise to steadily increasing costs of control and disposal. So one would not create pollutants unless it were unavoidable to do so with the available technologies, or because it would be cheaper to do so than not. If it is the latter case, then it may be unwise to seek to rule out this option by legislation, but it is not unreasonable for society to prohibit the release of pollutants into the environment, requiring instead their containment and approved means of disposal, unless the conditions of release can be shown to be within the parameters of acceptable risk.[60]

In fact the focus on creation rather than release is just another version of the confusion between hazard and risk which lies at the heart of what is wrong with "CEPA-toxic." At bottom, a ban on creating new risks means that, despite pretences to the contrary, its champions do not trust the risk assessment process, which is, in common parlance, supposed to tell us whether there are any unacceptable risks arising out of our exposure to hazards.[61] So "release," not "creation," is the real environmental protection issue when it comes to implementing pollution prevention.

CONCLUSION: TRANSITION TO "USER/PRODUCER RESPONSIBILITY"

There is a sentence in the Standing Committee Report that reads as follows: "[U]sers/producers must ensure that the substances they produce, use or sell do not pose an unacceptable risk to the environment or human health." This is intriguing, surprising, and puzzling, because in deceptively simple language it takes us straight out of the command-and-control framework that otherwise pervades the whole of the Standing Committee Report and its toxic-substances mentality! Is it possible that the authors of this sentence did not realize what they were saying? In fact its thrust is inconsistent with the underlying philosophy of CEPA as a whole, which puts the burden on government to find out everything that may be harmful in the environment, then how to regulate it effectively, and finally how to monitor everyone's compliance with all of the foregoing. This was never a realistic scenario, and its chances of success grow fainter with each passing year. For example, in his 1999 report, the commissioner of the environment and sustainable development found "significant weaknesses" in the federal environmental effects-monitoring effort. The sentence is, however, the philosophical basis of a very different approach, where primary responsibility for environmental protection is rooted in a "managerial ethic."[62]

A general managerial ethic oriented towards pollution prevention is based on the simple idea that the unwanted by-products of human activity (garbage from individuals as well as industrial wastes) may be presumed to be harmful to the environment *in some measure* and therefore that, in principle, all such by-products should be prevented from entering the environment except under deliberately planned conditions. In seeking to realize this ideal, pollution prevention incorporates a hierarchy of preferred options with respect to unwanted substances, namely, prevention, control, and disposal, including a number of subsets:[63]

PREVENTION	1	Prevent Creation/Use
	2	Prevent Release
CONTROL	3	Reuse/Recycle
	4	Manage *in situ*
DISPOSAL	5	Manage externally
	6	Remediation of prior stocks

Thus the preferred courses of action are ranked hierarchically from 1 to 6.

A general pollution prevention framework requires all agents who are thought to be releasing substances into the environment in significant amounts to be working from a prevention plan, which could, for example, be based on a concept of continuous improvement (that is, progressively lower impacts, or lower overall risk, of releases to all media per unit of production). The plan would also entail a continuing effort to move up the hierarchy, from number 6 towards number 1, for each logically distinct production sub-unit within a facility or operation. In such a scheme it would be the prerogative of the polluting agent to seek to demonstrate, for any operation, credibly and to public satisfaction, that a threshold of acceptable risk (i.e., acceptable harm) had been reached, and that no further effort or investment in pollution prevention for that operation was desirable. This would be done through a properly conducted risk assessment.

The managerial ethic would shift the burden of proof from the regulator to the regulated, and presumably it would be cost-effective for the polluting agent to conduct such a risk assessment. Of course, society and governments also have an interest in cost-effective risk management, that is, in seeking to ensure that resources for risk reduction are allocated as wisely as possible. Therefore the regulator might share the initiative and the cost of the risk assessment, if through voluntary negotiation there was an agreement in place to allocate risk reduction resources saved in one area to another domain. And, so far as the generation of new risks is concerned, if these are thought to be advantageous in achieving lower overall risk, the risk initiator can be asked to provide, or to share the cost of (as above), the proof of same in a proper risk assessment.

9 Voluntary Instruments

ÉRIC DARIER AND
DEBORA VAN NIJNATTEN,
WITH AN ADDENDUM
BY WILLIAM LEISS

By their very nature, environmental problems tend to be riddled with scientific uncertainties and complexities which require Herculean solutions. Yet these solutions must be formulated by multiple institutions and processes which do not themselves possess an obvious mandate, set of responsibilities, political will, legitimacy, or even practical expertise to tackle the apprehended environmental problem. Consequently, most attempts to address environmental problems in the real world are dealt with in a "muddling-through" approach, one that is readily observable in the reactions to the emergence of voluntary non-regulatory initiatives (VNRIs) as environmental policy instruments in Canada.[1]

The shift from an almost complete reliance on government-centred, "command-and-control" instruments – which have characterized environmental policy making over the past three decades – to more diffuse sets of practices, including relying on industry goal setting and self-enforcement, is part of an international trend. As a result, a wide variety of non-regulatory instruments have appeared in various jurisdictions, including:

- management standards such as BS 7750 in the UK, Denmark, and the Netherlands, ISO 14001 in (mainly) North America, and eco-audit programs such as EMAS (Eco-Management and Audit Standards) at the European Union level;[2]
- market instruments using fiscal incentives/disincentives such as product stewardship systems or emissions trading regimes;[3]

- industry-government convenants, contracts, or memorandums of understanding with specific environmental targets;[4] and
- voluntary challenge programs in which industry sets and achieves goals independently of government.[5]

In Western European countries and in the US, by and large, experimentation with VNRIs has been undertaken with due regard to the established policy and regulatory framework. For example, in the Netherlands pollution reduction "covenants" – agreements between industry and the national government specifying actions to be taken to reduce emissions – have been brokered within a framework of government-mandated targets, parliamentary oversight, and credible regulatory threat. In the US the adoption of VNRIs has been quite selective and the VNRIs themselves are intended only as experiments to supplement existing and new regulatory activities. In Canada, however, VNRIs at the federal level and in a number of provinces (especially Ontario) have been adopted rather haphazardly within an explicitly deregulatory context and alongside considerable reductions in environmental protection budgets. In some cases, environmental protection tasks formerly performed by government institutions are being shifted to individual companies or industry associations with little public debate; in others, VNRIs are being used more explicitly as an alternative to regulations.

In the ongoing debate, proponents argue that VNRIs are more flexible than regulations and can be targeted more directly, that they are more cost-effective and more amenable to quick design and implementation, and that they are also more likely to lead to a co-operative working relationship between government and industry. Critics counter that VNRIs are not necessarily as efficient and effective as established regulatory instruments[6] and that they are fundamentally inappropriate for environmental protection tasks.[7] In addition, some believe that these mechanisms represent an attempt by industry to avoid existing and new environmental regulations, or to reduce, even eliminate, the monitoring and enforcement capability of environmental agencies.[8] Critics also note that voluntary initiatives are usually unenforceable and subject to the free-rider problem, public accountability structures are largely non-existent, and the targets – because they are often set by industry – are unlikely to be particularly stringent.[9] Finally, much has been made of the tendency for voluntary initiatives to be formulated "behind closed doors" by industry and government, unlike the environmental regulations of the more recent past.[10]

After years of cuts to environmental protection budgets in Canada, successive rounds of deregulation or privatization of numerous environmental protection tasks by federal and provincial governments, and public concern about other issues such as health care, VNRIs are probably here to stay, at least for the medium term. The increased use of such mechanisms reflects these realities more than any coherent attempt to integrate new, effective environmental protection instruments into the policy toolkits of governments.

One significant problem is that the linkages between VNRIs and the Canadian environmental protection policy framework are tenuous at best. If VNRIs continue to be employed, as seems likely, they will need to be more explicitly and more effectively linked to public environmental protection goals and to policy/regulatory frameworks. Without such linkages, it will be difficult to ensure that voluntary initiatives are designed to (and in actuality do) deliver effective action. Moreover, if VNRIs continue to exist at the margins of the policy framework, as they do now, they also will continue to suffer from a lack of credibility in terms of their ability to deliver acceptable levels of environmental protection in a transparent and inclusive manner. Public credibility is unlikely to follow, and industry actors will not receive credit for real environmental gains. Nor will industry laggards be censured.

The so-called "ARET Challenge," one of Canada's most high-profile VNRIs, has been at the centre of debates about the place of VNRIs in the environmental policy framework. Indeed, this particular VNRI appears to represent much of what is possible through voluntary initiatives and, simultaneously, much of what is wrong with them. ARET (Accelerated Reduction/Elimination of Toxics) initially took the form of a multi-stakeholder consultation process which aimed to rethink toxic substances management in Canada and evolved into the ARET Challenge, a voluntary toxics reduction initiative undertaken by industry. However, the original ARET process laboured under a lack of policy guidance by government, which was at least partly responsible for the eventual breakdown of the process over questions of policy goals (reduction vs. elimination of toxics) and instrument choice (regulatory vs. voluntary measures). The ARET Challenge, brought into being after environmental stakeholders left the process, has likewise existed in a policy "purgatory." The Challenge suffers the fate of VNRIs in Canada generally, namely that governments utilize them but have not specified where and how such instruments fit into the environmental protection regime. Neither has the link between the ARET Challenge and federal toxic substances policy been properly defined, although some efforts in this direction have been made more recently. ARET Challenge participants and other stakeholders have been contemplating a redesign of the program under which its requirements and program components would be explicitly linked to government's toxic substances management objectives and a clear policy regarding instrument choice.

ARET'S HISTORY

The ARET initiative originally arose out of the work of the New Directions Group (NDG). The NDG is an independent, voluntary network of concerned Canadians from industry, environmental groups, and other non-governmental organizations which first came together in November 1990. The group's formation was spurred by the desire to establish a forum that "actively uses cooperative, non-adversarial methods of identifying and providing leadership in addressing significant environment-economy issues."[11] NDG activities were to be guided by four principles: the goal of sustainable development; a commitment to pollution prevention (where minimizing the generation of pollution takes priority over controlling discharges by end-of-pipe treatment); a cross-media approach (air, water, land, and biota) to reduction, not just shifting toxic substances from one medium to another; and a commitment to public participation in decision making.[12]

The first problem that the NDG chose to address, owing to the immediacy of the issue, was toxic substance emissions. During the 1980s, discussion had turned to the possible "sunsetting" or elimination of chemicals considered toxic through phase-outs and bans. In this vein, the NDG sought alternative methods to "reduce and eliminate emissions of toxic substances." The objective of the group was not to substitute these alternative policy instruments for environmental regulation. Rather, additional initiatives were to complement government and industry programs. In September of 1991, the group called on the federal government to initiate a process for targeted reductions including phasing out of some substances. The federal minister of the environment responded by launching a group that became known as "the ARET Committee."

The ARET Committee, although brought to life by the NDG initiative, was quite a different entity. Whereas the NDG had consisted of industry CEOs and executive directors of NGOs, ARET was composed of representatives of broad-based industry associations, ENGO representatives nominated by the Toxics Caucus of the Canadian Environmental Network, representatives of labour and aboriginal peoples, federal and provincial government officials, and representatives from health and professional groups. The ARET Committee had three main objectives: (a) to establish criteria for defining and measuring toxicity; (b) to compile a list of target substances based on these criteria; and (c) to devise a means by which industry could address its toxic emissions. The first two objectives were realized in the course of a series of intensive meetings of the ARET Committee and its subcommittees held throughout 1992. First, there was multi-stakeholder consensus on the criteria chosen: toxicity, persistence, and bioaccumulation. Second, the three-criteria approach resulted in multi-stakeholder consensus regarding the categorization of substances into five lists:

- List A-1 for 30 substances which met the persistence, bioaccumulation, and toxicity criteria;
- List B-1 for 8 substances which met the toxicity and bioaccumulation criteria;
- List B-2 for 33 substances which met persistence and toxicity criteria; and
- List B-3 for 44 substances which met only the toxicity criterion.

List A-2 contains 2 substances which met the three criteria but failed to gain consensus on reduction targets (total substances listed = 117).[13]

In late 1992 and early 1993, however, rifts among the stakeholders concerning the third task became evident, and in September 1993 the environmental and labour groups withdrew from the ARET Committee. A letter sent to Environment Canada by representatives of the Canadian Labour Congress, Great Lakes United, Pollution Probe, Toxics Watch Society of Alberta, and the West Coast Environmental Law Association outlined the reasons for their decision to withdraw from the ARET process.[14] First, the NGOs had believed that the original purpose of ARET was to "identify the most hazardous toxic substances and then develop strategies for their phase-out." For the NGOs, there were "no safe levels" and elimination was the "only appropriate long-term strategy." This meant uncompromising attempts to reduce both the generation and use of persistent toxic chemicals by identifying substances for phase-out. According to the NGOs, the ARET process did not seem to be moving in this direction. Secondly, the NGOs felt that Environment Canada failed to demonstrate proactive leadership in the process, viewing itself instead as a "stakeholder" and providing little policy guidance for the process. It is important to note, however, that ENGO and labour representatives continued to work on the Substances Selection Subcommittee, which finished its work in November. This allowed ARET to secure agreement on a substantial list of targeted substances that was truly based on a multi-stakeholder consensus.

It was decided by the remaining ARET Committee members that ARET should continue with industry and government participation. Then in March of 1994 the ARET Challenge to industry – voluntarily to reduce or eliminate toxic emissions – was issued. More specifically, the Challenge sought the virtual elimination of substances in list A-1 (90 per cent reduction by the year 2000) and a 50 per cent reduction in the same period for substances on the other lists. Industry was challenged to achieve these targeted reductions by means of voluntary action. Since the ARET Challenge was issued after the withdrawal of ENGOs and labour representatives from the ARET Committee in September of 1993, it was (and is) not supported by these sectors.

PHASE I OF THE ARET PROCESS:
ON THE LEADING EDGE, WITHOUT A MAP

The ARET process was initiated at a time when multi-stakeholder consultation was widely accepted as an integral part of environmental decision making, especially at the national level. However, whereas other multi-stakeholder processes had been clearly oriented towards the formulation of new legislative or regulatory mechanisms – e.g., a National Pollutant Release Inventory – ARET was different. The ARET Committee's work would be groundbreaking, defining toxicity and categorizing an incredible array of substances on the basis of the harm they posed to humans and the environment; but the final objectives of the ARET process were less clear.

When the ARET Committee first began its deliberations, government was in the process of formulating a number of different policies and contemplating various instruments in the area of toxic substances management. Perhaps as a result of this, government representatives adopted an ambiguous role in the ARET process and failed to provide guidance concerning overall policy goals, i.e., reduction or elimination, and the type of instrument that should result, i.e., a regulatory or voluntary program. In fact, representatives of Environment Canada behaved more as observers in the process than as policy makers or even stakeholders. This led to some frustration among the different stakeholder groups, who felt that Environment Canada was abrogating its responsibility to "govern." Moreover, because of the relatively open-ended nature of the ARET process, participants had different understandings of the terms of reference and goals of the process. Finally, any confusion about the framework for deliberation was exacerbated by process difficulties including unclear decision rules and complex participant-constituency relations.

The following discussion of these process-related issues draws on material gleaned from interviews with ARET Committee participants.[15]

1 Vague Terms of Reference

There was considerable misunderstanding surrounding the mandate of the original ARET Committee, despite the fact that successive draft versions of an ARET "Strategic Plan and Decision-Making Framework" were circulated to stakeholders. One version of the plan laid out three key objectives for the ARET Committee: (1) to develop an action plan with specific milestones that would result in accelerated, substantial, measurable reduction or elimination of selected bioaccumulative persistent toxic substances emissions from significant sources in Canada by the year 2000; (2) to develop challenges to industry and other sources of toxics, either by individual source or sector, for generalized reductions of emissions of substances or classes of substances; and (3) to demonstrate the successful use of a consensus approach to decision making.[16] In fact, the ARET Committee's mandate has been variously described by stakeholders as "fuzzy," "well defined," "broad," "very complicated," "naïve," and "unclear." Examples of more specific interpretations included the following:

- "a program to prove the validity of voluntary action in environmental policy,"
- "a program to eliminate the use of certain persistent, toxic chemicals,"
- "a talk shop geared towards understanding where the different interests were coming from on the issue of toxics use,"
- "a means of tackling toxic emissions through reductions and eliminations without a regulatory framework, although regulation might prove necessary in the end," and
- "a voluntary emission reductions plan implemented through industry associations who would then move their members to deliver."

The most contentious aspects of the mandate concerned the emphasis to be placed on the reduction vs. the elimination of substances deemed toxic and on voluntary vs. regulatory efforts to achieve this. Some stakeholders thought that ARET "included elimination by definition," while others disagreed. The problem, according to one stakeholder, was that there were different definitions of elimination; elimination was taken to mean either end-of-pipe treatment or complete phase-out, depending on who was doing the defining. Furthermore, some stakeholders wanted to address toxics use, as well as toxic emissions, as they believed pollution prevention was impossible without examining the use of toxic chemicals. Others preferred the focus on emissions, however. In addition, stakeholders disagreed on whether or not ARET was intended as a voluntary reductions program. Opinion was divided on the role regulation should play in a voluntary program – no role at all; as a backdrop to set minimum standards and ensure a level playing field; or as a proactive framework with extensive reporting requirements. Many believed that the regulatory stick was "in there somewhere," "sort of agreed to" or "implicit" in the mandate. Yet this was not clear.

One stakeholder summed up the problem with the ARET Committee's mandate as follows: "The 'if' question has to be resolved before the process starts, because multi-stakeholder projects can only deal with 'how' to get there." In the ARET process, the 'if' question was never resolved. A number of stakeholders used the National Pollutant Release Inventory (NPRI) as an example of a multi-stakeholder process that contained clear terms of reference provided by a supportive government. In this case, stakeholders hammered out the details of reporting requirements; there was no debate about whether there should be requirements in the first place. This can be compared with the ARET process in which "Environment Canada laid down no givens, so that stakeholders wandered forever," as one stakeholder put it.

2 Decision-Making Difficulties

The lack of an authoritative policy framework, evident in the ill-defined mandate of the ARET Committee, affected stakeholder discussions. Many participants doubted the usefulness and purpose of their participation in a process with uncertain goals. Indeed, there were various levels of suspicion concerning the "real" agenda behind the ARET initiative and who would be most likely to benefit. For example, some saw ARET as a "platform for industry in anticipation of regulation" and believed that the process was an "attempt to head off regulation." The frustration expressed by a number of stakeholders was summed up by one: "The process didn't seem to be getting anywhere, there was too much disagreement on fundamental issues." One stakeholder noted that repeated attempts were made by stakeholders to clarify the use of terms such as "reduction," "elimination," and "pollution prevention" during the course of meetings, which might have helped to clarify the project's mandate. Process facilitators also seemed unable to resolve continuing points of tension.

Interviewees reported uncertainty about how decisions were to be made. One interviewee stated: "There were no formal rules for consensus/agreement, just a willingness to participate." The method for reaching agreement was variously described as "fighting it out," "general agreement around the table," "not necessarily requiring unanimity," "implicitly requiring unanimity," and "can everyone live with that?" One stakeholder also pointed out that decision-making processes were quite different in the main ARET Committee and the subcommittees. The former was mainly concerned with value-laden policy issues and the latter with technical questions. It thus appeared much easier to make decisions in the subcommittees. An effort to streamline and facilitate "political" decision making by creating a smaller decision-making subcommittee concerned with the more contentious issues proved unsuccessful, however.

The lack of clear decision-making rules, coupled with underlying suspicion, fostered "an initial distrust and prudence" among stakeholders, a sense of caution, and a lack of respect for the process. The various represented interests took to forging mini-consensuses among themselves within caucuses (e.g., the industry "Friday Group"), or in "corridor negotiations" before or during the committee meetings. One interviewee noted that groups would get up in the middle of the meeting and consult in caucus.

The uncertainty about goals and rules and the climate of suspicion also may have complicated participant-constituency relations. Difficulties in getting the constituencies "on line" seemed to be an issue for a number of stakeholders. In particular, there was frustration on the part of some stakeholders about the inability of environmental representatives to "make deals" with others around the table. The self-perceived role of environmental representatives, however, was to act as "facilitators for the environmental perspective," rather than deal makers. The representation of environmental interests in ARET was co-ordinated by the Canadian Environmental Network (CEN), which does not take positions on behalf of its members, although issue-based working groups or caucuses of CEN may do so. On the industry side, difficulties in representative-association relations were also referred to. Indeed, it would appear that the boundaries defining what representatives of some associations could agree to on behalf of their constituency were restrictive, and this factor might have hindered discussions at the table.

The Canadian experience with multi-stakeholder consulation has shown that an important ingredient for a successful multi-stakeholder consultation is the provision by government of a policy framework within which consultation can occur. The outcomes of consultation should be consistent with and inform the larger decision-making process and priorities already set by government. Moreover, this framework should be clear to participants from the beginning of the consultation so that they know what is expected from them and what results to expect from their work. In the case of the ARET process, policy guidance by government was especially needed in light of new initiatives in the area of toxics reduction and the possibility of employing a voluntary instrument. Environment Canada accepted the challenge of the NDG to set up a multi-stakeholder process dealing with the important

problem of toxic substance discharges, but after the project was initiated, the agency's role was unclear. Moreover, multi-stakeholder processes can only work if the representatives of each constituency taking
part are committed to the process and work at convincing their constituencies that the process is worthwhile and that compromises must be
made. In the ARET case, the ambiguity inherent in the process and its
goals may have weakened any incentive for representatives to try to
convince their constituencies that compromises were worthwhile, a
difficult task under any circumstances.

Both the confusion surrounding ARET's mandate and the process and
decision-making difficulties were symptomatic of a larger dilemma –
uncertainty concerning where the ARET process was going to lead and
the means that would be used to get there. This uncertainty carried
over into the formulation and implementation of the voluntary ARET
Challenge.

PHASE 2, THE ARET CHALLENGE: A VOLUNTARY INITIATIVE IN POLICY PURGATORY

The ARET Challenge, issued by the remaining industry and government
stakeholders after the departure of the NGOs, has existed at the margins
of Environment Canada's toxics policy framework. Certainly, Environment Canada's response to the ARET Challenge was initially ambiguous
– which is perhaps not surprising, given the departure of the environmental non-governmental interests. A number of stakeholders initially
believed that the outcome of the ARET process would guide Environment Canada's approach to toxic emissions, whether this approach was
a regulatory one or support for voluntarism or some combination of the
two. Some sort of policy support was expected. It was the case that the
original letter sent to industry CEOs encouraging them to participate in
the Challenge was signed by all remaining stakeholders on the ARET
Committee, including the deputy minister of Environment Canada.
Moreover, the new minister of the environment who stepped into the
portfolio after the federal election in November 1993 increased the reduction target for emissions A-I substances from 50 per cent to 90 per
cent by the year 2000, a move which was praised by some stakeholders
and criticized by others. Overall, however, ministerial and public recognition of the Challenge was muted and the project seemed to float
somewhere in the public sphere, largely unacknowledged by the federal
government and thus difficult to sell to potential industry participants
or the provinces.

1 *Purported Environmental Gains*

Industry and some government representatives emphasize the industry-reported figures for toxics reduction as evidence of the Challenge's environmental success. Since the ARET Challenge was launched in March 1994, 316 organizations have agreed to participate. Collectively, these organizations have reduced their overall emissions by 26,358 tonnes from base year to the end of 1998 and were forecast to reduce their emissions by a further 3052 tonnes through 1999–2000.[17] An Environment Canada consultation paper notes: "By the time ARET runs its course, it is expected that participants will have reduced their emissions of 30 of the most harmful toxic substances by 71% (short of the 90% target) and emissions of 87 less hazardous substances by about 80% (well above the original 50% target)."[18] The average level of participation among the eight industry sectors who have signed on is 85 per cent, with 100 per cent participation for the Canadian Chemical Producers' Association (CCPA), 100 per cent for electrical utilities, and 97 per cent for mining and smelting.[19] Companies representing approximately half of Canadian industrial production have publicly committed themselves to the program.

In addition to the improved emission reduction results, participating companies report that they have derived numerous benefits from ARET, such as the development of effective toxics management strategies, reduced chemical spills, process and product cost reductions, and improved leak detection and repair programs.[20] In more general terms, one stakeholder has said that "ARET made us ask some questions we hadn't asked before and helped us uncover some problems we didn't think we had." It would appear that accepting the ARET Challenge has resulted in little change to administrative and management structures at the organizational level, however. Co-ordinating the association response to the ARET Challenge and selling it to members have been accomplished mainly through existing management structures and communication channels within industry sectors. In one example, the CCPA piggy-backed the ARET project onto management structures put in place for the "Responsible Care" Program, namely regional leadership groups of CEOs. In addition, the Canadian Manufacturing Association had previously compiled a database of 800 environmental co-ordinators within member companies, to whom information on ARET could be passed on and from whom feedback could be received.

Some ARET participants believe that industry willingness to participate in the ARET Challenge could reflect a change in attitude which is taking place within industry. As one stakeholder noted, even if the ARET

Challenge is only a reporting forum for industry, it could potentially become "a catalyst for other environmental initiatives." It is also argued that the ARET Challenge has been useful in demonstrating to more sceptical members of the industrial community what might be achieved through voluntary initiatives. One stakeholder noted that "ARET increased our commitment to voluntary initiatives."[21] Still others have emphasized that the ARET Challenge has reinforced the notion that government and industry can work together. Moreover, industry reports that participation in ARET has been less costly than would have been the case under regulatory compliance, while Environment Canada's investment in the Challenge has been relatively minimal.[22]

Problems with the reporting and verification structures of the ARET Challenge have attracted criticism, however, as have difficulties in gaining full industry participation in the program.

2 Questionable Emissions Claims[23]

ARET's emissions reductions claims have been questioned, owing to disparate data collection methods and reporting timelines as well as a lack of third-party verification. First, the reported reductions in emissions of ARET-targeted substances calculated from base year levels may be misleading. Although ARET officially commenced in March of 1994, participating companies were allowed to select a base year as early as 1988. Thus, a company could count its reductions from an emission baseline chosen up to seven years prior to commencement of the program. In addition, companies have adopted different base years. For example, if a company's emissions were higher in 1988 than in 1990, the company could pick 1988 as the base year from which to begin calculating its reductions, which would then appear to be larger than they actually were. Moreover, some reductions attributed to ARET might have been driven by earlier regulations or other motivating factors.

The ARET Secretariat reports that "estimating emissions is not an exact science" and acknowledges that they receive data generated in a number of ways, from direct periodic monitoring and sampling protocols to extrapolation.[24] While general guidelines exist, the reporting format for the presentation of ARET action plans is not prescribed. In fact, measurement of some ARET-targeted substances has required new data collection and reporting methods on the part of companies. The result is that reduction estimates are often difficult to compare. Moreover, some companies report only through the NPRI, which uses definitions and reporting formats which may be different from those employed by ARET. It is thus difficult for the secretariat to achieve a high level of accuracy in calculating the numbers at present.

The credibility of ARET data is further diminished by a lack of outside verification. Indeed, this aspect of the program has attracted perhaps the most criticism. It is widely acknowledged that verification is essential to gaining public trust and realizing the full benefits of a voluntary approach; it is, in fact, the link between credibility and effectiveness.[25] Challenge participants point out that various verification efforts are already taking place in the form of publicly available reports, third-party audits ("Responsible Care"), internal audits (in some larger companies), and through NPRI (it is possible to verify some releases by comparing NPRI and ARET data). It has also been noted that current reporting procedures under ARET might have greater validity than those associated with existing environmental regulations. Under ARET, it is a senior CEO in industry who signs the report instead of an employee in charge of reporting to environmental regulators. The CEO, then, is making a personal and public commitment to the program. The problem, however, it that there is very little consistency; ARET participants verify their reductions in various ways using different methods that are not always comparable.[26]

Some ARET participants are opposed to outside verification because of the associated costs. For nearly all other stakeholders, however, credible verification mechanisms need to be in place to gain the confidence of environmental regulatory agencies, politicians, and the public generally. As one stakeholder has noted: "It is up to industry to convince the regulator that voluntarism can be as efficient as regulation." The chemical industry, when designing their "Responsible Care" voluntary program, recognized the importance of outside verification.[27] "Responsible Care," participation in which is a requirement of membership in the Canadian Chemical Producers' Association, employs four-person verification teams comprising community members, industry representatives, environmentalists, and academics who are wholly independent of the companies being verified. The teams prepare a report on their findings for public, employee, and peer scrutiny. No other industry sectors involved in ARET have undertaken similar programs. Indeed, the absence of an independent verification mechanism hampers the government's ability to recognize the emissions reductions that are actually achieved by industry participants under ARET.

3 The Problem of Non-Participation

In addition to concerns about reporting and data collection by ARET participants, an inability to achieve the full participation of all industry sectors presents a significant obstacle to the realization of program goals. ARET, as it has developed, might be regarded as a case study in free riding. Almost as many companies have abstained from the program as have chosen to join it; in 1997, there were 250 non-participants compared to 278 members.[28] By the year 2000, there were expected to be more non-participants than participants and the annual toxic emissions of companies not participating in ARET were expected to be approximately equal to those of participants. Moreover, participation is uneven across industry sectors, and certain industry leaders appear to be carrying the brunt of the load in meeting the reduction targets. Within some industry sectors, there are companies that refuse to participate in the ARET Challenge, although this number varies according to sector. There are no penalties on those companies that refuse to participate in ARET or do little to meet their commitments. In fact, these companies might be able to gain a competitive advantage, or benefit from an improved public image through their association, while in actuality changing very few of their practices.

Certainly, the ARET program is commendable in that it requires and tallies participating companies' reductions of identified toxics. Other voluntary programs, such as the Voluntary Challenge and Registry Program (VCR) to meet Canada's commitment to reducing green house gas emissions, simply require that participants register action plans.[29] However, despite the strong stance by some industry associations that their member companies should participate in ARET, participation remains variable. This fact, combined with disparate data collection, unclear reporting methods, and a lack of third-party validation, have led some to question the credibility of the Challenge's reported successes.

PHASE 3: REDESIGNING THE ARET CHALLENGE

Where does ARET go from here? Critics continue to ask whether the basic goals of ARET and the program used to achieve these goals are sound. Certainly, one of the significant results of the original ARET process was the drafting of a list of toxic substances to be reduced/eliminated. Considering the relative time and resource constraints, the identification and classification of an impressive number of toxic substances were remarkable. However, has the ARET Challenge served as an adequate instrument to move industry towards the reduction (and the elimination where necessary) of those substances classified as persistent, bioaccumulative, and/or toxic? How should one view the Challenge's emissions claims, the lack of independent verification of these claims, the program's inability to attract significant numbers of new participants, and the apparent difficulties of achieving the 90 per cent virtual elimination goal for the most hazardous substances?

Aware of such questions, the ARET Stakeholders Committee – consisting of representatives of business and government organizations participating in the Challenge – decided to sponsor a one-day workshop on the future of ARET in late 1997. The objective of the workshop was "to identify and discuss issues, ideas and actions that must be addressed in developing a path forward for ARET as a voluntary initiative beyond 2000."[30] Representatives from a variety of stakeholder groups who had a interest in ARET were invited, along with Challenge participants. All participants attending the workshop agreed that verification of the reported releases of ARET substances was critical for ensuring the credibility of the program, and a number of verification formats were suggested, such as tracking ARET releases through NPRI, independent "hard audits" carried out on a random basis, and a system of peer audit.[31] It also was emphasized that government needs to be active in setting future directions for the ARET program, that it needs to specify how ARET fits into the larger policy framework, and that it needs to act to address weaknesses in the Challenge, i.e., the problem with free riders. Perhaps most important, however, all participants expressed strong support for a comprehensive, independent, third-party evaluation of the ARET program before any decisions were taken on the program's future.[32]

In response to the strong consensus at the workshop, the Review Branch of Environment Canada undertook an evaluation of the ARET Challenge in 1998 in collaboration with an Advisory Committee composed of one industry and one non-governmental organization representative. The ongoing evaluation is examining four issues: (1) the effectiveness of the program or the extent to which ARET is reducing/eliminating emissions of toxic substances; (2) the efficiency of the program or the cost of the program vs. the outcomes achieved; (3) the "market share" of the program and the issue of expanding participation; and (4) "other impacts" ARET may have had on participating companies.[33] Interviews, case studies, and departmental databases are being used as information sources.

Although the evaluation is not yet complete, preliminary results appear mixed. The ARET Challenge appears to be useful in helping to set priorities and in advancing pollution control investments, but the actual impact of the program on industry behaviour appears marginal. In addition, the most recent and highly critical report of the commissioner of the environment on federal toxic substances management policy stated: "Existing [voluntary] programs do contribute [to achieving reductions in the release of toxic chemicals] but lack effective accountability, reporting and monitoring arrangements. We are concerned that existing voluntary programs alone may not be sufficient to effectively manage priority substances."[34]

The findings from these two evaluations will certainly be taken into account in the current redesign of the program also being undertaken by Environment Canada over 1999–2000. The findings also may provide fuel for those who argue that the Challenge would be more effective with a regulatory backdrop. ARET's relationship to the existing regulatory framework is unclear, and it might be argued that many of its weaknesses pertaining to reporting and verification requirements as well as levels of participation stem from its non-regulatory, unenforceable status. Studies show that compliance with regulations has been thus far the most important factor motivating industry to undertake environmental protection activities.[35] Even the successful "Responsible Care" and Blue Box voluntary programs were initiated under the threat or in anticipation of regulatory action. It is less clear what role other drivers – including a desire to improve public image, attaining efficiencies that improve income generation, liability requirements, and the presence of "environmental leaders" within organizations[36] – play in encouraging environmentally friendly activities.[37] This is not to suggest that regulations are always the panacea. As F. Bregha and J. Moffet have pointed out: "The federal government would not have been able to achieve the reductions realised under ARET by relying on the *Canadian Environmental Protection Act*, which regulates less than 10 percent of ARET's 117 substances: it has neither the procedural tools to assess quickly the toxicity of so many substances, nor the necessary enforcement capacity to apply a purely regulatory approach."[38] However, it is also likely that the easiest emission reductions have already been achieved and any reductions made beyond current targets will take longer and be more costly. A recent report by Pollution Probe, which surveys a range of voluntary initiatives in Canada, notes: "The first round of ARET achieved a reasonable participation rate and good performance. A renewed ARET faces greater challenges since motivated companies already tend to participate and since these companies may have made the relatively easy reductions (i.e., the 'low-hanging' fruit)." This would imply that a more formalized approach in necessary.

The key issue with ARET continues to be its relationship to publicly articulated environmental protection goals and preferred instruments. Where does the Challenge fit into the federal government's toxics management framework? ARET's approach was adopted in Environment Canada's Toxic Substances Management Policy in 1995, although it is clearly different from the "list-screen-regulate" approach in the Canadian Environmental Protection Act (discussed in chapter 8). It has been suggested that ARET might be used to spur reductions in toxic substances which – when a certain percentage of industry has met agreed-upon targets – would then be incorporated under CEPA's umbrella. No official proposal outlining such an approach has been formulated, however. Moreover, there are still no firm guidelines regarding the use of voluntary initiatives at the federal or provincial levels in Canada, although Environment Canada is currently formulating policy in this area. Neither has the department adopted a uniform policy on pollution prevention vs. emission reduction across programs. Indeed, even as Environment Canada undertakes a redesign of ARET and indicates that it will assume a leadership role in this redesign process, departmental stances on voluntary initiatives generally, on the role of VNRIs in toxic substances management, and even on the reduction vs. elimination question have yet to be unveiled.

This instability may at least partly explain the relatively slow progress to date in renewing ARET. Over the period July 1999 to September 2000, the ARET Secretariat had planned to consider redesign options internally (in conjunction with consultants preparing an "Options" paper), conduct bilateral meetings with stakeholders, and then launch a Stakeholder Workshop at which reform options would be presented and negotiated. After final approval was obtained from Environment Canada, ARET 2 was to be launched in September 2000. Considerable work was indeed carried out in 1999, with reformers considering the addition of new substances to the program while dropping others, changing the reporting structure such that ARET reporting could be piggy-backed onto NPRI, adding incentives to participation, and adopting a new verification process. However, the Stakeholder Workshop, originally scheduled for the fall of 1999, then early 2000, was postponed, and the future of the ARET program remains largely in limbo. The reasons for this delay are likely varied. Certainly, the political context has changed. Yet another a new minister, focusing on priorities other than toxic substance reduction, staff turnover within the ARET Secretariat, a slight increase in support for regulatory and enforcement initiatives (in the face of budgetary surpluses and increased public concern about the environment), and the fall 2000 federal election have all conspired to shift the spotlight from ARET. Yet it also would appear that Environment Canada and certain provinces are now leaning towards a different approach to encouraging industry performance, one inspired by the American "environmental management systems" approach designed to achieve "beyond compliance" targets. The ARET of the new millennium may thus evolve into a very different creature or, perhaps just as likely, it may die a slow death.

ADDENDUM: INTEGRATING VOLUNTARY AND REGULATORY (BY WILLIAM LEISS)

What has been said so far is designed to pose a single question: Who among the major social actors, operating on the national stage, should accept responsibility *in the first instance* for environmental protection?

If one does not have the authority to command, then one should negotiate, especially when there are other parties willing to do so with you (which is the case). This is the situation of the federal power with regard to environmental management issues, broadly considered. The design of the 1999 CEPA, like that of its predecessor, is deficient mainly because of a lack of a comprehensive directive to seek negotiated solutions for such issues. This is especially disappointing because the time is right for choosing such a path, since momentum is building in industrial sectors to recognize responsibility for good environmental management and to engage in co-operative strategies for implementing them. The process leading to ARET began in 1991, and ten years later we still do not have another one. This is simply unacceptable. I believe that, in order to ensure that this neglect is not allowed to continue, our basic environmental protection legislation, at both federal and provincial levels, ought to incorporate provisions recognizing the usefulness of this type of approach and encouraging its wider use.

This proposal certainly will be regarded as controversial in some quarters, because opinion appears to be polarized on the subject. However, I think that this is based on a fundamental misconception of what it is all about. For example, this is often called a "voluntary" approach (or VNRI, "voluntary non-regulatory initiative"), and some persons claim that as such is it inappropriate in principle for something so important as environmental protection. But used in this context, "voluntary" – in the sense of "discretionary" – is simply a misnomer: of course attention to environmental protection should not be regarded as "voluntary" in this sense! That is why using this terminology should be avoided. Terms that have more appropriate connotations are ones such as "self-initiated" or "proactive"; the key is to indicate where the responsibility for ensuring adequate environmental protection *begins*, not where it *ends*.

It begins properly with those organizations which undertake activities that have or are likely to have adverse impacts on the environment; these are largely industrial actors, but governments are also heavily implicated in Canada, owing to their deep involvement in economic development initiatives. The key first step is for those organizations to acknowledge their responsibility for those impacts; next, to implement programs to manage those impacts adequately; and third, to co-operate with a wide range of stakeholders in ensuring compliance, through those programs, with socially validated environmental protection goals and a credible verification of performance in meeting them. Because the most important aspects of these initiatives (namely, the goals and the credible verification of performance) must win the approval of others outside the organization, I refer to them as "negotiated frameworks" for environmental protection.

A very common misunderstanding is that these frameworks are the "opposite" of legal and regulatory structures. In fact they only work well, and they also work best, in tandem with an overriding legal-regulatory structure (largely because of "free rider" issues); no important advocate of negotiated frameworks, so far as I know, has called for the repeal of such structures. The misunderstanding and its correction can be illustrated in two simple diagrams. (See figure 4.)

Without a doubt still the best example to date of a self-initiated organizational commitment is the "Responsible Care" program in the chemical industry, now a worldwide initiative in which the Canadian Chemical Producers' Association took the lead beginning in the mid-1980s.[39] It is also an evolving rather than a static framework, since CCPA member companies are now embarked on a process to "raise the bar" for acceptable environmental goals and performance. But, again, just as in the case of ARET, the great disappointment is that, more than ten years after "Responsible Care" got off the ground, the chemical industry remains the only national industrial sector in Canada to have made a solid commitment to a very broad "ethic" of responsible environmental management. Other sectors have begun to follow this path to a certain extent, but in my opinion progress is too slow, too half-hearted in some cases, and too unimaginative. This is unacceptable. But at least there is a partial explanation, in that there has been insufficient recognition so far of the merits of this approach (and, too often, downright hostility in some quarters) by governments and other stakeholders.

Opinion is polarized to the extent that so-called "voluntary initiatives" are seen as an industry agenda motivated by a wish to avoid statutory obligations for good environmental management. On the evidence we have before us, this is nothing short of absurd. In the first place, the "template" for such frameworks, "Responsible Care," includes a general stricture that all legal and regulatory obligations must be met. *All of the codes of practice then go beyond those obligations to create higher levels of organizational commitment and managerial responsibility.* In short, this self-initiated ethic in the chemical industry is in its entirety an incremental effort, over and above everything required of it in Canadian regulatory structures. (It would be advisable to specify, at least in general terms, a template for such agreements, to

Figure 4
Negotiated and regulatory frameworks

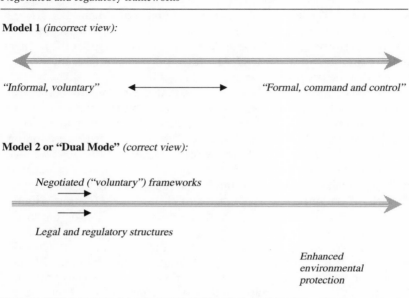

Model 1 *(incorrect view):*

"Informal, voluntary"   *"Formal, command and control"*

Model 2 or "Dual Mode" *(correct view):*

Negotiated ("voluntary") frameworks

Legal and regulatory structures

*Enhanced
environmental
protection*

reduce the confusion that might otherwise result from having too many quite dissimilar types of agreements all purporting to aim at the same objectives.)

There is still much to be done in solidifying the basis for this approach. For example, in general industry spokespersons tend to regard verification as a relatively unimportant aspect of the whole process, because they think that, once commitments are made, the modern corporate culture will ensure that they are honoured. However, the problem is that they are seeing the situation from the "inside." In the public mind generally, there is great distrust of corporate actors so far as environmental protection is concerned. Verification is a matter of perception; and perception is reality. Therefore, as an integral part of any statutory recognition of the types of initiatives represented by ARET and "Responsible Care," a credible verification scheme must be provided. In my opinion, the only really credible scheme is one that provides for independent third-party audit of performance claims and adherence to appropriate management procedures. There are good models for such audits and they would not be hard to design in this case.

Environmental protection legislation (federal and provincial) should incorporate a general provision to recognize, encourage, and "regularize" negotiated agreements for enhanced environmental performance, which would in no way detract from the other powers in the acts or, more important, their objectives. Quite the contrary, such additions could only improve the chances for those objectives to be realized. Here is a hypothetical legal structure.[40]

1 A statute such as CEPA should provide a broad grant of *authority* and direction to encourage the development of negotiated environmental performance agreements.
2 It is imperative that this statutory authority should mandate a high level of transparency for all transactions done under its wing. Therefore, there should be a *public registry* in which is deposited every negotiated agreement under this authority, including of course all commitments of actions for environmental protection that go beyond regulatory requirements.
3 The statute should provide certain benefits or *incentives* for parties to undertake such public commitments.
4 Attention should be paid to the procedural mechanisms for efficiently *integrating* the operational structures of registered Negotiated Agreements with all regulatory requirements.

The statute should provide a mechanism for periodic public *review and consultation* on the set of registered agreements, to discuss procedural and fairness matters, to examine verification issues, to encourage continuous improvement in all sectors and firms, and so forth.

10 Tobacco Uncontrolled

The global public health menace of tobacco use, as tallied in smoking-attributable illness and death, is still gaining strength, for earlier declines in the developed countries have been dwarfed by epidemic surges elsewhere in the world. Fittingly, the risk issue management and health policy dilemmas are no less intractable than smoking behaviour itself. Because the pool of victims has remained so large over such a long period of time, no risk factors are ever likely to be better described by the powerful tools of risk assessment than are those related to tobacco use. Despite this, tobacco control policy in Canada, where over 30 per cent of the adult population still smoke after decades of intensive risk information campaigns, has been handcuffed by these issues for the past decade and cannot seem to unshackle itself. Tobacco use patterns constitute an open rebuke to the rational paradigms of risk management decision making, which are premised on the assumption that from better risk assessments will flow wiser personal choices among relative risks. Until the conundrum of persistent tobacco-related risk taking is solved, modern risk management as a whole will remain in the shadow of that failure.

In particular, tobacco use (and now ETS, environmental tobacco smoke) issues present a significant challenge to conventional notions of risk communication, which were originally formulated in the late 1980s in the context of involuntary public exposures to chemicals, nuclear power, hazardous waste facilities, and similar technologies. Conventional wisdom on this subject encourages us to concentrate on risk message design and delivery parameters, such as source credibility and empathy, in order to maximize persuasive effectiveness and the elicitation of trust and believability. However, none of the elements in this conventional wisdom is applicable to the case at hand.

"Rational-format" risk messages themselves, as well as the conventional forms of message delivery (based on marketing communications strategies), appear to fail utterly in the case of tobacco use. In fact, all of the notable decreases in use among the general population in industrialized countries occurred before the onset of massive, government-financed campaigns against tobacco; and, of course, the more recent rise in youth smoking has occurred in open defiance of the messages in those campaigns. An examination of the obstacles to successful risk communication for tobacco use shows why this has happened: in general, rational-information risk message campaigns are unable to break through the social, educational, attitudinal, psychological, and other barriers that exist in the lives of the smoking subpopulations today. In addition, the "iconic" status of tobacco in modern society inhibits governments from taking the more drastic types of actions they would otherwise choose to carry out if there were any other risk factor of similar consequence within their purview.

If the tobacco case teaches us one thing about communication, it is that we must broaden considerably our notion of what constitutes effective risk communication practice. Communication is not just about messages and their delivery; rather, society communicates its changing conceptions of acceptable behaviour in many different ways, of which rational-format messages are perhaps the least important. Recognizing the truth of this proposition is essential for directing social resources for risk reduction towards areas of wise investment and away from unprofitable ones. Following Zimring, I argue that most of the victories that have been won so far in North America on curtailing tobacco use, and confronting the matter of involuntary exposure to environmental tobacco smoke, have occurred because social elites have been mobilized to drive smoking out of public spaces, one after the other.[1] These campaigns do not address smokers directly; rather, they are demands by the non-smoking majority to the effect that conditions in the public sphere should mirror the decisions that the majority have made in their private lives. The experience to date confirms that this is a highly successful way to reduce exposure for everyone. This leaves only the private domestic sphere, representing a particularly severe risk for children of smokers, as the major setting for ETS exposure yet to be dealt with.

TOBACCO USE PATTERNS

Tobacco use around the world shows different patterns in recent years. In Canada, population-average smoking rates declined roughly from one-half to one-third of the total population in the last thirty years and then levelled off with little appreciable further fall; on the other hand, an earlier dramatic fall in smoking rates among adolescents has been reversed, with rates in Canada showing a sharp increase after 1993, meaning that recruitment of new smokers remains highly successsful.[2] The story is the United States is about the same.[3] Many Western European countries started with smoking prevalence rates much higher than was ever the case in North America, and in most cases they are still higher today. In other nations, population-average rates have declined more slowly, stayed the same, or increased – sometimes dramatically.

In many parts of the world, tobacco use is the single greatest risk factor in population health and likewise the leading cause of preventable mortality and morbidity; at the same time, we probably have more reliable and extensive scientific knowledge about tobacco use risk than we do for any other human health risk factor. In this light, the reversals in tobacco use patterns in countries such as Canada and the United States during the last decade are shocking in the extreme. For young persons, all of the gains in reducing smoking prevalence made during the decades of the 1970s and 1980s have been reversed; for example, "during 1988–1996 among persons aged 12–17 years, the incidence of initiation of first use increased by 30% and of first daily use increased by 50%."[4]

Everyday risk communication practice spans everything from informal negotiation about lifestyle choices in private among family members to large-scale public health campaigns organized by governments. If we consider the latter rather than the former, it is clear that risk communication campaigns have been and remain a spectacular failure. For in those countries where population-average smoking rates show the steepest decline after 1970, all of the gains were made before 1990 – that is, well before the aggressive public-education programs were launched. Moreover, these gains were made before the explicit hazard warnings that now adorn tobacco packages in Canada appeared (until 1989 the single warning, which was almost unreadable in any case due to its placement on the package, advised smokers to "avoid inhaling," which in retrospect seems more amusing than irresponsible). And of course the so far relentless upturn in adolescent tobacco use has occurred amidst an attitude of blissful indifference or defiance towards the contrary messages circulating in the social environment.[5] A review article sketches this point – and the implications for conventional "rational-format" risk messages – in stark relief: "Controlled trials, chiefly in the USA, have shown that the provision of information on smoking and health has no effect on teenage prevalence."[6]

In fact the fall in tobacco use among former smokers in the adult populations in some countries represents a triumph of *informal* risk

communication, where individuals in collaboration with a newly mili-
tant medical community absorbed the increasingly abundant new
information about tobacco risk and made personal choices to discontinue use. During this entire period (1965–90), there were virtually no
direct and high-profile government challenges to the tobacco industry.
The difference between this situation and that of the last decade could
not be starker: the industry is under siege and yet it retains its tremendous profitability, is expanding its global markets rapidly, and is able
to recruit new users by the hundreds of thousands annually even where
its attackers are most active.[7] For anyone concerned with good risk
communication practices in general and their relevance to tobacco use
in particular, the beginning of wisdom is to recognize and acknowledge
just how daunting the obstacles are. For all in all tobacco use represents a standing refutation to any belief that we know how to carry out
effective risk communication practice.

OBSTACLES TO RISK COMMUNICATION ABOUT TOBACCO USE

Tobacco use is powerfully resistant to countervailing information and
educational campaigns.[8] Some of the most important reasons for this
are: (1) the nature of the demographic and psychographic profiles of
the "residual" user population; (2) the falling age of smoking initiation and the consequences of early onset; (3) the enduring "iconic"
status of smoking in popular culture; (4) the inherent difference between tobacco and all other consumer products; (5) the "discounting"
of tobacco use risk messages by smokers; (6) a failure to recognize explicitly in public health campaigns the underlying medical basis of the
problem (i.e., drug dependency); and (7) a monumental level of official
hypocrisy in society's "mixed messages" about drug use.

1 The Residual User Population

The one-third of the population who are still regular tobacco users, in
comparison with the other two-thirds, have on average lower household incomes (and thus also have poorer diets); are less well educated in
terms of formal schooling and have poorer school performance; have
relatively higher levels of emotional and psychological disorders, including major depression; are more subject to chronic stress; and even
may have a genetic predisposition to addiction.[9] Moreover, many of
these factors are correlated more highly with heavy smoking (more than
twenty cigarettes per day) and inversely correlated with quitting, with
some significant different between men and women in these respects.

Finally, since there are also environmental factors – such as being in the presence of smokers – in the causes of smoking behaviour, there is a higher likelihood of perpetuating it among these subpopulations from one generation to the next.[10] But all of these factors also represent *prima facie* strong obstacles to the chances for success of the "rational-information" rhetorical structure which is the dominant format used in public-health persuasive communications campaigns. With respect to this format, all of the easy victories have already been won, and we really have very little to rely on in terms of trying to "reach" the residual population of dedicated smokers directly with risk messages that are likely to have any attitudinal or behavioural impact at all.

2 Falling Age of Onset

The relationship between age of initiation and later smoking patterns is this: "The earlier in life a child tries a cigarette the more likely he or she is to become a regular smoker ... Furthermore, the earlier a youth begins smoking, the more cigarettes he or she will smoke as an adult."[11] In the Canadian survey data from 1994/95, "16% of 21- to 39-year-olds who had ever smoked daily reported that they had started to do so at age 13 or younger" and "55% reported ages 14 to 17."[12] It is likely that the reality is worse than the reported data indicates, since there is abundant anecdotal evidence about the dropping age of onset for a range of behaviours, including sexual activity and use of alcohol and other drugs. (Yet the most detailed Canadian effort on smoking prevalence, Health Canada's "Survey on Smoking in Canada," still does not collect data from persons under the age of fourteen.) Whatever the current state of affairs, the falling age of initiation also serves to block the prospects for successful risk communication, since the combination of factors (age plus those listed in the previous section) results in a profound indifference to long-term health effects.

3 The Iconic Status of Smoking

Having surmounted early attempts by the temperance forces to link cigarettes with alcohol in their prohibitionist campaign, the tobacco industry gradually achieved for its premier product a status in popular culture rivalled only by the automobile.[13] Hollywood films played a major role in disseminating positive images of smoking, beginning in the 1930s and continuing down to the present.[14] Some of the strongest images relate smoking to "outlaw" and "tough-guy" behaviour. Therefore, as tobacco use increasingly becomes marginalized in two senses – driven out of public spaces and confined to the less fortunate social groups – its own outlaw status will prove to be attractive, especially to the younger inititates: risk taking through tobacco use will be part of the product glamour. The outlaw appeal of smoking for youth actually could be enhanced if industry were ever forced by governments to put a skull-and-crossbones motif on its packages, as is sometimes mooted.[15] In addition, the iconic status of smoking provides a conscious and subconscious rationale for resistance to messages about health effects.

4 *Tobacco as a Unique Consumer Product*

In such areas as consumer product safety, recreation, and occupational health and safety, risk communication through hazard warnings is based on the paradigm of the rational-informed ("sovereign") consumer or worker. This paradigm assumes the desirability of individual choice and responsibility in the face of well-documented risks, even where those risks are relatively high. The proviso is that those sovereign individuals can become well informed as to the nature and relative severity of risk factors, can exercise good judgment in the light of adequate information, and can undertake the appropriate behavioural modifications. But there is another assumption built into this paradigm as well, namely, that the risks are incidental to the product use or the activities associated with the product. In other words, in most cases a reasonable level of care and attention is sufficient to control the risks attendant upon product use or activity within generally "acceptable" bounds.

Thus whether we are considering relatively hazardous recreations such as sky-diving, skiing, or spelunking, or occupations that require handling toxic chemicals, or the domestic use of hazardous machines such as chainsaws, society's expectation is that a judicious combination of general education, effective hazard warnings, specialized training, use of safety devices, care and attention, plus common sense – and the availability of prompt medical attention for the accidents that inevitably will occur – , can control the attendant risks satisfactorily. But not for tobacco.[16] Tobacco is the great anomaly: it has been marketed as an "ordinary" consumer product throughout this century, available in every corner store and gas station, but its use does not fit within the paradigm sketched above – perhaps the only case of its type in modern history.[17] This is because the risks are not incidental to product use, but are an inherent function of "normal use" (i.e., the regular pack-a-day smoker) itself. In other words, the associated risks cannot be controlled within acceptable limits, given normal use patterns, no matter what ostensible risk control strategies are employed by the consumer (smoking "light" cigarettes or whatever).

Owing to the anomalous nature of tobacco as a consumer product, none of the normal risk communication strategies is applicable. This includes the mandating of hazard warnings by governments on tobacco packages: survey data in Canada demonstrates that about half of the population of smokers cite the package hazard warnings as raising their risk awareness; however, only one-fifth say that those messages were a factor in their attempts to quit or to smoke less. Smokers also say that they are mostly in favour of getting more risk information on packages, specifically, lists of toxic ingredients; however, honesty prevails here, because most of the same respondents also "said that they would not be influenced in their smoking behaviour by a list of toxic ingredients."[18]

5 Discounting of Tobacco Risk Messages

One of the most interesting research results reported in recent years was a study that shows how smokers' risk awareness is effectively cancelled out by what is called "self-exempting beliefs."[19] These beliefs amount to artfully constructed rationales as to why the acknowledged risk factors, which are of course based on population averages, are offset (in the individual smoker's mind) by the particular circumstances of that individual's behaviour with respect to tobacco use. This important study undermines one of the ostensibly strongest arguments made by the tobacco industry, namely that its customers are fully aware of the health risks of smoking (these arguments are made every other day, alternating with statements calling into question the scientific basis of the risk assessments for tobacco use). It also calls into question the usefulness of the survey research results, some of which were referred to earlier, in which smokers report their desire to quit and their gratitude for the health risk information they receive from government-mandated hazard warnings. These beliefs represent deeply entrenched lines of resistance among tobacco users against the message content of risk communication campaigns.

A new dimension in the propaganda war against smoking was opened in Canada in late 2000, when the tobacco industry was required by the government of Canada to carry dramatic new warning illustrations and messages on their packaging.[20] The four-colour illustrations include for the first time graphic representations of tobacco-related diseases, and package inserts carry much more detailed information on the most serious risk factors than are conveyed in the one-sentence warning messages used so far. The follow-up evaluation studies which will attempt to measure the impact of these new formats will be of great interest, of course. Based on what we know about smoking behaviour, however, we may hazard a prediction that the new formats will harden attitudes among non-smokers, leading to demands on governments for other actions against tobacco use, but will not have much of a direct impact on the behaviour of existing smokers and those young persons now being recruited into smoking.

Among the other actions to be demanded in Canada and elsewhere are programs to match both the scope and the tone of the huge anti-tobacco campaign mounted by the state of California over the last few years. This campaign has been funded by a 25-cent-per-pack special levy on tobacco products authorized by Proposition 90, passed by the state's voters in 1988 (followed by an additional 50-cent levy introduced in 1998), which has generated an enormous revenue stream: in the year 2000 California spent US $136 million on its programs. California pioneered the use of very aggressive advertising directed against the tobacco industry itself, as well as multifaceted information programs, but it also has taken specific measures on ETS, as described by an official with the state department of health: "California has the most comprehensive program for protecting nonsmokers from second-hand smoke. Restaurants, bars and almost all indoor workplaces are smoke-free."[21] The decline in smoking rates in California is now matched in the lung cancer statistics, where California shows a 14 per cent decrease over the past ten years (compared with a 2.7 per cent decrease in other parts of the US).[22]

A comparable initiative for Canada has been led in the last few years by Senator Colin Kenny, who introduced a bill in the Senate in 1998 (Bill S-13, the "Tobacco Industry Responsibility Act") – even attracting the public support of some tobacco firms – that would impose a special levy on tobacco products to fund a large anti-tobacco information campaign.[23] To date the government refuses to accept the bill as government legislation, apparently because some in the Department of Finance dislike targeted tax levies. Meanwhile youth smoking rates escalate.

6 Tobacco Use as a Drug Dependency Issue

Anyone who has suffered through the calm mendacity of presentations by tobacco industry representatives appearing before legislative committees is bound to find the 1963 statement (made in private, of course) by Brown and Williamson's legal counsel refreshing: "We are, then, in the business of selling nicotine, an addictive drug effective in the release of stress mechanisms."[24] Society's continued tolerance of the virtually unrestricted marketing in massive quantities of a substance with powerfully addictive properties is the ultimate proof of tobacco's iconic status. The government of Canada, for instance, has been essentially paralysed for the past decade because it insists on fighting the tobacco industry on the territory of that industry's own choosing – namely, the absurd presumption that tobacco is an ordinary, "legal" consumer product to which the normal rules of economic intercourse apply.

Apparently to avoid the charge that it is *permitting* the provisioning of a hazardous substance (which of course it does by default), the government declines to use its authority over health protection to regulate nicotine as a drug.[25] For the same reasons, Canadian provincial governments pussy-foot around the matter of tobacco retailing, not wishing to offend the legions of small businesses for whom this is highly profitable. Every "sting" operation designed to test the efficacy of the age restrictions on tobacco purchase in corner stores has shown that consumers under the legal age can supply themselves with what they want quite nicely. But all of this elaborate political fan-dancing extracts its price: why should any of the committed users take their governments' dire health hazard warnings seriously, when this drug product, whose health toll is unlike any other by many orders of magnitude, is so freely available, compared with others of comparable potency – whose toll from abuse pales into comparative insignificance – that have been outlawed?[26]

7 Mixed Messages in the "War on Drugs"

The absurd and self-defeating criminalization of certain types of addictive substances extracts a huge price in the tacit downplaying of tobacco risk. The indefensible incommensurability between society's attitudes towards tobacco on the one hand, and the now-criminalized so-called "hard" and "soft" drugs on the other, robs government of the moral authority and clarity of purpose necessary to achieve its health protection objectives where adult use of the whole set of addictive substances is concerned. It also inserts massive confusion into government's ostensible role in health protection, because there cannot possibly be a rational defence for the profound anomalies that exist in the relationship between comparative health consequences, on the one hand, and the set of social and legal controls, on the other, across the whole set of potentially addictive substances. This is especially relevant to the marginalized subpopulation of young people who are most likely to take up smoking at an early age, for we now realize that this is part of a behavioural pattern that includes early initiation of (unsafe) sexual activity and the use of numerous other dangerous substances. So again, the stark difference between tobacco and all other substances (including alcohol) is impressed upon its users by the forces of law every day of the week. Something so easily tolerated by society cannot be *that* bad.

OVERCOMING THE OBSTACLES TO RISK
COMMUNICATION FOR TOBACCO

In many of the industrialized countries today, smoking prevalence has stabilized at varying percentages of the overall population; in other countries, smoking rates are rising, sometimes at a rapid pace. In both cases, but for somewhat dissimilar reasons, there are powerful currents of resistance to risk messages about tobacco use. Owing to accidents of history, tobacco has achieved an iconic status which serves it as a protective shield against which the rational content of risk communication messages is relatively powerless. For an analogous case which has equally disastrous health consequences, one thinks of the AIDS epidemic in Africa, for there, it seems, powerful taboos (especially among men) against discussions of sexual behaviour with medical professionals mean that not even the simplest risk reduction messages about this modern plague can penetrate the socially mandated veil of silence.[27] In any case, the preceding discussion gives many of the reasons why campaigns with risk messages directed at smokers – especially young smokers – have low chances of success and are thus relatively poor domains for the investment of scarce public health resources.[28]

But the failure of government-mandated anti-smoking campaigns in the 1990s is only one side of the story. For society sends its "messages" about behavioural norms in many ways, only one of which is through public health propaganda. The important message about tobacco use in the past decade in North America has been the ever-widening support for the eviction of smoking from public spaces, including workplaces, public facilities, and other social spaces. With respect to workplaces and public facilities, the main battles have been won, in Canada at least; controversy still is heated when it comes to restaurants and especially bars and lounges, although even in those cases the strong arguments based on ETS and occupational health eventually will prevail.[29] With specific reference to ETS and child health, all of the victories in evicting smoking from public facilities provide a direct benefit to children, of course. Exposures in the home, therefore, are the last major battlefield over ETS and child health in countries such as Canada.[30]

Although government-run campaigns with risk messages directed at smokers have low chances of success and are thus relatively poor domains for investment of scarce public-health resources, society sends its messages about acceptable and unacceptable behaviours in a wide variety of ways. What reaches and influences most people, especially populations in dynamic, market-based economies, are subtle signals about trends in behavioural norms that are identified with perceived indicators of success, high status, and novelty. Social norms govern the actions of individuals as they take place primarily in public rather than private spaces; changes in those norms first are worked out in private among higher-status groups and then "socially enforced" in the public sphere. So the dramatic changes in tobacco-use behaviour in Western Europe and North America beginning after 1965 started with highly literate strata in the population, reflecting the impact of new risk assessment information and the new militancy of medical researchers and practitioners. Governments played a relatively minor role in these transactions.

These behavioural changes preceded, and were the necessary precon-ditions for, both government propaganda campaigns and government's use of legal instruments to restrict tobacco use. This is the common pattern in the changes over time not just for tobacco but for all psycho-active substances, according to Franklin Zimring, and I think he is cor-rect. Governments take such steps after the high-status groups have altered their private behaviours and have insisted that behaviour in the public sphere should reflect the new choices they have already made in their private lives, including enforcement of the newer norms against those lower-status groups which by and large persist in the old ways. As Zimring puts it, bluntly but accurately: "Socially caused decreases in drug and tobacco use, particularly those that remove large numbers of high-status users, prepare the way for the adoption of get-tough programs by government."[31]

Most of these "get-tough" programs, beginning the late 1980s, have to do with the eviction of smoking from public spaces, either com-pletely or with the provision of separately ventilated rooms: offices and other workplaces, all types of facilities open to and frequented by the public, common carriers in transportation, and others, irrespective of whether they are publicly or privately owned.[32] In Canada today it is possible for a non-smoker to avoid encountering smokers entirely in-side virtually every space accessible to the public, with the exception of restaurants, bars, and entertainment clubs. This experience is striking, especially for anyone who grew up in the tobacco-rich environment of the 1950s and 1960s, and who as a non-smoker often wound up in confined spaces such as elevators and poorly ventilated airplanes cheek by jowl with users who were blissfully indifferent to their discomfort. Even in Western European countries today, and much more elsewhere, one's experience is far different.

The sequence of events in North America indicates clearly that the non-smoking majority began to flex its muscle to drive smoking from the public sphere well in advance of scientific determination, confir-mation, and quantification of the particular health risks associated with exposure to environmental tobacco smoke. It would be fair to say that there was certainly an intuition of harm, as well as the expectation that precise scientific characterization of the hazards was sure to follow, but the impetus for both regulatory and non-regulatory action was in no way dependent upon having the type of "proof" on this score that would satisfy a scientist – much less a tobacco company. Rather, almost certainly the non-smoking majority's belief in the legitimacy of proscribing smoking in public places is based on the simple proposition that the environmental conditions established for its private spaces should be replicated in the public sphere – certainly in that case, or cases, where it is impossible for non-users who are in proximity to users to avoid being exposed to the side-effects of the users' behaviour.[33]

Thus for the ever-widening campaign to proscribe smoking in public spaces, in areas where it is already well under way (such as many parts of North America), it is and will remain a matter of indifference when, and to what degree, further scientific research will provide definitive characterization and confirmation of particular ETS risk factors.[34] This is not to say that perception of risk *per se* is unimportant: given the uncertainties in risk assessments, as they are widely recognized, those who support this campaign have ample grounds, even on the basis of what is known to medical science now, and even more on the basis of what is reasonably suspected, to base their demands in risk terms. In any case, within many regions in North America there is a firm social consensus around the main objective – proscription of smoking in public spaces – with some disagreement at the margins (restaurants and bars, etc.), and greater uncertainty still as to how far to push the agenda with respect to more problematic spaces, particularly outdoors. This is the primary way in which the non-smoking majority, using both government and private resources, communicates its understanding of unacceptable risk.

TOBACCO: WHAT IS TO BE DONE?

In Canada we have been collectively spinning our wheels on the tobacco issue for ten years and counting.[35] The basic reason is that we have misclassified tobacco use as a social policy issue, treating tobacco as if it were just a slightly hazardous but otherwise ordinary consumer product, such as a household cleaner, which should carry a warning sign and be kept out of the reach of children, rather than what it is in fact: namely, a product containing a highly addictive drug whose easy availability is anomalous in relation to the way we treat all similar substances. Tobacco products are drug-delivery devices.

The drug in question (nicotine) has remarkable properties and a versatile set of effects as a psychoactive substance. For a long time already, medical science has classified the addictive properties of nicotine as comparable with those of heroin and cocaine.[36] And yet we continue to pretend that tobacco is completely different from other addictive drugs and that, despite our utter failure to achieve decreases in population-average smoking rates for the past decade, we can deal with the problem of tobacco use within a legal and policy framework that has demonstrated its ineffectiveness for everyone to see.

The failure of tobacco control policy in Canada and elsewhere to date – like the failure of risk communication practice (hazard warnings and associated health promotion literature) – is largely a function of the narrowness of the frameworks in which they have been cast. To repeat, those frameworks are too narrow to address the public-health challenge of tobacco use because, essentially, they treat tobacco products as if they were just another freely available consumer item rather than drug-delivery devices that enable users to gain access to a highly addictive substance (namely, nicotine) through means (smoking and chewing) that are extremely hazardous to health. Those frameworks are also too narrow because they do not relate tobacco use, as a problem of drug addiction (or dependence), to similar problems with other dependence-causing substances, namely, alcohol, certain prescription drugs, and the illicit drugs scheduled under the Controlled Drug and Substances Act (heroin, cocaine, etc.).

As a result of the narrowness of the policy and legislative frameworks prevailing in Canada and elsewhere, control over tobacco product advertising is pursued wrongly as an independent goal, rather than being integrated into a more comprehensive framework for control over all aspects of the provisioning, marketing, use, and abuse of tobacco products. To overcome this excessive narrowness, and following the model of the control of alcohol use as an illustration, tobacco products could be and should be

a) offered for sale only in licensed outlets;
b) consumed in public only in licensed premises;
c) forbidden to be used in private vehicles;
d) forbidden to be possessed by anyone under the age of legal majority.

After a transition period in which tobacco product use is controlled on the model of alcohol, tobacco products should be available only by medical prescription in licensed pharmacies or other licensed outlets. And, ultimately, society will have to find an appropriate policy mechanism by which to regulate tobacco use in private spaces, because of the serious, and well-documented, adverse health consequences to children of smoking behaviour in the home.

APPENDIX: ENVIRONMENTAL TOBACCO
SMOKE AND CHILD HEALTH

The preceding analysis suggests that a country which wishes to "get the message across" that children's exposure to ETS ought to be reduced would be well advised to concentrate its public-health resources on evicting smoking from public spaces. This is no less a risk communication objective than is the designing and disseminating of media-based propaganda campaigns, and the experience in North America shows, I believe, that it can be done. It is, however, a very different *type* of risk communication, namely, one that depends for success on the mobilization of social elites, ideally under the leadership of the professional medical community. It is, perhaps, an indirect form of communication, in the sense that it does not target directly those smokers whose behaviour is the source of the problem at hand; rather, it targets those already committed to a non-smoking lifestyle in their "private spaces" and seeks to galvanize their support for making non-smoking the social norm in public spaces as well.

Only after substantial victories have been achieved in the public sphere is it feasible to think of turning attention to private domestic spaces, where there are obviously significant exposures for children and other non-smokers to ETS in smoking households. Here too it is a waste of time and resources, in my opinion, to target directly – through media-based government propaganda campaigns – the smokers who are and must be in a state of denial about the adverse health effects of smoking, both for themselves and their children, whatever their self-reported awareness levels of risk factors are.[37] A more indirect approach is preferable in this case as well, again with the lead involvement of the professional medical and educational communities. Visits to doctors and clinics for medical care at the time of pregnancy and early childhood in families provide one good opportunity for risk communication discussions framed broadly in terms of multiple risk factors, including ETS. Certainly school-based risk communication programs for youth about tobacco use can include issues of ETS in the home. Finally, the issue of ETS in the home – certainly in North America – should be wrapped into the larger matter of indoor air quality generally, which is gaining increasing attention as a generic health risk factor, especially for children; this too has the advantage of sidestepping a direct challenge to domestic smoking behaviour in isolation. Using these and other avenues, the messages about ETS and child health gradually will reach many in the target audience.

The general conclusion from the foregoing analysis is that tobacco use, considered as an attitudinal and behavioural phenomenon, is fundamentally different from every other form of risk-taking activity in modern society. What follows from this perspective is the presumption that "applied" behavioural change intervention strategies – including risk communication campaigns of every sort – that have been developed for other types of health and environmental risks, including exposure to industrial chemicals and the use of seat belts in automobiles, as well as literally dozens of other such situations, are inapplicable to the case of tobacco use. The correctness of this presumption is borne out in the published evaluations and meta-analyses of the many unsuccessful experiments with intervention strategies designed to change smoking behaviour.

An up-to-date, exhaustive review of both published literature and written reports on risk communication and intervention strategies for tobacco use among youth was completed in Canada in 1998, and its conclusions confirm the correctness of the general diagnosis on obstacles to tobacco risk communication contained in the main body of this chapter. For example, the review summarizes the results of five meta-analyses, published in the period 1992–97, that encompassed individual studies on school-based programs designed to communicate health risks associated either with tobacco alone or with the "nexus" of tobacco, alcohol, and other drugs. There were no fewer than 428 individual studies included in the five meta-analyses; the author's general summary of their findings is stated as follows: "The magnitude of the positive effects of these programs is believed to translate into approximately a 5% reduction in smoking. *Further, these effects have been found to endure for only one or two years post-intervention.*"[38]

However, in addition to school-based communication approaches, the paper's author considers also mass media approaches and health warning labels, and these three are taken as the dominant types of sources of health risk information for youth. Taking all three together, and summarizing the overall tenor of a huge number of intervention strategies in applied risk communication, she concludes: "For the most part, efforts by the health sector to prevent or reduce risk behaviours among youth, such as smoking, alcohol, and other drug use, have been unsuccessful."[39]

Turning now to ETS specifically, two of Canada's leading authorities on tobacco use behaviour have noted the absence of evaluation data on the programs in which considerable, and growing, public resources are being invested: "Very few public education resources regarding ETS exposure appear to have undergone formal evaluation with regard to effectiveness in raising public awareness. We are not aware of any published evaluations of material used in Canada."[40] They also note that, in Canada at least, with respect to implementing smoking restrictions, there is noticeably lower public support for imposing such restrictions in the home as opposed to both workplaces and public spaces.[41] The primary reason for the difference was indicated in the results of a small pilot study: "Findings indicated that relatively high levels of participant awareness about health risks associated with ETS did not translate into the creation of 'smoke-free' home environments, although many participants did report various restrictions on smoking in the home. In this study, participants' concern for the risk of their children's health appeared to have been offset by their view that smoking is an individual choice exercised in a private domain."[42]

There are now a number of specific studies on educational programs, clinical interventions, and other strategies employed in an effort to change smokers' behaviour and thus children's exposure, a fair sample of which is summarized in the endnote.[43]

All in all, in the evaluation literature on trials in applied risk communication to date, whether they have addressed smoking behaviour generally, youth or adolescent tobacco use, behaviour relative to environmental tobacco smoke and passive smoking concerns, or, specifically, ETS and child health, there is a clear overall sense of the lack of effectiveness of intervention programs, policies, and strategies. At the same time, it is just as important to remember that many important battles against smoking prevalence and passive smoking exposure have been won, and are still being won, especially in North America, irrespective of the failure rate of specific interventions.

The single most important strategy that can be pursued to lower smoking prevalence and smoking exposures is "elite mobilization" against all smoking in public spaces, with a priority give to spaces where children might be exposed. Experience to date shows clearly that this is a battle which can be won, and won decisively; and without a doubt it is the single most important source to date of reductions in children's ETS exposure. In addition, these clear victories legitimize the broader objectives of encouraging smoking cessation among smokers and eliminating passive smoking among non-smokers.

However, no such victories are complete just because ordinances or regulations have been put into effect. Practical compromises among competing social interests commonly result, in this case, in the designation of smoking and no-smoking zones within public spaces. Although this solution satisfies demands of fairness, it is far from achieving the real and legitimate objective of preventing all passive smoking exposures among non-smokers. One study observes: "A common strategy designed to protect non-smoking patrons of public places is to designate smoking and non-smoking areas ... The results [of a survey] suggest that the practice of designated non-smoking areas in restaurants,

258   Governments in the Labyrinth

mall food courts, pool halls and bingo halls [does] not completely protect patrons and employees from exposure to ETS. In many cases, in
fact, the exposure may be nearly as great as that found in the smoking
areas of other locations."[44]

Completely eliminating passive smoking exposures in public spaces
clearly ought to be the first priority for public-health practitioners.

11 Into the Maze of Moral Risks

By now our society's commitment to sustained technological innovation is so much taken for granted, and so fundamental a part of our economy and well-being, that if we were to be deprived of it suddenly, the world would no longer make sense to most of us.[1] No one in his or her right mind would willingly revert to the world as it was when the story I tell in this chapter begins, in sixteenth-century Europe. For then every commonplace "natural" risk in the lives of individuals, rich and poor alike – an infected tooth or limb, a difficult childbirth, a failed crop, indeed, just the first five years or so of life itself – occurred under the shadow of pain, suffering, and death. And so it had been for much of previous human history, ruled by the Four Horsemen of the Apocalypse. Beginning in the seventeenth century, this pattern was broken by the project we have come to know as the "conquest of nature," or more prosaically as modern technology. The trajectory of modern Western technology over the last three centuries is this: Extending "outward" from the human intellect and will to the mastery over "external nature," and – in the capacity of bioengineering, soon to be realized, to construct novel quasi-human entities – returning back again to confront us with questions about our human nature and destiny. We are faced – literally – with this trajectory when we gaze at the visage of "Rachel" in Ridley Scott's film *Blade Runner* (1982), because "Rachel" is an entity designed by human technology to be, in the words of "her" Maker, the president of the fictional Tyrell Corporation, "more human than human."[2]

If this prospect appears too fantastical to be taken seriously, it becomes less so in the context of the news items from November 1998 about research breakthroughs on the cloning of "stem cells," cells which can differentiate into any kind of tissue. One research team reported successfully fusing material from a cow and a human to create stem cells, which led one well-known Canadian scientist to speculate that it would be possible to create a "hybrid" entity – known as a chimera – which would be part human and, say, part chimpanzee. Indeed, it now appears to be possible to do so relatively soon. And then what?

Modern science and technology have given us the power to exploit and manipulate nature's energy and resources beyond anything dreamt of earlier. In the form of genetic engineering they even promise to allow us to stand in God's place and to reshape the work of Creation. Humanity embarked on this mission under the terms of an epic wager: in effect, we "bet" that, if such enhanced power fell into our possession, we could handle it wisely and steer it according to morally worthy purposes. In other words, we bet that we could minimize the generic "downside risk" inherent in modern technology – the risk that this new power would escape from control by our own will (remember the broom in the tale of the sorcerer's apprentice), and lead us down dubious or evil paths on a journey from which there may be no safe return.[3]

In the ultimate promise of genetic engineering – to reshape the work of Creation – we come face to face with ourselves, i.e., with the meaning of human existence on earth, or with what was meant traditionally by the human "soul." When we are presented by bioengineering technology with the power to do whatever we want with organic life – that of our own species and indeed of all species, plant and animal alike – the first question is: What do we want to do? But the next and more fateful questions are: What ought we to do? What is the ethically appropriate action? If we are presented with the "option" of, say, engineering half-human, half-chimpanzee chimeras, to serve us perhaps as intelligent but obedient domestic servants (think of the "Deltas" in Aldous Huxley's *Brave New World*), the questions will be: *Should we go down this path?* And: *If we do, and by so doing we encounter great evils along the way, will we be able to abandon the journey and find our way back?* The downside risk is the probability – however we may estimate it – that we will indeed encounter those evils and will not be able to undo them.

It is my contention here that at present we cannot be sure that we can manage this most fateful and problematic downside risk inherent in modern technology. Speaking of the potential applications of current research in human genetics, one of Canada's leading geneticists, the University of Toronto's Lap-Chee Tsui, discoverer of the defective gene for cystic fibrosis, says: "This particular wave is moving too fast. The technology is leading us."[4] Another way of expressing this thought is to say that a new dimension of risk has been opened up as a result of our technology's capacity to engineer life, what I call (following Margaret Somerville) "moral risk," which is discussed later in this chapter. If you will allow only that there is some probability of our losing control over the direction of technological innovation, my question is: What should we do *now* in the face of this possibility? At least one good answer is that we should embark now on a serious public dialogue about risk and technological progress, for the answers to the questions I have posed can only emerge from policy choices supported by a well-informed citizenry. A model for such a discussion is presented in later sections of this chapter.

PASCAL'S WAGER

The most influential thinkers at the dawn of the modern era held firm to a religious world-view in which earthly existence was and always would be a "vale of tears," a punishment for original sin. Accordingly the population was discouraged from thinking that achieving happiness and well-being on earth was a worthy project – that is, a prize worthy of taking risks for – when the only true goal was the salvation of souls. This way of thinking is summed up in a famous "bet," known as "Pascal's Wager," after a seventeenth-century thinker. Blaise Pascal (1623–1662) was a French mathematician and philosopher whose wager is noteworthy because for the first time belief in God was put in terms of probability theory and decision theory, both of which are fundamental parts of our contemporary risk management.[5] In section 233 of his *Pensées* Pascal wrote: " 'God is, or He is not.' But to which side shall we incline? Reason can decide nothing here. There is an infinite chaos which separates us. A game is being played at the extremity of this infinite distance where heads or tails will turn up ... Which will you choose then? ... Let us weigh the gain and the loss in wagering that God is ... If you gain, you gain all; if you lose, you lose nothing. Wager, then, without hesitation that He is." The wager sets up a decision matrix with four outcomes, as follows:

A. Suppose that God exists:
   Outcome #1: If we have wagered on this, we win an infinite benefit (immortality).
   Outcome #2: If we have bet against this, we are left with infinite loss (eternal damnation).[6]
B. Suppose that God does not exist:
   Outcome #3: If we have wagered on this, we have saved some time and resources.

Outcome #4: If we have bet against this, we have wasted some finite amount of earthly time and resources in practising our belief
(for the average person, it is not a great investment of time and
there were in Pascal's time few resources in such hands anyway).

On the "upside" the comparative stakes are infinite benefit (immortality) vs. finite benefit (some saving of time and resources). However,
comparing the two forms of the "downside risk" – infinite vs. finite loss
– renders our decision an easy one: Belief in God is the safest bet. The
stakes in the "larger" downside risk are just too high to take a gamble
on not believing in God.

BACON'S WAGER

Pascal's Wager, although modern in form, was backwards-looking in
spirit and sought vainly to bolster an old tradition whose vitality had
been slipping away for some time. Its force depended on the huge gap
that appears to separate the relative benefits between the first and third
outcomes.

But the tradition represented in Pascal's Wager had been challenged
rudely a few decades earlier by another influential thinker of the early
modern era, the English philosopher Francis Bacon (1551–1626). Bacon argued that we should encourage the applied sciences to expand the
scope of the human understanding about how nature "works"; in turn,
this enhanced understanding would lead to a greatly improved ability
to exploit natural resources for human benefit. He reversed the terms of
the wager: If we gamble on applying human ingenuity and applied science to the conquest of nature, to seek the betterment of earthly life, we
need not fear that we are risking our souls thereby, for religion will control and superintend the uses to which we put our science. In other
words: *Religion will control the downside risk of modern technology.*
As Bacon himself wrote: "Only let the human race recover that right
over nature which belongs to it by divine bequest, and let power be
given it; the exercise thereof will be governed by sound reason and true
religion."[7]

Bacon's wager was seductive and eventually trumped Pascal's. But the
rest of us lost the bet. Religion was not able to maintain control. Rather,
its secular authority crumbled under the weight of the materialistic
economy that modern technology made possible. Now we shy away
from erecting other institutional controls over our prodigious scientific
and technological imagination, because we are addicted to its output,
and those who drive that project on warn us that they will not tolerate
external controls – and besides, they say, it is futile even to contemplate

them, because the enterprise will just pick up and move to a more congenial (i.e., unregulated) location on the globe.

Has "society" stepped into religion's place as the controlling agent which will ensure that science only pursues goals deemed "appropriate"? One of the present-day battlegrounds in which this question has been put to the test is called "human germline gene modification," which "can be defined as the genetic manipulation of human germ cells, or of a conceptus, resulting in inherited changes in DNA."[8] The "humane" purpose of germline therapy, which in effect would change every cell in an organism (such as a human fetus), would be to eliminate an inherited disease; however, the technology itself is in no way restricted to such particular applications, but rather can introduce any number of desired modifications to the organism, by adding or subtracting genes. Some contend that the strongest interest in such therapy has to do with the possibilities for "genetic enhancement," that is, the desire of parents to produce children with better genetic endowments in terms of intelligence, physical appearance, athletic traits, blood type, or any number of other characteristics that have a genetic basis – what have been called "designer babies." Critics say this is simply a eugenics program under another name.[9]

The crucial point is that any such changes would become part of the inheritable genetic structure of the organism, which would pass on those changes to any of its offspring; thus the modifications would enter the genome of that species. One US scientist has submitted a proposal to the National Institutes of Health that, if approved, would represent a step towards perfecting this approach; the proposal is being opposed publicly by other scientists on a number of grounds, including the following: "If germline manipulation is attempted, there will be mistakes or errors in its application."[10] Since any such mistakes would be, as mentioned above, inheritable traits and thus potentially become part of the human genome, it is clear why there is a sense of urgency in the debates among both scientists and ethicists about these matters – at least, the matters that the public has an opportunity to learn about before they become a reality. A science fiction writer who talks to genetics researchers frequently says that many of them no longer speak publicly about their research, lest the public become alarmed and call upon their governments to put a stop to things they find disquieting or morally offensive.[11]

Thus Bacon's wager represents unfinished business for the citizens of the twenty-first century. Whether or not contemporary society actually now has the capacity to exert effective control over the global scientific enterprise, in terms of permitting or forbidding certain lines of inquiry or applications of knowledge, is uncertain. Indeed, there are some who would assert either that society does not have the right to do so; or that it would not be in society's best interests to do so, because any research it sought to forbid would be "driven underground" and carried out in secret; or that society is in no position to do so, as a practical matter, since no effective international controlling capacity is or can be put in place. The consequences flowing from any of these three suppositions are that society needs the capacity to respond effectively and promptly to the stream of scientific discoveries and applications as it appears before us, and to take counteracting measures against troubling developments where it is thought wise to do so.

If we were to put Bacon's wager into Pascal's format, the "downside risk" is the possibility that future developments will occur, say in genetics or nanotechnology, which so alarm us, in terms of the threat they pose to the continued viability of human life and civilization, that we resolve to stop them – only to discover that it is too late, that they cannot be stopped. How should we wager on this possibility? Before presenting the options we have, I would like to present the concept of "moral risks" by referring back to one of the great imaginative works of the modern era.

MARY SHELLEY'S *FRANKENSTEIN*: RAISING THE ANTE

"Did I request thee, Maker, from my clay / To mould me Man, did I solicit thee / From darkness to promote me?" Milton, *Paradise Lost*, x, 743–5 (epigraph on the title page of Mary Shelley's *Frankenstein; or, The Modern Prometheus*)

In proceeding down the path towards the construction of chimeras made up partly of human genetic material and partly of that of other animals, say, we risk – to use an old-fashioned phrase – losing our souls. Think about "Rachel" again: is she "human" or not? We may be able to understand the nature of this risk better if we read carefully Mary Shelley's profound and far-seeing novel, *Frankenstein*, written in 1816 and first published two years later. Reflection on this remarkable work helps us to imagine the nature of the moral risks we would take, in constructing certain types of chimeras, by manipulating the boundary that separates human consciousness from animal sentience.[12]

The book by Mary Shelley (1797–1851) was a literary success in its day but fully entered popular culture in its cinematic version (directed by James Whale, 1931), thanks in large part to the brilliant portrayal of the monster by Boris Karloff – so great a success that it has led to a confusion between the monster and his creator, Dr Frankenstein. The confused name of "Frankenstein" now serves as both label and metaphor in the popular media's coverage of genetic engineering stories, as well as in the environmental movement's campaign against food products containing bio-engineered ingredients, where the term "Frankenfood" has taken root.[13]

But *Frankenstein* is not a "science fiction" story. We recognize the true genius in Mary Shelley's imagination when we see that the act of creation in the laboratory where Dr Frankenstein stitches together his monster is of so little interest to her that she devotes barely a paragraph of her novel to it, something the movie script writers felt they had to improve upon. Rather, as is widely recognized in commentaries on the novel, Mary Shelley's primary interest is in the monster's own consciousness or "spirit."[14] His consciousness, formed by music and Milton's poetry, self-destructs in response to the reactions of horror and fear elicited in people – whom he mistakenly regards as his fellow-creatures – by the monster's appearance, and finally turns into a boundless, murderous rage when Dr Frankenstein condemns his creation to cosmic loneliness by refusing his demand that he construct a female companion of the same type. Milton's three lines given in the novel's epigraph infuse every sentence of the monster's narration of his self-consciousness in the six chapters that are, in Harold Bloom's words, "the finest achievement of the novel."[15] The query that Milton's Adam addresses to God – "did I solicit thee / From darkness to promote me?" – is also the monster's challenge to his maker, who rejected his creation at the moment of its awakening to consciousness by fleeing from his laboratory in shame and disgust, and who in effect abandoned all responsibility for its fate.

Let us return to "Rachel" for a moment, because "Rachel" appears to solve the problem that destroyed Frankenstein's creation, whose appearance so frightened the people he encountered that they could not accept him as a member of the human community. The advanced models of replicants in *Blade Runner* are so human-like that their lack of a capacity for empathy is the only trait distinguishing them behaviourally from those who are "really" human.[16] "Rachel" has a full set of memories (these have been input at the factory using the life-history of a "real" human) and a wide complement of emotional resources, including a desire for intimacy and (apparently) a capacity for love. So: Is "Rachel" human, or can she at least *become* "human"? Alongside the ordinary reality in everyday human awareness there now appears a technologically induced "virtual reality" that mimics it. The better the technology, the better the mimicry: we already have "virtual advertisements," in which computer-generated imagery has been superimposed upon the broadcast feed of a live audience at a sporting event, making it appear to the TV viewers as if certain things are taking place in the live event which are not "really" happening.[17] "Rachel" would be right at home in this setting.

Milton uses the potent metaphor of "darkness" to refer to the non-conscious state of organic matter, and his inspired word "promote" alludes to the shadowy zone of being that separates the non-conscious sphere of organic life from the proto-conscious state of animal sentience and that distinguishes both of those in turn from the full self-awareness which we associate with human consciousness. Everything that we cherish in human civilization and that infuses meaning into the concept of the "human spirit" for us is dependent upon the meaningfulness of those three gradients of being, dependent upon the radical difference between Milton's "darkness" and the "light" of self-awareness. We toy with those differences at our peril. But certain prospects that are on the horizon will toy with those differences.

CLONING: SHOULD THERE BE LIMITS TO TECHNOLOGICAL INNOVATION?

Cloning is "the production of a precise genetic copy of a molecule (including DNA), cell, tissue, plant, animal or human ... [or] the process of producing individuals genetically identical to some other living or dead individual." In nuclear transfer cloning, the technique which gave us the most famous sheep in the world, Dolly, all genetic material is removed from an egg and is replaced by a nucleus from a donor cell.[18] The donor and recipient material are fused – in the case of mammals – by passing an electrical current through them, which makes a nice link with the famous laboratory scenes in the movie *Frankenstein*.

There are three major applications for nuclear transfer cloning: production of animals, creation of human cell lines, and production of a human being. Following the news about "Dolly," most attention focused naturally on the last-mentioned of these, and many governments (France, Germany, Canada, the US, and others) and other bodies (WHO, American Medical Association, Council of Europe, and others) have either implemented or proposed an outright ban on the production of humans by cloning. But in December 1998 doctors at a clinic in South Korea reported taking the first steps towards cloning a human, prompting a US cloning expert to remark: "[Human cloning] is going to happen sooner or later. You'd better get used to it."[19]

Patricia Baird, one of Canada's best-known experts in these matters, has listed and discussed the major concerns with the prospect of creating human "replicands," including physical harm (it is not known how clones will age, for example); the likelihood of psychological and social harm; and the manipulation of individuals by third parties. She concludes: "It would seem the wisest policy is to prohibit reproductive cloning that is aimed at producing a liveborn human infant."[20] Margaret Somerville, one of Canada's leading ethicists, has framed her reflections in broader terms, prompted in part by the media coverage during late 1998 about the cloning of stem cells.[21] She writes: "Nature never contemplated needing safeguards against science such as human cloning. It was thought that there was a natural barrier, that genetic material in a somatic cell was irreversibly modified in such a way that you could not obtain a clone from it. [Scientists] showed, in creating Dolly, that this was not true. What does this new power require of us in terms of our human responsibility to hold nature 'in trust,' in particular, for future generations, and especially that part of nature that constitutes the fundamental nature of us? If we were to undertake human cloning, what kind of creatures might we become?"[22]

The strong feelings of aversion that the prospect of human cloning stirs in many people will act temporarily as a barrier to this technology, but in my opinion human cloning will not in the end be prevented from happening. Other types of cloning experiments – particularly with animals – will continue, which will be justified by the experimenters on the grounds of anticipated human health benefits; they will refine the technologies and smooth the way for eventual human cloning.

Margaret Somerville asks: "What would happen, for instance, were we to combine the technology for genetic enhancement of intelligence, with that which makes possible a half-human half-chimp, with … the artificial uterus which would make ectogenesis possible?" This is just a sample of what is possible, of course, for it is precisely the unique potentiality of genetic engineering, which can now be foreseen clearly in the stem cell research, to open up the set of almost unlimited possibilities for the reshaping of biological life on earth. And this unique scientific capability in turn opens up an entirely new dimension of risk, which Somerville calls "moral or existential risk."[23] We encounter a state of moral risk when we pose certain options for ourselves, as goals which might be realized by using science to manipulate nature, that imply fundamental changes in the "order of being" as it has been experienced by humans until now. With respect to the potential for human cloning *per se*, this order of being includes the reproduction of human life through the random mixing of genetic material. In Patricia Baird's words: "The lottery of reproduction has been a protection against people being pre-determined, chosen, or designed by others – including parents."[24]

Moral risks also are entailed by manipulations in what I called earlier the "shadowy zone of being" that separates the non-conscious sphere of organic life from the proto-conscious state of animal sentience, on the one hand, and that distinguishes both of those in turn from the full self-awareness which we associate with human consciousness, on the other. We do poorly enough as it is with respect to the ethical treatment of animals, for example, both domesticated and wild. But these deficiencies pale into insignificance beside the great evils that could result, say, from manipulating the intelligence of chimpanzees or other non-human primates.

Genetic engineering technologies open a moral chasm before our feet so vast that (ironically) only the terms of Pascal's Wager can encompass it. For moral risks are not like the other risks associated with modern technologies – the familiar health and environmental hazards – each of which, however serious, is limited to finite types of harm. Rather, like the "negative infinity" of outcome #2 in Pascal's Wager, there is the potential for *infinite harm* here. In other words, were we to be tempted to redesign sentient life, both our own and that of other animals, we risk not just particular kinds of harm (well described by Patricia Baird), although these are onerous enough. In so doing we risk nothing less than "losing the thread" that connects us with the past trajectory of human civilization. Once we turn down that new path there is a substantial risk we could not find our way back, and there is no saying – in response to Margaret Somerville's question – what kind of creatures we might become.[25]

A NEED FOR EFFECTIVE RISK COMMUNICATION

To return to the question posed earlier: How shall we – collectively, in our societal decision-making processes – wager with Francis Bacon? Are we actually in any position to make a good bet on our capacity to steer our potent scientific research and development capacity to worthy ends, as we approach the shoals of moral risks? I think not, primarily because most citizens would be hard-pressed to say what germline gene therapy is, or what genes are and do for that matter. My presumption is that in a democratic society we cannot have sensible risk management decision making, or public policy development, where citizens have utterly inadequate information resources at their disposal for such issues. The first requirement, therefore, is for policies that promote good risk communication practice.

Risk communication is the process of engaging responsibly and effectively in public discussions about the risk factors associated with industrial technologies, natural hazards, and human activities. These responsibilities arise for all those who are developers and managers of industrial technologies, as well as for those who have public-health and environmental management oversight for technologies, natural hazards (including diseases), wildlife and natural habitat management, and risky behaviours (smoking, etc.). Good risk communication practice amounts to conducting a reasoned dialogue among stakeholders on the nature of the relevant risk factors and on acceptable risk management strategies. This includes: (1) interpreting the results of scientific risk assessments in terms that are appropriate for non-expert audiences; (2) understanding the basis of public risk perceptions; (3) working with interested parties towards a shared understanding of the risk factors.

From the standpoint of public policy, risk assessments are a means to the ultimate goal of reasoned public dialogue, wise risk management, and sensible priority setting in the allocation of resources to risk control and reduction. Given both the inherent limitations of risk assessments, especially the irreducible uncertainties usually associated with them, as well as legitimate differences in society over how to assign priorities for risk reduction, however, even the best risk assessments cannot lead automatically to wise risk management decisions. Informed public understanding of risk factors is the key to achieving broad support for and trust in risk management strategies, and this in turn depends upon an abundance of good risk communication practice. The responsibility to carry out good risk communication practice is a matter of creating specialized professional skills and an appropriate level of organizational commitment. It is emphatically not a matter of finding a way to emerge unscathed from a community meeting where outraged citizens voice their grievances. Rather, it can only be discharged through activities that go on every day and which endure as long as do the risk factors themselves for which the organization is responsible.

RISK DIALOGUE PROJECTS

Risk dialogue projects, which I advocate here as a way of responding to society's need for good risk communication practices, seek to establish and maintain a public resource for authoritative, fair, disinterested, and comprehensive information about, and for the exchange of views on, specific risk issue domains. A "risk issue domain" is defined as a discrete set of concerns about risks and risk management strategies associated with a natural hazard (e.g., viruses), an industrial technology (e.g., genetic engineering), an industrial substance or product (e.g., chlorine and plastics), or a personal activity (e.g., smoking), or some combination of sources of risk factors. Risk factors sometimes combine aspects of natural hazards with technologies. For example, radiation risks include a large number of particular risks associated with different parts of the spectrum of electric and magnetic fields, including UV-B from sunlight, X-rays, radio-frequency fields, and domestic electricity supply. Or, an industrial process may magnify the hazards from a natural pathogen, such as the disease agents implicated in transmissible spongiform encephalopathies such as "mad cow disease." Or, the effort to reduce some risk (*E. coli* O157:H7) by applying a new technology (food irradiation) may give rise to other concerns.

Risk issue domains include all factors of interest or concern identified by participants in an area of debate, whether or not the evidence about any of the adverse effects in question has been validated through accepted scientific research protocols. A major aspect of risk dialogue projects is to provide resources for citizens to become better able to evaluate the conflicting information they may encounter in many risk issue domains. Risk dialogue projects are designed to evolve from a starting-point in improved risk communication, through a better understanding of the range of public policy options for dealing with risk issues, to an informed consensus on preferred options for risk management decision making.

The three principal aspects of risk dialogue projects are diagrammed below (figure 5).

Endocrine-modulating (EM) substances – also called endocrine disruptors or "hormone mimics" and "estrogen mimics" – are chemicals (either natural or industrial in origin) that are known to have, or are suspected of having, effects on the endocrine systems of humans and other mammals at relatively low doses. The industrial chemicals that have been identified by some parties as possible culprits in adverse effects include substances, such as plasticizers, that have been widely used in consumer products and have been dispersed in the environment in small quantities. A great deal of scientific research is being done in this area, and there is a comprehensive review of research in a 1999 report from the US National Research Council, *Hormonally Active Agents in the Environment*. At the same time, many of the possible adverse effects that have been identified (falling sperm counts, breast cancer, compromised immune systems, or problems in childhood development) are greatly feared, and the public has been alerted to these effects by media reporting on scientific studies, by the activities of groups such as the World Wildlife Fund, and by influential publications, especially the book by Theo Colborn, *Our Stolen Future*.[26]

"EM-Com" (endocrine-modulators communication) is an example of a risk dialogue project and is based on a conceptual design or template

Figure 5
EM ⇔ Com: A representative risk dialogue process

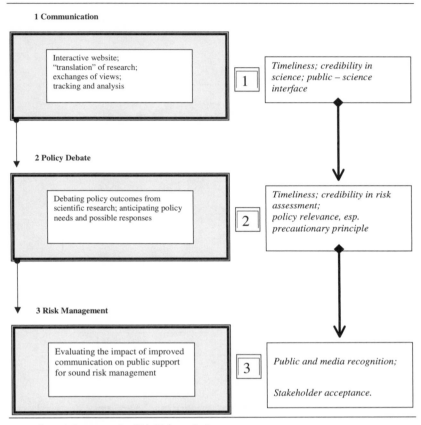

1 Communication

| Interactive website; "translation" of research; exchanges of views; tracking and analysis | 1 | *Timeliness; credibility in science; public – science interface* |

2 Policy Debate

| Debating policy outcomes from scientific research; anticipating policy needs and possible responses | 2 | *Timeliness; credibility in risk assessment; policy relevance, esp. precautionary principle* |

3 Risk Management

| Evaluating the impact of improved communication on public support for sound risk management | 3 | *Public and media recognition;*
 Stakeholder acceptance. |

EM ⇔ Com: A Representative Risk Dialogue Project

for an Internet-based public information resource with the generic URL of "riskcom.ca." The following diagrams show an illustrative architecture for such a resource. (See figures 6, 7, 8.)

DESIGN FOR AN "INTERNET LEARNING COMMUNITY"²⁷

We are designing and building an online educational community to share and communicate knowledge, through a useful and trustworthy Internet information resource, about several important environmental and health risk issues. Despite the masses of information available to

Figure 6
EM ⇔ Com: A public risk dialogue project for endocrine-modulating substances

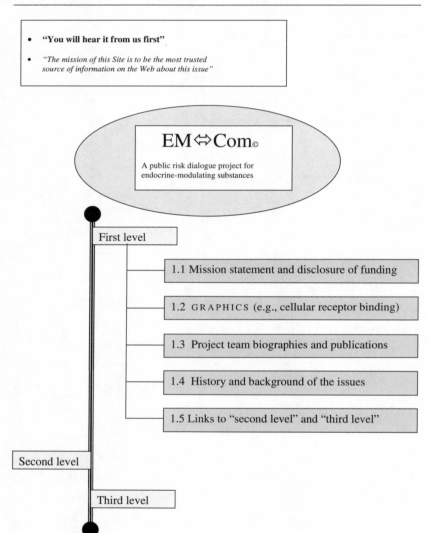

- **"You will hear it from us first"**
- *"The mission of this Site is to be the most trusted source of information on the Web about this issue"*

EM⇔Com©

A public risk dialogue project for endocrine-modulating substances

First level

1.1 Mission statement and disclosure of funding

1.2 GRAPHICS (e.g., cellular receptor binding)

1.3 Project team biographies and publications

1.4 History and background of the issues

1.5 Links to "second level" and "third level"

Second level

Third level

Figure 7
Second level: information resources

Second level: information resources

2.1 "What's new?"
Science translation of current research summaries

2.2 "What's happening?"
EM-Net, a weekly digest of current events, drawn from on-line searches of global media coverage and intermediate scientific journals (*Nature*, *Science*, etc.)

2.3 E-mail and feedback
Responses to queries and referrals to sources

2.4 Links
Hot links to preferred sites elsewhere on the Web

2.5 Sources
Bibliography of key documents (science and policy)

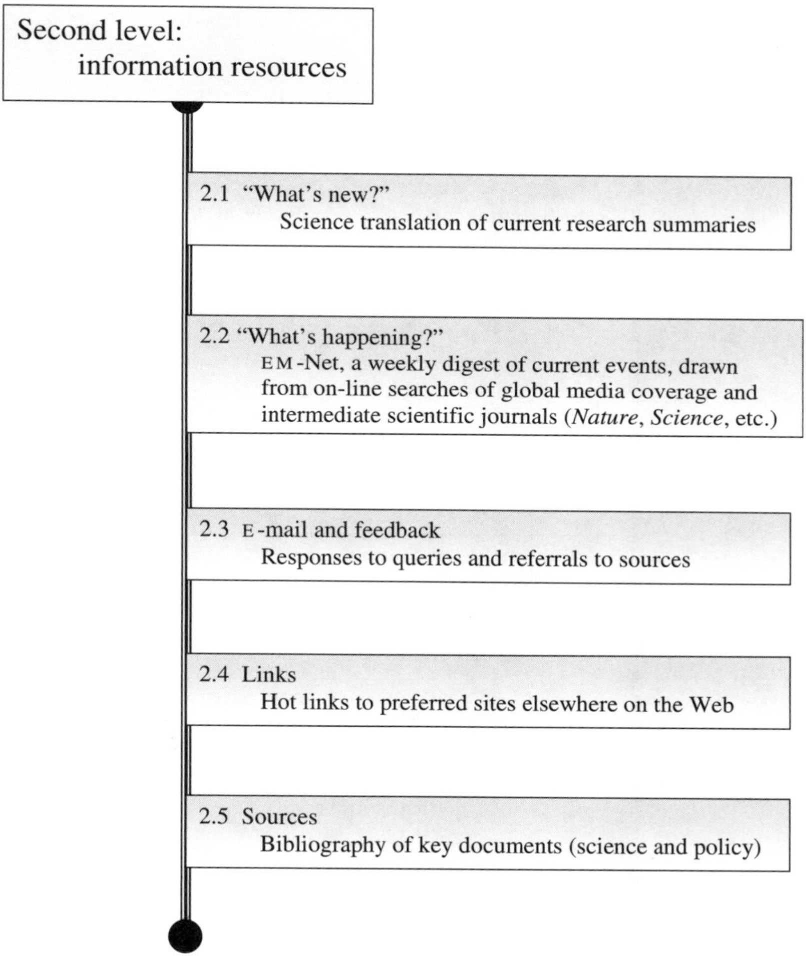

Figure 8
Third level: dialogue resources

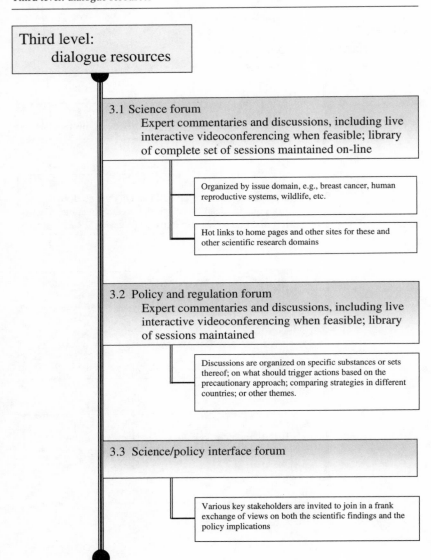

inquiring minds through the Web, search results on the issues addressed by the "riskcom.ca" project yield little of direct use to ordinary individuals. Existing material falls into one of three categories:

1 Scientific and academic papers posted on the Web, which seldom have a visual aspect and are often intimidating and impenetrable to lay audiences.
2 Special-interest sites (usually set up and maintained by a passionate individual), which lack peer review and provide neither a credible nor a complete resource for concerned individuals.
3 Sites hosted by non-government groups, such as Greenpeace or the World Wildlife Fund, which provide the most accessible information, but which also, as expected, cover risk issues in ways which encourage public support for their campaigns.

Expanding this already copious technical content is of limited value to concerned citizens. The real gap in current offerings is the lack of resources to help ordinary individuals understand the underlying science and thereby interpret the risks and the risk issues at hand.

The "riskcom.ca" group of sites aims to create and provide a trellis or infrastructure on which a Web-based educational community can grow and prosper. This infrastructure has three elements:

1 Carefully crafted interactive animations and diagrams which seek to attract interest, provide entry-level understanding of the key issues, and help users understand the science underlying the risks as well as the relationship between themselves and the environment; clearly communicate the scientific concepts; and establish a professional tone for the sites.
2 Easy-to-navigate interface and search facilities, enabling users to quickly zero in on the aspects of the topic that interest them, and presenting each topic and risk issue using clear and consistent conceptual models to aid users in digesting and interpreting the information.
3 Sophisticated database-backed community discussion resources so that users can (a) discuss and annotate the links and articles; (b) ask questions, and receive informed responses from both researchers/editors working on the project and other members of the community; (c) read comments by experts (and community members) on the articles linked to the site; (d) scan recent news releases relating to the risk factors and risk issues.

"Riskcom.ca" is about developing a new breed of educational Web portal, one that strives to build a learning community around a shared educational interest and to provide high-powered interactive multime-dia animations to assist interested and concerned individuals in gaining facility with navigating scientifically complex (and emotionally charged) topics.

1 Learning Communities

Database-backed, Web-based education has several advantages over traditional one-to-many media (e.g., lectures, books, or videos). Two-way information exchange allows dynamic personalization of content and presentation. We are exploring and researching how to best lever the opportunities and challenges of providing public education through the Web.

Though not formally enrolled in a course, most users of our site will come with specific learning objectives. Additionally, we as educators and publishers have clear ideas of what we'd like users to learn during their (we hope) repeated visits to our site. So both the users and Web educators have educational objectives. However, surfing the Web can seem like an aimless, unproductive activity. Our Web curriculum system allows Web educators to identify up to a dozen or so important areas of content we'd like our users to visit eventually, and it even allows the users to design their own curriculum and educational objectives.

Problem: Suppose that "Joe" comes to "www.em\com.ca" hoping to learn something about endocrine modulators. He sees a group of articles which interests him and is excited about what he can learn through our site. But after reading an article or two Joe is distracted by another task. Three months later, he returns to "www.em\com.ca" to continue his education, but cannot remember which articles he has read or which ones he wanted to read. The home page has been freshened with news so that the links are not in familiar places. Joe doesn't know what he should read next and, worse, doesn't feel that he is progressing towards any goal. *Solution/Implementation:* Our system provides a cur-riculum bar on each page Joe views on "www.em\com.ca." The bar shows a condensed description of the articles that "riskcom.ca" wants everyone to read, with little checkboxes by the ones that he has read already. Also Joe can personalize his curriculum by checking next to all the articles he would like to read in a "design your curriculum section." As Joe finishes a section, it is clear from referring to the curriculum bar which section to read next.

2 Interactive Visual Explanations

We are exploring the potential of Web-delivered interactive animations as tools for self-education about risk issues, in particular simultaneously communicating micro-level processes (biological and molecular) and macro-level relationships (human interaction in the environment). The animated learning resource should be useful for people of varying backgrounds ranging from concerned individuals with no special education or knowledge to students in the health, biological, or environmental sciences.

3 *Interaction as Feedback*

The third area of exploration and innovation, in addition to providing us with both valuable information on the public's risk concerns, provides a means of evaluating the success of our work. We will be achieving this through comprehensive analysis of server logs and click-through records. This will give us a feel for

- the popular and unpopular areas of our site, information on search engine referrals, and the types of search terms our visitors are entering into the search engines;
- information on which links people are using when they leave our site;
- the number and frequency of visits from registered and non-registered users.

User feedback through online forms will point out the strengths and weaknesses of our content and may suggest areas of expansion for the services and content provided through the "riskcom.ca" group of sites. It will also tell us the degree of success we had in addressing user concerns; what are the areas of greatest concern; and what type of information users are looking for. Questions asked by our users will direct our attention to areas in which we can expand our coverage, or improve our information presentation. We may eventually implement a quizzing system through which users can test their knowledge, and we (as publishers) can gauge the effectiveness of our learning materials.

12 Towards Competence in Risk Issue Management

Competence in risk issue management starts with an ability to understand that risk controversies have common structures and evolve over time in distinctive stages. The particular type of risk issue that becomes controversial is of fundamental importance to risk managers, because it determines which industrial sector and government agency is answerable to the public about its concerns. But, although controversies originate with the products and processes of many different industrial technologies and sectors (chemicals, tobacco, nuclear energy, forestry, telecommunications, petroleum, agriculture, to name but a few), the risk controversies themselves have many features in common.

THE EARLY STAGE

The early stage of every risk controversy has the following features. *First*, there is an incomplete hazard characterization, because scientific studies are inadequate, and sometimes scientists do not know at that point even what types of studies will clarify the concerns. At this stage it is not clear what is the range of adverse effects the public should be worried about, or sometimes whether anyone should be worried at all. These large unknowns are compounded by the propensity of spokespersons for industry, often seconded by their government counterparts, either to downplay or deny the scope of the hazards, to be reluctant to initiate adequate funding programs for the science that needs to be done, and to make soothing noises to dampen public concerns.

Second, there is poor or non-existent exposure assessment: it is not clear who (if anyone) is at risk of harm from many of the suspected effects, nor is it readily apparent how to resolve this question. Providing an answer necessitates being able to separate out specific sets of factors from the entire gamut of the hundreds or indeed thousands of relevant risk factors impinging upon the lives of individuals in modern societies. Epidemiological studies that attempt to do this are notoriously hard to construct and carry out, and the results from such studies are fought over by specialists sometimes for decades. Compounding these intrinsic difficulties is the reluctance of industry and governments to provide early funding for these studies, which are often inconclusive and always expensive.

Third, in the early stage the industrial and government institutions which eventually will be answerable for the issue have a strong desire to avoid calling attention to it, in the hope that there will never be a major controversy. Their motto for this stage is "Let sleeping dogs lie." Their fear is that, if they take the initiative to call attention to the newly suspected but poorly understood risk factors, they will raise alarms that might be unfounded and cause unnecessary worry in a population perhaps predisposed to worry needlessly about certain types of hazards. So, typically, little or no effort is made in risk communication, that is, explaining the nature of the hazards and the scientific studies being done to clarify them.

Fourth, and following directly from the third, throughout the early stage there is the possibility of "issue capture" and "stigma." Issue capture refers to the process whereby one party seizes the initiative and succeeds in raising the profile of an issue, to the point where others can no longer pretend it is unimportant and are required to respond. Since there are tremendous advantages to be reaped by the party which succeeds in this endeavour, this is a point where the strategic competence of ENGOs is put to the test, because like all other organizations they have limited resources at their disposal which must be deployed in an efficient way. One of the most potent devices for issue capture is to find a way to brand the risk source with a stigma, that is, an image with strongly negative connotations and having dramatic power to make something intuitively obvious and easily remembered; examples abound, ranging from dioxins in the 1970s ("the deadliest chemical known to mankind") to today's "Frankenfood" label for genetically modified crops.[1]

The early stage of a risk controversy can last for ten or fifteen years, as was the case with dioxins (c. 1970–85) and endocrine disruptors (c. 1990–2000); other risk issue domains such as cell phones and wireless telecommunications, global climate change, and agricultural biotechnology are still in this formative period. It is certain that many other applications of genetic engineering, especially as they apply to human health (xenotransplantation, animal cloning) and to manipulations of the human genome (germline gene therapy, genetic screening), will generate significant risk controversies. In addition, there will be efforts to win support for the intensive engineering of plants and trees both for enhanced carbon sequestration (to offset greenhouse gas emissions) and to provide biological feedstocks which promise far lower environmental impacts than conventional fossil fuels have had (so-called "cleaner production" technologies), and this too can be expected to be controversial.[2]

In general the early stage in risk controversies is marked by a very high degree of volatility. One aspect of this volatility is a phenomenon which could be named "issue cascading," where for purely accidental reasons intense concerns are transported across the boundaries that would otherwise separate them into distinct compartments.[3] The best example of this occurred when public dissatisfaction with government authorities over the mismanagement of "mad cow disease" in the UK spilled over shortly thereafter into distrust of the authorities' messages about the safety of genetically modified foods. Food was of course the link between the two uproars, but there was no other common factor between them in either the nature of the risks or the technologies which lay behind them. Issues can also "leak" across the boundaries that separate related technologies, and when that happens the newer phases of public controversy carry on some of the issues raised in earlier ones, even if the industrial players are quite different. In the case of electric and magnetic fields (EMF), the first phase of controversy involved the electrical utility industry's high-voltage transmission lines and the extremely low frequency fields (ELF) used in domestic electricity supply. In the second phase, although the frequencies of the EMF spectrum utilized by cell phones and other products of the wireless telecommunications industry are considerably higher than those in the ELF fields, and generally involve a somewhat different set of risk factors, there are enough similarities in the issue profiles to result in some spillage across the two sets of issues, as was shown earlier in our "Internet map" (figure 2).

There is also a type of volatility that arises when new events become connected with a long-standing source of risk controversy, and in this case the issues usually spin out of control so fast that authorities are forced to take actions to bring a quick resolution irrespective of costs. In Belgium in April 1999 the agricultural food sector suffered a case of accidental dioxin contamination, and when it was over probably not more than a few litres of waste oil containing PCBs inadvertently mixed into animal feed resulted in over one billion dollars of losses to that sector (and to the taxpayers).[4] Even the corporate history of organizations or industrial sectors identified with risk controversies can lead to cross-fertilization of the issues and contribute to institutional responses that aggravate the situation. Again, the controversy over genetically modified foods provides a good illustration: many of the firms prominent in agricultural biotechnology during the 1990s either had their origins in the chemicals sector, as in the case of Monsanto, or were subsidiaries of conglomerates in which the dominant members were chemical or pharmaceutical firms. In the opinion of some informed observers, the many key personnel in the new ag-biotech companies did not understand either the farming or the food sectors, which are rather old lines of business into which they had leaped rather hurriedly, and this unfamiliarity hindered their ability to understand the nature and seriousness of the GM foods controversy as it was gathering steam.[5]

THE MIDDLE STAGE

The middle stage of every risk controversy has the following features. *First,* large-scale scientific research programs designed to produce a definitive hazard or risk characterization are well under way but remain incomplete, and early epidemiology studies (if they exist) are likely to be inconclusive as well. Typically, there is little, if any, effective communication to the public of the research program objectives, the reasons why certain programs and not others are under way, or how the results are expected to be applied to a surer understanding of the hazards.

Second, there are initial risk assessments, giving some quantitative expression to the magnitude of the hazard, which tend to be expressed in technical jargon; to invent an example, "excessive daily alcohol consumption [a measure which differs significantly for males and females] is estimated to represent an annual incremental risk of breast cancer on the order of 2×10^{-5} in the exposed population." In addition, often the uncertainties, which may or may not be specified clearly, remain rather large, or the initial estimates are challenged by subsequent findings. Typically, no decent effort is made to explain clearly to the public either the great complexities in the risk assessment exercises, or the strengths and weaknesses of competing assumptions and approaches. This failure can be quite serious for the public if citizens miss some key information in the risk assessments, for example the finding that women who smoke have a risk of lung cancer *four times* higher than men do, for comparable patterns of tobacco use, owing apparently to differences in physiology.

Third, the risk information vacuum that is pervasive in the middle stage helps to keep an issue "in play," as it were, with various stakeholders jockeying for position and leverage during the ebb and flow of events such as the publication of key studies, calls for regulatory action, protests, closed-door negotiations, and lobbying. With respect to both the scientific programs and the risk assessments, throughout this phase the strongest inclination of industry and government, in most cases, is to continue to downplay concerns, to keep a low profile, and to pray that the issue just goes away of its own accord. There is a different kind of inherent volatility in this stage, compared with the earlier one, which rules out reliable predictions about the future course of the issue agenda. For example, the release of a long-awaited major scientific study can generate competing efforts by opposed factions to provide the "spin" (interpretive context) that will define the public attitudes of the great majority of the population who will never see the study itself; this happened during 1999 in the risk issue domain of endocrine disruptors with the release of a major report by the National Research Council in the United States.[6]

Fourth, and increasingly, in the middle stage an issue may be "bounced" around the globe as the contending parties (industry, governments, ENGOs, academics) find different venues in which to mount their campaigns in strategic issue management. Globalized business strategies mean that the same technologies are deployed around the world, and, in reaction to this, many ENGOs have become highly adept at internationalizing their own operations and matching the capacities of multinational firms to operate on a world scale. This has happened repeatedly in the disputes over forestry practices (clear-cutting, logging of old-growth stands, unsustainable harvests, etc.). During the height of its campaign against GM foods in 1999, Greenpeace's issue leader, based in Germany, held a daily two-hour strategy session, using the Internet, with his campaign leaders in seventeen countries around the globe.[7] Electronic mass communications and above all the Internet promote the increasingly sophisticated co-ordination of marketing campaigns for both products and issues.

Dioxins passed through the middle stage of controversy in the period 1985–99, but Greenpeace keeps the dioxin issue alive today by focusing on Japan, which uses incineration for its garbage because there are no landfill sites, and waste incineration is now the largest human source of dioxins. Issues about risks associated with extremely low frequency electric and magnetic fields in household electricity supply (ELF/EMF) and with high-voltage transmission lines also diminished during the decade of the 1990s; however, a continuing stream of epidemiological studies, many of which have quite different and even contradictory outcomes, keeps some controversy brewing. The intense international controversies over forestry practices also seemed to enter the mature stage in the late 1990s, after activists had developed the strategy of promoting consumer boycotts of lumber supplied by companies whose forestry practices allegedly do not respect certain standards of appropriate environmental management. This controversy has matured in the sense that the major forestry companies have agreed to respect externally generated forest practices codes, and the remaining disputes (which will endure for some time yet) have to do with which codes will be adopted and how conformity with them will be monitored and enforced. The international mining industry is in pretty much the same situation and, as with the forestry industry, the most important focus is on the operations carried on in Third World countries.[8]

THE MATURE STAGE

Among major risk controversies reviewed in this and earlier volumes, tobacco use and nuclear power probably entered the mature stage first (of course these two are among the oldest risk controversies), sometime in the 1980s, followed by asbestos risk and many aspects of pesticide use in agriculture in the 1990s. And it seems likely that both dioxins and most ELF/EMF issues have now entered this stage.

The mature stage of every risk controversy has the following features. *First,* large scientific research programs maintained by industry and governments are scaled back to a "maintenance" state, although they never stop entirely for major risk domains, as the full hazard characterization is increasingly well understood. *Second,* exposure measures become more and more sophisticated, and therefore the quantitative risk assessments are more reliable, with the most troubling uncertainties being reduced to tolerable levels. However, large epidemiological studies often continue, and in cases of very complex risk domains such as smoking, important discoveries about previously unrecognized risk factors continue to be made. But for the most part the public can expect few great surprises from the ongoing scientific programs in these areas, although essential new knowledge will be gained continuously, some of which can lead to important modifications in risk assessments even for relatively well described risks. For example, both geological radon and food- and water-borne pathogens (especially *E. coli* O157:H7 and *Cryptosporidium parvum*) appear to be more serious hazards than they were thought to be sometime earlier.[9]

Third, in most case the long-standing inadequacies in risk communication typically are never repaired and therefore continue to take their toll, in that the framing of issues is frozen in time and cannot respond to changing circumstances. For example, there are those in Canada and elsewhere who now would like to see the generation of electricity from nuclear power reconsidered as a newly desirable option in an era of concern about lowering atmospheric greenhouse gas emissions, by using alternatives to the burning of fossil fuels. But there is an enormous weight of resistance to this option in public opinion to be dealt with, the legacy of decades of appallingly inadequate risk communication from the nuclear industry. Another prime example is afforded by asbestos, which became notorious in the 1970s and 1980s when the terrible legacy of industrial deception about occupational risks in the preceding half-century finally was exposed. As noted in chapter 7, Canada (a major producer of this mineral for many years) has been unable to stop the closing of its markets in Europe to asbestos products in recent years, despite having made a good case for their acceptability on the basis of current occupational exposure standards and credible scientific risk assessments for public exposures.[10]

Fourth, there is a shifting stakeholder interest profile in the mature stage, as businesses, governments, and non-governmental organizations make strategic choices about allocations of time and resources to a variety of risk issues. In addition, by the time the mature stage is reached for a risk domain, the controversial aspects of the issue usually are firmly controlled by a small number of interested parties, who may be said to "own" the issues and who cannot easily be dislodged from that position.[11] However, I shall argue in the following pages that, no matter how adept the organizations are which assume control over risk issues, their ascendancy owes at least as much to the mistakes, inattention, indifference, and arrogance of their opponents – organizational behaviour traits that are, in principle, remediable.

For example, Greenpeace International has owned the issues around dioxin for over ten years, a position it earned by virtue of the consistency of its active involvement, its ability to stage high-profile public events, and its extensive series of publications in which scientific issues are expressed clearly for a non-specialist public. The World Wildlife Fund has the pre-eminent position with respect to endocrine disruptors issues, by virtue of both its early entry into the fray with the influential book *Our Stolen Future* and the consistency of its subsequent attention to the accelerating scientific research developments; like Greenpeace, it presents this information in an easily accessible form. Indeed to date few organizations anywhere, of any kind, can match the ability of Greenpeace and the World Wildlife Fund to maintain an effective activity profile worldwide on so many different contentious issues.[12] Of course there are many other influential non-governmental organizations actively engaged in these and other issues, as well as local and

regional citizens' groups, and even individuals, who are often important players in certain types of controversies (for example, facility siting issues, which inevitably have a specific locational focus).

By no means does this suggest that industry and governments are
less important players in risk controversies. On the contrary, both have
essential roles, but their actions are at once both more highly constrained, and more determinative of outcomes, compared with those of
NGOs. More highly constrained, because their places in institutional
power structures are more clearly defined by legal frameworks and social conventions. But also far more determinative, because the facilities
and technologies that jointly they operate (as businesses) and ultimately control (as government regulators) actually drive the economic
engines of the global economy, generating profits for firms and tax
revenues for governments. All current risk controversies are about
practices and technologies that actually continue to operate widely in
the world, although the operators may suffer a good deal of grief as a
result of the controversies, and even have to change the way they
manage them (sometimes substantially). For an adept and innovative
company such as DuPont, such an issue is a challenge to be overcome,
as happened when it developed replacement products for the chlorof-
luorocarbon refrigerants that were indicted and then banned as ozone-
depleting substances. Rarely are the controversies themselves the occasion of disruptions that threaten the viability of firms or governments
in power, but this can happen, as is illustrated by the story of Monsanto, and the public outrage over the handling of "mad cow disease"
in the UK, which discredited the ruling Conservative government.

RISK MANAGEMENT VS. RISK ISSUE MANAGEMENT RESTATED

The comment from Deutsche Bank's investment banking group quoted
among the epigraphs for chapter 2 – "GMOs are good science but bad
politics" – sums up in a single pithy sentence the essential difference between risk management and risk issue management, which was introduced at the beginning of this book. *Risk management* relies on
scientific risk assessment to estimate the probable harm to persons and
environments resulting from specific types of substances or processes.
These assessments by risk managers, which are highly technical in nature, normally occur well outside of public view and often rely on commercial confidential information which cannot be disclosed by the
governments that must evaluate it. Using those estimates, industry and
governments set allowable limits of exposure, regulate, permit or ban
substances and facilities, manage stocks of natural resources, and carry

out other actions, all designed to provide certain protections for public health and the environment and to ensure a sustainable resource base for future economic activity.

As such, even when risk managers seek honestly to take into account varying perceptions of the risk in question among different sectors of the public, they are constrained by the scope and limitations of scientific knowledge and probabilistic risk assessment to favour certain specific courses of action. They must take into account the uncertainties that are always a factor in risk estimates, but they are also obliged to render "yes/no" decisions even where substantial uncertainties exist, because interested parties – including employees and citizens as well as corporations and government departments – demand access to the economic benefits that arise in risk-taking activities.

Risk issue management is fundamentally different.[13] The most important difference is that risk issues, as they play out in society at large, are not primarily driven by the state of scientific risk assessments. Rather, such assessments are just one of a series of "contested" domains within the issue. Risk issues are configured by the competing attempts of various stakeholder interests to define or control the course of social action with respect to health and environmental hazards. Issue management refers to the relation between an organization and its larger social environment and is inherently governed by strategic considerations as developed by an organization or even loose collections of individuals. (See table 4.) All those who wish to become skilled interveners in risk controversies, such as ENGOs, as well as those who will inevitably be caught up in them, namely industry and governments, become risk issue managers (by choice or default). To do so entails understanding the internal dynamics of risk controversies and seeking to influence them towards some final resolution; in most cases this will be called the "public interest," although inevitably there will be diverse definitions of what this means in practice.

Whereas risk management seeks to assess and control the hazards that make up a risk domain, risk issue management responds to a public controversy about the adequacy of the risk management measures and approaches. A risk controversy is a risk domain which becomes the subject of a protracted battle among stakeholder interest groups, some of whom will challenge the entire basis of the risk assessment that has been accepted by both industry and governments. No matter how well the risk assessment exemplifies the best practices of professional risk managers, its entire basis and results often will be simply dismissed by the opposing side. The evolution of a risk controversy is determined primarily by the competing strategies of whatever groups or organiza-

Table 4
Contrast between risk management and risk issue management

	Risk Domain	Risk Controversy
Type of responsibility	Risk management	Risk issue management
Type of expertise required	Risk/benefit assessment	Risk communication
Key activities	Hazard characterization Exposure assessment Benefits assessment Uncertainty analysis Options/decision analysis	Science explanations Science/public interface Science/policy interface Explaining uncertainties Stakeholder relations
Orientation of activities	"Substantive"	Strategic
Principal "language"	Technical/probabilistic	Non-technical/graphics

tions choose to, or are compelled to, enter into it; as mentioned earlier, the objective of these strategies is to steer the outcome of the controversy towards some preferred risk management option, which may include the rejection of the entire technology (as in the cases of agricultural biotechnology and nuclear power).

Since by definition a risk controversy is an area of competing visions about where an optimal resolution lies, competence in risk issue management should not be understood as seeking to "control" the outcome. Rather, it means in general being able to compete successfully with other influential stakeholders within the zone of controversy, in a way that is appropriate to the specific positioning of an organization and its lines of accountability within society. Industry, ENGOs, and governments all have quite diverse situations in this regard. Governments' positioning is defined primarily by their responsibility to define and defend "the public interest" as such; for example, to seek to be as "inclusive" as possible in relation to the spectrum of social interests. ENGOs are accountable to the particular constituencies which support them, morally and financially, including individuals, charitable foundations, wealthy benefactors, high-profile public figures, and in some cases both businesses and governments. Among these major players it is industry which finds itself at a decisive crossroads, deliberating between the traditional path of following exclusively shareholder interests, on the one hand, and a newer path of multifaceted accountability known as the "triple bottom line," where both responsible environmental management and social or community responsibility have been added to profitability requirements.[14]

At one time or another, intense and persistent risk controversies have affected, or are likely to affect, most major industrial sectors and many different government agencies. Traditionally the instinctive response of managers within those organizations, when a brewing risk controversy first threatens to engulf them, is one of denial: Denial, that the *issues* as represented by other interested parties are at all significant – and that those parties have any business meddling in such matters anyway; denial, that the management of the risk factors in question is or should be open to dispute by those who are not "experts" in the relevant scientific disciplines; and denial, that "the public" really needs to be involved in the intricacies of evaluating scientific research results, assessing the credibility of experts, figuring out exposures and uncertainties, doing quantitative risk estimates, and exploring risk-benefit trade-offs among the decision options for risk control.

The case studies of risk controversies to date show, alas, that those instincts are unreliable guides to effective risk issue management. In all cases the opposite propositions are the better guides – namely, that public perceptions of risk are legitimate and must be treated as such, that risk management subsists in an inherently disputable zone, and that the public ought always to be involved (through good risk communication practices) in discussions about the nature of risk evaluation by scientists and risk managers. The concluding section offers some specific guidelines on how to carry out this preferred strategy.

DEFINING COMPETENCE
IN RISK ISSUE MANAGEMENT

As mentioned in chapter 1, "perceived managerial incompetence" has been identified in public opinion surveys as a primary factor in the loss of trust, on the public's part, in the ability of government and industry to manage risks well. The inadequate responses of risk managers to public concerns arising in risk controversies have been solidly documented in case studies, referred to throughout the preceding chapters. On the other hand, competence in this domain has not been described systematically anywhere, to the best of my knowledge. The four dimensions outlined below are at least some of the minimal requirements for anyone hoping to manage risk issues competently. Arranged sequentially they are: (1) accepting responsibility; (2) addressing uncertainties; (3) managing the science/policy interface; and (4) communicating risks appropriately. I have illustrated the workings of those various dimensions by referring back to the case studies presented earlier.

1 Accepting Responsibility

This is the first and greatest test and to pass it one must overcome the denial phase, described above. This means in the first place accepting the reality and the legitimacy of public controversy about technologies. It also means being willing to engage the public fairly and openly, in a timely fashion – on the issues as they are perceived by citizens and opposition groups – as well as to carry out one's share of an obligation to manage the risks, described in scientific language, that are identified with an industrial sector or an area of government regulatory jurisdiction. In conventional wisdom, deliberately setting out to raise the profile of a set of risk issues in one's own area would be regarded as nothing short of heresy: seeking to engage the public early in the developing stage of a risk controversy contradicts one of the strongest tenets in the prevailing doctrine of issue management, that is, doing everything possible to avoid calling attention to oneself and identifying one's organization with a potentially troublesome set of issues. And yet, I suggest, competent risk issue management demands just such a stance, because it affords an organization or sector a chance to occupy the "high ground" on a set of issues, demonstrating through early engagement its commitment to doing everything in its power to resolve the public's concerns, as they are perceived, as well as to help manage the risks, relevant to those concerns, as they are characterized by science.

The irony is that, these days, there are forces at work in the institutional arrangements between industry and governments that for the most part lead to more prudent risk management – in other words, a greater margin of public safety – than was ever the case in earlier periods. However, most risk managers still seek to avoid raising the risk issue profile in their area because they fear that they might lose control over the management of the risk factors; this imprudent attitude towards good risk issue management increases the probabilities that they will indeed do so. The chemical industry's "Responsible Care" program is still the best example of taking the initiative to accept responsibility broadly for all aspects of risk in its sphere of activity, although, fifteen years after its inception, no other important industry sector operating internationally has yet followed this path unequivocally.[15]

2 Addressing Uncertainties

Persistent uncertainty among the public about the potential scope and impact of feared hazards is by far the most important single dimension in all risk controversies. This is perfectly understandable, because whereas the hazard characteristics can be specific, graphic, and dreaded (as with neuro-degenerative diseases or cancer), people ordinarily have no way of knowing *how much* they should worry about some risk factors, that entail those types of possible outcomes, in comparison with others. As a result, it is likewise understandable if they should react to the impoverished state of their knowledge about relative uncertainties with a demand for protection against any exposure at all to certain risk factors (i.e., "zero risk"), even if this demand cannot possibly be met at any cost by any conceivable risk control scheme. Avoidance of appropriate discussions of uncertainties by responsible authorities was a major factor in the disastrous mismanagement of the "mad cow disease" episode in Britain; it is now commonly found in representations of the risks associated with radio-frequency fields made by the wireless telecommunications industry.

The nature of uncertainties in risk assessments, and the reasons why they may persist for long periods despite the most intensive programs of scientific research, are among the most difficult matters to explain well to the non-expert public; as a result, few honest attempts to do so have ever been undertaken. For many members of the public, who have only a passive relation at best to an industrial sector (as consumers of its products), a "natural" response to persistent uncertainties in risk assessments is to advocate a "wait and see" strategy – that is, delay implementation of new technologies until a desirable level of certainty about possible adverse effects has been realized. However, this is a truly frightening prospect that jeopardizes the realization of adequate returns on capital investment within an industrial sector. So the only proper alternative is to confront the existence and implications of persistent uncertainties early and openly, through (for example) an intense and fair dialogue about comparative risks, reasonable risk-benefit trade-offs, and possible cost-effective risk reduction strategies.

3 Managing the Science/Policy Interface

This requirement follows directly from the first two. Both an unwillingness to accept responsibility for timely engagement with the public on risk issues and an unwillingness to represent uncertainties fairly constitute near-fatal errors at the interface of science and public policy. The importance of this interface as such is indicated by the simple observation that all environmental and health risks must have, by definition, a scientific and technical description on which a risk assessment (and therefore any feasible risk control options) is based. Societies seek to control risks by means of risk management decision making, which ultimately produces – implicitly or explicitly, usually the former – a judgment on what levels of risk are publicly "acceptable" in specific cases. But what is "acceptable" is *always* a policy decision, and ultimately a political one, rather than a scientific or technical judgment. In other words, science and policy meet in risk management.

Many risk controversies are exacerbated because some technical specialists insist on passing judgment, not only on hazard characterization and exposure estimates, but also on what level of risk for a particular technology or practice the public should regard as acceptable (say, a one-in-a-million risk), and some among them become openly contemptuous of the public if the latter is flatly rejected, as it often is. (This failing has been endemic in the civilian nuclear industry, for example; the fact that, all too often, uncertainties have been poorly characterized and communicated by these same specialists has played a part in forming the public's poor view of their arguments.) It matters not at all even if the public is found to be arbitrary and inconsistent in making comparative risk judgments, as is often just the case, seemingly tolerating easily higher risks in some areas of life than in others. Such is democracy. The public very well may damage its own self-interest in this way, because some benefits from technologies may go unrealized owing to an arbitrarily high perception of risk. The only good countermeasure is for the risk managers to mount a consistent, long-term, and fair public risk dialogue process, providing clear and pertinent information on the relevant scientific research, the hazard and exposure characterization, the risk assessment and uncertainties, risk control options, economic and health benefits, and comparative risk and risk-benefit profiles of competing technologies. To date no such process has ever been initiated for a controversial technology.

The case studies of MMT and AOX, in chapters 4 and 6 respectively, present a striking contrast with regard to competence in risk issue management, in terms of managing the science/policy interface. In the former, the ultimately disastrous end result is attributable chiefly to the inability of the five federal ministers, who had collective responsibility for the issue, to insist that the troublesome point (the auto manufacturers' claims about emissions systems fouling) be resolved by a credible technical review. In the absence of such a resolution, there was no way to resolve the inconsistencies of judgment at the interface of science and policy. In the AOX case, on the other hand, Environment Canada's lead scientists insisted, over many years and in the face of some determined opposition, that the developing scientific analysis was credible and should guide the policy process; ultimately they succeeded in their own domain, and through no fault of their own other agendas, developed at the provincial level, produced unnecessary policy confusions in this file.

4 *Communicating Risks Appropriately*

At the end of the previous chapter a sketch is given of what a fair and appropriate risk dialogue process could look like. Every one of the high-stakes, international risk controversies that are intense at the time of writing – greenhouse gas emissions and global climate change, genetically modified foods, radio-frequency fields, endocrine-disrupting chemicals – as well as some older ones still simmering in the background (nuclear energy, forest practices) could benefit from a dedicated effort in good risk communication practice, along the lines of what is sketched there, or in some arguably more effective design. The key point in the design offered there can be summed up in a single message: The institutional actors in charge of the risk management process (industry and governments) ought to surrender control over the related process of engaging the public in long-term risk dialogues. Put directly, those actors should surrender control over the process of consensus building for risk understanding, as well as the risk messages themselves that emerge from that process. These tasks should be entrusted to independent and credible third parties who are capable of demonstrating to the wider public that they can be trusted to create a fair, informed, and disinterested forum for these risk dialogues. We will never know if it could make a difference until it is tried.

The discussion of cloning and related technologies in chapter 11 suggests that, in the technologies of genetic engineering applied to the manipulation of animal and human genes, we shall soon face dimensions of risks – there labelled "moral risks" – that take us far beyond what we have had to deal with in modern industrial technologies to date. We cannot learn how to manage those risks sensibly unless we can first understand their full implications through an intensive public risk dialogue. The alternatives are almost too abhorrent to contemplate.

Appendix:
Providing Independent
Expert Advice to Government
and the Public

There are almost a hundred national or regional academies in the world, affiliated through the InterAcademy Panel on International Issues. Most of them have some kind of official recognition and sustaining funding by government: "Almost all Academies are explicitly or implicitly recognised in national legislation. Indeed, many owe their existence to Government initiative. Others have secured the endorsement, and often the explicit patronage, of Government or Head of State along the way ... Some Academies – e.g. the Royal Society of Canada – receive no regular funding from Government, but most receive significant sums."[1] Academies perform a number of functions and services, but the one which stands out from the rest, in relation to the "official" recognition of academies by nations, is the provision of expert advice to governments and the public. In some cases, notably for the US National Academy of Sciences, there is a statutory mandate to do so, and in many other cases, this has evolved to become a customary activity. Sometimes the advice is solicited for specific purposes by government agencies, and in other cases the activity is self-initiated by the academy. Resources to discharge these functions are provided either by a general and regular stipend or by funds allocated to specific projects, or both.

There are a number of special qualities attached to the provision of expert advice which are intrinsically related to the unique characteristics of academies. Some of these are: (1) independence, objectivity, and "disinterestedness"; (2) the high professional standing of the individuals who are called upon to serve as advisors; (3) "balanced" judgment with respect to competing views; and (4) placing results before the public to encourage discussion and further consideration.[2] A Canadian study commissioned by Industry Canada in 1993 looked at the activities of twenty-five academies and institutes in five countries, and its findings generally confirm what is outlined above.[3] The key points noted are the regular activities in the area of science policy and public policy; the "high profile" of the advice function; the importance of clear independence from government; and the prestige of the academies. In all five of these countries, the academies proper receive some part of their regular funding from government, an arrangement that has been in place for a very long time (in most cases a century or more). Of all the academies in the world, those in the United States and Great Britain appear to be the most active in the role of providing advice to the public and to government.[4] In others, particularly France's Académie des Sciences, there are initiatives under way to increase the academy's role in the provision of advice.[5]

SCOPE OF THE ROLE OF PROVIDING ADVICE

The activities of the four US institutions that make up the academy in that country (National Academy of Sciences, National Academy of Engineering, Institute of Medicine, National Research Council) are considerable in scope, with an output of about two hundred reports a year.[6] More suitable models for most other countries, including Canada, are the Royal Society of London and the Académie des Sciences (Institut de France), two of the oldest academies in the world, which have for some time identified "advice/le conseil" as one of their key roles. Since 1849 the Royal Society of London has administered an annual "Parliamentary Grant-in-Aid" which is dedicated to specific purposes; in 1998 this grant amounted to £23.85 million. As of 1998 the society had a total staff of 117 and an annual operating budget in excess of £30 million, including over £1.5 million dedicated towards "enhancing science education, understanding, or advice." Eight full-time staff were employed in its science advice function in that year, which is described as follows: "The Royal Society's authority and independence give it a unique role in science policy advice. In discharging this responsibility the Society makes full use of its extensive networks and of all available quantitative data in order to establish and present to Government and others the informal views of the scientific community on a wide variety of policy issues."[7]

In 1997 the Académie des Sciences (Institut de France) had a total budget of 41,8 million francs, of which 45 per cent was received from the ministère de l'éducation nationale, de la Recherche et de la Technologie; 12 per cent of expenditures (5 million francs) were allocated to the "Conseil des applications études-rapports." The académie published five major reports in 1997 on topical issues and sponsored many colloquia and conferences to which the public was invited. These functions are co-ordinated by Le Conseil pour les applications de l'Académie des Sciences and a number of committees (Comité 2000, Comité de l'environnement, Comité de la recherche spatial, Comité des études et rapports, and Comité de défense des hommes des sciences). The government of France recognizes the role of the académie by regularly charging it with certain missions of a highly visible nature.[8]

The Royal Society of Canada has been very active in providing advice to governments and the public in Canada during the last quarter-century. During the decade of the 1980s, for example, perhaps the most high-profile activity was that of the Commission on Lead in the Environment, chaired by Dr Kenneth Hare; but there was also important similar work done in the areas of nuclear safety, acid deposition, the Great Lakes Water Quality Agreement, "nuclear winter," AIDS, and tobacco. The society has also administered two long-term efforts, the Canadian Program for the International Decade for Natural Disaster Reduction (1990–2000, jointly with the Canadian Academy of Engineering) and the Canadian Global Change Program (1985–99), both of which have produced many well-regarded reports and other documents containing policy advice.

In 1996 the society adopted formal guidelines for the conduct of expert panel processes, which are one of the main instruments used in various formats by academies in providing advice to government and the public.[9] Since late 1996, three important reports have been completed by panels using these procedures, and the fourth and fifth panels are completing theirs early in 2001:

1 "A Review of the INSERM Report on the Health Effects of Asbestos," December 1996;
2 "Recommendations for the Disposition of the Health Canada Primate Colony," November 1997;
3 "A Review of the Potential Health Risks of Radiofrequency Fields from Wireless Telecommunication Devices," May 1999;
4 "Review of Methods Used to Estimate and Compare the Costs and Benefits of Particulate Matter and Ozone Reduction" (panel appointed October 1999);
5 "The Future of Food Biotechnology" (panel appointed February 2000).

Some indication of the impact of these reports is given by the large number of combined "hits" for the third report on the websites of the society and of Health Canada, where the report is available (over seven thousand in the period May–November 1999).

WHAT DO EXPERT PANELS DO?

Reports of expert panels provide a distinctive type of public policy guidance to governments and other parties, on occasions where the advice sought depends on the application of highly specialized knowledge. Any domain of knowledge may be pertinent to the issues placed before such panels, ranging from engineering and natural sciences through medicine and social welfare to ethics, culture, and law. What distinguish expert panel reports from the usual types of scholarly publication are two main features: (1) some acknowledged matters of public policy decision making are related, directly or indirectly, to the panel charge, and (2) some agency whose responsibilities lie in that policy domain has explicitly asked for the panel's contributions.

The way in which expert panels are constituted and operate is another one of their essential features. In short, such panels always function strictly at arm's-length from the agency which commissions and receives their outputs. The reason for this is bound up with the very qualities that differentiate expert panel processes from the many other forms of policy advice. For their outputs are the ideal type of policy advice that can claim to be uninfluenced by "extrinsic" or externally imposed considerations. The work of expert panels, then, is determined by the occasional needs of governments and other parties for a specific type of policy-relevant guidance, namely, one that has a claim to a degree of broad credibility based on the reputations and autonomy of its authors. In one sense it is the professional reputations of the panellists themselves that are supposed to buttress such a claim to autonomy and to guard against any attempted manipulation of the outcome by special interests. However, in practice this claim needs to be supported also by some kind of publicly visible procedural framework which plausibly legitimizes the panel's special status and guarantees its independence from direct control by a sponsoring agency. Policy-relevant guidance is given by recognized experts in a variety of settings that may be represented as a spectrum defined by the degree of autonomy, in each case, from both sponsors and particular interests (see figure 9).

In all such settings there are legitimate claims to the provisioning of expert, policy-relevant advice to governments and other parties, and all forms of such advice giving can be invaluable to modern governments, in view of the daunting array of issues confronting them which have some form of technical complexity or scientific description.

HOW DO EXPERT PANELS FUNCTION?

1 Overall Panel Composition

The most important criterion for overall panel composition is "balance." The search for a "balanced" panel arises out of the recognition that experts often or always have strongly held views, arising directly out of their detailed knowledge and long study of an area, and that there may be quite different "points of view" in any group of equally qualified individuals within a specialized area of knowledge. It is expected, of course, that such differing viewpoints within a field are well known to others through published commentaries and debates; a common problem is methodological disagreements which persist over long periods. The rule, in this case, is that panel membership must be balanced with

Figure 9
[Appendix] Degrees of autonomy in expert panels

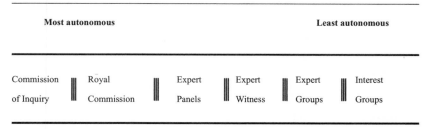

Notes to Figure 9:

- A "Commission of inquiry" is constituted under the Inquiries Act and usually headed by a judge or lawyer who has great autonomy.
- A Royal Commission is nominally quite independent, but it often has a "political" mission and so is under some general policy direction.
- Expert panels are the subject of this section.
- An expert witness is a single individual with special qualifications, usually serving a client.
- Expert groups are, for examples, members of recognized professions.
- Interest groups often have specialized expertise by virtue of the qualifications and experience of their staff, but they do not pretend to be "neutral" on issues.

respect to the established range of viewpoints commonly acknowledged to exist within a field. Obviously, in any field of inquiry there may be "marginal" or idiosyncratic viewpoints that are held by some highly distinguished authorities, and not all of these can be accommodated in a panel. The sponsoring body must be prepared to make judgments in these matters, and, if and when challenged, to defend its selection of panellists publicly and credibly.

2 *Selecting Panellists*

In particular, the choices should reflect the predominant purposes that motivate the use of such bodies in the first place – namely, the provision of advice which has a special claim to objectivity and disinterestedness. This consideration is fundamental to the meaning of expert panels. Members of such panels always serve in an individual capacity, and *never* as representatives of organizations, stakeholders, or interest groups. Their appointments are justified and given credibility by their publicly validated specialized expertise that is directly relevant to the issues which the panel is to consider. This rule cannot be violated even occasionally, in response to special circumstances that seem to justify it, because then and thereafter all other organized bodies which have a stake in an issue will have a legitimate claim to such consideration. And at that point one is no longer running expert panels. The sponsoring body may and should seek the advice of interested parties and even solicit names of individuals for consideration for appointment. However, it must make clear to all others that final selection is its prerogative alone and is not subject to prior review or approval by any other agency or party. Violation of this rule too is inevitably fatal to the credibility of the sponsoring body and its panels.

3 Bias and Conflict of Interest Review

After potential panels members are identified, panel composition is approved, nominated panel members are approached, and the panel is assembled, a review of bias and potential conflict of interest is undertaken.[10] Direct conflict of interest in the matter at hand is good grounds for exclusion from panel service. But it is necessary to define this quite narrowly (in monetary or organizational terms), because to allow more nebulous criteria, such as "perceived" conflict of interest, to constitute grounds for exclusion can be most unfair. Again, the sponsoring body should be aware, to the greatest extent possible, of any objections to its selections that are likely to be raised in some quarters, and to be prepared to defend its selection process – if necessary, publicly.

4 Panel Deliberations

When there is complete agreement on all of the above, the panel is ready to begin its work. From this point on, and until its report is delivered to the sponsor, the panel works in confidence, and no one apart from panel members and the support staff is privy to either the nature of its deliberations or its tentative conclusions. No one other than the panel's own designated support staff attends its meetings. In particular, although the panel may receive written communications from anyone interested in its mandate (and indeed, may invite such communications if it wishes), including the sponsor and any agency which is supporting the panel process, there must be no "informal" or "off the record" contacts or discussions about the issues before it. This autonomy of the panel deliberations themselves is perhaps the most important aspect of expert panel processes, and it is what distinguishes them most clearly from most other forms of policy guidance by experts. It is also the most important defence of the panel's objectivity and freedom from external influence.

5 Peer Review and the Final Report

The panel's report, once drafted, is then submitted to peer review. All of the panel's findings, conclusions, and recommendations are subject to review by anonymous experts who have prior involvement in that particular panel process. The selection of these individuals is ratified by the oversight committee. Peer review is the final quality control procedure in the process.

Panel reports are solely the product of the panel members. Although they may be submitted confidentially in draft form to peer reviewers, under appropriate procedures, this is the only type of prepublication review that is permitted for expert panel reports. It is also part of the nature of expert panel processes themselves that the reports emanating from them are public documents. The text of the final report that is approved by the panellists is the text that is published, and it is the responsibility of the sponsoring agency to make a reasonable effort to disseminate the report to external parties.

6 Dissemination and Public Access

The final report is issued by the organization governing the panel process. This document is made available to the public at the same time as it is transmitted to the sponsor. Meetings convened by the panel may be held in public forums to discuss the findings of the report. This provides interested individuals as well as the sponsor an opportunity to comment openly on the findings of the panel for public record. The panel is not required to make public other documentation that may have been generated throughout the course of its deliberations. The final report is the only documentation that is published.

Notes

CHAPTER ONE

1 Codification occurs when practices are put into the form of quasi-official standards, such as that of the Canadian Standards Association's 1997 document, *Risk Management*.

2 Doll and Hill, "Smoking and Carcinoma of the Lung."

3 "The Multidimensional Nature of Risk," 61ff. in US National Research Council, *Understanding Risk*; and see especially Slovic, *The Perception of Risk* and Wilde, *Target Risk*.

4 The story of BSE is told in chapter 1 of Powell and Leiss, *Mad Cows and Mother's Milk*; for France see Charles Bremner, "France Falls Victim to Mad Cow Panic," *Ottawa Citizen*, 10 November 2000, A7 (reprinted from *The Times*, London). A full story on the reaction to genetically modified foods is in chapter 2, and the cell phone example follows in chapter 3.

5 Mad cow disease: personal communication, Health and Safety Executive, Government of the UK, September 1999; Atlantic cod fishery: Harris, *Lament for an Ocean*; Weyerhauser: *http://www.weyerhauser.com*; silicon breast implants: Powell and Leiss, *Mad Cows and Mother's Milk,* chapter 5; Monsanto: see chapter 2. For the beginnings of the current European struggle with mad cow disease, see Charles Bremner, "France Falls Victim to Mad Cow Panic," *Ottawa Citizen*, 10 November 2000, A7 (reprinted from *The Times*); within two weeks the French government had made its first "down payment" on the costs, a $400 million subsidy to farmers and traders to offset plummeting beef prices (*Globe and Mail*, 22 November 2000, A15).

6 See chapter 2.

7 See James Rodger Fleming, *Historical Perspectives on Climate Change*, and Dotto, *Storm Warning*.

8 Compare the current and extensive discussion of climate change issues on the British Petroleum (BP) website:
http://www.bp.com/alive/index.asp?page=/alive/performance/
health_safety_and_environment_performance/issues/climate_change
with Imperial Oil's website, *http://www.imperialoil.com/news/globe-wrm.htm*, which has a single paper dated October 1998, a text that is not particularly easy to find on the site in any case. However, nothing at all about climate change appears on the website of Imperial's US parent, Exxon Mobil, *www.exxon.com* (all were accessed 23 November 2000).

9 Dotto, 101.

10 I am indebted to my colleague Dr Hadi Dowlatabadi, director of the Center for Integrated Study of the Human Dimensions of Global Change at Carnegie Mellon University and University Fellow at Resources for the Future, Washington, DC, for providing figure 1 and an accompanying explanation. Dowlatabadi comments (personal communication, 4 December 2000): "My rule of thumb is that we need to get to less than 3 GtC/yr to have a hope of stabilizing CO_2 concentrations at 500ppm or lower."

11 For further reading: Bostrom et al., "What do people know about climate change? Part I"; Read et. al., "What do people know about climate change? Part II"; Thompson and Rayner, "Risk and Governance Part I"; Thompson, Rayner, and Ney, "Risk and Governance Part II."

12 See generally Leiss and Chociolko, *Risk and Responsibility*, chapter 2, "Managing Risks."

13 It is derived from the approach taken in Heath, *Strategic Issues Management*.

14 Burns et al., "Incorporating Structural Models into Research on the Social Amplification of Risk," 621; the second is Renn et al., "The Social Amplification of Risk."

15 My colleagues and I have explored this difference in an extensive series of case studies, both in previously published books and in the new cases presented in the present volume, and other relevant studies appear in the published literature: alar, pentachlorophenol and related fungicides, and electric and magnetic fields (power line frequencies), in Leiss and Chociolko, *Risk and Responsibility*; "mad cow disease," dioxins and chlorine, "hamburger disease," silicon breast implants, bovine growth hormone, plant biotechnology, and PCBs, in Powell and Leiss, *Mad Cows and Mother's Milk*; genetically modified foods, radio-frequency fields (cellular telephone technologies), MMT (a manganese-based gasoline additive), nuclear power, pulp and paper mill effluent, and tobacco, in this volume; climate change and endocrine disruptors (ongoing studies).

Other sources include: Krimsky and Plough, *Environmental Hazards*; the case studies on Dow Chemical Canada (Edmonton) and CXY Chemicals (Calgary) in Leiss, "Three Phases in the Evolution of Risk Communication Practice"; Chess et al., "The Organizational Links between Risk Communication and Risk Management"; Flynn et al., "The Nevada Initiative"; Flynn and Slovic, "Yucca Mountain"; Wildavsky, *But Is It True?*

CHAPTER TWO

1 Harrison McCain: quoted in the *National Post*, 30 November 1999, A9; Deutsche Bank: Ramey et al., "GMOs Are Dead"; Dan Ferber, "Monarch Press Release Raises Eyebrows," *Science Magazine*, 26 October 1999, 1663; *Globe and Mail*, 30 November 1999, A14; Douglas Powell, *National Post*, 4 December 1999, D5.

2 Among Monsanto's acquisitions was the cotton seed producer Delta and Pine Land Co., owner of the so-called "terminator gene," which genetically engineers crops that produce seeds that are reproductively sterile in the second generation. This would make it impossible for farmers to save and replant seeds, making them dependent on commercial seed suppliers. The public backlash associated with Monsanto's terminator gene patent and its potential impact was enormous; genetic engineering of plants to produce sterile seeds was denounced as a "morally offensive application of agricultural biotechnology." Intense hostility worldwide towards this developing technology was a public relations disaster for Monsanto, which eventually announced – *after* great damage had been done to its corporate reputation – that it would abandon the technology. For an early Canadian story see Kim Honey, "Genetic Engineering Threatens Traditions on the Farm," *Globe and Mail*, 16 November 1998, A11; on 6 December 2000 Canada's National Farmers' Union called (*http://www.planetark.org/ dailynewsstory.cfm?newsid=9237*) for an indefinite moratorium on GM foods. A record of the controversy can be found at: *http://www.rafi.org/ web/allnews-one.shtml?dfl=allnews.db&tfl=allnews-one-frag.ptml& operation=display&ro1=recNo&rf1=112&rt1=112&usebrs=true.*

3 Mark Tran, "Monsanto Merger Creates a Life-Sciences Monster," *Guardian*, 2 June 1998, 20; Joan Magretta, "Growth through Global Sustainability: An Interview with Monsanto's CEO, Robert B. Shapiro," 82, 87.

4 An excellent account of Greenpeace's strategic capacity to mount a global "issue campaign" will be found in Pauline Tam, "Greenpeace's Food Fight," *Ottawa Citizen*, 5 January 2000, A4.

5 On Greepeace, see the list of events at *www.greenpeace.org/~geneng*; opinion poll: *Guardian*, 4 June 1998, 14–15.

6 Mitsch and Mitchell, "DuPont, Ag Biotech." Ramey et al., "GMOs Are Dead" is appendix 2 in this report, and the quotation will be found on p. 18.

7 Frankel, "Food, Health and Still Hopeful," 7 (the title is a play on Monsanto's corporate motto, "Food, health, hope").

8 Gordon Conway, "Statement on Plant Biotechnology," delivered on 24 June 1999 (*www.consecol.org/Journal/vol4/iss1/art2/index.html*). Conway urged Monsanto's board to do the following: "label; disavow gene protection (terminator) systems; phase out use of antiobiotic resistance markers; agree (with big seed companies) to use the plant variety protection system, rather than patents, in developing countries; establish an independently administered fellowship program to train developing-country scientists in crop biotechnology, biosafety, and intellectual property; donate useful technologies to developing countries; agree to share financial rewards from intellectual property rights on varieties such as basmati or jasmine rice with the countries of origin; and finally, develop a global public dialogue that treats developing-country participants as equal partners." In December 1999 Conway "said that he is earmarking $3 million for a broad new effort that will, pending board approval, include: funding a mediation and conflict-resolution firm to study how warring factions can be brought together; funding consumer activists who want strict labelling of products containing genetically modified ingredients, which the biotech industry opposes; supporting bioethicists to study the ethical implications of bioengineered food (as well as other biotech issues such as cloning); and sponsoring a global 'dialogue' about genetically modified food geared mainly toward giving the opposition a public forum" (quoted in Lucette Lagnado, "Raising the Anti," *Wall Street Journal*, 14 December 1999).

9 Perhaps the company just could not change. A story in the *New York Times* around this time (8 December 1999, C1, "Monsanto Campaign Tries to Gain Support for Gene-Altered Food"), says that the image-management consultants Burson-Marsteller, acting on Monsanto's behalf, recruited "pro-GM" support among labour, church, and other groups, including a group of elderly Baptist church members who were induced to mount a counter-demonstration against anti-GM advocates in Washington, DC, including the carrying of signs saying, "Biotech saves children's lives." If this is an accurate report, this is very much the old style of confrontation and spin doctoring, not any new style as promised in the speech Shapiro had sent to Greenpeace UK a few months earlier (see note 11).

10 *Economist*, 23 December 1999, 33.

11 *http://www.monsanto.com/monsanto/mediacenter/speeches/ 99oct6_Shapiro.html* (accessed 6 December 1999, no longer on the Monsanto website as of 24 November 2000). There is a German phrase, which may be translated as "going to Canossa," to describe a situation where one undertakes a journey to capitulate in public to critics or enemies – although Shapiro did not actually go to London to deliver this address. For additional background see Ann Thayer, "Ag Biotech Food," *Chemical and*

Engineering News, 1 November 1999, 11–20, and Martin Enserink, "Industry Response: Ag Biotech moves to mollify its critics," *Science Magazine*, 26 December 1999, 1666–8.

12 *Financial Post*, 21 December 1999, C10; Julian Borger, "How the Mighty fall," *Sunday Observer*, 21 November 1999; "Aventis to Sell Ag Chems and Focus on Drugs," *Reuters*, 15 November 2000, and the press release from Aventis of the same date (*www.aventis.com/press/press_161.htm*).

13 Referring to emerging public concerns about biotechnology, in an earlier book my co-author and I remarked in a passage written towards the end of 1996: "But neither the agricultural biotechnology industry in Canada nor the main regulatory agency (Agriculture Canada) wants to talk about any of this with the public. The operative philosophy appears to be 'let sleeping dogs lie.' A vacuum is developing which almost certainly will be filled in the future with worrisome events, possibly causing significant damage to the industry." Powell and Leiss, *Mad Cows and Mother's Milk*, 33.

14 CBC television, "The National" (*http://www.tv.cbc.ca/national/trans/T990927.html*, 27 September 1999); and in Pauline Tam, "Genetically Modified Foods: The Battle Comes to Canada," *Ottawa Citizen*, 3 January 2000, A1. For an account of the transfer of the controversy from Europe to Quebec see C. Beaulieu, "Une bombe dans votre assiette?" *L'actualité*, August 1999. A number of foundations in the United States have decided to fund groups associated with the campaign against GM foods, and some US observers believe that the campaign against GM foods will become as intense in North America as it has been in Europe (Lucette Lagnado, "Raising the Anti," *Wall Street Journal*, 14 December 1999). In February 2000 the world's largest manufacturer of snack foods, the US company Frito-Lay, announced it would no longer buy GM corn for its products.

15 *http://www.tv.cbc.ca/national/trans/T991103.html*; Pauline Tam, "Farmers Caught in Middle of Raging GM Debate," *Ottawa Citizen*, 7 January 2000, A5; Heather Scoffield, "Farmers Face a Growing Problem," *Globe and Mail*, 10 January 2000, B8.

16 Barrett, "Canadian Agricultural Biotechnology."

17 Moore, "Science, Internationalization, and Policy Networks," especially chapter 5, "The Role of Science in Plant Biotechnology Regulation," and pp. 372–7.

18 Moore, 275 and note 33. Perhaps the most powerful constraint on the Canadian regulators was their perceived need to conform (for trade harmonization reasons) to the US model, which first made the choice on how to approach the regulation of the new biotechnology. So far as excluding the public is concerned, it is likely that this was not at all an explicit decision; rather, it is the "normal" procedure for governments to make policy choices first and then to design a public consultation process that leaves out the most basic issues from consideration.

19 Asked to respond to a newspaper story about the unwanted invasion of GM canola plants into neighbouring fields, a spokesperson for the Canadian Food Inspection Agency stated: "Certainly it's a question that's been raised. That's my answer." Heather Scoffield, "Canola Farmer Fights Seed Invasion," *Globe and Mail*, 14 August 2000, B4.

20 The version circulated by e-mail attachment carries the electronic "tag" of the crisis management firm Fleishman-Hillard International Communications of St Louis, Missouri, which was asked to organize a press conference for its release.

21 The Royal Society of London, "Genetically Modified Plants for Food Use," sections 4 and 5; benefits are also discussed. A well-balanced short account is Dan Ferber, "Risks and Benefits: GM Crops in the Cross Hairs," *Science Magazine*, 26 December 1999, 1662–6.

22 I received a copy from one of the signatories, Professor Marc Fortin of McGill University.

23 The letter reads in part: "As a scientist, I am concerned about the tactics recently employed by Dr. David Suzuki in the debate over genetically modified food. Many concerned scientists do not support a method of public debate that places a premium on generating public fear and hysteria. Those of us who have studied the issue in detail understand the labyrinthine complexities of modern genetic science. Without doubt there are real benefits from genetically improved foods including fewer allergens, greater resistance to insects, and enhanced nutritive value. The laboratory may be the true testing ground for scientific truth, but the opponents of biotechnology have chosen the ground of hearsay and half-truths to fight this battle. I have no doubt that foods from biotechnology are safe, healthy and have been rigorously tested by Health Canada and the Food Inspection Agency. Moreover, I am a scientist who believes in the future possibilities of biotechnology. There are thousands of like-minded scientists around the world who understand that biotechnology represents an astonishing breakthrough in the field of crop science – indeed it could represent another Green Revolution that would benefit subsistence agricultural economies." (I received the text in an e-mail transmission from a trusted source. WL)

24 Since this act apparently will cost the student an additional year of work, it is especially unfortunate that, according to Professor Lemaux, the plants in question were not genetically engineered.

25 *http://www.aspp.org/pubaff/issues.htm* (this and all other websites listed in the remaining notes to this chapter were accessed 6 December 1999).

26 John Greenwood, "Canadian Food Producers in Disarray," *National Post*, 27 December 1999, C1.

27 Robin Pomeroy, "Novartis Conceals Its Seedy Side," *Globe and Mail*, 4 August 2000, B5 (from Reuters News Agency, Belgium).

28 Mark Kennedy, "Biotech Advances Spook Canadians," *Ottawa Citizen*, 8 January 2000, A1. Another polling firm, Angus Reid Group, undertook an eight-country opinion survey at the same time (Germany, UK, Japan, Australia, France, Canada, US, and Brazil). This poll, which confirmed the Canadian results reported by Pollara, showed that only Brazil appeared relatively unconcerned, and that even in the US, the home of agricultural biotechnology, 57 per cent of respondents said that knowing a food contained GM ingredients would make them less likely to purchase it. Anne McIlroy, "Canadians Wary of Genetically Altered Foods," *Globe and Mail*, 15 January 2000, A2.

29 Readers who are interested in studying the activist role of plant scientists in the risk controversy over GM foods should subscribe to the invaluable Internet list-serve, "AgBioView," which has many daily postings. For example, scientists (most of whom are university-based) regularly encourage their peers to sign petitions responding quickly to specific actions, such as when companies such as Frito-Lay and Novartis (notes 14 and 27 above) announce that they will stop using GM ingredients in their products.

30 See the "Factsheet: The Federal Regulatory System," included on the National Biotechnology Strategy's site: *http://www.ic.gc.ca/cmb/ welcomeic.nsf/558*. The best detailed studies of the development of this regulatory system done so far are the doctoral theses of Katherine Barrett and Elizabeth Moore, referred to earlier (notes 16, 17); see also S. Jasanoff, "Product, Process or Programme."

31 US National Academy of Sciences, *Introduction of Recombinant DNA-Engineered Organisms into the Environment*; US National Research Council, *Genetically Modified Pest-Protected Plants*. The quotations in the text are from p. 44 of the latter report. Some of the broader issues involving the international context are briefly noted in the report, *Transgenic Plants and World Agriculture*, issued in July 2000 by the national academies of seven countries and regions and published by the US National Academy of Sciences.

32 Cf. the distinction made by David Dennis on his website: "[B]iotechnology is defined as the transfer of genes using the techniques of molecular biology to generate transgenic plants. It does not refer to methods used by modern plant breeders." *http://www.performanceplants.com/FAQ.htm*

33 Contrast the definition given by David Dennis (note 32) with the following statement from material (dated August 1997) posted on the CFIA website: "Biotechnology involves using biological processes to produce substances beneficial to agriculture, the environment, industry, and medicine. In fact, we have used biotechnology to make everyday products for thousands of years." *http://www.cfia-acia.agr.ca/english/ppc/biotech/whatbio.htm*

34 House of Commons, Standing Committee on Environment and Sustainable Development, transcript of hearing, meeting no. 19 (16 May 1996),

testimony of Dr Brian Morrissey, AAFC. The current wording on the traditional vs. new biotechnology distinction is on the CFIA website at *http://www.cfia-acia.agr.ca/english/ppc/biotech/geninfo.htm* (last updated August 1997).

35 Canada, Agriculture and Agri-Food Canada, *Biotechnology in Agriculture*.
36 For further discussion see Barrett, "Canadian Agricultural Biotechnology."
37 "Eurobarometer," *Nature* 400 (26 June 1997).
38 For detailed background discussion of these issues I recommend the following selection of sources, which includes some diversity of viewpoint: May, "Genetically Modified Foods," a superb short statement; McHughen, *Pandora's Picnic Basket*; *Journal of Risk Research*, special issue: "Precautionary Regulation: GM Crops in the European Union," vol. 3, no. 3 (July 2000); Mehta and Gair, "Social, Political, Legal and Ethical Areas of Inquiry in Biotechnology and Genetic Engineering"; Miflin, "Crop Biotechnology"; Conway and Toennissen, "Feeding the World in the Twenty-First Century"; Leiss and Tyshenko, "Some Aspects of the 'New Biotechnology' and Its Regulation in Canada"; and the other publications mentioned in the notes to follow.
39 For a discussion of an earlier stage of these developments see Powell and Leiss, *Mad Cows and Mother's Milk*, chapter 7: "Gene Escape, or the Pall of Silence over Plant Biotechnology Risk." See also the response from the Canadian Food Inspection Agency: *http://www.cfia-acia.agr.ca/english/ppc/ biotech/madcow.html*. For many issues related to agricultural biotechnology go to: *http://www.gmissues.org/*
40 For the best in-depth analysis of public understanding yet published, which accurately forecast the nature of the controversy to come, see Robin Grove-White et al., "Uncertain World." See also Global Environmental Change Program (UK), "The Politics of GM Food: Risk, Science and Public Trust," October 1999 (*http://www.gecko.ac.uk*); numerous related publications are listed on this website. In March 1999 Sir Robert May, chief scientist of the UK government, said of the former: "I now have had a chance to read 'Uncertain World,' which I wish I had indeed read earlier. It is in many ways a remarkably prescient document."
41 *http://www.tv.cbc.ca/national/trans/T990427.html*; BIOTECanada's website is at *www.biotech.ca*
42 There is a useful overview of labelling options for the current generation of products in a speech given by Ian Lindenmayer, managing director, Australia New Zealand Food Agency on 3 November 1999, published at: *http://www.anzfa.gov.au/documents/sp008_99.asp*. A group of Canada's most famous chefs joined with an industry association, Canadian Organic Growers, to organize a national media event in December 1999 to complain about the failure of government and industry in Canada to provide mandatory labelling of food products containing genetically modified ingredients

(Dawn Walton, "Canadian Chefs Trash Frankenfood," *Globe and Mail*, 14 December 1999, B7). On a national television program one chef who sells his own proprietary brand of prepared food was quoted on camera as detailing how he had, with considerable effort, persuaded a supplier of cooking oils to furnish him with a canola product that was certified not to contain genetically modified ingredients (*http://www.tv.cbc.ca/national/trans/T991213.html*).

43 The government of Canada has inched its way to the position of mildly encouraging the food industry to do something called "voluntary labelling," a silly attempt to duck the issues that will make no one happy.

44 Three examples: A document on the CFIA website entitled "General Questions and Answers on Biotechnology" (*http://www.cfia-acia.agr.ca/english/ppc/biotech/fqas.htm*) opens with a section on benefits; these and other sections mention specific benefits in detail. However, the word "risks" is not used until the very end ("some people are concerned about the possible environmental and health risks"), but no specific risks are referred to there. (This material was last updated in August 1997 and is therefore also very much out of date.) Second, the news release for the renewal of the federal "Canadian Biotechnology Strategy" in August 1998 refers enthusiastically to a number of specific economic and health benefits, but mentions unspecified "social and ethical considerations" without giving a clue what they might be. The five "factsheets" there include "Biotechnology: The Benefits" – but there is no corresponding document on risks. (*http://www.ic.gc.ca/cmb/welcomeic.nsf/558*). This is exactly mirrored in the expensive new operation being run by the Council for Biotechnology Information, which is funded by a consortium of the large plant biotechnology companies. Both the website (*www.whybiotech.com*) and a set of print brochures dated May 2000 have large sections on "the benefits of biotechnology," but neither uses the word "risks" at all, and the brief discussions of what just about everyone else would call "risk issues" dismisses all concerns in a few brief sentences. In view of the protracted controversy that has existed, it is almost as if those responsible for this truncated communications exercise are living on a different planet.

45 "Frequently Asked Questions," *www.whybiotech.com*, the website of the Council for Biotechnology Information (accessed 26 November 2000). See the comments on labelling by Elizabeth Moore (above note 17), 376–7.

46 The industry and government publicists should pay attention to this guidance from the foreword to von Wartburg and Liew, *Gene Technology and Social Acceptance*: "The seven attitudinal sins which tend to further inhibit the societal acceptance of biotechnology: (1) The 'wait and see' attitude: Too often a 'let us not be bothered by critical opposition' attitude still prevails in academic and industrial circles which further impedes the acceptance of biotechnology by society at large. (2) The 'belittling' attitude:

Euphemistic language and derisory risk comparisons may contribute to the emotional rejection of biotechnology. (3) The 'everything under control' attitude: The denial of uncertainty in science and with respect to industrial activity undermines trust and credibility. (4) The 'we know best' attitude: Knowledge as power needs to be shared to be effective. Arrogance of knowledge is perceived as arrogance of power. (5) The 'you have to believe me' attitude: Trust is a matter of experience and cannot be asked for only in critical situations. (6) The 'freedom works best' attitude: Laws and regulation reflect the social consensus about the necessary level of control of a new technology. (7) The 'discredit the critics' attitude: Critical opposition groups enjoy the highest level of credibility. Attacking them usually destroys the value of one's own arguments." (I owe this reference to Douglas Powell.)

47 Gibbons, "Science's New Social Contract with Society," c81–4.

48 In personal e-mail communications to me, David Dennis (Biology, Queen's University) and Douglas Powell (Plant Agriculture, University of Guelph) have described the plant genetic mutations carried out with older technologies, predating molecular biology, including bombardment with high-energy radiation or chemically induced mutagenesis, producing hybrids by repeated crossing with wild relatives of domesticated plants, and somoclonal variation through hormonal modifications. By comparison with all of these, Dennis remarks, the newer techniques offer "a much more precise transgenic route to genetic diversity," and – arguably – to a lower risk profile. Another senior Canadian plant biologist commented to me, however, that "more precise" in this context does *not* mean that the results of the molecular genetic manipulations carried out in the laboratory are completely predictable. With respect to the last point, there is a report from the scientists at the Roslin Institute (Scotland), where "Dolly" was cloned, to the effect that more recent animal cloning experiments have shown that clones are not identical "carbon copies" of the parent and that there is random genetic and behavioural variation in the cloned offspring. Jonathan Leake, "Differences between Clones Baffles Science," *Ottawa Citizen*, 26 December 1999, A1 (reprinted from the *Sunday Times*, London).

49 The Royal Society of London, "Genetically Modified Plants for Food Use," 21. See also the Royal Society of London, "Scientific Advice on GM Foods" (April 1999): *http://www.royalsoc.ac.uk./st_pol52.htm*).

50 *http://www.health.gov.au/tga/gene/gmac/gmactor.htm*. In April 2000 the government of New Zealand appointed a Royal Commission on Genetic Modification.

51 On 17 December 1999 three federal ministers (health, agriculture, and environment) announced that the government of Canada had asked the Royal Society of Canada to establish an expert panel on the future of food bio-

technology. See *http://www.rsc.ca/foodbiotechnology/indexEN.html* for the full text of the panel's report, issued in February 2001. See chapter 3 for references to the contributions of expert panels to the discussion of issues about radio-frequency fields.

52 See chapter 11. Michael Mehta suggested to me that the aspects of the Frankenstein imagery which give rise to feelings of dread may be related to the *process* of the monster's creation out of dead flesh. This is relevant to the process/product distinction discussed earlier in chapter 2.

53 Regular news about new stages of completion in the Human Genome Project will produce, among other things, an enormous increase in public concerns about genetic manipulation.

54 The involvement of members of the Natural Law party, best known for its doctrine of "yogic flying," shows just how convoluted the strategic organizational line-ups can be in public controversies over risks. First, they have designed their Internet-based document formatting so that a query using some Internet search engines will yield about 30 per cent of the top 100 "hits" for their material. Second, they initiated (through testing in a scientific laboratory controlled by the party's leaders) the series of events that led to the "StarLink" corn episode in September 2000, where a variety of genetically engineered corn, not approved for human consumption, was found in taco shells sold by Kraft Foods on store shelves, leading to a major product recall. The story broke in the *Washington Post* on 17 September 2000, citing laboratory work done by a firm called "Genetic ID." On 18 September it was revealed that this firm is partly owned by John Fagan, who is dean of the graduate school at Maharishi University of Management (Fairfield, Iowa) and advisor to Dr John Hagelin, who was at that time the Natural Law party candidate for US president. On 27 September Aventis announced it was suspending sales of its "StarLink" seed; by that time other testing done for Kraft Foods had confirmed that the original analysis was correct. A full record of the press coverage and commentaries on this story can be found, starting with the date 17 September 2000, in the archives of the list-serve "AgBioView" at *http://agbioview.listbot.com.*

CHAPTER THREE

1 Clearnet PCS, Inc., "PCS: What Is It?" pamphlet, December 1997; Ericsson Radio Systems AB, "Health and Safety in Mobile Telephony," pamphlet, 1997.

2 Canada, Health Canada, "Safety Code 6 – Limits of Human Exposure to Radiofrequency Electromagnetic Fields in the Frequency Range from 3 kHz to 300 GHz"; Industry Canada, "Environmental Process, Radiofrequency Fields and Land-Use Consultation." At least some provincial governments,

such as British Columbia, maintain staff with technical expertise in EMF and RF, but this level of government does not have an official role in siting decisions.

3 Church steeples are a preferred site for wireless telecommunications equipment locations, and in the United States some consultants are making hefty fees advising church congregations on how to bargain effectively with the industry representatives. Jon G. Auerbach, "Steeple Chase a Serious Business for U.S. churches," *Globe and Mail*, 1 January 1998, B5. Cf. Kevin Marron, "Antenna on Church is a Test of Faith," *Globe and Mail*, 2 September 1997.

4 Professor Henry Lai, quoted in the *Vancouver Sun*, 10 July 1997.

5 Interviews with community members, Vancouver, BC, March 1998.

6 The consultant, Professor Maria Stuchly of the University of Victoria, has a special significance in this controversy, because at an earlier stage in her career she was the federal government employee who was chiefly responsible for preparing the original version of Safety Code 6 (see note 8).

7 Traditional print-based publications are still important in the electronic age: *Microwave News* was a key source for the citizen interveners in the early stages of their investigations into the health risk issues.

8 Safety Code 6 is officially a guideline, not a regulatory instrument; federal officials maintain that this is actually an advantage, since guidelines can be changed far more easily than regulations. However, it did have the character of a "static" document, since no new material appeared in the booklet betweeen 1991 and 1999. With the single exception of a 1990 publication which did not deal with health issues, there was no publication dated later than 1988 in the list of references in the version of Safety Code 6 then in force (an updated version appeared in October 1999).

9 One week earlier (16 July 1997) another municipal official, the medical health officer at the Vancouver/Richmond Health Board, had issued a one-page sheet supporting Health Canada's position: "[T]he general scientific consensus holds that the power from cellular base stations is far too low in the community to result in adverse impacts." There was also a very pertinent comment on prudent avoidance, to which I shall return later; but this document does not appear to have exerted any influence on the course of the debate.

10 Interview with Rick Cluff, "Early Edition" program, CBC-AM (Vancouver), 24 October 1997.

11 Leiss and Chociolko, *Risk and Responsibility*, chapters 4–5.

12 Citations in this paragraph are from the nearly identical stories published in many western Canada newspapers on 20 December, all based on a Reuters wire story from Geneva.

13 Madelaine Drohan, "How the Net Killed the MAI," *Globe and Mail*, 29 April 1998, A1.

14 This exercise was carried out in February 1998. The result is a "phenome-nological topography" (snapshot, in common parlance) of the Internet "map" on RF and EMF issues; or, in plain language, it is *one* version of what a person would get if, starting at *any* entry-point, using a search en-gine, he or she followed the links among various websites. It is important to know that this is one possible snapshot out of an almost infinite number of possible "experiences" one could have in surfing the Web for these issues. On the other hand, it is not "arbitrary," since any dedicated Internet search on these issues would come up with the same set of boxes, more or less – although they would be arranged differently, since the connections between them do not constitute any kind of "logical" framework. For a sample of what may be found on the Internet see: *http://www.cruzio.com/~rbedard/waveguide/library.html.*

15 "Science is a hard taskmaster, and in the light of mounting evidence that suggestions of toxicity are for the most part ultimately confirmed by pains-taking scientific inquiry, perhaps it is time to reexamine whether scientific standards of proof of causality – and waiting for the bodies to fall – ought not to give way to more preventative health policies that are satisfied by more realistic conventions and that lead to action sooner" (New *England Journal of Medicine* 19 April 1987).

16 In European countries the term "electrosmog" is a catchy shorthand phrase to denote the sum total of electrical and magnetic fields (EMF) disseminated through the operation of all communications-related technologies – cellular phones, short-wave radio, radio and television broadcasting, radar and other microwave installations. "Electrosmog" is not yet a prominent part of the lexicon of public controversy in Canada. See Wiedemann and Schütz, "The Electromagnetic Fields Risk Issue."

17 The history is chronicled in Brodeur, *The Zapping of America.*

18 Press release, Royal Society of Canada, Ottawa, 4 August 1998 (*www.rsc.ca*).

19 The senior author was at the time chair of the society's Committee on Expert Panels which screens and appoints panellists and oversees the proce-dures by which panels operate.

20 The best single guide to general work on the subject is US, National Research Council, *Improving Risk Communication.*

21 This is just one in an almost endless list of such cases, where governments think they have finished their work after their risk assessment is completed, having devoted little or no effort to risk communication, including con-fronting the matter of credibility only after a controversy has erupted, when it is virtually impossible to get one's message across.

22 "The signal from a cellular or PCS base station antenna is essentially directed toward the horizon in a relatively narrow beam in the vertical plane. For example, the radiation pattern for an omni-directional antenna

might be compared to a thin doughnut or pancake centered around the antenna while the pattern for a sector antenna is fan-shaped, like a wedge cut from a pie ... Consequently, normal ground-level exposure is much less than exposure very close to the actual antenna." US Federal Communications Commission (FCC), Office of Engineering and Technology, "Information on Human Exposure to Radiofrequency Fields from Cellular and PCS Radio Transmitters," 2 (*OET Bulletin* no. 56).

23 "Thermal effect" (or "thermal biological effect") refers to the well-known capacity of microwave radiation, at certain frequencies and a specific threshold of power, to raise the temperature of exposed organic matter (as in a microwave oven). "Non-thermal (biological) effects," which occur below the threshold for the thermal effect, are thought to be very diverse (see the list in the text that follows); some on that list are regarded by scientific specialists as reasonably well established, and others are not (or not yet), and there is considerable scientific uncertainty and dispute in this area, which is only to be expected, since the research effort is relatively new.

24 The FCC has useful and up-to-date documents on its website that are written in a reasonably accessible style (*www.fcc.gov/oet/rfsafety*), especially *OET Bulletin* no. 56, "Questions and Answers about Biological Effects Potential Hazards of Radiofrequency Radiation."

25 Ibid., 5

26 (i) *Vancouver Sun*, 10 July 1997; (ii) *Province* (Vancouver), 2 July 1997; (iii) *Vancouver Courier*, 8 June 1997.

27 See note 18 above.

28 WIC Connexus press release, Toronto, 19 August 1998.

29 Corporation of the District of West Vancouver, BC, "Council Report: Personal Communication Service (PCS) Antenna Cell Sites Approval Process" (1997).

30 Leiss and Chociolko, *Risk and Responsibility,* chapter 9.

31 This is not the same as demanding consent from everyone who might be exposed at any level, because no new technology ever could be introduced under such a requirement, and on the whole, and collectively, citizens derive significant net benefits from them.

32 Cited in Kevin Marron, "Antenna on Church is a Test of Faith," *Globe and Mail,* 2 September 1997 and in other news stories.

33 Circular prepared by the medical health officer at the Vancouver/Richmond Health Board, 16 July 1997.

34 Swiss Reinsurance Company, "Electrosmog – a phantom risk," 4–5 (italics in original).

35 The senior author's e-mail address was given on the press release from the Royal Society of Canada; within days there was a regular return flow of communications about RF issues, containing among other things detailed cases about alleged adverse health effects for both humans and farm animals in Australia, Canada, Germany, and the former Yugoslavia.

36 "A Review of the Potential Health Risks of Radiofrequency Fields from Wireless Telecommunications Devices" (May 1999), available at *www.rsc.ca*.

37 Ibid., 2–3.

38 *http://www.cwta.ca/safety/health/effects/positions/royal.php3* (accessed August 1999).

39 Much of this battle is fought out on the Internet. See *www.microwavenews.com/www.html* for a directory of Internet sites and *www.wired.com/news/* for current news.

40 Cherry Norton and Richard Woods, "Are We Being Told the Truth about Mobile Phones?" *Sunday Times*, 20 December 1998; CBC TV, "The Fifth Estate," "Cone of Silence" (with Victor Malarek), broadcast 9 February 1999.

41 *www.wtrllc.com/* (accessed 15 August 1999; as of 30 August 2000, this site was no longer accessible on the Web).

42 This comment is not at all meant to disparage the Royal Society of Canada panel: expert panels are given different mandates, and also may use different "strategies" in interpreting their mandates.

43 Independent Expert Group on Mobile Phones (Sir William Stewart, chair), National Radiological Protection Board (UK), "Mobile Phones and Health," 11 May 2000: *http://www.iegmp.org.uk/* The "clarification" also will be found on this site (accessed 30 August 2000).

44 *http://www.hc-sc.ca/ehp/ehd/rpb/index.htm* (accessed 1 December 2000). The "What's New" section of the Radiation Protection Bureau contained no entry on cellular phones for the entire period since May 2000, when (following the release of the Stewart Report in the UK) there has been intense scientific discussion and media reporting, especially on the issue of children and cell phones. A query for "cellular telephones" using the "search" function on this site yields, for the top two responses, documents dated 1993 and 1996.

45 *http://www.wirc.org/FAQ/2final-faq.html#q16* (accessed 30 November 2000). There is nothing in the "What's New" section on the Stewart report or on the other developments related to that report; there is no reference to it in the "Links" section, and the user can only find the Web link for the report by following the subsidiary link from question #16 under "FAQ." Under question #8 in "FAQ" there is a single quotation from the Stewart Report: "[T]he balance of evidence to date suggests that exposures to RF radiation below NRPB and ICNIRP guidelines do not cause adverse health effects to the general population." (The reader could compare this with the quotations from the report given in the text.) In the "FAQ" section the user also will find this additional comment at question #16: "The Independent Expert Group in the UK appears to accept the view that children absorb more energy (paragraph, 4.37, 6.63 and 6.90). Note that this conclusion is based upon unpublished and non-peer reviewed conclusions." This is

accurate and fair comment, although it should also be noted that a certain authority attaches to an expert group report, by virtue of the members' qualifications, and that they decided to make the recommendation in question after considering the evidence base for it. To be equally fair, it should also be noted that the report on which WIRC bases its FAQ section, "Wireless Telecommunications and Health," has never – as judged by the documentation provided there – been published and shows no evidence of having undergone a normal peer review, despite the statement on the WIRC home page that all material referred to on the site "must be peer-reviewed-research."

46 *http://www.cwta.ca/safety/health/effects/positions/wirc.php3*. The most recent information under "health effects" on the CWTA site (accessed 30 November 2000) is dated November 1998, and its last position statement is dated October 1999. Thus there is no easily accessible and timely health-related information for consumers on the site.

47 Both the CWTA and WIRC sites rely primarily on the same scientific unpublished document for guidance on health effects issues (see also the comment above, end of note 45): Brian F. Habbick and Michele L. Masley, "Wireless Telecommunications and Health," n.d. [September 2000]. This is primarily a review of scientific studies, although it also draws on various expert panel reports. From a technical perspective what is interesting is that, although it relies heavily on the Royal Society of Canada (RSC) report (above, note 36), the following sentence from the concluding section (p. 50) of the Habbick/Masley paper appears to contradict the passage in the RSC report quoted in the text (note 37): "There is still no convincing evidence of non-thermal biological effects of near-field and far-field RF exposure." More important, the Habbick/Masley report does not offer any reflection on the "precautionary" approach taken in the Stewart report, and so it is of limited usefulness to ordinary consumers.

48 *http://www.abcnews.go.com/onair/2020/PrimeTime_001123_cellphones_feature.htm* has the story, which also shows the intense disagreement between two leading North American authorities on the subject, George Carlo and John Moulder.

49 Hyland, "Physics and Biology of Mobile Telephony."

50 *http://www.dti.gov.uk/cii/regulatory/telecomms/telecommsregulations/mobilephones_and_health.shtml*

CHAPTER FOUR

1 CBC TV, "The National Magazine," 2 November 1998 (host: Leslie Mackinnon), summary 981027 (*www.tv.cbc.ca/national/*). The text of the parenthetical remark in the seventh sentence in the original – "(the by product of burnt of MMT)" – is obviously incorrect and we have substituted what we believe is correct wording.

2 Letter from Leader of the Opposition Jean Chrétien to the Honourable Doug Lewis, minister of transport, 17 April 1991.

3 There is a story worth telling the reader about our assembly of documentation for this case study. We first approached Environment Canada, the lead federal department in the MMT affair, for assistance; after some preliminary discussions we were advised that to get what we wanted we would have to file formal access-to-information (ATI) requests. Those who have some experience in such matters know that this route is a long and agonizing one, necessitating the filing of repeated requests as each batch of information yields new leads; the junior author feared that, under this scenario, he would expire long before the last batch had been given up. As an alternative we asked for and were provided access to a set of documents made public through ATI requests by Ethyl Canada Inc. We received valuable documentary materials from the Canadian Petroleum Products Institute; we wish to thank Mark Nantais of the Canadian Vehicle Manufacturers' Association for assisting us with an interview and documentation. We are grateful to Marika Egyed of Health Canada for her responsiveness to our questions, and to Morrie Kirshenblatt of Environment Canada for the small amount of assistance he was permitted to extend to us. We have circulated drafts of this chapter to knowledgeable persons in industry and government, asking to be advised of any errors or omissions in our account, but we assume complete responsibility for the interpretation of the case that is presented here. The authors are maintaining a file of reference materials used in this chapter which can be made available to others for research purposes.

4 MTBE is methyl tertiary butyl ether and it is derived from methanol, which like MMT is an octane-enhancing additive for gasoline; a Canadian methanol producer, Methanex Corporation of Vancouver, has filed a NAFTA claim for US $970 million in compensation over the State of California's proposed ban on MTBE because of concerns over water contamination. There is a lovely irony in all this, because Methanex is using some of the same legal framework (international trade agreements) to bring its action as Ethyl Corporation did in its fight against the Canadian government's ban on MMT. Not only that, Methanex is embroiled in a dispute with the US EPA at the same time, because the EPA has called for reductions in the use of MTBE on environmental protection grounds, which, Methanex claims, is inconsistent with the findings and recommendations of a panel report on the subject commissioned by EPA. See the Canadian Press story, "Methanex Calls EPA Move 'Misguided'," *Globe and Mail*, 3 August 1999, B14.

5 US *Federal Register*, 17 August 1994 (59 FR 42227). One of the April 1991 "Chrétien letters" (addressed to Robert de Cotret, then minister of the environment) notes "the fact that the first cases of manganese poisoning by inhalation were reported in 1837" (!).

6 Colmenares et al., "Analysis of Manganese Particulates from Automotive Decomposition of Methylcyclopentadienyl Manganese Tricarbonyl."

7 A. P. Jaques, *National Inventory of Sources and Emissions of Manganese (1984),* cited in Wood and Egyed, *Risk Assessment for the Combustion Products of Methylcyclopentadienyl Manganese Tricarbonyl (MMT) in Gasoline* (cited hereafter as *Risk Assessment of MMT*).

8 Pellizzari et al., "Executive Summary: Manganese Exposure Study (Toronto)."

9 Robert Routs, president, Shell Canada Products Ltd., before the Standing Senate Committee on Energy, the Environment and Natural Resources, *Evidence*, 4 February 1997, 0800- 23.

10 A second, and perhaps less obvious, motivation for the oil industry was to help set the terms of reference for the debate on sulphur levels in gasoline. In an interview with the authors, Mark Nantais of the Canadian Vehicle Manufacturers' Association stated that, "although the costs for removing MMT were not trivial, the real motivation for the CPPI's position on MMT may have been to establish a favourable procedure and frame the future debate over the much bigger item of sulphur, potentially a billion dollar cost for the oil industry" (personal interview, 18 and 23 August 1999). Even the oil industry suggested this motive in their appearances before the Senate Standing Committee on Energy, Environment and Natural Resources, although their concerns were different. Alain Perez, president of the CPPI, when asked about whether MMT was a financial or technical issue, stated: "It is a financial issue. It is not huge, like sulphur or others would be, but it is significant for some refiners, particularly the small ones. It is not an overwhelming financial issue; it is money wasted. It is a technical issue because we cannot get the answers. More importantly, it is legislation which creates a precedent. Instead of letting the two industries negotiate ... the Government of Canada has clearly taken sides. It has interrupted a negotiating process which was not going well, I agree, and removed any motivation for the auto industry to continue negotiating with us. What truly terrifies us ... is that the precedent will then be used on other components of gasoline. The real issue for us is whether we will be footing the next $5 billion of environmental bills without a chance for study, without a chance for rationale, and without any chance for negotiating because a precedent has been set" (remarks made by Alain Perez, president, Canadian Petroleum Products Institute, to the Standing Senate Committee on Energy, the Environment and Natural Resources, *Evidence*, 4 February 1997, 1010- 28.)

11 Elizabeth May, Executive director, Sierra Club of Canada, before the Standing Senate Committee on Energy, the Environment and Natural Resources, *Evidence*, 5 February 1997, 1940- 63. Most of Ms May's remarks dealt with health risk issues.

12 Wood and Egyed, *Risk Assessment of MMT*.

13 Personal communication from Marika Egyed, Health Canada, February 1999.

14 US *Federal Register*, 17 August 1994 (59 FR 42227).

15 The US EPA reviewed and accepted data submitted by Ethyl showing that MMT in unleaded gasoline reduced nitrogen oxide emissions between 5 and 20 per cent, depending on how the reductions were calculated. In any case, this represented a significant direct reduction in emissions with accompanying environmental benefits. For more information see the US *Federal Register*, 17 August 1994 (59 FR 42227).

16 US *Federal Register*, 17 August 1994 (59 FR 42227). It should be noted that although the EPA decided that MMT did not cause or contribute to emission control system failure, some reservations about this decision remained. In particular, the EPA felt that the statistical tests used to substantiate the "cause or contribute" requirement might not represent sufficiently stringent criteria, and shift the burden of proof away from the waiver applicant. The EPA was revisiting these statistical tests but did not think it was appropriate or fair to require Ethyl to resubmit their data under these new criteria.

17 US *Federal Register*, 17 August 1994 (59 FR 42227).

18 US *Federal Register*, 18 September 1978 (43 FR 41424).

19 US *Federal Register*, 1 December 1981 (46 FR 58360).

20 US *Federal Register*, 17 August 1994 (59 FR 42227).

21 Martha Hamilton, *Washington Post*, 9 June 1998, F1: "Honda Settles Suit on Pollution Control; Ford Also Agrees to Pay Government Fine."

22 *United States of America v. Ford Motor Company*, US District Court for the District of Columbia, Consent Decree (Judge Royce C. Lamberth), 8 June 1998.

23 US *Federal Register*, 17 August 1994 (59 FR 42227).

24 US *Federal Register*, 17 August 1994 (59 FR 42227).

25 EPA Press Release, "Statement by EPA Administrator Carol M. Browner regarding Advertisement by Ethyl Corporation," 3 July 1996.

26 Personal communication from Joe Sopata, Office of Air and Radiation, US EPA, March 1999.

27 US *Federal Register*, 9 February 1999 (64 FR 6294). See also *www.epa.gov/ OMSWWW* for full notification, "Statement of Alternative Tier II testing requirements by EPA," January 1999.

28 Health and Welfare Canada, *Methylcylcopentadienyl manganese tricarbonyl (MMT): An Assessment of the Human Health Implication of Its Use as a Gasoline Additive*, cited in Wood and Egyed, *Risk Assessment of MMT*, i.

29 Holtz, *Alternatives to Lead in Gasoline*, 8.

30 Health Protection Branch, Health and Welfare Canada, "Issues: MMT – Gasoline Additive," 27 November 1992, 3.

31 Wood and Egyed, *Risk Assessment of MMT*, 69.

32 For a discussion of "CEPA-toxic" see chapter 8.

33 Roels et al., "Assessment of the Permissible Exposure Level to Manganese in Workers Exposed to Manganese Dioxide Dust."

34 Wood and Egyed, *Risk Assessment of* MMT, 45.
35 Dr Daniel Krewski, acting director, Bureau of Chemical Hazards, Health
Canada, before the Standing Senate Committee on Energy, Environment
and Natural Resources, *Evidence*, 6 February 1997, 1020- 2.
36 US *Federal Register*, 17 August 1994 (59 FR 42227).
37 Wood and Egyed, *Risk Assessment of* MMT, 64.
38 Frank Vena and Chandra Prakash, Industrial Sectors Branch, Environment
Canada. Internal Briefing (advice to the minister for anticipated November
meeting with CPPI Board), "Removal of MMT from Canadian Gasoline,"
24 October 1994.
39 Remarks made by Senators Ron Ghitter and Colin Kenny, the Standing
Senate Committee on Energy, the Environment and Natural Resources,
Evidence, 6 February 1997, 1020- 13.
40 When an Ethyl Corporation official wrote to a newspaper complaining of
the confusion between MMT and MTBE, MP Clifford Lincoln (Lac-Saint-
Louis), who is widely respected for his commitment to environmental protection, could not resist returning to the previous battle: "Count me among
the large majority of Canadians, including credible scientists ... who believe
... that manganese is bad for us and that therefore we should stop using
MMT. And the sooner the better." *Globe and Mail*, 6 July 1999, B2.
41 To be sure, no agency is always right. The point here is that there is a consistent record of scientific assessment over a long period of time that remains publicly uncontradicted by any other expert body of similar repute.
42 The Standing Senate Committee on Energy, the Environment and Natural
Resources, *Evidence*, 6 February 1997, 1020- 3.
43 Letter from Leader of the Opposition Jean Chrétien to the Honourable Don
Mazankowski, deputy prime minister, 17 April 1991.
44 Barrie McKenna, *Globe and Mail*, 3 October 1994, B1: "Ethanol Plan
Sees Cash in Corn: Proposal to Build $170-million Plant Awaits Ottawa's
Guarantee."
45 Liberal party of Canada, "Liberals Announce Agriculture Policies,"
10 May 1993, "Backgrounder." The ethanol part of the story remained an
ongoing subtext thereafter; for example, as the draft legislation banning
MMT was nearing completion in 1994, MP Julian Reed (Halton–Peel) and
the "Ethanol Task Force" peppered Minister Copps with arguments for
using ethanol instead of MMT. (Ethyl Corporation said that both could be
used advantageously together.) A nice twist on the current controversy over
MTBE is that in the same correspondence Reed was busily attacking this
Canadian product as well as MMT, since MTBE competes with ethanol-
derived ETBE (ethyl tertiary butyl ether); Reed referred to comments in the
US, including a resolution of the American Medical Association, that
portrayed continued use of MTBE as representing unacceptable health and
environmental risks.

46 J.A. Buccini to the US EPA, 17 July 1990. This is the earliest-dated correspondence we have seen in the documents on MMT that we have examined.

47 Quoted in Shawn McCarthy, "Gas War: The Fall and Rise of MMT," *Globe and Mail*, 24 July 1998, A1.

48 Minutes of the 21 June 1993 meeting of the Joint Government-Industry Committee on Transportation Fuels and Motor Vehicle Control Technologies.

49 Minutes of the 30 June 1993 meeting of MVMA and CPPI executives, compiled by MVMA President Norman A. Clark.

50 Transport Canada, "Working Group Report on MMT and Motor Vehicle Emissions." Prepared for the Joint Government-Industry Committee on Transportation Fuels and Vehicle Emissions Control Technology and tabled at the 17 August 1993 meeting.

51 Minutes of the 10 December 1993 meeting of the Joint Government-Industry Committee on Transportation Fuels and Motor Vehicle Control Technologies.

52 Minutes of the 9 September 1994 meeting of the Joint Government-Industry Committee on Transportation Fuels and Motor Vehicle Control Technologies. During the Senate hearings, much was made of a Transport Canada memo of 19 July 1994 dealing with Toyota's study, which concluded: "Toyota did not find any evidence that false detections made by the catalyst monitoring system occurred as a result of using MMT" (reprinted in part in "Submission by the Complaining Party, the Government of Alberta, under the *Agreement on Internal Trade*, in the matter of a Dispute Regarding the *Manganese-based Fuel Additives Act*, filed 1 December 1997": Supporting Documents, vol. 2, tab. 21). However, the president of Toyota Canada, testifying before the committee, stated: "Since then, we have also conducted additional research which confirmed that, in fact, it is a serious problem." The Standing Senate Committee on Energy, Environment and Natural Resources, *Evidence*, 4 February 1997, 32324- 40.

53 Indeed, the federal government followed just such a process for determining levels of sulphur in gasoline, perhaps learning from the MMT débâcle. The sulphur case illustrates how rigorous and public assessments of the contentious risk issues, in this case by expert panels, can provide a substantive basis for the decision. While the debate here was still contentious, the decision-making process was clear to all the players involved. The Environment Canada website contains more information: *www.ec.gc.ca/ceparegistry/regulations* under Current Regulations, Sulphur in Gasoline.

54 CPPI Technical Task Force Report, "Review of MMT Claims Made by MVMA, AIAMC, and Ethyl," Ottawa, 28 February 1995. This document contains an extensive summary of all of the technical aspects of the dispute about the emissions control systems. A similar, albeit opposing, document was prepared by the MVMA titled "The Impact of Manganese-Based Fuel

Additives on Vehicle Emission Control Technology in Canada," 24 October 1995, and submitted to the House of Commons Standing Committee on Environment and Sustainable Development.

55 See the Appendix for a full discussion of expert panels. The CPPI first approached the Royal Society of Canada with this request in November 1994, and the society agreed to undertake the project pending a final agreement, which never occurred, since both the auto industry and the federal government refused to participate.

56 Dan Westwell, "Additive Fuels Big Three Drive," *Globe and Mail*, 29 October 1994, A6.

57 Jack Knox, *Canadian Press article,* 13 October 1994: "Fuel Industry Warned to Stop Using Additive."

58 CPPI press release, 27 October 1994.

59 Internal government e-mail message by Michael Caplan, 14 December 1994: "Submission by the Complaining Party, the Government of Alberta, under the *Agreement on Internal Trade*, in the matter of a Dispute Regarding the *Manganese-based Fuel Additives Act*, filed 1 December 1997": Supporting Documents, vol. 1, tab. 14.

60 Internal memo to CPPI Board of Directors, 31 October 1994.

61 As noted above, the CPPI approached the Royal Society of Canada for this purpose. As is detailed more fully in the Appendix, the society's procedures require that the panel be chosen and operate in complete independence from the sponsors, which have no control over the selection of panel members and cannot see or comment on the panel's report before it is released to the public.

62 Internal government e-mail message by Michael Caplan, 14 December 1994, in "Submission by the Complaining Party, the Government of Alberta, under the *Agreement on Internal Trade*, in the matter of a Dispute Regarding the *Manganese-based Fuel Additives Act*, filed 1 December 1997": Supporting Documents, vol. 1, tab. 14. Representatives of all five concerned federal departments were present at the December 1994 meeting.

63 Jenefer Curtis, "Big Oil vs. Big Auto," *Report on Business Magazine,* March 1999, 62–71.

64 The Senate of Canada, "Interim Report concerning Bill C-29," 4 March 1997, 21–49.

65 The Standing Senate Committee on Energy, Environment and Natural Resources, *Evidence*, 11 February 1997, 900-11 to 900-12. A Transport Canada ministerial briefing note dated 1 March 1995 contains the following statement: "The GM strategy seems designed to protect GM from warranty claims whether attributable to MMT or not." "Submission by the Complaining Party, the Government of Alberta, under the *Agreement on Internal Trade*, in the matter of a Dispute Regarding the *Manganese-based Fuel Additives Act*, filed 1 December 1997": Supporting Documents, vol. 2, tab. 22.

66 The Standing Senate Committee on Energy, Environment and Natural Resources, *Evidence*, 11 February 1997, 900- 25 to 900- 26.

67 Nicole Pageot, director general, Road Safety and Motor Vehicle Regulations, Transport Canada before the Standing Senate Committee on Energy, Environment and Natural Resources, *Evidence*, 6 February 1997, 1020- 15 and following.

68 In government documents obtained through the Access to Information Act and made available to us, the large majority of references to the legal justifications behind the bill were deleted pursuant to the act.

69 Jenefer Curtis, "Big Oil vs. Big Auto," *Report on Business Magazine,* March 1999, 62–71.

70 Letter from Arthur Eggleton, minister for international trade, to Sergio Marchi, minister of the environment, 23 February 1996.

71 Environment Canada, news release, "Government Reintroduces MMT Bill C-94," 18 April 1996.

72 Letter from Prime Minister Jean Chrétien to John Manley, minister of industry, 31 June 1996.

73 45–6 Elizabeth II, c. 11, "An act to regulate interprovincial trade in and the importation for commercial purposes of certain manganese-based substances," authorizes control over any substance specified in the Schedule to the act, and MMT is the only substance so specified.

74 "Report of the Article 1704 Panel concerning a dispute between Alberta and Canada regarding the *Manganese-based Fuel Additives Act,*" Winnipeg, 12 June 1998.

75 Shawn McCarthy, "Gas War," *Globe and Mail,* 24 July 1998, A1.

76 Environment Canada, news release, "Government to act on Agreement on Internal Trade (AIT) panel report on MMT" (*www.ec.gc.ca/press/mmt98_n_e.htm,* 20 July 1998). In order to give legal effect to the settlement, all the government had to do was to remove MMT from the Schedule of the Manganese-based Fuel Additives Act; although it became at that point an empty shell, since MMT was ever the lonely occupant of that Schedule, the act itself remains on the books, mute but enduring testimony to a colossal failure in Canadian public policy.

77 Dan Westwell, "Additive Fuels Big Three Drive," *Globe and Mail,* 29 October 1994, A6.

78 Internal CPPI memo to board members, requesting their views on a reduction in the Canadian maximum concentration of MMT in gasoline, 27 July 1993.

79 Concerning the merits of public consultation in defining the scope and issues of a health risk assessment, see the US National Research Council's thoughtful report on the need for including the public in characterizing risks, entitled *Understanding Risk.*

80 One can find anywhere from 2.5 to 5mg of manganese sulfate as an ingredient in common multivitamin preparations sold in Canada. (Such

preparations also include other metals such as zinc and selenium, all of which would be toxic at sufficiently high doses.) However, exposure to manganese by the inhalation route has a much different risk profile from exposure through ingestion. The only point in mentioning this is to emphasize once again the complexity of risk management decision making.

81 The precautionary principle was defined in Principle 15 of the 1992 United Nations Rio Declaration on Environment and Development: "Where there are threats of serious of irreversible damage, lack of full scientific certainty shall not be used as a reason for postponing cost-effective measures to prevent environmental degradation."

CHAPTER FIVE

1 Mehta, "Risk and the Canadian Nuclear Industry: The Democracy-Technocracy Quandary."
2 Jasanoff, *Risk Management and Political Culture.*
3 Brickman, Jasanoff, and Ilgen, *Controlling Chemicals: The Politics of Regulation in Europe and the United States.*
4 Sclove, "Scientists in the US Nuclear Debate."
5 Plough and Krimsky, "The Emergence of Risk Communication Studies," 4.
6 Ibid.
7 Otway and Ravetz, "Technology."
8 Nelkin, *Controversy.*
9 Douglas, *Risk and Blame.*
10 Mehta, "Environmental Risk."
11 Luhmann, *Risk*, 91.
12 Mehta, "Risk Assessment and Sustainable Development."
13 Joppke, *Mobilizing against Nuclear Energy.*
14 Marshall, *Class, Citizenship, and Social Development*; Lipset and Rokkan, *Party Systems and Voter Alignments.*
15 Dahrendorf, *The Modern Social Conflict*, 37.
16 Beck, *Risk Society.*
17 Ibid., 183.
18 Joppke, *Mobilizing against Nuclear Energy.*
19 Dunlap, Kraft, and Rosa, *Public Reactions to Nuclear Waste.*
20 Sclove, "Scientists in the US Nuclear Debate."
21 Olsen, Lodwick, and Dunlap, *Viewing the World Ecologically.*
22 Doern, "The Atomic Energy Control Board."
23 Torgerson, "Contextual Orientation in Policy Analysis," 245.
24 Linnerooth, "The Political Processing of Uncertainty."
25 Rudolph and Ridley, *Power Struggle.*
26 Paehlke, *Environmentalism and the Future of Progressive Politics.*
27 Giddens, *The Return of Grand Theory in the Human Sciences.*

28 See Touraine, *Anti-Nuclear Protest*; Price, *The Antinuclear Movement*; Nelkin and Pollak, "Problems and Procedures in the Reevaluation of Technological Risk"; Sugai, *Nuclear Power and Ratepayer Protest*; Mattausch, *A Commitment to Campaign.*

29 Price, *The Antinuclear Movement.*

30 Ibid.

31 Parsons and Shils, *Toward a General Theory of Action.*

32 Parkins, *Middle-Class Radicalism.*

33 Sugai, *Nuclear Power and Ratepayer Protest.*

34 Babin, *The Nuclear Power Game.*

35 Switzer, *Environmental Politics.*

36 Hare, "The Management of Canada's Nuclear Waste."

37 Olsen, Rosa, and Dunlap, "Public Opinion versus Government Policy on National Energy Issues."

38 Greer-Wooten and Mitson, "Nuclear Power and the Canadian Public."

39 McKay, *Electric Empire.*

40 N.H. Richardson, "Land Use Planning and Sustainable Development in Canada."

41 Beanlands and Duinker, "An Ecological Framework for Environmental Impact Assessment in Canada," 37. Beanlands and Duinker's faith in science as arbitrator between values and scientific investigation is familiar and appears somewhat misplaced. If risk assessment is an indispensable part of social impact assessment, then the polarities between "expert" and "non-expert" ensure that public opinion and social values are subsumed by the values of science and technocracy.

42 Sadler, "Impact Assessment in Transition," 103.

43 Notzke, *Aboriginal People and Natural Resources in Canada.*

44 Lipset, "Canada and the United States."

45 According to section 3 of the Guidelines Order, agencies like the AECB shall ensure that environmental implications of all proposals for which they have authority are fully considered. This section stressed that the self-assessment review process should occur early on so that irreversible decisions are made with full knowledge of their environmental consequences. Section 12 of the Guidelines Order specified the type of environmental consequences which required review by an environmental assessment panel. They included such things as adverse environmental effects which are "significant" or "unacceptable."

46 Doern, "The Atomic Energy Control Board."

47 Ashforth, "Reckoning Schemes of Legitimation," 2.

48 Wynne, *Rationality and Ritual.*

49 Ibid., 160–1.

50 Richardson, Sherman, and Gismondi, *Winning Back the Words.*

51 Schumpeter, *Capitalism, Socialism and Democracy.*

52 Hiskes, "Emergent Risks and Convergent Interests."
53 Fiorino, "Technical and Democratic Values in Risk Analysis."
54 Habermas, *Toward a Rational Society*, 68.
55 Ibid., 69.
56 Ibid., 92.
57 Bobrow and Dryzek, *Policy Analysis by Design*.
58 Roszak, "The Monster and the Titan," 31.
59 Halfmann and Japp, "Modern Social Movements as Active Risk Observers."

CHAPTER SIX

1 Initial research in this area was carried out some years ago at Simon Fraser University and was supported by a SSHRC Strategic Grant (1991–94) to William Leiss, "The Flow of Science into Public Policy." Christina Chociolko, a Ph.D. student in the School of Communication, served as a research assistant for this phase of the project and also provided support for the Multi-Stakeholder Working Group on Pulp Mill Effluent. The second phase of the research effort (1996–99) was led by Debora VanNijnatten and was supported by the research funds of the Eco-Research Chair Program, Environmental Policy Unit, School of Policy Studies, Queen's University. The authors would like to thank those representatives of the environmental movement, government, and industry who generously gave of their time during interviews in 1996 to speak with us about this issue.
2 AOX (Adsorbable Organic Halogen) is a gross measurement applied to pulp mill effluent to represent the total amount of organochlorine compounds. The AOX parameter is non-specific, i.e., it does not differentiate among the chlorinated organic compounds making up AOX. A large fraction of the organically bound chlorine in AOX is attached to high molecular weight (HMW) material, which is too large to penetrate living cells, is highly water soluble and so will not bioaccumulate, and has a relatively low chlorine content (10 per cent). Some of the low molecular weight (LMW) compounds, however, are known to be toxic and persistent, to bioaccumulate, and to include chlorinated dioxins and furans and chlorophenols. There are a number of ways to determine the associated impacts with AOX: AOX per air-dried metric tonne (ADT), which bears no relation to the environment; AOX concentration in effluent; AOX concentration in the environment; and AOX concentration in organisms.
3 The term "toxicity" is used throughout this paper and requires some discussion here. It is important to differentiate between acute toxicity, causing lethality after brief exposure to chemicals or effluents, and chronic, sublethal effects. Untreated pulp and paper mill effluents are generally acutely toxic owing to low dissolved oxygen, resin acids, and a variety of other

wood extractives. It has been well known that proper and thorough secondary treatment generally removes acute toxicity. The main concern with dioxins, furans, and other organochlorines are chronic, sublethal toxicity which affects the growth, survival, and reproduction of aquatic organisms.

4 The term "Compound x," which has been widely used in discussions of pulp mill effluent, may be a misleading one, since it implies that, just as in the case of dioxin, we will eventually find a single, new chemical which has significant environmental impacts. Instead, the search for "Compound x" has been for the compound or compounds responsible for sublethal effects in fish. There may not be a "Compound x"; there may be a synergism among many compounds, all individually at well below known effect levels, or even below detection levels, which in their cumulative interactions cause toxic or developmental problems.

5 This is not to suggest, however, that the science-policy relationship is unidirectional. For example, the research undertaken in the third stage by Canadian federal scientists was in response to policy debates in stage 2, themselves engendered by the Swedish scientific findings.

6 See the detailed account of the dioxins controversy in Powell and Leiss, *Mad Cows and Mother's Milk*, chapter 3.

7 2,3,7,8-TCDD (tetrachlorodibenzo-*p*-dioxin) is the most toxic of the dioxin family of seventy-five related compounds.

8 Van Strum and Merrell, "No Margin of Safety"; von Stackelberg, "White Wash," 7.

9 Van Strum and Merrell, 11-11.

10 Environment Canada's monitoring program, conducted in co-operation with industry, became the Dioxin and Furan Monitoring Program in 1990. Under the program, the data collected was referred to Health Canada for human health risk assessment, and Health Canada then made the determination of whether fishing should be restricted in the areas sampled.

11 Berry et al., "Toward Preventing the Formation of Dioxins during Chemical Pulp Bleaching."

12 Södergren et al., "Summary of Results from the Swedish Project 'Environment/Cellulose,'" 49–60; Hansson, "Effects of Pulp and Paper Mill Effluents on Coastal Fish Communities in the Gulf of Bothnia," 344–8; Andersson et al., "Physiological Disturbances in Fish Living in Coastal Water Polluted with Bleached Kraft Pulp Mill Effluents," 1525–36; Neuman and Karas, "Effects of Pulp Mill Effluent on a Baltic Coastal Fish Community," 95–106; Sandstrom and Thorensson, "Mortality in Perch Populations in a Baltic Pulp Mill Effluent Area," 564–7; Sandstrom, Neumann, and Karas, "Effects of a Bleached Pulp Mill Effluent on Growth and Gonad Function in Baltic Coastal Fish," 107–18.

13 Hodson et al., "Canada and Sweden – Contrasting Regulations for Chlorine Discharge from Pulp and Paper Industries," 4–5.

14 MFO induction refers to increased activity of enzymes that facilitate excretion of organic chemicals and is believed by scientists to be a marker for both chemical exposure and possible toxicity.

15 Hodson et al., "Canada and Sweden – Contrasting Regulations," 1.

16 Södergren, "Biological Effects of Bleached Pulp Mill Effluents." These findings also supported earlier laboratory studies which had provided clear support for a cause-effect relationship between effluent from a mill using a traditional bleaching sequence involving elemental chlorine and effects on fish.

17 By way of comparison, Hodson et al. note that older mills using molecular chlorine for bleaching and having little waste treatment release as much as 8–10 kg AOX/ADT.

18 NCASI, "Effects of Biologically Treated Bleached Kraft Mill Effluent on Warm Water Stream Productivity in Experimental Streams – Third Progress Report," 414 (it should be noted that MFO induction was not measured in this study); NCASI, "Effects of Biologically Treated Bleached Kraft Mill Effluent on Cold Water Stream Productivity in Experimental Streams – Fifth Progress Report," 566.

19 Mehrle et al., "Pulping Effluents in the Aquatic Environment"; Eysenbach, Neal, and Owens, "Pulping Effluents in the Aquatic Environment," 104–6.

20 The bleached mill under investigation was in start-up, had no secondary treatment, and was discharging large quantities of unchlorinated organic compounds. Also, the unbleached reference mill was discharging lower loadings into higher dilutions. This prompted some questions concerning the methodology of the Swedish studies.

21 Forlin et al., "Biochemical and Physiological Effects of Pulp Mill Effluents in Fish."

22 Lehtinen, "Environmental Effects of Chlorine Bleaching – Facts Neglected?" 715–19.

23 Holloran et al., "Estimating Effluent Toxicity from Molecular-Chlorine Gas-Free Bleaching in Terms of Toxicity Equivalence."

24 Wilson and Holloran, "Decrease of AOX with Various External Effluent Treatments," 139.

25 Fleming et al., "A Discussion of the Use of the AOX Parameter as a Tool for Environmental Protection"; Craig et al., "Toxicity and Bioaccumulation of AOX and EOX," 39–45; NCASI, "A Review of the Characteristic and Significance of Adsorbable Organic Halide (AOX) in Wastewaters from U.S. Pulp and Paper Mills."

26 Hall et al., "Organochlorine Discharges in Wastewaters from Kraft Mill Bleach Plants," 53–9; Gergov et al., "Chlorinated Organic Compounds in Effluent Treatment at Kraft Mills," 443–55; Firth and Blackman, "A Comparison of Microtox Testing with Rainbow Trout Acute and Ceriodaphnia Chronic Bioassays Using Pulp and Paper Mill Wastewaters," 621–30.

27 Garden and Tsang, "Baseline Levels of Adsorbable Organic Halogen in Treated Wastewaters from Bleached Kraft Pulp Mills in Ontario." (Based on Environment Canada, Conservation and Protection/Environmental Protection, Ontario Region/Pollution Abatement Division, "Levels of Adsorbable Organic Halogen in Wastewaters from Ontario Bleached Kraft Mills," April 1990.)

28 Owens, "The Hazard Assessment of Pulp and Paper Mill Effluents in the Aquatic Environment," 1511–40.

29 Taken from Hodson et al., "Canada and Sweden – Contrasting Regulations," 11.

30 Canada, Environment Canada and Health Canada, "Effluents from Pulp Mills Using Bleaching."

31 MacKinnon, "AOX as a Regulatory Parameter," 79.

32 It should be noted that these results were from lab tests, the total exposure time of the fish exposed and affected was limited (less than six months), and there were no environmental stresses present that could enhance the responses.

33 O'Connor et al., "A Study of the Relationship between Laboratory Bioassay Response and AOX Content for Pulp Mill Effluents," A165.

34 MacDonald, "Product Challenges in the Marketplace."

35 B. Parfitt, "Cleanup Priorities Criticized," *Vancouver Sun*, 3 February 1991, D1.

36 S. Bell, "Life in the Dirty Shadow," *Probe Post*, 1991, 8.

37 Inquiries made at that time, however, indicated that this type of research was not being conducted by universities in the province.

38 Bell, "Life in the Dirty Shadow," 9.

39 G. Scotton, "Pulp Mills Clean Up Their Act," *Financial Post*, 2 October 1991, 5.

40 Luthe, Wrist, and Berry, "An Evaluation of the Effectiveness of Dioxins Control Strategies on Organochlorine Effluent Discharges from the Canadian Bleached Chemical Pulp Industry," 46.

41 These estimates were provided by Roy Parker, environmental effects officer, Environmental Protection Branch, Atlantic Region. Although Environment Canada was not informed as to the actual costs of each mill's EEM study, anecdotal information has indicated that costs per study have ranged from about $65,000 to a high of just over $250,000. According to CPPA's figures, the average cost per study has been $85,000, or $28,000 per year.

42 WCELA, letter to Hon. Jean Charest, 31 January 1992, re: Pulp and Paper Science Forum.

43 Memorandum from John Carey, RRB – NWRI to Laura Tupper, CCB – EP re: letter from W.J. Andrews (WCELA) concerning the Pulp and Paper Science Forum, 3 March 1992.

44 H. Hart, "Pulp Industry Cleans Up Its Act," *Financial Post*, 25 March 1992, 10.

45 British Columbia, Ministry of the Environment, *Environmental Compliance Report*, February 1992.

46 B. Williamson, "B.C. Sets New Limits on Waste," *Globe and Mail*, 17 January 1992, B1, B2.

47 T. McFeely, "B.C. Pulp: A Furor over Zero," *Financial Times of Canada*, 3/9 February 1992, 11.

48 Cormick and Associates, "Proposed Consensus Process: AOX Regulations."

49 Cormick and Associates, "Summary Report: Convening of Consensus Process for AOX Regulations," 2.

50 One of us (WL) had set up this stakeholder group in 1991, after a broad spectrum of stakeholder representatives from all sectors had agreed that it was a good idea. A number of meetings were held over the ensuing year, consisting of exploratory discussions and presentations, including technical presentations on technology control options. During this time the BC Ministry of Environment played a cat-and-mouse game with the stakeholder group, refusing to commit itself to recognizing the legitimacy of its participation in the developing decision making within the ministry, while also encouraging the group to meet and discuss the issues. Then the ministry devised its plan to consult the group officially *after* it had made its regulatory choice! Little wonder that the stakeholders were not inclined to regard this charade very sympathetically.

51 Background files on MSWG, Centre for Policy Research on Science and Technology, Simon Fraser University, 1991–92.

52 B. Williamson, "Proposed B.C. Bleach Ban Trouble for Mills, Study Says," *Globe and Mail*, 6 October 1991, B5.

53 B. Williamson, "Pulp Cleanup May Be Waste of Money," *Globe and Mail*, 23 December 1991, A1.

54 NLK Consultants, "Market and Economic Research on Current and Future Demands: AOX Free and Low AOX Kraft Pulp," i.

55 British Columbia, Council of Forest Industries, "B.C. Pulp Sector Position on Zero AOX" (June 1992), 1.

56 Canadian Press, "Campaign against Chlorine Bleach Isn't Based on Science, Report Says," *Vancouver Sun*, 19 September 1992, H9.

57 B. Williamson, "Proposed B.C. Bleach Ban Trouble for Mills, Study Says," B5.

58 MacKinnon, "AOX as a Regulatory Parameter" (July 1992), concluded that "the AOX parameter is limited in its use for regulating the discharge of chlorinated organic substances," although it went on to say that "nevertheless, the AOX parameter appears to provide a gross measure of environmental protection when it is used to monitor the progressive elimination of organochlorine discharges." (63) This sentence does not appear in the September draft.

59 Letter to Dr William Leiss, 1 October 1992 from Dr Jon O'Riordan, ADM, BC Ministry of the Environment.

60 Letter from the office of the ADM, Dr Jon O'Riordan, 29 October 1992.
61 M. Mittelstadt and C. Mahood, "Industry Denounces Chlorine Cuts,"
   Globe and Mail, 3 February 1993, B3. A particularly sordid aspect of the
   battle over AOX in Ontario was the attempt by some parties to malign the
   reputation of Environment Canada's John Carey, because of their perceived
   need to seek to discredit the pathbreaking (and ultimately vindicated)
   research on the sources of pulp mill effluent toxicity undertaken by him and
   his group at NWRI. See the two columns by Terence Corcoran in the *Globe
   and Mail,* 3 February and 13 April 1993.
62 Stevenson, "Bleaching Is More Than Brightening," 13.
63 Liebergott, Van Lierop, and Fleming, "Methods to Decrease and Eliminate
   AOX in the Bleach Plant," 35.
64 PAPRICAN, "Alternative Bleaching Technology and the Environment," 2.
65 Solomon et al., "A Review and Assessment of the Ecological Risks Associated with the Use of Chlorine Dioxide for the Bleaching of Pulp," 1–4.
66 Editorial, "BC May Reconsider Chlorine Ban," *Papermaker,* 16 January
   1995.
67 *Water Policy Report,* 3 March 1993, 1.
68 F. Shalom, "Industry Comes Out Swinging in Battle over Bleached Pulp,"
   Edmonton Journal, 13 February 1993, B4.
69 S. Strauss, "Pulp-Mill Waste Research Challenged," *Globe and Mail,*
   28 January 1993, A5.
70 B. Williamson (note 53), "Pulp Cleanup May Be Waste of Money," A1.
71 Ontario Ministry of Environment, "Clean Water Regulation: Pulp and
   Paper Sector," 2 February 1993.
72 Mittelstadt and Mahood (note 61), "Industry Denounces Chlorine Cuts," B3.
73 D.W. Reeve, "Banning AOX Is Not Justified: A Response to the Draft
   Effluent Limits Proposed by the Ontario Ministry of the Environment for
   the Pulp and Paper Sector." University of Toronto, Pulp and Paper Centre,
   1993.
74 C. Mahood, "Ontario Group Fights Pollution Rules," *Globe and Mail,*
   21 July 1993, B15.
75 C. Mahood, "Pulp Mill Effluent Rules Clarified in Final Draft of Law,"
   Globe and Mail, 27 November 1993, B5.
76 Stevenson, "Bleaching Is More Than Brightening," 16.
77 Bohn, "Pulp Industry Accused of Stalling on Cleanup," *Vancouver Sun,* 1
   December 1993, B2.
78 D.W. Schindler, letter to Clifford Lincoln, parliamentary secretary to deputy
   prime minister and minister of the environment.
79 Carey, Memorandum to Garth Bangay, director general, Ecosystem Conservation, Environment Canada.
80 R. Sarti, "Pulp Mills Get Gold Stars for Contaminant Cleanup," *Vancouver
   Sun,* 8 April 1995, A8; P. Lush, "B.C. Pulp and Paper Mills Pumping Less
   Pollution," *Globe and Mail,* 8 April 1995.

81 Bureau of National Affairs, "Research on Environmental Effects From Pulp Mills Shifting, Conference Told."

82 B. Williamson, "B.C. Open to Change on Chlorine Ban," *Globe and Mail*, 9 April 1995, B1.

83 W5, "Science vs. Politics," CTV Television Network, 13 January 1995.

84 Note by WL: The senior author of this chapter (Debora VanNijnatten) and I have disagreed politely for years about whether or not it is appropriate to comment on the minister's statement. I believe that it is, and I make the following comment, for which I take full and sole responsibility: Since the minister's statement about the comparative size of the two "stacks" of evidence is contrary to all of the documentary record reviewed exhaustively in this chapter, this cannot be considered a plausible claim, at least not without a convincing re-enactment of this drama in full public view by the minister's successor in that portfolio.

85 Alliance for Environmental Technology, "Stellar Surge Continues in ECF Pulp and Paper Markets" (1995). It should be noted that different sources have different estimates for world demand for TCF pulp, e.g., some claim one-half of 1 per cent, others 3 per cent, still others 7 per cent.

86 Fleming and Sloan, "Low Kappa Cooking, TCF Bleaching Affect Pulp Yield, Fiber Strength," 95–6.

87 Gandhi, "Research Points to Better Pulp Bleaching Process," 1, 6.

88 B. Williamson, "NDP Chlorine Ban Ignites Pulp Friction," *Globe and Mail*, 1997, B10.

89 This information was obtained from the BC Council of Forest Industries. The US regulations call for an AOX level of 0.6 kg/ADT.

90 Winfield and Jenish, "Ontario's Environment and the 'Common Sense Revolution': A Third Year Report," 59.

91 There is some uncertainty on the part of industry concerning whether EEM is geared towards primarily providing information on the current state of affairs, or whether it is a program to monitor industry compliance.

92 This research is being carried out by Peter V. Hodson and others in the School of Environmental Sciences at Queen's University.

93 Axelgard et al., "Minimum-Impact Mills," 1.

94 Ibid., 1, 6.

CHAPTER SEVEN

1 Allan Robinson, "Ottawa, NWT to Pay for Giant Cleanup," *Globe and Mail*, 28 August 1999, B1.

2 According to the conventional scripting, public-interest groups want to "tighten" control over environmental impacts, whereas industry wants to "loosen" them.

3 Pollster Doug Miller was reported as presenting the following analysis to environment ministers at the Canadian Council of Ministers of the

Environment (CCME) meeting in Whitehorse in October of 1995: "Although several polls have shown that the environment is no longer one of Canadians' top concerns, having fallen behind jobs and other economic issues, it remains 'a potent issue just below the radar screen.'" Robert Matas, "Environmental Protection a Priority for Canadians," *Globe and Mail*, 24 October 1995, A13.

4 As reported by Tom Spears in the *Ottawa Citizen*, 11 March 1998.

5 Canada, Commissioner of the Environment and Sustainable Development, *1999 Report*, "The Commissioner's Observations – 1999, Forward and Main Points," 10 (paragraph 21).

6 There is a useful review of developments in an earlier period in the article by Nemetz, "Federal Environmental Regulation in Canada."

7 M. Paul Brown, "Organizational Design as Policy Instrument: Environment Canada in the Canadian Bureaucracy," chapter 2 in Boardman, ed., *Canadian Environmental Policy*; Doern and Conway, *The Greening of Canada*.

8 Some of the results surfaced in a leaked memo reported in the article by Robert Matas, "MPs Environmental Proposals Planned," *Globe and Mail*, 16 October 1995, A3. As discussed in chapter 2, the Canadian government has made a policy choice whereby biotechnology applications are assessed under a variety of statutory instruments, depending on the type of application (pharmaceutical, agricultural, forestry, etc.).

9 Doern and Conway do not mention one other source of internal disarray, namely, the strong regional makeup of the department (divided into five regions: Pacific and Yukon, Western and Northern, Ontario, Quebec, and Atlantic). In areas such as pesticides, regional personnel have fought with their own headquarters staff, as well as with other federal and provincial departments, over policy issues.

10 This history is described and analysed in Skogstad and Kopas, "Environmental Policy in a Federal System," chapter 3 in Boardman, ed., *Canadian Environmental Policy*; see also Harrison, "Prospects for Intergovernmental Harmonization in Environmental Policy," 180ff, and Harrision, "Intergovernmental Relations and Environmental Policy." A good study of interjurisdictional confusion is Day and Gamble, "Coastal Zone Management in British Columbia."

11 Doern and Conway, *The Greening of Canada*, 74–7.

12 See Vanderzwaag and Duncan, "Canada and Environmental Protection," chapter 1 in Boardman, ed., *Canadian Environmental Policy*.

13 For a sampling of coverage on Windy Craggy: "BC Copper Mine Faces US Review," *Globe and Mail*, 9 April 1992, B1 and 8 July 1993, B8; on the last acts in Kemano: Ross Howard, "Largest Project in BC Blocked," *Globe and Mail*, 24 January 1995, A1 and Craig McInnes, "Autopsy Sure to Follow the Killing of Kemano," *Globe and Mail*, 30 January 1995, A5. Cheviot Mine: The Federal Court decision can be found on the Internet at: *http://www.fja.gc.ca/en/cf/1999/orig/html/1999fca24281.0.en.html*.

A balanced perspective will be found in Kennett, "Meeting the Intergovernmental Challenge of Environmental Assessment."

14 Fafard, "Groups, Government and the Environment"; Harrison, "Prospects for Intergovernmental Harmonization in Environmental Policy," 199n47; Doern and Conway, *The Greening of Canada*, 208–9.

15 There is a "harmonization" agreement between the federal government and Alberta for conducting environmental impact assessments (EIAs) under the respective legislation of the two parties: *http://www.mbnet.mb.ca/ccme/ 3e_priorities/3ea_harmonization/3ea.html*. This is a great step forward (or, if what was said earlier in the text is correct, a progressive and beneficial step backward). Now all the public needs to see is an actual EIA carried out, credibly and completely, on an important proposed project where the provincial government has a stake, for the first time in Canadian history.

16 For an overview see Stavins and Whitehead, "Dealing with Pollution." Economic instruments themselves are a subset of a wider category of forms of "commercial activity which can further the interests of environmental protection": Grabosky, "Green Markets."

17 Canada, House of Commons, Standing Committee on Environment and Sustainable Development, *It's about Our Health!* 86.

18 Doern and Conway comment: "It [DOE] has failed over most of its existence to consider seriously the role of market instruments such as taxes, charges, and so-called tradeable-pollution permits to augment and complement its traditional regulatory urges." Doern and Conway, *The Greening of Canada*, 238. Fully *fifteen* years ago Peter Nemetz ("Federal Environmental Regulation in Canada," 605) wrote: "The literature is replete with compelling demonstrations of the savings to society inherent in the adoption of market or quasi-market mechanisms for pollution control."

19 Doern and Conway, *The Greening of Canada*, 74.

20 Ibid., 78.

21 There are many individual exceptions to any general rule, including the one just stated. Also, there are major subsystems within Environment Canada as a whole to which the rule does not apply, the best example of which is the Atmospheric Environment Service, where in general policy-making needs have been minimal (however, global climate change issues are changing this context).

22 Peter Hodson of Queen's University has some considerable experience in these matters and submits the following alternative view: "The only area where I have really strong opinions is the notion that Environment Canada needs more policy and less science. I think the opposite is true. Too often, Environment Canada generates policies that are technically not defensible and impractical to implement – hence CEPA. From my view of the CEPA process, the scientists involved in advising the policy makers often had very similar views to your own, particularly concerning the futility of one

chemical at a time and the definitions of 'toxic'. There are models that allow prediction of chemical fate and effects that have been validated for large numbers of compounds. Using models to predict which compounds should be on lists of different hazards and risks is technically defensible, but requires the government to stand tough with industry. One could imagine that a technical advisory group could review and revise such models for use by the government. If industry did not like the outcome for specific compounds, then an appeal process could be devised to allow submission of data on compounds believed not to fit the mould. The technology is there, but the policy is not! The bottom line is that the policy makers in Ottawa need to listen to their own scientists. I think there are two reasons for a lack of communication between the two: First, industries have an enormous influence and use it to reduce the effectiveness of new programs (the environmental effects monitoring program was a good example). Second, policy makers and managers are afraid of science and scientists. Fear of science arises from the power derived from knowledge, and policy makers in Environment Canada often seem afraid that they will be upstaged or blind-sided by their own scientists. The result is that Environment Canada's scientists are an under-utilized resource who are kept in the dark and are often very poorly managed within the context of Environment Canada's mandate."

23 Source: Environics "Environmental Monitor Survey," December 1993, reproduced with the permission of Environics Research Ltd. The numbers on the horizontal axis represent percentages of respondents. These data are a bit old, but there are no more recent results, according to Environics (D. Miller, personal communication); however, Environics plans to include questions relevant to this measure in future surveys. Miller believes that the line-up in the 1993 chart still represents public thinking on the subject.

24 Council of Science and Technology Advisors (CSTA) Secretariat, Industry Canada, 5 May 1999. See also the two useful background studies by Janet Halliwell, Willie Smith, and collaborators: (1) "Scientific Advice in Government Decision-Making – the Canadian Experience," and (2) "Principles and Practices for Using Scientific Advice in Government Decision-Making: International Best Practices" (both June 1999).

25 The Health and Safety Executive, Government of the UK, currently has a project under way entitled "Policy, Risk and Science: Securing and Using Scientific Advice."

26 The brief case studies in the background papers for the CSTA report (note 24 above) do not draw lessons that are applied to comparable current cases for Canada. Yet this is just what is needed, for the simple reason that everyone, from children to governments, ought to learn from prior mistakes how to do things better. Indeed, the failure to incorporate a "learning" mode within the internal decision-making structures of government is, in my opinion, one of the most serious deficiencies in the conduct of public policy today.

27 Hutchings, Walters, and Haedrich, "Is Scientific Inquiry Incompatible with Government Information Control?"

28 I have deliberately changed "control" to "management" with respect to the use of information by governments. There is far too much (attempted) information control, and far too little intelligent information management, in today's government practices. The need for confidentiality should be restricted to a tightly circumscribed sphere of "advice to ministers" for policy formation and implementation. Most of the other policy-oriented information circulating in governments – so much of which is of dubious quality anyway – should be available to the public without the need to invoke access-to-information legislation, which is far too weak in Canada in any case.

29 My policy expertise is in the area of health and environmental risk management, and in this chapter I will be confining my illustrations to this area.

30 On 2 February 1998 the University of Ottawa hosted a panel discussion on the role of scientists in government. A discussant who was formerly a senior government scientist took the position that science differed from policy in that the former was based on "fact," whereas the latter includes a large dose of opinion. This is a surprising notion and, in my view, a most imprecise characterization of the relation between the two.

31 By the same token, this confidentiality should be relaxed when a period of policy development has been completed; the ministerial advisors would benefit from external, critical reviews of the advice they have been given by their experts.

32 Not to mention the exercise of police authority to inhibit spontaneous disclosures to the public.

33 I distinguish between the always evolving scientific characterization of hazards, on the one hand, and risk assessment on the other. The latter takes the former into account, along with exposure information, and applies complex models for estimating probabilities of harm. The very nature of risk assessment methods, and their direct bearing on the setting up of choices among risk management options, means that governments must have competent risk assessment expertise among their staff resources. But none of the basic science needs to be done in-house.

34 One of the main challenges undermines the very basis of the older model, which was based on expertise arrayed in watertight bureaucratic compartments. Today sensible risk management requires that we do relative risk comparisons across the domains that separate departments and agencies (food, transportation, chemicals, drugs, infectious disease, and so forth). More on this later.

35 The older model is still resilient today, but it is beginning to break down.

36 The same is true for industrially generated environmental hazards as they affect other species. The best study of the relation of science to policy in risk

management under the older model is Salter, *Mandated Science*. The more general relation between science and policy, which is known as "science policy," is a quite distinct subject, with its own literature, that is not discussed here.

37 Powell and Leiss, *Mad Cows and Mother's Milk*, ch. 1; see also E. Millstone and P. van Zwanenberg, "Bovine Spongiform Encephalopathy (Mad Cow Disease): Lessons for Public Policy," which comes to a similar conclusion, in Doern and Reed, eds., *Risky Business*, chapter 4. As does the sixteen-volume official UK report, *The BSE Inquiry*, issued in October 2000.

38 Horace Krever, *Commission of Inquiry on the Blood System in Canada*; Harris, *Lament for an Ocean*; Terry Glavin, "Salmon's Sea Change," *Globe and Mail*, 18 July 1998, D1; and chapter 5 above.

39 Hutchings, Walters, and Haedrich, "Is Scientific Inquiry Incompatible with Government Information Control?" Hutchings, "Presentation to the House of Commons Standing Committee on Fisheries."

40 Hutchings, Walters, and Haedrich, "Is Scientific Inquiry Incompatible with Government Information Control?" 1204.

41 References to those replies and a criticism of this belief will be found towards the end of the paper by D.E. Lane, "Fisheries and Oceans Canada: Science and Conservation," in Doern and Reed, eds., *Risky Business*, chapter 11; however, that paper contains no rebuttal of the substantial case made by Hutchings, Walters, and Haedrich. The nastiness continues. An article in the *Globe and Mail*, "B.C. Fish Study Worthless, Official Says," 9 October 2000, citing a DFO official who criticized the scientific work of Mr John Volpe, a graduate student at the University of Victoria, incited this rejoinder from Mr Volpe: "[T]o date, the entire DFO has not produced a single piece of empirical research on Atlantic salmon in the Pacific drainage. How dare your paper attack my science armed only with the secondhand vitriol of a mechanical engineer, and then not extend to me an opportunity to respond? Over the course of my research, I have tested some of the many government and industry assumptions that accompanied Atlantic salmon during their introduction to B.C. (no formal assessment was done before 1997 – more than a decade after the fact). Every assumption I have tested has fallen." "Letters to the Editor," *Globe and Mail*, 17 October 2000, A18.

42 It sometimes seems as if the older model is unravelling completely in a very public fashion at the federal level. Newspaper coverage during the fall of 1998 was filled with stories of disarray among the science staff in the Health Protection Branch at Health Canada, including allegations of destruction of documents and suppression of evidence in the evaluation of rBST, a product to increase milk production in cows. Powell and Leiss, *Mad Cows and Mother's Milk*, chapter 6; P. McIlroy, "Approval for Bovine Growth Hormone Hits Roadblocks," *Globe and Mail*, 4 December 1998,

A4; see also the essay by M.R. MacDonald, "Socioeconomic versus Science-Based Regulation," in Doern and Reed, eds., *Risky Business*, ch. 7.

43 See Brodeur, *Outrageous Misconduct.*

44 A small part of that story is told in Glantz et al., *The Cigarette Papers.*

45 See further the Appendix: "Using Expert Panels."

46 Leiss and Chociolko, *Risk and Responsibility*, chapter 6. At about the same time, the Canadian regulatory system for pesticides at Agriculture Canada began voluntarily to transform its original, equally secretive process (where only industry sat down at the table with governments) and reach out to a broader set of stakeholders.

47 Governments will still protect the commercial confidentiality of scientific studies undertaken in support of new products in those cases where regulatory approval is required prior to marketing – primarily in the cases of pesticides and prescription drugs. But even in these cases good ways can be found to permit (under confidentiality rules) disinterested parties to review the scientific studies and report their findings to the public.

48 In the current case about health risks associated with the radio-frequency fields that are generated by the operation of wireless communications technologies (chapter 3 above), national governments sell to industry the permits to construct the wireless networks, getting a huge, unearned financial windfall in the process. These same governments are the risk regulators who set the exposure limits for those fields. It is no longer acceptable for them to conduct in secret the evaluations of the scientific studies on which the health risk assessments are made. It would be better still if they were to offload completely – to credible independent bodies – the making of those evaluations.

49 Leiss, "Down and Dirty."

50 As a general rule, the type of risk factors that are most significant for the average person in industrial societies has shifted, over the course of the preceding 150 years, from occupational and public-health domains to that of individual lifestyle choices. (It has also shifted owing to the huge rise in average income or standard of living.) This shift is so difficult and complex a matter for societal intervention, however, that an adequate exposition of it cannot be undertaken here.

51 Royal Society of Canada, "A Review of the INSERM Report on Health Effects of Exposure to Asbestos." See also the article on asbestos and lung cancer by Camus et al., "Nonoccupational Exposure to Chrysotile Asbestos and the Risk of Lung Cancer," which says that the US EPA's risk assessment methodology overstates the risk of lung cancer for some populations by a factor of 10 (a contention that was not at all well received by some of the best-known experts in the US).

52 Powell and Leiss, *Mad Cows and Mother's Milk*, chapter 3.

53 The same is true for another notorious group of substances, PCBs. See ibid., chapter 8.

54 Kavlock and Ankley, "A Perspective on the Risk Assessment Process for Endocrine-Disruptive Effects on Wildlife and Human Health."

55 Frustrating because one is never done: dioxins are now regulated at the picogram (parts per trillion) level and detected at even lower (nanogram) levels; but if there were to be a campaign launched to "virtually eliminate" dioxins at the nanogram level, those compounds would still be among us, somewhere, to be detected and virtually eliminated once again, in an endless hunt for the last molecule on earth. (On virtual elimination see further chapter 8.)

56 During the recent internal federal government discussions of the role of science in the public sector, the idea of a government-wide "science advisor" position was floated; this notion quickly floundered on the shoals of departmental autonomy.

57 Even the first generation of modern chemical pesticides developed during the 1940s, which were later deemed to engender unacceptable levels of risk, represented a huge advance over the compounds they replaced, such as arsenic.

58 In government departments which are responsible for sets of risk factors that are both extensive and varied in nature, such as food-borne pathogens or industrial chemicals, the question about efficiency in the allocation of resources is also an internal matter.

59 In principle it might be possible to calculate the lost health benefits to Canadians that resulted, for example, from the fact that, within a specific span of time, the federal minister of environment chose to focus on MMT rather than on sulphur in gasoline. There are many who will not like the implications of this example, for quite different reasons, but such is the nature of risk management.

60 Natural ecosystems are always changing irrespective of human impacts. The reference here is to the type of impacts implied in the sustainable development concept – namely, those which might fatally impair the ability of humans to create a desirable quality of life indefinitely into the future.

61 Terry Glavin, "Salmon's Sea Change," *Globe and Mail*, 18 July 1998, D1.

62 The word "safe" is the simple expression for the more accurate phrase, "not an unacceptable probability of harm."

63 Of course one has the solemn duty to be as clear and careful as is humanly possible in carrying out responsible risk communication: The word "unlikely" indicates that *every* risk factor is a matter of probabilities and ranges of uncertainties. This must be stated openly and repeatedly. The statements "There is no risk" and "The public is perfectly safe" should be banished from our lexicon.

64 The best example is the federal government's "national biotechnology strategy." Why anyone thinks that the same government that is supposed to regulate dispassionately the relevant risks should become an ardent promoter

for the industry is a profound mystery – especially when it is abundantly clear that private industry is doing a perfectly adequate job of promotion all by itself. (See further the discussion in chapter 2 above.)

65 There is some as yet unspecifiable probability that the Canadian government's risk reduction strategy, implied in its commitments at Kyoto, will turn out to have been exactly the right response to the nature of the relevant risk factors; however, if it comes to pass this would be a purely accidental phenomenon. The nasty exchanges among some scientists in this debate are all the more reason for governments to "let it all hang out" so far as the science is concerned, and some scientists themselves seem to have fallen victim to others' "political" agendas. A brief glimpse into this big story is contained in Stephen Strauss, "Discrepancy Cools Down Climate Debate," *Globe and Mail*, 13 August 1998, A3.

66 Canada, Treasury Board Secretariat, "Getting Science Right in the Public Sector."

67 The perceived conflict of interest that governments have with respect to risk-relevant science is not dissolved by creating new crown agencies that have "presidents" rather than deputy ministers. There may be many administrative advantages to be realized from such creations, but no one will believe, nor should they, that they are qualitatively different from government departments.

68 Leiss and Cairney, "Feasibility Study on Expert Panels"; Smith, "A Review of Expert Panels for Provision of Scientific and Technological Advice for Development of Public Policy."

69 Royal Society of Canada, "A Review of the INSERM Report on the Health Effects of Exposure to Asbestos"; Royal Society of Canada, "Recommendations for the Disposition of the Health Canada Primate Colony"; Royal Society of Canada, "Expert Panel on Potential Health Risks of Radio-Frequency Fields from Wireless Telecommunications Devices."

70 Canada, Federal Environmental Assessment Review Agency, *Nuclear Fuel Waste Management and Disposal Concept*, 2; Government of Canada, "Response to Recommendations"; Berger, *Northern Frontier, Northern Homeland*.

CHAPTER EIGHT

1 For a full background treatment see Leiss and Chociolko, *Risk and Responsibility*, ch. 8, "Antisapstain Chemicals."

2 Documentation on this issue will be found in the report by Envirochem Special Projects Inc., North Vancouver, BC, "Antisapstain Chemical Technical Review" (December 1996), appendix 1.

3 EVS Environmental Consultants, North Vancouver, BC, "Investigations into the Causes of Toxicity and Potential Environmental Effects Associated with Stormwater Discharge from Sawmills" (March 1998).

4 See generally Webb, *Pollution Control in Canada*.

5 Webb points out (chapter 2) that intensive negotiation between regulators and regulated, as well as intensive collaboration in finding new technological solutions to pollution problems, is a necessary part of implementing environmental protection regimes, even under command-and-control (or "command-penalty" in his terms) approaches. This observation is of course quite correct.

6 Bill C-32 passed the House in June 1999 and the Senate in September; the full text may be found at: *http://www.ec.gc.ca/cepa/index_e.html*.

7 *Canada (Attorney-General) v. Hydro-Québec*, SJC 76 (1997). See Lucas and Sharvit, "Underlying Constraints on Intergovernmental Cooperation in Setting and Enforcing Environmental Standards."

8 This explains the relative strength of the Fisheries Act as compared with CEPA, since the former is a statute founded solidly on prohibition (see further note 29 below), which also explains why Environment Canada has relied on it for important matters such as pulp mill effluent. Cf. Webb, "Gorillas in Closets?"

9 This judgment, albeit seemingly harsh, is reinforced by the fact (clearly articulated by the justices) that the federal authority rests squarely on its strong suit, from a constitutional standpoint: its criminal law power. However, environmental management, in any kind of sensible legal framework, is almost entirely a civil law matter, that is, a matter of reasonable differences of opinion and interests, rather than one of moral depravity, which is what attends criminality.

10 Most people can think of the qualifiers for this statement. For example, we wish to prohibit certain weapons of war (although their constituent components are substances that in other contexts are good for us). Or, we wish to "ban" substances for which we can find no useful properties, and which are harmful to us in certain doses, such as dioxins. Or to ban certain types of substances because of their effects in particular zones of our ecosystems, such as some chlorinated compounds known as "ozone depleting substances." But all these are exceptions to the general rule stated in the text.

11 The "bizarre" note was the recommendation by the Senate that the next CEPA review process should begin immediately upon passage of C-32. Senate of Canada, Standing Senate Committee on Energy, the Environment and Natural Resources, *Seventh Report* (9 September 1999), "Appendix: Majority Observations," ii. One could imagine hearing groans of dismay from the officials who would have been assigned this task, had the recommendation been accepted by the government (it was not).

12 Later environmentalists accused chemical industry lobbyists of trying to block passage of the bill entirely and rallied to its support (*Globe and Mail*, 23 March 1997, A7). This was a curious development, given the December 1996 statements, but there were very many curious aspects to the CEPA review process.

13 This Standing Committee has been chaired by Charles Caccia and its report
   will be referred to hereafter as the "Standing Committee Report." For a
   glimpse at the backstage bureaucratic combat see Robert Matas, "MPs
   Environmental Proposals Planned," *Globe and Mail*, 16 October 1995, A3
   and Robert Matas, "Environment Comes First, Caccia Says," 19 October
   1995, A12. In CEPA *Review: The Government Response*, issued on
   15 December 1995, the ministers of health and environment replied to the
   report on behalf of the government; this document is cited hereafter as
   Government Response.
14 The six principles will be found in the Standing Committee Report,
   chapter 4, 39–58. A rather intemperate editorial, "A Polluted Report"
   (*Globe and Mail*, 18 October 1995, A14), dismissed this list of principles
   out of hand; see Mr Caccia's reply, 31 October 1995, A24. The real problem is that the Standing Committee, like the child set free in the candy store,
   could not make a judicious selection but instead included everything it
   considered to be a good idea.
15 M'Gonigle et al., "Taking Uncertainty Seriously."
16 Mendeloff, *The Dilemma of Toxic Substances Regulation*.
17 Bosso, *Pesticides and Politics*; the legislation is FIFRA, the Federal Insecticide, Fungicide, and Rodenticide Act. See generally US, National Research
   Council, *Toxicity Testing*.
18 Ross Hall and Donald Chant, cited in Doern and Conway, *The Greening of
   Canada*, 218.
19 Hall, "Why the EPA [CEPA] Won't Work."
20 Ibid. As an alternative, he argued for what would now be called a pollution-
   prevention approach.
21 The wording is identical in the 1999 CEPA, section 64, except for the addition in 1999 of the phrase "or its biological diversity" at the end of subsec-
   tion (a). It is also very close to the mandate wording in its predecessor, the
   Environmental Contaminants Act (1975), SC 1974–75, c. 72.
22 Standing Committee Report, 66.
23 *Government Response*, 70.
24 Standing Committee Report, 66. The Health Canada brief is entitled "The
   Role of Human Health in CEPA," 4 April 1995; on p. 10 it recommended
   eliminating the use of the word "toxic" from section 11 of the act, due to
   the amount of confusion that this idiosyncratic usage has engendered!
25 Standing Committee Report, 67.
26 Environment Canada, "Canadian Environmental Protection Act: Report
   for the Period April 1993 to March 1994," 15. Schedule 1 of Bill C-32 now
   lists 45 substances or groups thereof (see further note 35 below).
27 Standing Committee Report, 67.
28 Ibid., 68, 69, 71.
29 It is sometimes incumbent upon a critic to come up with a plausible alternative to something which he or she dislikes, although one can usually plead

343 Notes to pages 208–9

lack of time or space for the exercise. Is there a good alternative to the cumbersome process that we know as "CEPA-toxic"? One always thinks of the marvellous simplicity of section 33(2) of the Fisheries Act (RSC 1970, c. F-14): "[No] person shall deposit or permit the deposit of a deleterious substance of any type in water frequented by fish or in any place under any conditions where such deleterious substance or any other deleterious substance that results from the deposit of such deleterious substance may enter any such water."

Of course, Environment Canada is a co-administrator of this section, and has made numerous regulations under its authority, controlling discharges from chlor-alkali plants, pulp and paper mills, petroleum refineries, and other facilities. See Nemetz, "Federal Environmental Regulation in Canada," 554–5. Regulating discharges to air with the same broad language and operative terminology ("deleterious substance") might withstand a constitutional challenge on jurisdictional grounds, since air pollutants from major facilities almost always cross a provincial or national boundary, or both, and thus could fall within the federal power. (But see Versteeg, "Examining the Current and Proposed Potential of the Canadian Environmental Protection Act to Incorporate Pollution Prevention Principles and Strategies," 75, who notes the traditional provincial primacy in this area, also recognized in section 61(2) of CEPA.) Under this approach, for regulatory purposes one would not have to go through elaborate proofs of toxicity, but rather merely demonstrate harm or presumption of harm. However, all this is properly in the domain of legal scholars, and I shall say no more.

30 Standing Committee Report, 70.

31 In the United States, where carcinogenic risk is a major factor in regulatory schemes, there are "expedited" estimates of carcinogenic risk based purely on laboratory animal studies. See Hoover et al., "Improving the Regulation of Carcinogens by Expediting Cancer Potency Estimation." But it is hard to know if this is what the passages quoted in the text are aiming at.

32 M'Gonigle et al. end up with the following proposition: "Thus, a major theme of the precautionary principle is the control not merely of toxic substances, where the toxicity (or persistence or bioaccumulative character) has already been demonstrated, but of *any substances*, whose 'safety' has not yet been demonstrated" (159, italics in original). "Safety" is a traditional term which is still found in the Pest Control Products Act; as the authors recognize (127–8), it has been interpreted (in the regulations pursuant to that act) to mean "acceptable risk of harm." More modern usage has equated "safety" with "acceptable risk" simply because the traditional term cannot be operationalized or quantified satisfactorily. The main federal regulator, Health Canada's Health Protection Branch, also has come to use a broad "risk management" approach, for similarly pragmatic reasons, even though none of its legislation (or any other legislation) uses the term "risk" except incidentally. M'Gonigle et al. do not fully appreciate, it seems

to me, the fact that there is only a very small class of substances, out of the huge number of available industrial chemicals, for which the manufacturer must demonstrate "safety" (i.e., acceptable risk) prior to market use (i.e., where "preventative design" now applies): primarily, pesticides, food additives, and prescription drugs. These demonstrations are very costly, both for the manufacturers and the regulators. For everything else, unacceptable levels of harm are discovered *post hoc*, when humans, other species, or ecosystems are revealed, retrospectively, to have become victims of unwise practices. This is a harsh reality, but one which is not easily altered. The authors write (161): "The precautionary principle thus presumes that any regulatory procedure should begin with a presumption against the discharge of wastes unless the proponent can adequately demonstrate that harm is not likely to occur." Demonstrate *to whom*? Who will review and assess the scientific adequacy of the demonstration? Surely this cannot be applied to the tens of thousands of substances already in use; and, if it is applied only to all new substances, which now tend to be on average less harmful than those already in use, it will discourage innovation of less harmful substances. What we really need is (a) a much better "early warning" system overall for spotting potential trouble with hazardous substances (on the model of "adverse drug reaction" reporting for prescription drugs); and (b) a credible, negotiated problem-solving process, wherein manufacturers are strongly pushed to find cost-effective alternatives for identified problem cases, even knowing that there will be ones where more evidence does not bear out the initial suspicions. Together these would constitute a healthy precautionary principle in action.

33 One of the unrecognized drawbacks of this three-step process is that those who make or use substances that *might* be regulated, after having been listed and assessed, have a rational interest in slowing down the progress from step 1 to step 3, because they have no idea what regulatory terms they might end up with once it is all over.

34 I have time here only for a very brief account of what is a long story. I am indebted for information supplied by Christina Chociolko, who is undertaking a full analysis of the PSL process as part of her Ph.D. thesis in progress at Simon Fraser University.

35 C-32, as passed by the House of Commons on 1 June 1999, lists 26 substances in schedule 1. An additional 18 were added to schedule 1 in March 1999; the total of 45 includes a mystery substance (#27) that is nowhere clearly identified in the documentation that is easily accessible on Environment Canada's websites (accessed 27 December 1999): *http://www.ec.gc.ca/cepa/schedule1/18_subst.html* and *http://www.ec.gc.ca/press/18psl_b_e.htm*.

36 Canada, Environment Canada, "Canadian Environmental Protection Act: Report for the Period April 1993 to March 1994," 15. The majority of the

regulations now in force under CEPA are "rollovers" from earlier legislation (Canada Water Act, Clean Air Act, Environmental Contaminants Act, Ocean Dumping Act, etc.).

37 So far as pulp and paper effluent is concerned, the most important regulations are those made pursuant to the Fisheries Act; in existence since 1971, they were amended in 1992 to control biochemical oxygen demand and total suspended solids and to require extensive effects monitoring.

38 "Pulp and Paper Mill Effluent Chlorinated Dioxins and Furans Regulations" (SOR/92–267) and "Pulp and Paper Mill Defoamer and Wood Chip Regulations" (SOR/92–268), both issued on 7 May 1992. The latter prohibits use of defoaming agents containing dioxins and furans as part of the bleaching process, and also the use of wood chips made from wood treated with polychlorinated phenols. See generally Doern, "Sectoral Green Politics: Environmental Regulation and the Canadian Pulp and Paper Industry."

39 Canada, Environment Canada, "Canadian Environmental Protection Act: Report for the Period April 1993 to March 1994," 15. Ross Hall's comment (note 18 above) about the number of new chemicals that might have appeared in the marketplace in the meantime is still relevant here.

40 Standing Committee Report, 67.

41 A well-articulated proposal for an environmental risk priority-setting process for Canada will be found in an unpublished paper by Chociolko and Smith, "Setting Environmental Management Priorities."

42 Tengs et al., "Five Hundred Life-Saving Interventions and their Cost-effectiveness."

43 The "substance" approach can reach a state of absurdity, when regulators put controls on certain chemicals because they are already known to be present, even when it is acknowledged by those same regulators that at certain concentrations the controlled chemicals may not be the source of the observed adverse environmental effects. Such cases exist in the areas of pulp mill effluent and stormwater effluent containing antisapstains, as was noted at the beginning of this chapter.

44 See the full discussion in chapter 9.

45 With respect to the capacity for finding advantageous trade-offs, mentioned above, note that the 90 per cent and 50 per cent ARET targets are for the lists as a whole, not for the individual substances named. The latest numbers are in the Canadian Chemical Producers' Association report, "Reducing Emissions 9" (November 2000), available on the Web at *www.ccpa.ca*.

46 This assumes that the targets will be met, of course; while there are potential problems about reporting and compliance with such approaches, they are by no means insuperable. The statement in the text is without prejudice to the argument that there is a need for government to have legislative and regulatory authority in these matters (a need which I accept). The point is,

there must be greater encouragement in the current legislation for initiatives such as the ARET process. Versteeg, "Examining the Current and Proposed Potential of the Canadian Environmental Protection Act to Incorporate Pollution Principles and Strategies," maintains that section 8 of the original CEPA "is well-suited to the development of voluntary pollution-prevention strategies." It is still the case that in practice, so far, adequate encouragement for co-operative approaches has been lacking. The terms "negotiated" and "cooperative" are preferable to "voluntary" in that they are almost always set in motion by a legislation, regulatory, or policy imperative.

47 It is characteristic of the approach taken in the Standing Committee Report that, in recommending the incorporation of the "precautionary principle" into the act (56), it dropped the reference to cost-effectiveness which is included in the original UNCED "Rio Declaration," which runs as follows: "When there are threats of serious or irreversible damage, lack of full scientific certainty shall not be a reason for postponing cost-effective measures to prevent environmental degradation." Without the test of cost-effectiveness, the principle simply cannot be acted upon; the reason is that the majority of environmental management issues are characterized by "lack of full scientific certainty" in the accepted sense of that phrase. Thus, absent cost-effectiveness, in theory the principle would apply to almost every issue, none more so than those (such as "environmental estrogens") where the potentially high level of public concern is mirrored by the low level of scientific certainty. In practice, however, it would apply to none, since it would be impossible to tell where a sensible investment in risk reduction could be made. This did not stop the House Committee chair, Mr Caccia, from fighting the government on this point right through the final vote on the Bill in the House.

48 House of Commons, Bill C-32 (first session, thirty-sixth Parliament), passed 1 June 1999. The official French version of the phrase is "quasi-élimination," which has a more mysterious ring. Much of this started with the International Joint Commission's Virtual Elimination Task Force and its unpublished "Draft Final Report" dated 31 March 1993. Environment Canada scientists are seeking to operationalize VE: Servos et al., "Developing Biological Endpoints for Defining Virtual Elimination."

49 This is because of a cunning evasion tucked away in section 77(4)(c) of the new CEPA, which exempts a substance from being virtually eliminated if it is a "naturally occurring radionuclide or a naturally occurring inorganic substance." Such substances may well be "naturally occurring," but in many cases it is human technologies and uses that are responsible for much or all of the potential exposure to them. Dioxins are also formed by natural (as well as industrial) processes, but, unlike asbestos, dioxins are subject to VE. "Go figure," as they say.

50 Governments of Canada and Ontario, "The Canada-Ontario Agreement respecting the Great Lakes Basin Ecosystem," 1994. It is a characteristic of those who wish to deliberately use vague terminology to repeat the same expressions, rather than to elucidate them further, by simply changing the order of words.

51 Senate of Canada, testimony on Bill C-32 by Dr Harvey Lerer of Environment Canada, before the Senate of Canada, Senate Standing Committee on Energy, the Environment and Natural Resources, *Proceedings* (first session, thirty-sixth Parliament), 15 June 1999, 19: 8. During this exchange Mr Lerer added: "The basis of toxics management in Canada is risk assessment and risk management."

52 See my discussion at the Senate hearings on Bill C-32: Senate of Canada, Standing Senate Committee on Energy, the Environment and Natural Resources, *Proceedings* (first session, thirty-sixth Parliament), 26–7 August 1999, 21: 118–34.

53 CEPA defines "environment" as "air, land, water, all layers of the atmosphere, [and] all organic and inorganic matter and living organisms."

54 Misunderstandings will arise unless one important caveat is noted immediately: pollution prevention (itself strongly based on co-operative thrusts), negotiated compliance, and market-based instruments all require, in order for their benefits to be realized, a strong regulatory framework that creates incentives for these other forms of action. (Among other things, this is necessary to avoid "free rider" and "bad actor" cases.) But the reverse is also true: such a regulatory framework must include clear and positive incentives for these alternatives.

55 A multi-stakeholder process preceded the preparation of this document. See Canada, Environment Canada, "Pollution Prevention Legislative Task Force: Final Report" and "Pollution Prevention: Issues Elaboration Paper."

56 M'Gonigle et al., 155 remark with respect to pollution prevention policy and legislation elsewhere: "Both conceptually and in practice, Canadian legislative policy lags far behind these initiatives."

57 Since this is a fundamental point, and one that is potentially misunderstood, I have devoted some more attention to it a little further on. Note that the later version (June 1995) of the federal strategy paper, as well as the *Government Response*, dropped this notion, substituting the phrase "and reducing overall risk" for the words "without shifting or creating new risks" in the definition quoted earlier. This is important, and correct. However, I have left stand the remarks in the text, because the view that we should not create any new risks in pursuing better environmental protection is still widely held.

58 A full and proper discussion would contain the usual caveats. For example, we would need to know whether the risk assessment for the new substance or practice had a very much wider error or uncertainty range.

59 In principle, of course, "not to create" is preferable to "not to release," because inevitably, in practice, there will be accidental releases and also some evasions of pollution controls. In practice, however, the creation of hazardous substances in the process of making useful things is just a generally inescapable fact of industrial life.

60 See further the remarks below, which seek to unite the process of creating new risks with a shift in the "burden of proof" for environmental protection in a pollution prevention context.

61 There very well may be good reasons not to trust any specific risk assessment process, but this is a separate problem, and there are also remedies for it. See Leiss, "Down and Dirty."

62 "Managing Toxic Substances," chapter 3, paragraph 3.95ff. For further thoughts along the lines suggested in this section see the Addendum at the end of chapter 9.

63 See, e.g., Standing Committee Report, 49, which puts reuse and recycle between prevention and control. The role of reuse/recycling in pollution prevention is the source of some disagreement; they are included here for illustrative purposes only, without prejudice to the merits of the various arguments.

CHAPTER NINE

1 See the following sample of the literature: special issue, "Voluntary Agreements and Environmental Policy," *European Environment: Journal of European Environmental Policy*, vol. 9, no. 2 (March–April 1999); Gibson, ed., *Voluntary Initiatives*; Graham and Hartwell, *The Greening of Industry*; Conference Board of Canada, "The Optimal Policy Mix" and "Case Studies in Voluntary and Non-Regulatory Environmental Initiatives"; Sinclair, "Self-Regulation versus Command and Control?"; Harrison, "Talking with the Donkey"; King and Lenox, "Industry Self-Regulation without Sanctions"; Nash and Ehrenfeld, "Codes of Environmental Management Practice"; Sharma and Vredenburg, "Proactive Corporate Environmental Strategy"; Fung and O'Rourke, "Reinventing Environmental Regulation from the Grassroots Up"; Antweiler and Harrison, "Environmental Regulation vs. Environmental Information"; VanDuzer, "To Whom Should Corporations Be Responsible?"; and the following source list: *http://www.feem.it/gnee/direc/ref2.html.*

2 See, for example, Zito and Egan, "Environmental Management Standards, Corporate Strategies and Policy Networks," 94–117.

3 See, for example, Howes et al., *Clean and Competitive?*; Arnold, *Economic Analysis of Environmental Policy and Regulation*; Kosobud et al., *Market-Based Approaches to Environmental Policy.*

4 van Dunné, ed., "Environmental Contracts and Covenants."

5 Examples include the US 33/50 Program, the National Packaging Protocol in Canada, and, of course, Canada's ARET.

6 See, for example, Gallon, "Voluntary Environmental Measures"; Krahn, "Enforcement vs. Voluntary Compliance"; Lukasik, "Dofasco Deal Cuts Pollution and Controls," 8.

7 For a critique of economic instruments see Foster, ed., *Valuing Nature?*.

8 Economic Government Group (*http://www.economic.net/*); Muldoon and Nadarajah, "A Sober Second Look."

9 Gibson, "Questions about a Gift Horse"; Muldoon and Nadarajah, "A Sober Second Look."

10 VanNijnatten, "The Day the NGOs Walked Out," 101–10.

11 New Directions Group, news release, 26 September 1991, 2.

12 New Directions Group, "Reducing and Eliminating Toxic Substances Emissions," 1–2.

13 ARET Secretariat, *ARET Update: Addendum to Environment Leaders 1*.

14 "Position of Non-Governmental Organizations in the Accelerated Reduction/Elimination of Toxics (ARET) Consultation," letter to Assistant Deputy Minister Tony Clarke, Environment Canada, 17 September 1993.

15 The balance of this chapter draws on research undertaken on behalf of Environment Canada's ARET Secretariat by the Environmental Policy Unit of the School of Policy Studies at Queen's University. In the original study (Leiss, Darier, and VanNijnatten, "Lessons Learned from ARET: A Qualitative Survey of Perceptions of Stakeholders"), the authors sought to identify what could be learned from the ARET experience to render future initiatives potentially more effective. The objectives of the study were to identify ways in which stakeholders in the ARET process, as well as stakeholders familiar with that process (but not direct participants), perceived the nature of the consultative process (as well as any changes the respondents would recommend); the costs associated with the process; and the results of that process (in relation to the ARET Challenge). See also VanNijnatten, "The Day the NGOs Walked Out," 10–15.

16 ARET Committee, "Strategic Plan and Decision-Making Framework."

17 ARET Secretariat, *Environmental Leaders 3: Update*.

18 Environment Canada, "Consultation Paper on the Future of ARET," August 1999. *http://www.ec.gc.ca/aret/homec.html*.

19 ARET Secretariat, *Environmental Leaders 3*.

20 Roewade, "Voluntary Environmental Action."

21 Leiss et al., "Lessons Learned from ARET," 13.

22 Environment Canada has been able to support the Challenge through a modest investment of approximately $1 million.

23 See also VanNijnatten (with files from G. Gallon), "The ARET Challenge," 93–100.

24 Gallon, "Voluntary Environmental Measures," 11.

25 See the New Directions Group, "The New Directions Group Position," 229–38; VanNijnatten (with files from G. Gallon), "The ARET Challenge," 93–100; Leiss et al., "Lessons Learned from ARET."

26 VanNijnatten, "Group B – Workshop Discussion Notes," 7 December 1997, 4.

27 Moffat and Bregha, "Responsible Care," 69–92.

28 Bregha and Moffat, "From Challenge to Agreement?"

29 Hornung, "The VCR Doesn't Work," 134–40.

30 Versteeg, "Summary of Proceedings," 2.

31 VanNijnatten, "Group B – Workshop Discussion Notes," 6–7.

32 Versteeg, "Summary of Proceedings," 4.

33 Review Branch, Environment Canada, "Accelerated Reduction/Elimination of Toxics: Draft Evaluation Plan."

34 Commissioner of the Environment and Sustainable Development, *1999 Report*, part 4: "Managing the Risks of Toxic Substances."

35 See Davis, "Canadian Environmental Management Survey," i; Davis and Mazurek, "Industry Incentives for Environmental Improvement: Evaluation of US Federal Initiatives"; OECD, "Extended Producer Responsibility Programs."

36 Gallon, "Voluntary Environmental Measures," 4–6.

37 Indeed, determining the incentives to participate, or not participate, in the ARET program has proven difficult, despite considerable research on the part of the ARET Secretariat in this area.

38 Bregha and Moffat, "From Challenge to Agreement?" 2.

39 *www.ccpa.ca*. To date no other industry sector has made a set of voluntary performance commitments of comparable range and credibility, although some other industry associations, such as the Crop Protection Institute of Canada, are moving in this direction (*www.cpic.ca*). Another interesting development is in the climate change issue area, where some firms are attempting to overcome the policy lethargy which afflicts many governments: Guy Dixon, "Industry Joins Advocates to Cut Greenhouse Gas Emissions," *Globe and Mail*, 24 October 2000, B15.

40 I reproduce below relevant parts of the detailed proposal on recognizing "voluntary initiatives" from the submission by the Canadian Chemical Producers' Association on Bill C-32 to the House of Commons Standing Committee on Environment and Sustainable Development in April 1998. In my opinion this position meets many of the legitimate objections that have been lodged against the concept of VNRIs.
RECOMMENDATION.
Broad enabling powers should be provided in Bill C-32 to empower the Minister or the Governor-in-Council to recognize a wide range of non-regulatory instruments such as codes of practice, Responsible Care®, MOUs, etc. which, when specified by the Minister or the Governor-in-Council,

would be able to be treated as equivalent to meeting requirements under
CEPA.

For non-regulatory/voluntary initiatives that the Minister or Governor-in-Council could recognize as described above, there should have to be some criteria that would be prescribed either in the legislation or through regulation. Such criteria should include requirements for:

- a statement of the environmental improvement objective the agreement or initiative seeks to achieve;
- a public tracking mechanism of result that provides public accountability (possible mechanisms would include NPRI, or sectoral equivalents such as NERM-CCPA's annual Reducing Emissions Report which is more comprehensive than NPRI);
- public transparency, with possible mechanisms including use of community advisory processes and national advisory panels;
- industry participation in a particular voluntary initiative would be open and inclusionary on the basis of agreeing to the objectives and meeting the other elements of the agreement;
- voluntary initiatives should be results based, performance based, and verifiable."

The underlying philosophy in this recommendation is roughly consistent with the spirit of the document issued by the New Directions Group, "Criteria and Principles for the Use of Voluntary or Non-Regulatory Initiatives to Achieve Environmental Policy Objectives," November 1997. This document, the result of a multi-stakeholder deliberative process, is the best guide to the essential principles for what are here called negotiated environmental performance agreements.

CHAPTER TEN

1 Zimring, "Comparing Cigarette Policy and Illicit Drug and Alcohol Control," confirms that shifts in consumption patterns are responses to social trends, in the first instance (especially behavioural changes among "high-status" groups), and that government actions occur later.

2 Smoking prevalence in Canada in the population as a whole declined from 45 per cent in 1966 to 31 per cent three decades later; but the decline from 1990 to 1996/97, which is the last year for which statistics are available – from 29.5 per cent to 28.9 per cent – was insignificant. Among older teenagers (age fifteen to nineteen), from 1989 to 1996/97 smoking prevalence for males increased from 21.6 per cent to 27.2 per cent and for females, from 23.5 per cent to 31 per cent; almost certainly it is even higher now. Stephens and Siroonian, "Smoking Prevalence, Quit Attempts and Successes"; Health Canada: *http://www.hc-sc.gc.ca/hppb/wired/ smoking_stats/smoking_stats.htm* (accessed 6 December 2000).

3 In the US the percentage of smokers in the total population stopped falling at the 26 per cent level and has not declined since 1990: Lynch and Bonnie, eds., *Growing Up Tobacco Free*, 7. (But there is some increase in the use of smokeless tobacco in this same period.) Among teenagers, smoking prevalence stopped falling *in 1980* and has increased in every year from 1993 to 1996: US, National Cancer Policy Board, Institute of Medicine and National Research Council, *Taking Action to Reduce Tobacco Use,* 1. A study from the Centers for Disease Control found that US youth smoking rates had increased from 27.5 per cent to 36.4 per cent in the period 1991–97: *Wall Street Journal*, 3 April 1998, A8.

4 US Centers for Disease Control, "Incidence of Initiation of Cigarette Smoking – United States, 1965–1996," 838.

5 It is possible to imagine an argument to the effect that adolescent use rates might be higher still in the absence of the intensive propaganda campaigns, and thus that those campaigns dampen the rate of increase; however, the burden of proof for such a contention would lie with its proponents.

6 Reid, "Tobacco Control," citing Bruvold, "A Meta-Analysis of Adolescent Smoking Prevention Programs."

7 At current teenage prevalence rates in the US, "3,000 youths become *regular* smokers every day": Lynch and Bonnie, eds., *Growing Up Tobacco Free*, 8.

8 See further the summary of studies in note 43 below. It should be obvious that these comments are relevant to population-average smoking rates, not to the decisions by particular individuals to start or stop smoking, especially the latter, for which there are a number of approaches: Foulds, "Strategies for Smoking Cessation."

9 Clarke, "Tobacco Smoking, Genes and Dopamine." New research also shows the differential impact of nicotine on individuals: Colette Bouchez, "Thrill Seekers More Likely to Smoke, Studies Find," reporting on research done at the University of Pittsburgh: *http://www.healthscout.com/cgi-bin/ WebObjects/Af.woa/7/wo/df3000tp700a6400I6/51.2.5.21.9.70.3.3.7.8.3.1*

10 Lynch and Bonnie, eds., *Growing Up Tobacco Free*, 52–6; Chen and Millar, "Age of Smoking Initiation." In Canada the highest smoking rates for both adults and youth are among aboriginal peoples, especially those living in the far North.

11 Lynch and Bonnie, eds., *Growing up Tobacco Free*, 29; see 43–56 for the full account.

12 Chen and Millar, "Age of Smoking Initiation," 41.

13 Klein, *Cigarettes Are Sublime*; Franzen, "Sifting the Ashes."

14 Hazan, Lipton, and Glantz, "Popular Films Do Not Reflect Current Tobacco Use."

15 "Smoke Labels Getting Deadly," *Ottawa Citizen*, 8 July 1998, A1, citing Health Canada officials who were supposedly considering this option then.

16 Leventhal et al., "Is the Smoking Decision an 'Informed Choice'?"
17 Products are routinely removed from market circulation, usually voluntarily by manufacturers, when new risk assessments indicate unacceptable levels of consumer risk. Alcohol does not fit this description, since there does appear to be reliable evidence to the effect that moderate use confers a health benefit, and its use is otherwise controlled to limit (but not eliminate) the health damage that is attributable to abuse of the product. The rational basis for the controls on other addictive substances presumably is that individuals cannot exert sufficient personal control over their use to avoid unacceptable levels of health damage (but this objective can never justify criminalization for adult users).
18 Tandemar Research Inc., "Cigarette Packaging Study"; Environics Research Group, "Public Attitudes toward Toxic Constituent Labelling on Cigarette Packages."
19 Chapman et al., "Self-Exempting Beliefs about Smoking and Health."
20 Canada, Health Canada, "Health Warnings and Information for Tobacco Products."
21 Quoted in Jennifer Coleman, "Cancer Decline Linked to Anti-Tobacco Campaign," *Ottawa Citizen*, 1 December 2000, A12 (from the Associated Press), which is the source for the information in the preceding paragraphs.
22 Centers for Disease Control, "Declines in Lung Cancer Rates – California, 1988–1997," 1 December 2000 (*http://www.cdc.gov/mmwr/preview/ mmwrhtml/mm4947a4.htm*).
23 *http://www.sen.parl.gc.ca/ckenny/backgrou.htm*
24 Cited as the epigraph to chapter 3 in Glantz et al., *The Cigarette Papers*, 58; cf. Kluger, *Ashes to Ashes*, chapter 20. There is additional documentation on this point released as a part of the lawsuit filed against the industry by the state of Minnesota and available on the Internet, at *www. mnbluecrosstobacco.com*, under "trial news." For an overview of the Minnesota documents relating to addiction, see Hurt and Robertson, "Prying Open the Door to the Tobacco Industry's Secrets about Nicotine."
25 This reluctance sometimes appears to be based on the notion that there is some "moral hazard" in licensing the delivery of a drug that has no therapeutic benefits, but this is simply a canard, because of course tobacco provides through its nicotine content abundant therapeutic benefits for its committed users – as the tobacco industry was the first to discover (see Glantz et al., *The Cigarette Papers*, chapter 3).
26 The contrast with control over the use of alcoholic beverages is especially instructive. In Canada it is an offence to consume such beverages outside of a residence or a licensed establishment, but one can by contrast walk about freely with a lit cigarette. Moreover, whereas mere possession of alcohol by a minor is an offence, it is not so with tobacco, where only the act of purchase is regulated, although there are new laws imposing fines for

354   Notes to pages 251–5

possession in the US: "States and Cities Impose New Laws on Young Smokers," *New York Times*, 7 December 1997, A1.

27 Article in the *Globe and Mail*, 2 August 1998.

28 For one study of the actual failures see Murray, Prokhorov, and Harty, "Effects of a Statewide Antismoking Campaign on Mass Media Messages and Smoking Beliefs."

29 Canada's province of British Columbia followed the lead of California in announcing in late 1997 very comprehensive regulations covering ETS based on occupational safety. As of 1 January 2000 the total ban (except outdoors and in independently ventilated rooms) covers the few facilities exempted until then – bars, games rooms, long-term residential facilities, and prisons.

30 One of the remaining battlegrounds is outdoor public facilities used by children, such as playgrounds and recreation centres; municipalities in California have begun to pass ordinances in this area: "SF Playgrounds Likely to Go Smoke-Free," *USA Today*, 10 June 1998, A3.

31 Zimring, "Comparing Cigarette Policy and Illicit Drug and Alcohol Control," 95.

32 It goes without saying that one important form of eviction is the banning of *all* tobacco advertising and promotional campaigns; in countries such as Canada this has turned out to require a legal battle that sometimes appears to be eternal, but eventually it will be won. The old argument about whether or not it can be "proved" (to the satisfaction of a court) that advertising has an effect on behaviour is irrelevant; on health protection grounds society has a legitimate interest in proscribing publicity on behalf of a dangerously addictive substance.

33 Some commentators can become quite exercised, even frenetic, about the alleged "fanaticism" displayed by anti-smoking forces. And yet the desire to be reasonably free of undesirable effects from others' behaviour when one is frequenting public spaces is common to a whole range of impacts, not just the residue of smoking – for example, noise or offensive smells.

34 Except in the sole case of the United States, a nation cursed by litigiousness, where lawyers will be enriched for decades to come fighting these battles in the courts. See Law and Hackshaw, "Environmental Tobacco Smoke."

35 This section is extracted from Leiss, "The Censorship of Commercial Speech, with Special Reference to Tobacco Product Advertising," 114–23 passim; see also Leiss, "Tobacco Control Policy in Canada."

36 Royal Society of Canada, *Tobacco, Nicotine and Addiction*; Lynch and Bonnie, eds., *Growing Up Tobacco Free*, chapter 2, "The Nature of Nicotine Addiction."

37 Most if not all societies grant broad parental discretion in child raising, limited chiefly by protections (where they exist) against physical and sexual abuse and severe neglect. Exposure of children to ETS by parents is unlikely

to be regarded as an actionable form of abuse – except in the United States, where one would not be surprised to see lawsuits against parents by their children.

38 Paglia, "Tobacco Risk Communication Strategy for Youth," 11 (my italics WL).

39 Ibid., 28.

40 Ashley and Ferrence, "Environmental Tobacco Smoke in Home Environments."

41 Ibid., 32.

42 Ibid., 38. The pilot study is #7 in the list that follows.

43 This following list constitutes all of the relevant studies found in the "Abstracts on Tobacco" – a comprehensive bibliography of smoking-related literature – published by the Ontario Tobacco Research Unit in the years 1994–99:

1) P. Vineis et al., "Prevention of Exposure of Young Children to Parental Tobacco Smoke: Effectiveness of an Educational Program": "The intervention itself had limited effectiveness in decreasing the number of smokers."

2) M.F. Hovell et al., "Reduction of Environmental Tobacco Smoke Exposure among Asthmatic Children: A Controlled Trial": "This randomized clinical trial tested a behavioral medicine program designed to reduce asthmatic children's exposure to ETS in the home. Families were randomly assigned to an experimental preventative medicine counseling group, a monitoring control group, or a usual treatment group ... Exposure to parents' cigarettes in the home decreased for all groups. The experimental group attained attained a 79 percent decrease in children's ETS exposure, compared with 42 percent for the monitoring control and 34 percent for the usual treatment group." This result justifies others in looking at the specific program utilized in the trial. It should be noted that the study was done in California, which has the lowest smoking rates in North America (and thus arguably in the world), and was done among families with asthmatic children.

3) N.A. McIntosh et al., "Reducing Tobacco Smoke in the Environment of the Child with Asthma: A Cotinine-Assisted, Minimal-Contact Intervention": "More treatment (35%) than control (17%) subjects reported smoking outside their homes at posttest (and their children's cotinine levels were lower), but this difference was not statistically significant."

4) J.S. Kendrick et al., "Integrating Smoking Cessation into Routine Public Prenatal Care: The Smoking Cessation in Pregnancy Project": "Results. At the eighth month of pregnancy, self-reported quitting was higher for intervention clinics than control clinics in all three states. However, the cotinine-verified quit rates were not significantly different."

5) W. Eriksen et al., "Effects of Information on Smoking Behaviour in Families with Preschool Children": "We found no significant differences between the [intervention and control] groups with respect to changes in smoking behaviour."

6) R.A. Greenberg et al., "Evaluation of a Home-Based Intervention Program to Reduce Infant Passive Smoking and Lower Respiratory Illness": "Among the 121 infants of smoking mothers who completed the study, there was a significant difference in trend over the year between the intervention and the control groups in the amount of exposure to tobacco smoke; infants in the intervention group were exposed to 5.9 fewer cigarettes per day at 12 months. *There was no group difference in infant urine cotinine extraction*." (my italics WL)

7) S.J. Bondy et al., "Promoting Smoke-Free Families: Report of a Pilot Intervention Trial to Reduce Environmental Tobacco Smoke in Family Homes": "Our preliminary work here does not indicate that a full trial is warranted. We had difficulty achieving any indication of behaviour change, even when using highly motivated change agents."

44 Abernathy and O'Grady, "Exposure to ETS in Public Places: An Exploratory Study."

CHAPTER ELEVEN

1 A complete picture file of illustrations for an earlier version of this chapter will be found on my website: *http://www.leiss.ca* (click on "Inaugural Lecture"). The illustrations are:
- "Rachel," a Replicant in the film *Blade Runner* (1982)
- Replicants (*Blade Runner*)
- Blaise Pascal
- Francis Bacon
- Mary Shelley
- Boris Karloff in the film *Frankenstein* (1931)
- Boris Karloff in the film *Frankenstein* (1931)
- Dolly
- Immanuel Kant
- The Dioxin Molecule
- Global CO_2 Projection
- The Carbon Cycle
- Risk ⇔ Com: Risk Dialogue Projects
- Method for Risk Dialogue Projects
- EM ⇔ Com and CO_2 ⇔ Com (I)
- EM ⇔ Com and CO_2 ⇔ Com (II)
- EM ⇔ Com and CO_2 ⇔ Com (III)

Two of my accomplished associates (both Ph.D. candidates), Mike Tyshenko (Biology, Queen's University) and Alison Hearn (Communication,
Simon Fraser University), assembled the picture file and background
research for this chapter. Tim Griffin, a graduate student in the Faculty of
Environmental Design at the University of Calgary, did the website design.

2 The film is based on a novel by Philip K. Dick, *Do Androids Dream of
Electric Sheep?* The novel's title provides a nice link with Dolly, the cloned
sheep (see the section on cloning in the text).

3 Bill Joy, one of the founders of Sun Microsystems and the creator of the
"Java" language, describes the threat of a technological apocalypse (an end
to biological life on earth) that could arise out of future innovations in
nanotechnology in his April 2000 Web essay, "Why the Future Doesn't
Need Us."

4 Quoted in Margaret Wente, "The Human Genome, and Pandora's Box,"
Globe and Mail, 29 June 2000.

5 The following discussion, and the quotation from Pascal's *Pensées*, is based
on Hájek, "Pascal's Wager." See also Manson, "The Precautionary Principle, the Catastrophe Argument, and Pascal's Wager," which applies the
wager to current global climate change issues (I owe this reference to Marc
Saner).

6 I follow the interpretation which assigns a value of "negative infinity" to
outcome #2 (see Hájek, "Pascal's Wager," 5).

7 Bacon, *The New Organon*, cited in Leiss, *The Domination of Nature*, 50.

8 Billings et al., "Human Germline Gene Modification: A Dissent," 1873.
A British researcher has patented a technique for carrying out human germline gene therapy on male sperm: *Ottawa Citizen*, 10 December 2000, A1.

9 The first "designer baby" has been created in the US, albeit not with germline gene therapy. "Baby Adam" of Denver was the result of a process of
genetic screening, whereby fourteen fertilized embryos from a couple were
tested for the presence of specific genetic traits before the chosen one was
reimplanted in the mother's womb. The purpose was to provide a stem cell
transplant for Adam's six-year-old sister, who had been born with an inherited disease, with no known cure, that would inevitably kill her around the
age of seven; the transplant was indeed carried out when Adam was two
weeks old, and his sister now has a 90 per cent chance of survival. The possibilities are endless: "Meanwhile, couples with inherited disabilities such as
deafness say they welcome pre-implantation genetic screening, so they can
choose to have deaf children just like themselves." Margaret Wente, "Adam
Nash, Brave New Baby," *Globe and Mail*, 12 October 2000, A17.

10 Billings et al., "Human Germline Gene Modification: A Dissent," 1874;
see also Taylor, "Evolution Is Dead" and Baird, "Should Human Cloning
Be Permitted?" These references come from a useful information and

dissemination facility on germline therapy and related subjects which is being maintained by a group known as the "Exploratory Initiative on the New Human Genetic Technologies." The group and its co-ordinator, Richard Hayes, may be contacted at: *rhayes@publicmediacenter.org* and *teel@adax.com.* Sample websites are: *http://www.genewatch.org*, *http://www.ess.ucla.edu/huge/*, and *http://www.research.mednet.ucla.edu/ pmts/germline.*

11 David Stonehouse, "Keeping the Lid on Cloning," *Ottawa Citizen*, 14 September 2000, A5, citing an interview with science fiction writer Robert Sawyer.

12 There is a direct link from Francis Bacon to Victor Frankenstein: Bacon had opposed his natural philosophy to that of the alchemists, because he saw correctly that they had hoped to find too simple a solution to the problem of gaining access to nature's powers (see Leiss, *The Domination of Nature*, 40–61). When Victor goes to university, his teacher ridicules his early fascination with alchemy and converts him to the cause of modern science: Shelley, *Frankenstein; or, The Modern Prometheus*, 44–5.

13 Two illustrations: Margaret Munro, "Well, Hello, Dr. Frankenstein," *National Post*, 12 November 1998, A17; Christopher Shulgan, "Canada Blocks Move to Regulate Trade of 'Frankenfood,'" *Ottawa Citizen*, 26 February 1999, A1.

14 See the "Afterword" by Harold Bloom in Shelley, *Frankenstein*, 217–21.

15 Ibid., 219.

16 "Rachel" is a mechanical device, although she looks and feels (to us and, more important, to herself) as if she were a human being, which makes her somewhat ambiguous as an entity; but cloning technology promises to avoid this ambiguity and to be able to produce such a being as a completely biological entity.

17 John Heinzl, "Globe Hopes to Score with 'Virtual Ads,'" *Globe and Mail*, 23 January 1999, B1. Computer animation software has been used recently to create a television advertisement for a Canadian chocolate bar in which the head of a man is attached to the body of a small dog.

18 In technical language: "Cloning by nuclear transfer or substitution involves the complete removal of genetic material (chromosomes) from a matured oocyte or an egg to produce an enucleated cell (cytoplast). It is replaced by a nucleus containing a full complement of chromosomes from a suitable donor cell (the karyoplast) which is introduced into the recipient cytoplast by direct microinjection (in amphibians) or by fusion of the donor and recipient cells (in mammals)." Statement by the Council of the Royal Society of London, "Whither Cloning?" 2; the preceding quotation is from the same page.

19 Gina Kolata, "Human Cloning: The Race Is On," *Globe and Mail*, 18 December 1998, A19.

20 Baird, "Cloning of Animals and Humans."

21 See Krista Foss, "Cell Discovery a Major Step toward Human Cloning," *Globe and Mail*, 6 November 1998, A1; Nicholas Wade, "Human and Cow Cells Fused, Scientists Say," *Globe and Mail*, 13 November 1998, A9.

22 Somerville, "Human Cloning: The Ethics of Repairing, Replicating and Enhancing Us," 39. Cf. Russo and Cove, *Genetic Engineering*.

23 Somerville, "Human Cloning," 27; the preceding quotation is from 30.

24 Baird, "Cloning of Animals and Humans," 10.

25 Dixon, *Man after Man*, projects evolutionary and bioengineering possibilities into the near and far future and imagines all sorts of "post-human" humanoid creatures, including human-machine chimeras. The drawings in this provocative volume are quite striking and provide much food for reflection. (I owe this reference to Michael Mehta.)

26 *http://www.panda.org/resources/publications/sustainability/edo_disrupt/rv3_summary.htm* and *http://www.ourstolenfuture.org*

27 This section was written by Tim Griffin, a graduate student in the Faculty of Environmental Design at the University of Calgary.

CHAPTER TWELVE

1 See the volume *Risk, Media and Stigma*, edited by James Flynn, Paul Slovic, and Howard Kunreuther (London: Earthscan Publications, 2001).

2 OECD, "Biotechnology for Clean Industrial Products and Processes."

3 I owe some of the terminology in this section to my colleague Michael Mehta.

4 Lok and Powell, "The Belgian Dioxin Crisis of the Summer of 1999."

5 This perspective was explained to me in a private conversation with a plant scientist with over forty years of experience in both the government and the food-processing industry sides of the agricultural sector in Canada.

6 US National Research Council, *Hormonally Active Agents in the Environment*.

7 Pauline Tam, "Greenpeace's Food Fight," *Ottawa Citizen*, 5 January 2000, A4.

8 See the elaborate materials on both environmental and community issues on the website of Rio Tinto PLC, one of the world's largest mining firms: *http://www.riotinto.com/community/*. Not surprisingly, there are also "dissident" sites which are critical of the company's activities, for example: *http://www.cfmeu.asn.au/mining-energy/rio* and *http://www.rio-tinto-shareholders.com/default.htm*

9 On *E. coli* see Powell and Leiss, *Mad Cows and Mother's Milk*, chapter 4 and additional material at: *http://www.plant.uoguelph.ca/safefood*. See also *http://www.walkertoninquiry.com*, the website of the inquiry into the *E. coli* outbreak in Walkerton, Ontario in May 2000. For cryptosporidium:

E.A. Casman et al., "An Integrated Risk Model of a Drinking-Water-Borne Cryptosporidiosis Outbreak."

10 See *http://www.dfait.gc.ca/english/news/press_releases/98_press/ 98_135e.htm* and *http://www.dfait.gc.ca/english/news/press_releases/ 98_press/98_236e.htm*, two press releases in 1998 from Canada's Department of Foreign Affairs and International Trade.

11 The point made by Heath (*Strategic Issues Management*, 340) appears to reinforce this judgment: "The primary outcome of the management of risk issues is not understanding or agreement ... Rather, the outcome is control." However, the context makes it clear that Heath is referring to attempts by individuals, aided by good risk communication practice, to assume *personal* control over the issues that concern them.

12 Over the last few years, Greenpeace International and the World Wildlife Fund have played major roles, operating in many countries and regions around the world, on issues grouped into campaigns (Greenpeace: Oceans, Forests, GMOs, Toxics, Climate, Nuclear, see *http://www.greenpeace.org/ report99/index.html*; World Wildlife Fund: Living Planet, Climate Change, Endangered Seas, Forests for Life, Living Waters, see *http:// www.panda.org/*).

13 As noted at the outset, my concept of "risk issue management" is a further development of the perspective worked out in Robert L. Heath's important book, *Strategic Issues Management: Organizations and Public Policy Challenges*.

14 *http://www.nexeninc.com/home.htm*, *http://www.suncor.com*, *http:// www.transalta.com* are the websites of the Canadian firms Nexen Inc. (formerly Canadian Occidental Petroleum), Suncor, and Transalta, all of which have adopted this approach to corporate accountability.

15 See the website of the Canadian Chemical Producers' Association: *www.ccpa.ca/*

APPENDIX

1 Peter Collins (head, Science Advice, the Royal Society of London), "The Role of Academies in Advising National Governments," September 1998.

2 Leiss and Cairney, "Feasibility Study on Expert Panels"; Smith, "A Review of Expert Panels for Provision of Scientific and Technological Advice for Development of Public Policy."

3 Goss Gilroy, Inc., Management Consultants, "National Academy/Royal Society Review (Britain, Germany, Sweden, France, and the United States)," Ottawa, April 1993.

4 The website for the US institutions is: *www.nationalacademies.org*; for the Royal Society of London: *www.royalsoc.ac.uk*; for Académie des Sciences (Institut de France): *http://www.acad-sciences.institut-de-france.fr*

5 Michael Balter, "Blowing the Dust off the French Academy," *Science Magazine*, 23 April 1999.

6 Publications may be found at *www.nas.edu*

7 "Science policy" is emphasized here, of course, because of the structure of the Royal Society of London's membership, which is drawn exclusively from the natural sciences. But the Society also participates in the National Academies' Policy Advisory Group, which includes as well the British Academy, the Conference of Medical Royal Colleges, and the Royal Academy of Engineering, all of which "pool their expertise when addressing nationally-important policy issues which require a multi-disciplinary approach or are of common concern to the Academies." See *http:// www.royalsoc.ac.uk/rs_sas.htm* and the section on "Science Advice" in the *Year Book of the Royal Society 1999*, London, E33–E36. "The Parliamentary Grant-in-Aid represents that share of the Science Budget voted annually since 1849 by Parliament which is administered by the Society. The Grant-in-Aid is negotiated annually through the Office of Science and Technology (Department of Trade and Industry) to be used by the Society for a variety of agreed purposes. Expenditure is subject to review and examination by the Government's Office of Science and Technology and the National Audit Office" (F1).

8 Académie des Sciences (Institut de France), *Annuaire pour 1998*, Paris; "Avant-Propos," 5 and "Les Actions," 71–103.

9 "Manual of procedural guidelines for the conduct of expert panel processes," October 1996. Panels are selected and governed by the Society's Committee on Expert Panels. The best single overview of the functions of expert panels is Smith, "Review of Expert Panels for Provision of Scientific and Technological Advice for Development of Public Policy." See also New Zealand, "Independent Science Panels: A Handbook of Guidelines for Their Establishment and Operations."

10 In the US and Canadian systems, panellists are asked to complete a "Potential sources of bias and conflict of interest" form.

References

Aalders, M. "Regulation and In-Company Environmental Management in the Netherlands." *Law and Policy* 15 (1993): 75–94.

Aalders, M., and T. Wilthagen. "Moving beyond Command-and-Control." Amsterdam, The Netherlands: Centre for Environmental Law and Hugo Sinzheimer Institute for Socio-Legal Studies in Labour and Law, University of Amsterdam, 1995.

Abernathy, T., and B. O'Grady. "Exposure to ETS in Public Places: An Exploratory Study." Toronto: Ontario Tobacco Research Unit, 1996.

Andersson, T., L. Forlin, J. Hardig, and A. Larsson. "Physiological Disturbances in Fish Living in Coastal Water Polluted with Bleached Kraft Pulp Mill Effluents." *Canadian Journal of Fisheries and Aquatic Sciences* 45 (1988): 1525–36.

Antweiler, W., and K. Harrison. "Environmental Regulation vs. Environmental Information: A View from Canada's National Pollutant Release Inventory." Paper prepared for the annual meeting of the Association for Public Policy Analysis and Management, Washington, DC, November 1999.

Arnold, F.S. *Economic Analysis of Environmental Policy and Regulation*. New York: Wiley, 1995.

Ashforth, A. "Reckoning Schemes of Legitimation: On Commissions of Inquiry as Power/Knowledge Form." *Journal of Historical Sociology* 3 (1990): 1–22.

Ashley, M.J., and R. Ferrence. "Environmental Tobacco Smoke in Home Environments." Toronto: Ontario Tobacco Research Unit, 1996.

Axelgard, P., J. Carey, J. Floke, P. Gleadow, J. Gullichsen, D. Fryke, D. Reeve, S. Swan, and V. Uloth. "Minimum Impact Mills: An Examination of the Issues and Challenges." Ottawa: Environment Canada, 1997.

The BSE *Inquiry: Report, Evidence and Supporting Papers of the Inquiry into the Emergence and Identification of Bovine Spongiform Encephalopathy* (BSE) *and Variant Creutzfeldt-Jakob Disease* (VCJD) *and the Action Taken in Response to It up to 20 March 1996.* 16 vols. London: Stationery Office, October 2000.

Babin, R. *The Nuclear Power Game.* Montreal: Black Rose Books, 1985.

Baird, P.A. "Cloning of Animals and Humans: What Should the Policy Response Be?" *Perspectives in Biology and Medicine* 42 (1999): 179–94.

– "Should Human Cloning Be Permitted?" *Annals of the Royal College of Physicians and Surgeons of Canada* 33 (2000): 235–7.

Barke, R.P., and H.C. Jenkins-Smith. "Politics and Scientific Expertise: Scientists, Risk Perception, and Nuclear Waste Policy." *Risk Analysis* 13 (1993).

Barnes, B. *Scientific Knowledge and Sociological Theory.* London: Routledge and Kegan Paul, 1974.

Barrett, Katherine J. "Canadian Agricultural Biotechnology: Risk Assessment and the Precautionary Principle." Ph.D. Thesis, Department of Botany, University of British Columbia, 1999.

Bauer, Martin, ed. *Resistance to New Technology.* New York: Cambridge University Press, 1995.

Beanlands, G.E., and P.N. Duinker. "An Ecological Framework for Environmental Impact Assessment in Canada." Halifax and Hull: Institute for Resource and Environmental Studies and Federal Environmental Assessment Review Office, 1983.

Beck, U. *Risk Society: Towards a New Modernity.* London: Sage Publications, 1992.

Berger, P., and T. Luckmann. *The Social Construction of Reality.* Garden City, NJ: Doubleday, 1996.

Berger, Thomas R. *Northern Frontier, Northern Homeland: The Report of the Mackenzie Valley Pipeline Inquiry.* 2 vols. Ottawa: Minister of Supply and Services, 1977.

Berry, R.M., B.I. Fleming, R.H. Voss, C.E. Luthe, and P.E. Wrist. "Toward Preventing the Formation of Dioxins during Chemical Pulp Bleaching." *Pulp and Paper Canada* 90 (1989).

Billings, P.R., R. Hubbard, and S.A. Newman. "Human Germline Gene Modification: A Dissent." *Lancet* 353 (29 May 1999): 1873–5.

Boardman, Robert, ed. *Canadian Environmental Policy: Ecosystems, Politics and Process.* Toronto: Oxford University Press, 1992.

Bobrow, D.B., and J.S. Dryzek. *Policy Analysis by Design.* Pittsburgh: University of Pittsburgh Press, 1987.

Bondy, S.J., et al. "Promoting Smoke-Free Families: Report of a Pilot Intervention Trial to Reduce Environmental Tobacco Smoke in Family Homes." Toronto: Ontario Tobacco Research Unit, 1995.

Borgmann, A.I., S. Humphrey, and S. Michajluk. "Environmental Effects Monitoring at 22 Pulp and Paper Mills in Ontario. Cycle 2 Interim Report, Summary of Summer 1997 and Winter 1998 EEM Effluent Toxicity Results." Environmental Protection Branch – Ontario Region, Environment Canada, 18 February 1999.

Bosso, C.J. *Pesticides and Politics*. Pittsburgh: University of Pittsburgh Press, 1987.

Bostrom, A., M.G. Morgan, B. Fischoff, and D. Read. "What Do People Know about Climate Change? Part 1: Mental Models." *Risk Analysis* 14 (1994): 959–70.

Bregha, F., and J. Moffat. "From Challenge to Agreement? Background Paper on the Future of ARET." Ottawa: Resource Futures International, 1997.

Brickman, R., S. Jasanoff, and T. Ilgen. *Controlling Chemicals: The Politics of Regulation in Europe and the United States*. Ithaca: Cornell University Press, 1985.

Brodeur, P. *Outrageous Misconduct: The Asbestos Industry on Trial*. New York: Pantheon Books, 1985.

– *The Zapping of America: Microwaves, Their Deadly Risk, and the Cover-Up*. New York: W.W. Norton and Company, 1979.

Bruvold, W.H. "A Meta-Analysis of Adolescent Smoking Prevention Programs." *American Journal of Public Health* 83 (1993): 872–80.

Bureau of National Affairs, Inc. "Research on Environmental Effects from Pulp Mills Shifting, Conference Told." *BNA International Environment Daily*, 30 November 1994.

Burns, William J., et al. "Incorporating Structural Models into Research on the Social Amplification of Risk." *Risk Analysis* 13 (1993): 611–23.

Camus, M., J. Siemiatycki, and B. Meek. "Nonoccupational Exposure to Chrysotile Asbestos and the Risk of Lung Cancer." *New England Journal of Medicine* 338, no. 22 (1998): 1565.

Canada, Agriculture and Agri-Food Canada. *Biotechnology in Agriculture: General Information*. Ottawa, 1995.

– Commissioner of the Environment and Sustainable Development. *1999 Report*. Ottawa: Minister of Public Works and Government Services, 1999. *http://www.oag-bvg.gc.ca/domino/reports.nsf/html/c904me.html*.

– Canadian Council of Ministers of the Environment. "Environmental Management Framework Agreement (Discussion Draft)." Ottawa: CCME, 1995.

– Environment Canada, ARET Secretariat. "Environmental Leaders: Voluntary Commitments to Action on Toxics through ARET." Ottawa, 1995.

– Environment Canada. "Canadian Environmental Protection Act: Report for the Period April 1993 to March 1994." Ottawa, 1994.

– Environment Canada. "Pollution Prevention: Issues Elaboration Paper." Ottawa, 1994.

- Environment Canada. "Pollution Prevention Legislative Task Force: Final Report." Ottawa, 1993.
- Environment Canada. "Toxic Substances Management Policy: Persistence and Bioaccumulation Criteria." Ottawa, 1995.
- Environment Canada and Health Canada. "Effluents from Pulp Mills Using Bleaching." Ottawa, 1991.
- Federal Environmental Assessment Review Agency. *Nuclear Fuel Waste Management and Disposal Concept: Report of the Nuclear Fuel Waste Management and Disposal Concept Environment Assessment Panel.* Ottawa, February 1998.
- Government of Canada. "Government of Canada Response to Recommendations of the Nuclear Fuel Waste Management and Disposal Concept Environmental Assessment Panel." Ottawa, 1998.
- Government of Canada. *CEPA Review: The Government Response.* Ottawa, 1995.
- Health Canada. "Health Warnings and Information for Tobacco Products." Ottawa: 12 May 2000.
- Health Canada. "Risk Management in the Health Protection Branch." Ottawa, 1990.
- Health Canada, Radiation Protection Bureau. "Safety Code 6 – Limits of Human Exposure to Radiofrequency Electromagnetic Fields in the Frequency Range from 3 kHz to 300 GHz." *http://www.hc-sc.gc.ca/ehp/ehd/catalogue/rpb_pubs/99ehd237.htm.* Ottawa, October 1999
- Health and Welfare Canada. *Methylcylcopentadienyl Manganese Tricarbonyl (MMT): An Assessment of the Human Health Implication of Its Use as a Gasoline Additive.* Ottawa, 1994.
- House of Commons, Standing Committee on Environment and Sustainable Development. *It's about Our Health!* Ottawa: House of Commons, 1994.
- Industry Canada, Spectrum Management. "Environmental Process, Radiofrequency Fields and Land-Use Consultation." Ottawa: Industry Canada, 1995.
- Treasury Board Secretariat. "Getting Science Right in the Public Sector." Ottawa: Treasury Board Secretariat, Research and Analysis, Public Affairs, 1998.
- Canadian Standards Association. *Risk Management: Guideline for Decision-Makers (CAN/CSA-Q850-97).* Rexdale, Ontario: Canadian Standards Association, 1997.
- Carlo, G.L., N.L. Lee, K.G. Sund, and S.D. Pettygrove. "The Interplay of Science, Values, and Experiences among Scientists Asked to Evaluate the Hazards of Dioxin, Radon, and Tobacco Smoke." *Risk Analysis* 12 (1992): 37–44.
- Casman, E.A., B. Fischoff, C. Palmgren, M.J. Small, and F. Wu. "An Integrated Risk Model of a Drinking-Water-Borne Cryptosporidiosis Outbreak." *Risk Analysis* 20 (2000): 495–511.

Chapman, S., et al. "Self-Exempting Beliefs about Smoking and Health: Differences between Smokers and Ex-smokers." *American Journal of Public Health* 83 (1993): 215–19.

Chen, J., and W.J. Millar. "Age of Smoking Initiation: Implications for Quitting." *Statistics Canada Health Reports* 9 (1998): 39–46.

Chess, C., et al. "The Organizational Links between Risk Communication and Risk Management: The Case of Sybron Chemicals, Inc." *Risk Analysis* 12 (1992): 431–8.

Chociolko, C. "The Experts Disagree: A Simple Matter of Facts versus Values?" *Alternatives Magazine* 21, no. 3, (1995).

Chociolko, C., and W.G.B. Smith. "Setting Environmental Management Priorities: Rethinking Risk Analysis." Kingston: Environmental Policy Unit, School of Policy Studies, Queen's University, 1995.

Clarke, P.S. "Tobacco Smoking, Genes and Dopamine." *Lancet* 352 (1998): 98–9.

Colborn, Theo, et al. *Our Stolen Future.* New York: Penguin, 1996.

Cole, S. *Making Science: Between Nature and Society.* Cambridge, Massachusetts: Harvard University Press, 1992.

Collins, H. *Changing Order: Replication and Induction in Scientific Practice.* London: Sage, 1985.

Colmenares, C., S. Deutsch, C. Evans, A.J. Nelson, L.J. Terminello, J.G. Reynolds, J.W. Roos, and I.L. Smith. "Analysis of Manganese Particulates from Automotive Decomposition of Methylcyclopentadienyl Manganese Tricarbonyl." *Applied Surface Science* 151 (1999): 189–202.

Conference Board of Canada. "Case Studies in Voluntary and Non-Regulatory Environmental Initiatives." Final Report. Ottawa, February 1999.

– "The Optimal Policy Mix." Ottawa, June 2000.

Conway, Gordon. "Statement on Plant Biotechnology." Address to the Monsanto Board of Directors, 24 June 1999 (*www.consecol.org/Journal/vol4/iss1/art2/index.html*).

Conway, G., and G. Toennissen. "Feeding the World in the Twenty-First Century." *Nature* 402 (Supp., 2 December 1999): C55–8.

Council of Forest Industries. "B.C. Pulp Sector Position on Zero AOX." Vancouver: Council of Forest Industries, 1992.

Craig, G.R., P.L. Orr, J.L. Robertson, and W.M. Vrooman. "Toxicity and Bioaccumulation of AOX and EOX." *Pulp and Paper Canada* 91 (1990): 39–45.

Dahrendorf, R. *The Modern Social Conflict.* New York: Weidenfeld and Nicolson, 1988.

Darier, É. "Environmental Governmentality: The Case of Canada's Green Plan." *Environmental Politics* 5 (1996): 585–606.

– "The Politics and Power Effects of Garbage Recycling in Halifax, Canada." *Local Environment* 1 (1996): 63–86.

– "Foucault and the Environment: An Introduction." In: É. Darier, ed., *Discourses of the Environment*. Oxford: Blackwell, 1999.

Davis, A. "Canadian Environmental Management Survey." Toronto: KPMG Environmental Services, 1994.

Davis, D.L., and H.L. Bradshaw. "Can Environmental Estrogens Cause Breast Cancer?" *Scientific American* 273 (1995): 166–72.

Davis, T., and J. Mazurek. "Industry Incentives for Environmental Improvement: Evaluation of US Federal Initiatives." Washington, DC: Global Environmental Management Initiative, 1996.

Day, J.C., and D.B. Gamble. "Coastal Zone Management in British Columbia." *Coastal Management* 18 (1990): 115–41.

Dick, P.K. *Do Androids Dream of Electric Sheep?* New York: Doubleday, 1968.

Dixon, Dougal. *Man after Man: An Anthropology of the Future*. New York: St Martin's Press, 1990.

Dodd, Matt, and Doug Bright. "Scientific Overview of AOX Discharge Limits and Current Regulatory Approaches." Applied Research Division, Royal Roads University, Victoria. Prepared for the BC Council of Forest Industries, 23 August 1999.

Doern, G.B. "The Atomic Energy Control Board: An Evaluation of Regulatory and Administrative Processes and Procedures." Ottawa: Law Reform Commission of Canada, 1976.

– "Sectoral Green Politics: Environmental Regulation and the Canadian Pulp and Paper Industry." *Environmental Politics* 4 (1995): 219–43.

Doern, G.B., and T. Conway. *The Greening of Canada: Federal Institutions and Decisions*. Toronto: University of Toronto Press, 1994.

Doern, G.B., and T. Reed, eds. *Risky Business: Canada's Changing Science-Based Policy and Regulatory Regime*. Toronto: University of Toronto Press, 2000.

Doll, R., and A.B. Hill. "Smoking and Carcinoma of the Lung: Preliminary Report." *British Medical Journal* 2 (1950): 739–48.

Dotto, Lydia. *Storm Warning: Gambling with the Climate of Our Planet*. Toronto: Doubleday Canada, 1999.

Douglas, M. *Risk and Blame: Essays in Cultural Theory*. London: Routledge, 1992.

Dunlap, R.E., M.E. Kraft, and E.A. Rosa. *Public Reactions to Nuclear Waste: Citizens' Views of Repository Siting*. Durham, NC: Duke University Press, 1993.

Environics Research Group. "Public Attitudes toward Toxic Constituent Labelling on Cigarette Packages." Ottawa: Health Canada, 1996.

Eriksen, W., et al. "Effects of Information on Smoking Behaviour in Families with Preschool Children." *Acta Paediatrica* 85 (1996): 209–12.

Eysenbach, E.J., L.W. Neal, and J.W. Owens. "Pulping Effluents in the Aquatic Environment: Data Compilation and Scientific Panel Report." *Tappi Journal* (1990): 104–6.

Fafard, P.C. "Groups, Government and the Environment: Some Evidence from the Harmonization Initiative." In Fafard and Harrison, eds., *Managing the Environmental Union,* 81–101.

Fafard, P.C. and K. Harrison, eds. *Managing the Environmental Union: Intergovernmental Relations and Environmental Policy in Canada.* Montreal: McGill-Queen's University Press, 2000 (for the School of Policy Studies, Queen's University).

Finch, R. *Exporting Danger: A History of Canadian Nuclear Energy Export Programme.* Montreal: Black Rose Books, 1986.

Fiorino, D.J. "Technical and Democratic Values in Risk Analysis." *Risk Analysis* 9 (1989): 293–9.

Firth, B.K., and C.J. Blackman. "A Comparison of Microtox Testing with Rainbow Trout Acute and Ceriodaphnia and Chronic Bioassays Using Pulp and Paper Mill Wastewaters." In *TAPPI Conference Proceedings.* Atlanta: Tappi Press, 1990.

Fitzsimmons, G. "Harmonization Initiative of the Canadian Council of Ministers of the Environment." Ottawa: CCME Secretariat, 1995.

Fleming, B.I., T. Kovacs, C.E. Luthe, R.H. Voss, R.M. Berry, and P.E. Wrist. "A Discussion of the Use of the AOX Parameter as a Tool for Environmental Protection." Vancouver: PAPRICAN, 1990.

Fleming, B., and T. Sloan. "Low Kappa Cooking, TCF Bleaching Affect Pulp Yield, Fiber Strength." *Pulp and Paper,* December 1994.

Fleming, James Rodger. *Historical Perspectives on Climate Change.* New York: Oxford University Press, 1998.

Flynn, J., et al. "The Nevada Initiative: A Risk Communication Fiasco." *Risk Analysis* 13 (1993): 643–8.

Flynn, J., and P. Slovic. "Yucca Mountain: A Crisis for Policy." *Annual Review of Energy and Environment* 20 (1995): 83–118.

Forlin, L., T. Andersson, L. Balk, and A. Larsson. "Biochemical and Physiological Effects of Pulp Mill Effluents in Fish." In A. Södergren, ed., *Proceedings of an International Conference on the Fate and Effects of Pulp Mill Effluents.* Stockholm: Swedish EPA, 1992.

Foster, J., ed. *Valuing Nature? Economics, Ethics and Environment.* London: Routledge, 1997.

Foulds, J. "Strategies for Smoking Cessation." *British Medical Bulletin* 52 (1996): 157–73.

Frankel, Carl. "Food, Health and Still Hopeful." *Tomorrow: Global Environment Business* 11, no. 2 (April 2000): 6–8.

Franzen, J. "Sifting the Ashes." *New Yorker,* 13 May 1996: 40–8.

Freudenburg, William R., et al. "Media Coverage of Hazard Events." *Risk Analysis* 16 (1996): 31–42.

Fung, A., and D. O'Rourke. "Reinventing Environmental Regulation from the Grassroots Up: Explaining and Expanding the Success of the Toxics Release Inventory." *Environmental Management* 2 (2000): 115–27.

Funtowicz, S.O., and J.R. Ravetz. "Three Types of Risk Assessment and the Emergence of Post Normal Science." In S. Krimsky and D. Golding, eds., *Social Theories of Risk*.

Gallon, G. "Voluntary Environmental Measures: The Canadian Experience." Montreal: Canadian Institute for Business and the Environment, 1997.

Gandhi, P. "Research Points to Better Pulp Bleaching Process." *Georgia Environmental News* (Vancouver) (1995): 8.

Garden, A., and T. Tsang. "Baseline Levels of Adsorbable Organic Halogen in Treated Wastewaters from Bleached Kraft Pulp Mills in Ontario." *Chemosphere* 20 (1990): 1695–1700.

Gergov, M., M. Priha, E. Talka, O. Valttila, A. Kangas, and K. Kukkonen. "Chlorinated Organic Compounds in Effluent Treatment at Kraft Mills." In: *TAPPI Conference Proceedings*. Atlanta: TAPPI Press, 1988.

Gibbons, Michael. "Science's New Social Contract with Society." *Nature* 402 (supp., 2 December 1999): C81–4.

Gibson, R. B. "Questions about a Gift Horse." In R. B. Gibson, ed., *Voluntary Initiatives: The New Politics of Corporate Greening*, 3–12.

Gibson, R.B., ed. *Voluntary Initiatives: The New Politics of Corporate Greening*. Peterborough: Broadview Press, 1999.

Giddens, A. *The Return of Grand Theory in the Human Sciences*. Boston: Beacon Press, 1985.

– *The Consequences of Modernity*. Stanford: Stanford University Press, 1990.

Glantz, S.A., et al. *The Cigarette Papers*. Berkeley: University of California Press, 1996.

Global Environmental Change Program (UK). "The Politics of GM Food: Risk, Science and Public Trust." October 1999 (*http://www.gecko.ac.uk*).

Grabosky, P.N. "Green Markets: Environmental Regulation by the Private Sector." *Law and Policy* 16 (1994): 419–48.

Graham, J.D., and J.K. Hartwell. *The Greening of Industry*. Cambridge, Massachusetts: Harvard University Press, 1997.

Gray, P., R. Stern, and M. Biocca, eds. *Communicating about Risks to Environment and Health in Europe*. Dordrecht: Kluwer, 1998.

Greenburg, R.A., et al. "Evaluation of a Home-Based Intervention Program to Reduce Infant Passive Smoking and Lower Respiratory Illness." *Journal of Behavioural Medicine* 17 (1995): 272–90.

Greer-Wooten, B., and L. Mitson. "Nuclear Power and the Canadian Public." North York, Ontario: Institute for Behavioural Research, York University, 1976.

Grove-White, Robin, et al. "Uncertain World: Genetically Modified Organisms, Food and Public Attitudes in Britain." Lancaster University (UK), Centre for the Study of Environmental Change, 1997 (*http://www.lancs.ac.U.K./users/csec*).

Habermas, J. *Philosophical-Political Profiles.* Cambridge, Massachusetts: MIT Press, 1983.

– *Toward a Rational Society.* Boston: Beacon Press, 1971.

Hájek, Alan. "Pascal's Wager." In *The Stanford Encyclopedia of Philosophy*, 1998: *http://plato.stanford.edu/entries/pascal-wager/*

Halfmann, J., and K.P. Japp. "Modern Social Movements as Active Risk Observers: A Systems-Theoretical Approach to Collective Action." *Social Science Information* 32 (1993): 427–46.

Hall, F.R., J. Fraser, S. Garden, and L.-A. Cornacchio. "Organochlorine Discharges in Wastewaters from Kraft Mill Bleach Plants." In *CPPA Environmental Conference Proceedings.* Vancouver, 1988.

Hall, R.H. "Why the EPA Won't Work." *Probe Post* (Spring, 1987): 30.

Hansson, S. "Effects of Pulp and Paper Mill Effluents on Coastal Fish Communities in the Gulf of Bothnia." *Ambio* 16 (1987): 344–8.

Harding, S. *The Science Question in Feminism.* Ithaca: Cornell University Press, 1986.

Hare, R.K. *The Management of Canada's Nuclear Waste.* Ottawa: Supply and Services Canada, 1977.

Harris, Michael. *Lament for an Ocean: The Collapse of the Atlantic Cod Fishery.* Toronto: McClelland and Stewart, 1999.

Harrison, K. "Intergovernmental Relations and Environmental Policy: Concepts and Context." In Fafard and Harrison, eds., *Managing the Environmental Union*, 3–19.

– "Prospects for Intergovernmental Harmonization in Environmental Policy." In D.M. Brown and J. Hiebert, eds., *Canada: The State of the Federation 1994.* Kingston: Institute of Intergovernmental Relations, Queen's University, 1994.

– "Talking with the Donkey." *Journal of Industrial Ecology* 2 (1999): 51–72.

Hazan, A.R., H.L. Lipton, and S.A. Glantz. "Popular Films Do Not Reflect Current Tobacco Use." *American Journal of Public Health* 84 (1994): 998–1000.

Heath, Robert L. *Strategic Issues Management: Organizations and Public Policy Challenges.* Thousand Oaks, California: Sage Publications, 1997.

Hiskes, R. "Emergent Risks and Convergent Interests: Democratic Policy Making for Biotechnology." *Policy Studies Journal* 17 (1988): 73–82.

Hodson, P.V., J.H. Carey, K.R. Munkittrick, and M.R. Servos. "Canada and Sweden – Contrasting Regulations for Chlorine Discharge from Pulp and Paper Industries." Ottawa: Environment Canada, 1995.

Holloran, M.F., R.F. Willes, M.J. Palmiere, and D.G. Wilson. "Estimating Effluent Toxicity from Molecular-Chlorine Gas-Free Bleaching in Terms of Toxicity Equivalence." Pacific Paper Expo Technical Conference, Vancouver, 1990.

Holtz, Marcus C.B. *Alternatives to Lead in Gasoline: A Technical Appraisal.* Ottawa: Royal Society of Canada, Commission on Lead in the Environment, 1986.

Hoover, S.M., et al. "Improving the Regulation of Carcinogens by Expediting Cancer Potency Estimation." *Risk Analysis* 15 (1995): 267–80.

Hornung, R. "The VCR Doesn't Work." In R.B. Gibson, ed., *Voluntary Initiatives: The New Politics of Corporate Greening*, 134–40.

Houghton, R.A., and J.A. Hackler. "Carbon Flux from Land Cover Change." In *Trends: A Compendium of Data on Global Change*. Oak Ridge, Tennessee: Carbon Dioxide Information Analysis Center, Oak Ridge National Laboratory, US Department of Energy, 2000.

Hovell, M.F., et al. "Reduction of Environmental Tobacco Smoke Exposure among Asthmatic Children: A Controlled Trial." *Chest* 106 (1994): 440–6.

Howes, R., J. Skea, and B. Whelan. *Clean and Competitive? Motivating Environmental Performance in Industry.* London: Earthscan Publications, 1997.

Hurt, R.D. and C.R. Robertson. "Prying Open the Door to the Tobacco Industry's Secrets about Nicotine: The Minnesota Tobacco Trial." *Journal of the American Medical Association* 280, no. 13 (1998): 1173–81.

Hutchings, J.A., C. Walters, and R.L. Haedrich. "Is Scientific Inquiry Incompatible with Government Information Control?" *Canadian Journal of Fisheries and Aquatic Sciences* 54 (1997): 1198–1210.

Hyland, G.J. "Physics and Biology of Mobile Telephony." *Lancet* 356 (25 November 2000): 1833–36.

Jacob, G. *Site Unseen: The Politics of Siting a Nuclear Waste Repository.* Pittsburgh: University of Pittsburgh Press, 1990.

Jaques, A.P. *National Inventory of Sources and Emissions of Manganese (1984).* Report EPS 5/MM/1. Ottawa: Environment Canada, 1987.

Jasanoff, S. *The Fifth Branch: Science Advisors as Policymakers.* Cambridge: Harvard University Press, 1990.

– "Product, Process, or Programme: Three Cultures and the Regulation of Biotechnology." In Martin Bauer, ed., *Resistance to New Technology*, 311–31.

– *Risk Management and Political Culture.* New York: Russell Sage Foundation, 1986.

Joppke, C. *Mobilizing against Nuclear Energy.* Berkeley: University of California Press, 1993.

Joy, Bill. "Why the Future Doesn't Need Us." *Wired Magazine*, April 2000. *http://www.wired.com/wired/archive/8.04joy_pr.html*

Kansky, M. "Summary of the Federal Environmental Assessment and Review Process Procedures." Edmonton: Environmental Law Centre, 1997.

Kasperson, R., and P. Stallen, eds. *Communicating Risks to the Public.* Dordrecht: Kluwer, 1991.

Kasperson, Roger E. "The Social Amplification of Risk: Progress in Developing an Integrative Framework." Chapter 6 in S. Krimsky and D. Golding, eds., *Social Theories of Risk*.

Kasperson, Roger E., et al. "The Social Amplification of Risk: A Conceptual Framework." *Risk Analysis* 8 (1988): 177–87.

Kavlock, R., and G. Ankley. "A Perspective on the Risk Assessment Process for Endocrine-Disruptive Effects on Wildlife and Human Health." *Risk Analysis* 16 (1996): 731–7.

Kendrick, J.S., et al. "Integrating Smoking Cessation into Routine Public Prenatal Care: The Smoking Cessation in Pregnancy Project." *American Journal of Public Health* 85 (1995): 217–22.

Kennett, S.A. "Meeting the Intergovernmental Challenge of Environmental Assessment." In Fafard and Harrison, eds., *Managing the Environmental Union*, 105–32.

King, A., and M. Lenox. "Industry Self-Regulation without Sanctions: The Chemical Industry's Responsible Care Program." *Academy of Management Journal* 43 (2000): 698–716.

Klein, Richard. *Cigarettes Are Sublime.* Durham, NC: Duke University Press, 1993.

Kluger, R. *Ashes to Ashes.* New York: Alfred A. Knopf, 1996.

Knorr-Cetina, K.D. *The Manufacture of Knowledge: An Essay on the Constructivist and Contextual Nature of Science.* New York: Pergamon Press, 1981.

Kosobud, R.F., and J.M. Zimmerman, eds. *Market-Based Approaches to Environmental Policy: Regulatory Innovation to the Fore.* New York: Van Nostrand Reinhold, 1997.

Krahn, P. "Enforcement vs. Voluntary Compliance: An Examination of the Strategic Enforcement Initiatives Implemented by the Pacific and Yukon Regional Office of Environment Canada, 1983 to 1988." Vancouver: Environment Canada, 1998. *http:/www.pwc.bc.doe.ca/ep/programs/eppy/enforce/index.html.*

Kraus, N., T. Malmfors, and P. Slovic. "Intuitive Toxicology: Expert and Lay Judgements of Chemical Risks." *Risk Analysis* 12 (1992).

Krever, Horace. *Commission of Inquiry on the Blood System in Canada: Final Report.* 3 vols. Ottawa: Minister of Public Works and Government Services Canada, 1997.

Krimsky, S., and D. Golding, eds. *Social Theories of Risk.* Westport, Connecticut: Praeger, 1992.

Krimsky, S., and A. Plough. *Environmental Hazards: Communicating Risk as a Social Process.* Dover, Massachusetts: Auburn House Publishing Company, 1988.

Kuhn, T. *The Structure of Scientific Revolutions.* Chicago: Chicago University Press, 1962.

Latour, B. *Science in Action.* Cambridge: Harvard University Press, 1987.

Latour, B., and S. Woolgar. *Laboratory Life: The Construction of Scientific Facts.* Princeton: Princeton University Press, 1986.

Law, M.R., and A.K. Hackshaw. "Environmental Tobacco Smoke." *British Medical Bulletin* 52 (1996): 22–34.

Lehtinen, K.-J. "Environmental Effects of Chlorine Bleaching – Facts Neglected?" *Paperi Ja Puu – Paper and Timber* 74 (1992): 715–19.

Leiss, W. "The Censorship of Commercial Speech, with Special Reference to Tobacco Product Advertising." In K. Petersen and A.C. Hutchinson, eds., *Interpreting Censorship in Canada.* Toronto: University of Toronto Press, 1999, 101–28.

– *The Domination of Nature.* 1972. Montreal: McGill-Queen's University Press, 1994.

– " 'Down and Dirty': The Use and Abuse of Public Trust in Risk Communication." *Risk Analysis* 15 (1995): 685–92.

– "The Public Controversy over Genetically Modified Foods." *Isuma: Canadian Journal of Policy Research* 1, no. 2 (Autumn 2000): 80–5.

– "Three Phases in the Evolution of Risk Communication practice." In H. Kunreuther and P. Slovic, eds., *New Directions in Risk Management,* special issue, *Annals of the American Academy of Political and Social Science,* 545 (May 1996): 91–7.

– "Tobacco Control Policy in Canada: Shadow-Boxing with Risk." *Policy Options* 18, no. 5 (June 1997): 3–6.

– *Under Technology's Thumb.* Montreal: McGill-Queen's University Press, 1990.

Leiss, W., ed. *Problems and Prospects in Risk Communication.* Waterloo: University of Waterloo Press, 1989.

Leiss, W., and J. Cairney. "Feasibility Study on Expert Panels: Credibility in Risk-Based Decision Making." Kingston: Environmental Policy Unit, School of Policy Studies, Queen's University, 1995.

Leiss, W., and C. Chociolko. *Risk and Responsibility.* Montreal: McGill-Queen's University Press, 1994.

Leiss, W., É. Darier, and D. VanNijnatten. "Lessons Learned from ARET: A Qualitative Survey of Perceptions of Stakeholders." Kingston: Environmental Policy Unit, School of Policy Studies, Queen's University, 1996.

Leiss, W., and M. Tyshenko. "Some Aspects of the 'New Biotechnology' and Its Regulation in Canada." Chapter 16 in Debora L. VanNijnatten and Robert Boardman, eds., *Canadian Environmental Policy: Ecosystems, Politics and Process.* 2nd edition. Toronto: Oxford University Press, 2001.

Leventhal, H., et al. "Is the Smoking Decision an 'Informed Choice'?" *Journal of the American Medical Association* 257 (1987): 3373–76.

Liebergott, N., B. Van Lierop, and B.I. Fleming. "Methods to Decrease and Eliminate AOX in the Bleach Plant." *Pulp and Paper Canada* 94 (1993).

Linnerooth, J. "The Political Processing of Uncertainty." *Acta Psychologica* 56 (1984): 219–31.

Lipset, S.M. "Canada and the United States: The Cultural Dimension." In C.F. Doran and J.H. Sigler, eds., *Canada and the United States.* Englewood Cliffs, NJ: Prentice-Hall, 1985.

Lipset, S.M., and S. Rokkan. *Party Systems and Voter Alignments*. New York: Free Press, 1967.

Lok, Corie, and Douglas Powell. "The Belgian Dioxin Crisis of the Summer of 1999: A Case Study in Crisis Communications and Management" (1 February 2000): *http://www.plant.uoguelph.ca/safefood*.

Lucas, A.R. and C. Sharvit. "Underlying Constraints on Intergovernmental Cooperation Setting and Enforcing Environmental Standards." In Fafard and Harrison, eds., *Managing the Environmental Union*, 133–62.

Luhmann, N. *Risk: A Sociological Theory*. New York: Aldine De Gruyter, 1993.

Lukasik, L. "Dofasco Deal Cuts Pollution and Controls." *Alternatives Journal* (Spring 1998): 8–9.

Luthe, C.E., P.E. Wrist, and R.M. Berry. "An Evaluation of the Effectiveness of Dioxins Control Strategies on Organochlorine Effluent Discharges from the Canadian Bleached Chemical Pulp Industry." *Pulp and Paper Canada* 93 (1992).

Lynch, B.S., and R.J. Bonnie, eds. *Growing Up Tobacco Free*. Washington: National Academy Press, 1994.

MacDonald, I. "Product Challenges in the Marketplace: Public Perceptions and Mill Process." Montreal: Canadian Pulp and Paper Association, 1992.

M'Gonigle, R.M., T.L. Jamieson, M.K. McAllister, and R.M. Peterman. "Taking Uncertainty Seriously: From Permissive Regulation to Preventative Design in Environmental Decision Making." *Osgoode Hall Law Journal* 32 (1994): 120–63.

McHughen, Alan. *Pandora's Picnic Basket: The Potential and Hazards of Genetically Modified Foods*. New York: Oxford University Press, 2000.

McIntosh, N.A., et al. "Reducing Tobacco Smoke in the Environment of the Child with Asthma: A Cotinine-Assisted, Minimal-Contact Intervention." *Journal of Asthma* 31, no. 6 (1994): 453–62.

McKay, P. *Electric Empire: The Inside Story of Ontario Hydro*. Toronto: Between the Lines, 1983.

MacKinnon, L. "AOX as a Regulatory Parameter: A Scientific Review of AOX Toxicity and Environmental Fate (Draft)." British Columbia Ministry of the Environment, July and September 1992.

Magretta, Joan. "Growth through Global Sustainability: An Interview with Monsanto's CEO, Robert B. Shapiro." *Harvard Business Review*, January–February 1997. Reprinted in *Harvard Business Review on Business and the Environment*. Boston: Harvard Business School Press, 2000, 59–84.

Maier-Reimer, E., and K. Hasselman. "Transport and storage of CO_2: An Inorganic Ocean Circulation Carbon Cycle Model." *Climate Dynamics* 112 (1987): 63–90.

Manson, Neil A. "The Precautionary Principle, the Catastrophe Argument, and Pascal's Wager." *http://www.abdn.ac.uk/cpts/manson1.hti* (accessed 28 November 2000).

Marland, G., T.A. Boden, et al. "Global Regional and National CO_2 Emission." In *Trends: A Compendium of Data on Global Change*. Oak Ridge, Tennessee: Carbon Dioxide Information Analysis Center, Oak Ridge National Laboratory, US Department of Energy, 2000.

Marshall, T.H. *Class, Citizenship, and Social Development*. Westport, Connecticut: Greenwood Press, 1977.

Mattausch, J. *A Commitment to Campaign: A Sociological Study of the Campaign for Nuclear Disarmament (CND)*. Manchester: Manchester University Press, 1989.

May, Sir Robert. "Genetically Modified Foods: Facts, Worries, Policies and Public Confidence." February 1999. *http://www.dti.gov.uk/ost/ostbusiness/gen.htm*

Mehrle, P.M., K. Dickson, R. Hartung, R. Huggett, D. McLeay, A. Oikari, and J. Sprague. "Pulping Effluents in the Aquatic Environment: Data Compilation and Scientific Panel Report." Cincinnati: Procter and Gamble Company, 1989.

Mehta, M.D. "Risk and the Canadian Nuclear Industry: The Democracy-Technocracy Quandary." Ph.D. thesis, Department of Sociology, York University, 1995.

– "Environmental Risk: A Macrosociological Perspective." In M.D. Mehta and E. Ouellet, eds., *Environmental Sociology: Theory and Practice*. North York, Ontario: Captus Press, 1995.

– "Risk Assessment and Sustainable Development: Towards a Concept of Sustainable Risk." *Risk: Health, Safety and Environment* 8 (1997): 137–54.

Mehta, M.D., and J.J. Gair. "Social, Political, Legal and Ethical Areas of Inquiry in Biotechnology and Genetic Engineering." *Technology in Society* 23, no. 2 (forthcoming June 2001).

Mendeloff, J.M. *The Dilemma of Toxic Substance Regulation: How Over-Regulation Causes Under-Regulation*. Cambridge, Massachusetts: MIT Press, 1988.

Miflin, B.J. "Crop Biotechnology: Where Now?" *Plant Physiology* 123 (May 2000): 17–27.

Mitsch, F.J., and J.S. Mitchell. "DuPont. Ag Biotech: Thanks, but No Thanks?" *Deutsche Banc Alex. Brown research*, 12 July 1999 (*www.biotech-info.net/Deutsche.html*).

Moffat, J., and F. Bregha. "Responsible Care." In R.B. Gibson, ed., *Voluntary Initiatives: The New Politics of Corporate Greening*, 15–31.

Moore, Elizabeth L. "Science, Internationalization, and Policy Networks: Regulating Genetically-Engineered Food Crops in Canada and the United States, 1973–1998." Ph.D. Thesis, Department of Political Science, University of Toronto, 2000.

Muldoon, P., and R. Nadarajah. "A Sober Second Look." In R.B. Gibson, ed., *Voluntary Initiatives: The New Politics of Corporate Greening*, 51–65.

Mulkay, M. *Science and the Sociology of Knowledge*. London: George Allen and Unwin, 1979.

Murphy, R. "Sociology As If Nature Did Not Matter: An Ecological Critique." *British Journal of Sociology* 46 (1995).

Murray, D.M., A.V. Prokhorov, and K.C. Harty. "Effects of a Statewide Anti-smoking Campaign on Mass Media Messages and Smoking Beliefs." *Preventive Medicine* 23 (1994): 54–60.

Nash, J., and J. Ehrenfeld. "Codes of Environmental Management Practice: Assessing Their Potential as a Tool for Change." *Annual Review of Energy and the Environment* 22 (1997): 487–535

NCASI (National Council for Air and Stream Improvement). "Effects of Biologically Treated Bleached Kraft Mill Effluent on Warm Water Stream Productivity in Experimental Streams – Third Progress Report." *NCASI Technical Bulletin*, 1984.

– "Effects of Biologically Treated Bleached Kraft Mill Effluent on Cold Water Stream Productivity in Experimental Streams – Fifth Progress Report." *NCASI Technical Bulletin*, 1984.

– "A Review of the Characteristic and Significance of Adsorbable Organic Halide (AOX) in Wastewaters from US Pulp and Paper Mills." *NCASI Technical Bulletin*, 1990.

Neftel, A., H. Friedli, et al. "Historical CO_2 Record from the Siple Station Ice Core." In *Trends: A Compendium of Data on Global Change*. Oak Ridge, Tennessee: Carbon Dioxide Information Analysis Center, Oak Ridge National Laboratory, US Department of Energy, 2000.

Nelkin, D., and M. Pollak. "Problems and Procedures in the Reevaluation of Technological Risk." In C.H. Weiss and A.F. Barton, eds., *Making Bureaucracies Work*. Beverly Hills: Sage, 1981.

Nelkin, D., ed. *Controversy: Politics of Technical Decisions*. Beverly Hills: Sage, 1984.

Nemetz, P.N. "Federal Environmental Regulation in Canada." *Natural Resources Journal* 26 (1986): 551–608.

Neumann, E., and P. Karas. "Effects of Pulp Mill Effluent on a Baltic Coastal Fish Community." *Water Science and Technology* 20 (1988): 95–106.

New Directions Group. "Reducing and Eliminating Toxic Substances Emissions: An Action Plan for Canada." 1991.

"The New Directions Group Position." In R.B. Gibson, ed., *Voluntary Initiatives: The New Politics of Corporate Greening*, 229–38.

New Zealand, Ministry of Research, Science and Technology. "Independent Science Panels: A Handbook of Guidelines for Their Establishment and Operations." Report no. 74. Wellington, NZ, September 1998.

NLK Consultants. "Market and Economic Research on Current and Future Demands: AOX Free and Low AOX Kraft Pulp." 1992.

Notzke, C. *Aboriginal Peoples and Natural Resources in Canada*. North York, Ontario: Captus Press, 1994.

O'Connor, B.I., T.G. Kovacs, R.H. Voss, and P.H. Martel. "A Study of the Relationship between Laboratory Bioassay Response and AOX Content for Pulp Mill Effluents." In *Proceedings of Annual Meeting of CPPA Technical Section*. Montreal, 1993.

OECD (Organisation for Economic Co-operation and Development). "Biotechnology for Clean Industrial Products and Processes." Paris: OECD, 1998.

– "Extended Producer Responsibility Programs." Paris: OECD, 1995.

Olsen, M.E., E. Rosa, and R.E. Dunlap. "Public Opinion versus Governmental Policy on National Energy Issues." *Research in Political Sociology* 1 (1988): 189–210.

Olsen, M.E., D.G. Lodwick, and R.E. Dunlap. *Viewing the World Ecologically*. Boulder, Colorado: Westview Press, 1992.

Otway, H., and J. Ravetz. "Technology: Examining the Linear Model." *Futures* (June 1984): 1–9.

Otway, H., and D. von Winterfeldt. "Expert Judgement in Risk Analysis and Management: Process, Context, and Pitfalls." *Risk Analysis* 12 (1992).

Owens, J.W. "The Hazard Assessment of Pulp and Paper Mill Effluents in the Aquatic Environment: A Review." *Environmental Toxicology and Chemistry* 10 (1991): 1511–40.

Paehlke, R.C. *Environmentalism and the Future of Progressive Politics*. New Haven and London: Yale University Press, 1989.

Paglia, A. "Tobacco Risk Communication Strategy for Youth: A Literature Review." Ottawa: Health Canada, 1998.

PAPRICAN (Pulp and Paper Research Institute of Canada). "Alternative Bleaching Technology and the Environment: A Summary of Research and Development at PAPRICAN." Ottawa, 1992.

Parkins, F. *Middle-Class Radicalism: The Social Bases of CND*. Manchester: Manchester University Press, 1968.

Parsons, T., and E. A. Shils. *Toward a General Theory of Action*. Cambridge, Massachusetts: Harvard University Press, 1959.

Pellizzari, E.D., R.E. Mason, C.A. Clayton, K.W. Thomas, S. Cooper, L. Piper, C. Rodes, M. Goldberg, J. Roberds, and L. Michael. "Executive Summary: Manganese Exposure Study (Toronto)." Prepared by Analytical and Chemical Services, Research Triangle Institute, Research Triangle Park, North Carolina (RTI/6312/02–01F), 30 June 1998.

Plough, A., and S. Krimsky. "The Emergence of Risk Communication Studies: Social and Political Context." *Science, Technology and Human Values* 12 (1987): 4–10.

Powell, D., and W. Leiss. *Mad Cows and Mother's Milk: The Perils of Poor Risk Communication*. Montreal: McGill-Queen's University Press, 1997.

Price, J. *The Antinuclear Movement*. Boston: G.K. Hall and Company, 1982.

Rabin, R.L., and S.D. Sugarman, eds. *Smoking Policy: Law, Politics and Culture.* New York: Oxford University Press, 1993.

Ramey, Timothy F., et al. "GMOs Are Dead." Appendix 2 in "DuPont. Ag Biotech: Thanks, but No Thanks?" *Deutsche Banc Alex. Brown research,* 12 July 1999 (*www.biotech-info.net/Deutsche.html*).

Read, D., A. Bostrom, M.G. Morgan, B. Fischoff, and T. Smuts. "What Do People Know about Climate Change? Part II: Survey Studies of Educated Lay People." *Risk Analysis* 14 (1994): 971–82.

Reid, D. "Tobacco Control: Overview." *British Medical Bulletin* 52 (1996): 108–20.

Renn, Ortwin, et al. "The Social Amplification of Risk: Theoretical Foundations and Empirical Applications." *Journal of Social Issues* 48 (1992) 137–60.

Richards, D.A. "Human Rights, Public Health and the Idea of Moral Plague." *Social Research* 55 (1988): 492–528.

Richardson, M., J. Sherman, and M. Gismondi. *Winning Back the Words: Confronting Experts in an Environmental Public Hearing.* Toronto: Garamond Press, 1993.

Richardson, N.H. "Land Use Planning and Sustainable Development in Canada." Ottawa: Canadian Environmental Advisory Council, 1989.

Roels, H.A., P. Ghyselen, J.P. Buchet, E. Ceulemans, and R.R. Lauwerys. "Assessment of the Permissible Exposure Level to Manganese in Workers Exposed to Manganese Dioxide Dust." *British Journal of Industrial Medicine* 49 (1992): 25–34.

Roewade, D. "Voluntary Environmental Action: A Participant's View of ARET." Ottawa: Industry Canada, 1996.

Roszak, T. "The Monster and the Titan: Science, Knowledge and Gnosis." *Daedalus* 103 (1974): 17–32.

Royal Society of Canada, "Elements of Precaution: Recommendations for the Regulation of Food Biotechnology in Canada." Ottawa, 2001.

– "Recommendations for the Disposition of the Health Canada Primate Colony." Ottawa, 1997.

– "Report of the Expert Panel on Potential Health Risks of Radio-Frequency Fields from Wireless Telecommunications Devices." Ottawa, 1998.

– "A Review of the INSERM Report on the Health Effects of Exposure to Asbestos." Ottawa, 1996.

– *Tobacco, Nicotine and Addiction.* Ottawa, 1989.

Royal Society of London. "Genetically Modified Plants for Food Use." London, September 1998.

– "Whither Cloning?" London, 1998.

Rudolph, R., and S. Ridley. *Power Struggle: The Hundred Year War over Electricity.* New York: Harper and Row, 1986.

Russo, Enzo, and David Cove. *Genetic Engineering: Dreams and Nightmares.* New York: Oxford University Press, 1998.

Sadler, B. "Impact Assessment in Transition: A Framework for Redeployment." In R. Lang, ed., *Integrated Approaches to Resource Planning and Management*. Calgary: University of Calgary Press, 1990.

Salter, L. *Mandated Science*. Boston: Kluwer, 1988.

Sandstrom, O., and G. Thorensson. "Mortality in Perch Populations in a Baltic Pulp Mill Effluent Area." *Maritime Pollution Bulletin* 19 (1988): 564–7.

Sandstrom, O., E. Neumann, and P. Karas. "Effects of a Bleached Pulp Mill Effluent on Growth and Gonad Function in Baltic Coastal Fish." *Water Science and Technology* 20 (1988): 107–18.

Schumpeter, J.A. *Capitalism, Socialism and Democracy*. New York: Harper and Row, 1942.

Sclove, R.E. "Scientists in the u.s. Nuclear Debate: An Inquiry into the Structure, Evolution and Social Implications of a Sociotechnological Controversy." M. Sc. thesis, Nuclear Engineering, Massachusetts Institute of Technology, 1978.

Servos, M.R., J.L. Parrott, J.P. Sherry, and S.B. Brown. "Developing Biological Endpoints for Defining Virtual Elimination: A Case Study for PCDDs and PCDFs." *Water Quality Research Journal of Canada* 34 (1999): 391–422.

Sharma, S., and H. Vredenburg. "Proactive Corporate Environmental Strategy and the Development of Competitively Valuable Organizational Capabilities." *Strategic Management Journal* 19 (1998): 729–53.

Shelley, Mary. *Frankenstein; or, The Modern Prometheus*. Signet Classic ed. New York: Penguin Books, 1965.

Sinclair, D. "Self-Regulation versus Command and Control?" *Law and Policy* 19 (1997): 529–59.

Slovic, Paul. "Perception of Risk." *Science* 236 (1987): 280–4.

– *The Perception of Risk*. London: Earthscan Publications, 2000.

Smith, W. "A Review of Expert Panels for Provision of Scientific and Technological Advice for Development of Public Policy." Report no. 61. Auckland, NZ: Ministry of Research, Science and Technology, May 1997.

Södergren, A. "Biological Effects of Bleached Pulp Mill Effluents." Stockholm: National Swedish Environmental Protection Board, 1989.

Södergren, A., B.E. Bengtsson, P. Jonsson, S. Lagergren, A. Larsson, M. Olsson, and L. Renberg. "Summary of Results from the Swedish Project 'Environment/Cellulose.'" *Water Science and Technology* 29 (1988): 49–60.

Solomon, K., H. Bergman, R. Huggett, D. Mackay, and B. McKague. "A Review and Assessment of the Ecological Risks Associated with the Use of Chlorine Dioxide for the Bleaching of Pulp." Toronto: Alliance for Environmental Technology, 1993.

Somerville, M. "Human Cloning: The Ethics of Repairing, Replicating and Enhancing Us." Paper delivered at the annual meeting of the Royal Society of Canada, Ottawa, November 1998.

Stavins, R.N., and B. Whitehead. "Dealing with Pollution: Market-Based Incentives for Environmental Protection." *Environment* 34 (1992).

Stephens, M., and J. Siroonian. "Smoking Prevalence, Quit Attempts and Successes." *Statistics Canada Health Reports* 9 (1998): 32–3.

Stevenson, S.M. "Bleaching Is More than Brightening: It's Effluent Too." *Pulp and Paper Canada* 94, no. 2 (1993).

Sugai, W.H. *Nuclear Power and Ratepayer Protest: The Washington Public Power Supply System Crisis*. Boulder, Colorado: Westview Press, 1987.

Swanson, S., R. Shelast, R. Schryer, P. Kloepper-Sams, T. Marchant, K. Kroeker, J. Bernstein, and J.W. Owens. "Fish Populations and Biomarker Responses at a Canadian Bleached Kraft Mill Site." *Tappi Journal* (December 1992): 139–49.

Swiss Reinsurance Company. "Electrosmog – A Phantom Risk." Zurich: SwissRe, 1996.

Switzer, J.V. *Environmental Politics: Domestic and Global Dimensions*. New York: St Martin's Press, 1994.

Tandemar Research Inc. "Cigarette Packaging Study: The Evaluation of New Health Warning Messages." Ottawa: Health Canada, 1996.

Taylor, Robert. "Evolution Is Dead." *New Scientist* no. 2154 (3 October 1998): 25–9.

Tengs, T.O., et al. "Five Hundred Life-Saving Interventions and Their Cost-Effectiveness." *Risk Analysis* 15 (1995): 369–90.

Thompson, M., and S. Rayner. "Risk and Governance Part I: The Discourses of Climate Change." *Government and Opposition* 33 (1998): 139–66.

Thompson, M., S. Rayner, and S. Ney. "Risk and Governance Part II: Policy in a Complex and Plurally Perceived World." *Government and Opposition* 33 (1998): 330–54.

Torgerson, D. "Contextual Orientation in Policy Analysis: The Contribution of Harold D. Lasswell." *Policy Sciences* 18 (1985): 241–61.

Touraine, A. *Anti-Nuclear Protest: The Opposition to Nuclear Energy in France*. London: Cambridge University Press, 1983.

United States, Centers for Disease Control. "Incidence of Initiation of Cigarette Smoking – United States, 1965–1996." *Morbidity and Mortality Weekly Report* 47 (1998).

– Federal Communications Commission, Office of Engineering and Technology. "Information on Human Exposure to Radiofrequency Fields from Cellular and PCS Radio Transmitters." Washington, DC: Federal Communications Commission, 1998.

– National Academy of Sciences. *Introduction of Recombinant DNA-Engineered Organisms into the Environment: Key Issues*. Washington, DC: National Academy Press, 1987.

– National Academy of Sciences. *Transgenic Plants and World Agriculture*. Washington, DC: National Academy Press, 2000.

– National Cancer Policy Board, Institute of Medicine, and National Research Council. *Taking Action to Reduce Tobacco Use*. Washington, DC: National Academy Press, 1998.
– National Research Council. *Genetically Modified Pest-Protected Plants: Science and Regulation*. Washington, DC: National Academy Press, 2000.
– National Research Council. *Hormonally Active Agents in the Environment*. Washington, DC: National Academy Press, 1999.
– National Research Council. *Improving Risk Communication*. Washington DC: National Academy Press, 1989.
– National Research Council. *Toxicity Testing*. Washington, DC: National Academy Press, 1984.
– National Research Council. *Understanding Risk: Informing Decisions in a Democratic Society*, ed. Paul C. Stern and Harvey V. Fineberg. Washington, DC: National Academy Press, 1996.
van Dunné, Jan M. "Environmental Contracts and Covenants: New Instruments for a Realistic Environmental Policy?" Proceedings of an international conference held at the Institute for Environmental Damages, Erasmus University, Rotterdam, The Netherlands, October 1992.
VanDuzer, J. Anthony. "To Whom Should Corporations Be Responsible? Ideas for Improving Corporate Governance." In Gilles Paquet, organizer, *Governance in the Twenty-First Century*. Ottawa: Royal Society of Canada, 2000, 81–116.
VanNijnatten, D. "The Day the NGOs Walked Out." *Alternatives Journal* 24 (1998): 10–15.
– "The ARET Challenge." In R.B. Gibson, ed., *Voluntary Initiatives: The New Politics of Corporate Greening*, 93–100.
Van Strum, C., and P. Merrell. "No Margin of Safety: A Preliminary Report on Dioxin Pollution and the Need for Emergency Action in the Pulp and Paper Industry." Washington, DC: Greenpeace USA, 1987.
Versteeg, H. "Examining the Current and Proposed Potential of the Canadian Environmental Protection Act to Incorporate Pollution Prevention Principles and Strategies." Ottawa: Environment Canada, 1993.
– "Summary of Proceedings: Future of ARET Workshop." Ottawa: Environment Canada, 1997.
Vineis, P., et al. "Prevention of Exposure of Young Children to Parental Tobacco Smoke: Effectiveness of an Educational Program." *Tumori* 79 (1993): 183–6.
von Stackelberg, P. "White Wash: The Dioxin Cover-up." *Greenpeace* (March/April 1989).
von Wartburg, W.P., and J. Liew. *Gene Technology and Social Acceptance*. Washington, DC: University Press of America, 1999.
Webb, K. "Gorillas in Closets? Federal-Provincial *Fisheries Act* Pollution Control Enforcement." In Fafard and Harrison, eds., *Managing the Environmental Union*, 163–203.

– *Pollution Control in Canada: The Regulatory Approach in the 1980s*. Ottawa: Law Reform Commission of Canada, 1988.

Weber, M. "Science as a Vocation." In H.H. Gerth and C.W. Mills, eds., *For Max Weber: Essays in Sociology*. London: Routledge and Kegan Paul, 1961.

Weinburg, A. "Science and Trans-Science." *Minerva* 10 (1972): 209–22.

Wiedemann, P.M., and H. Schütz. "The Elecromagnetic Fields Risk Issue." *European Review of Applied Psychology* 45 (1995): 35–9.

Wildavsky, A. *But Is It True? A Citizen's Guide to Environmental Health and Safety Issues*. Cambridge, MA: Harvard University Press, 1995.

Wilde, Gerald J.S. *Target Risk*. Toronto: PDE Publications, 1994. *http://psyc.queensu.ca/target*

Wilson, D.G., and M.F. Holloran. "Decrease of AOX with Various External Effluent Treatments." *Pulp and Paper Canada* 93 (1992).

Winfield, M., and G. Jenish. "Ontario's Environment and the 'Common Sense Revolution': A Third Year Report." Toronto: Canadian Institute for Environmental Law and Policy, 1998.

Wood, Grace, and Marika Egyed. *Risk Assessment for the Combustion Products of Methylcyclopentiadienyl Manganese Tricarbonyl (MMT) in Gasoline*. Environmental Health Directorate, Health Canada, December 1994.

Wynne, B. *Rationality and Ritual*. Chalfont St Giles: British Society for the History of Science, 1982.

Zimring, F.E. "Comparing Cigarette Policy and Illicit Drug and Alcohol Control." In Rabin and Sugarman, eds., *Smoking Policy: Law, Politics, and Culture*, 95–109.

Zito, A.R., and M. Egan. "Environmental Management Standards, Corporate Strategies and Policy Networks." *Environmental Politics* 7 (1998): 94–117.

Index